D1143096

OS

AUTHOR	CLASS
BEARSHAW, B.	

TITLE

From the Stretford end

06 MAR 9

FROM THE STRETFORD END

Also by Brian Bearshaw

Lancashire Cricket at the Top
Waterside Walks in Lancashire
Towpaths of England
Flat Jack (with Jack Simmons)
The Big Hitters
The Great Towpath Walk

Fiction
The Day of Murder
Practice Makes Murder
The Order of Death

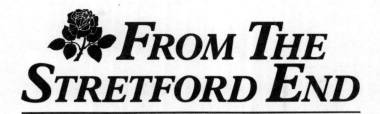

FROM THE STRETFORD END

The Official History of
LANCASHIRE
County Cricket Club

BRIAN BEARSHAW
Foreword by **Cyril Washbrook**

PARTRIDGE PRESS

LONDON · NEW YORK · TORONTO · SYDNEY · AUCKLAND

The Publishers have made every attempt to contact the owners
of the photographs appearing in this book. In the instances where
they have been unsuccessful they invite the coyright holders
to contact them direct.

TRANSWORLD PUBLISHERS LTD
61-63 Uxbridge Road, London W5 5SA

TRANSWORLD PUBLISHERS (AUSTRALIA) PTY LTD
15-23 Helles Avenue, Moorebank, NSW 2170

TRANSWORLD PUBLISHERS (NZ) LTD
Cnr Moselle and Waipareira Aves,
Henderson, Auckland

Published 1990 by Partridge Press
a division of Transworld Publishers Ltd
Copyright © Brian Bearshaw 1990

British Library Cataloguing in Publication Data
Bearshaw, Brian, *1932-*
From the Stretford End: the Offical history of the
Lancashire County Cricket Club.
1. Lancashire County cricket. Clubs: Lancashire County
Cricket club, history
I. Title
796.35′863′0942

ISBN 1-85225-081-X

Printed in Great Britain
by Mackays of Chatham, Chatham, Kent

*For Peter Smethurst, an
outstanding sportsman, a good
friend, a great guy, an immeasurable loss.*

Acknowledgements

When I started this book, many months ago, I decided to record every book, every publication, every smiling helper as I went along. Like many other worthy resolutions, I am ashamed to say this one soon bit the dust. In my frantic efforts now to catch up, I hope and trust I have not missed anybody. If I have, a special thank-you to you. I am sure you will understand.

People first. My thanks to Tom Alderson, Bob Barber, Bob Bennett, Jack Bond, Ken Cranston, Alan Crompton, Geoff Edrich, David Green, Stephen Green, Ken Grieves, Charlie Hallows, Derek Hodgson, Len Hopwood, David Hughes, Peter Lever, Lionel Lister, Clive Lloyd, David Lloyd, Malcolm Lorimer, Douglas McDonald, Arthur Mold, Buddy Oldfield, Reg Parkin, Eddie Paynter, Eddie Phillipson, Winston Place, Geoffrey Sharp, Jack Simmons, Brian Statham, Roy Tattersall, Mac Taylor, Chris Tyldesley, Bob Warburton, Cyril Washbrook, Alan Wharton, Len Wilkinson.

Newspapers were my main source of information and I remember with particular pleasure the many tranquil hours spent in Chetham's Library in Manchester, ploughing through those ancient newspapers with the occasional welcome cup of tea. Manchester Library, particularly the Local History section, must have grown sick of the sight of me. I learned more there about Lancashire cricket – particularly the early years – than anywhere else. *Wisden*, as ever, was invaluable and I found many references in the major cricket magazines, *The Cricketer* and *Wisden Cricket Monthly*. I tried hard to avoid the previous histories and referred to them only when absolutely essential. The main books used are listed in the bibliography.

Contents

Foreword by Cyril Washbrook, President

One of the proudest moments of my life came when I received my Lancashire county cap. That pride has never diminished, pride in being associated for nearly sixty years with one of the world's great cricket clubs.

I was born in Lancashire, in a village called Barrow, near Clitheroe, and left when I was twelve years old when the family moved to Bridgnorth in Shropshire. When I was eighteen I had the chance to play with Warwickshire and Worcestershire, whose representatives saw my parents and made an offer. But Lancashire was the county I wanted to play for and my father gave me twelve months to make good at Old Trafford. Luckily, things went right for me. I scored a double hundred for the second team against Yorkshire and hit a century, against Surrey, in my second game for the first team. That was the start of a long association with Lancashire as player, manager, committeeman and now as president. Pride, I should think, was born in me and it gave me tremendous pride to play for the county of my birth, while becoming president has been a great honour and an appointment which I have appreciated very much.

It is marvellous still to be connected with, and interested in, the game I love. I use the word love carefully because that is what it has always been. It was never a job of work, it was a pleasure and a love.

When I started there were still such famous old characters around the club as S. F. Barnes, Cec Parkin and Harry Makepeace, who were all coaches. Arthur Paul, who played with such people as A. N. Hornby, Johnny Briggs and Archie MacLaren in the nineteenth century, used to come into the dressing room and have a cup of tea. I had the great pleasure of playing, for a year or two, alongside Ernest Tyldesley, one of Lancashire's greatest-ever batsmen. He used to say he could not hold a candle to his brother, J. T., who died a couple of years before I joined the club. I am only sorry I was never able to see him and learn from him. Such names are known all over the world, solid Lancastrians along with people like Eddie Paynter, George Duckworth, Brian Statham, all part of Lancashire's rich history.

The history of a powerful club like ours is important. It is important for young players entering the game to know what great traditions they are upholding, it is important for us to be reminded of those fine players who represented Lancashire and the deeds that were performed in the county's name. So it gives me the utmost pleasure – and I would not have agreed to this Foreword if it had not been so – to be associated with this official history of Lancashire County Cricket Club. I have known Brian Bearshaw for more than twenty-five years, through all the years he has been writing about the county, and I am delighted he decided to record the club's history. I can think of nobody better qualified and I know he has put an enormous amount of time and effort into it. And I am sure that he, like me, feels pride in his connection with the county and cricket club of Lancashire.

Cyril Washbrook
April 1990

Introduction

For a county cricket club with so rich a history as Lancashire, it is surprising that the first history was not written until after the Second World War. There had been little before that. A. G. Steel wrote articles and books in the last century, but contributed little to the history of the club. A. N. Hornby, whose life was bound up with the club for more than half a century, once wrote a brief history for a periodical, but without going into detail. His batting partner, Dicky Barlow, became the first Lancashire player to write his own life story in 1911, and the only other player to get involved in a biography before the Second World War was Cec Parkin. The first serious attempts to get the history into book form did not arrive until the 1950s through Archie Ledbrooke, who wrote the first official history of the club, and Rex Pogson. Newspapers rarely interviewed sportsmen before the First World War, so there were few references to the early days. What a pity that Hornby never wrote a biography, that he never put his memories into print.

So when I researched the history of the club I went back to original sources, to the earliest newspapers in the county, to the late eighteenth and early nineteenth century for whatever references I could find. I had been led to believe that cricket flourished in the county around this time, yet I found nothing to support this. There was little organized cricket in Lancashire at the time and the county lagged far behind many others.

It took time to get going and for more than a decade after the club's formation in 1864, Lancashire county was in danger of fading away. Old Trafford was inaccessible, county cricket was less attractive than many other showier matches, and the gentlemen who formed the backbone of the game often could not give the time needed for several days away from business. Even men like Steel and Hornby, whose names are deeply associated with the county, were reluctant to play in their early years. Steel, in fact, played only forty-seven times over seventeen years, yet played in many bigger and more attractive games. The members of Manchester Cricket Club, whose home was Old Trafford, had to dig deep into their pockets at annual meetings to meet the high costs of county matches. And it was not until 1878, when W. G. Grace at last agreed to take his attractive Gloucestershire team to Old Trafford, that financial worries receded. But it was Hornby who made Lancashire county cricket a success, who got it onto the strong footing needed to take it into the twentieth century. It would be foolish to claim that all has been plain sailing since then. It has not. Lancashire, in common with every other club, have had problems, but thankfully there has always been enough sense about to see the club through the bad times.

This history is not just of a cricket club. It reflects the social history of the country, and particularly of Lancashire. The gulf between Players and Gentlemen, between professionals and amateurs, was the same one that separated squire from peasant, and as one was bridged, so was the other. Lancashire, though, it must be said, tended to drag behind and as recently as 1962 thought that the best man to lead a team of hardened professionals was a thirty-four-year-old amateur who had never played county cricket. And only two years before that, the captain, Bob Barber, who was also an amateur, was made to travel and live separately from his players. It needed something of a revolution then to catch up with time and throw off many of the old outdated ideals. One particularly prickly thorn that stuck in Lancashire's side for far too long was the question of women becoming full members with the right to vote and play a full part in running the club. Cricket clubs were founded in the last century by gentlemen for gentlemen. They had little to do with professionals and nothing to do with women, whose place belonged in the parlour. Women were allowed to adorn the club and to watch, but not to interfere. They were even allowed in the pavilion until interest in the club became so great and membership so high that in 1881 the committee decided they must keep to their own quarters. Happily, the 1989 annual meeting decided that women, for the first time in the club's history, should be entitled to full membership.

Watching the development of cricket unfold right from the start of the last century was fascinating. Lancashire is my county. I could not live anywhere but in a cotton mill town. My ancestors had hard lives in the mills and their struggle, their stubbornness, their strong will to see it through was epitomized in a less onerous way by the game of cricket. Lancashire and Yorkshire cricket mirrors the life of its people; so, too, I find, does the cricket of Kent and Somerset, of Glamorgan and Derbyshire. And so it should be. The game, like life, has its ups and downs and Lancashire's history has all the depressions and hallelujahs that we all experience. In fact, it is life all over.

FROM THE STRETFORD END

Chapter 1 1864

*'Lancashire boast many good cricketers but from the
fact of most of its towns being manufacturing ones, the
residents have but little or no time to devote to this
noble pastime.'*

On 25 April 1857, Manchester Cricket Club inserted a five-line
advertisement on the front pages of the *Manchester Courier* and
Manchester Guardian. It read:

> MANCHESTER CRICKET CLUB – The opening of the
> New Ground at Old Trafford, adjoining the Art Treasures
> Exhibition, is fixed for Saturday, 9th May. Wickets pitched
> at two. Dinner on the table at four.
> RICHARD HAMPSON, Treasurer M.C.C.

The Old Ground at Old Trafford had been swallowed up by the Art
Treasures Exhibition; just down the road the New Ground, which
was to become one of the most famous in the world and was to house
Lancashire County Cricket Club, was about to open. But what was
the opening of a mere cricket ground compared to the launching,
four days earlier, of the Art Treasures Exhibition, the biggest event
of its kind ever staged in Manchester? Prince Albert was to open it,
the Queen was coming; the newspapers and the people could think
of little else. The papers were full of it and there was no room in
the news columns for something as insignificant as the opening of
the town cricket club's new ground . . .

Cricket, born and nourished in the south of England, had been slow
to find its way into Lancashire. By 1800 the game was well-rooted
in several southern counties, particularly Kent, Hampshire, Sussex,
Middlesex and Surrey, but in Lancashire it was hard, almost impossible, to find mention of the game. G. B. Buckley, in his book *Fresh*

Light on 18th Century Cricket written in 1935, made no reference at all to Lancashire, although Durham, Northumberland, Nottinghamshire, Derbyshire and Yorkshire were among those well represented. Two years later he brought out a second book concerning pre-Victorian cricket with one mention of Lancashire in the eighteenth century, taken from the *Manchester Journal* of 1 September 1781: 'On Monday last was decided on Brinnington Moor (Cheshire) the cricket match between 11 men of the townships of Haughton (Lancashire) and Bredbury (Cheshire) and 11 gentlemen in the printing business, which was won by the former. The odds run 2–1 in favour of the printers.' Haughton was just across the Cheshire–Lancashire border, close to Denton and five miles out of Manchester.

Lancashire was largely an industrial society with little time or inclination for cricket. Manchester historian Thomas Swindells, writing at the end of the nineteenth century, said that in the early decades of the century the working class had few opportunities for enjoyment and little money to spend on pleasures. Mills worked on Saturday afternoons, so there were few chances for youths and men to indulge in cricket and football. In fact, such games were almost entirely confined to the wealthier classes. Football crowds were unknown and cricket had few supporters in Manchester.

An observer commented in 1827 that although Manchester was one of the most important, thriving and wealthy cities in the world, and the port of Liverpool second only to London, yet there were scarcely any signs of cricket life. Even in 1854, Frederick Lillywhite felt compelled to comment in his cricket annual: 'Lancashire boast many good cricketers but from the fact of most of its towns being manufacturing ones, the residents have but little or no time to devote to this noble pastime.'

Cricket, in the early part of the nineteenth century, was certainly hard to find in Lancashire. Fylde Cricket Club, on the west coast, claims to have been founded in 1810 but has no documented evidence to support it. And it appears that Liverpool can justifiably claim seniority among the cricket clubs of the county. The forerunner of Liverpool CC was Mosslake Field Society, formed in 1807, although it is said that cricket had been played before that on the Mersey Bowmen's Archery ground. The *Liverpool Mercury* in 1811 referred to a long poem about Liverpool CC which included this extract:

> White hats of scarce four ounces,
> A jacket smart, flesh coloured hose,
> A cricketer complete compose . . .

Liverpool, born out of Mosslake, had five homes before settling, in

1881, at Aigburth, the second oldest to Old Trafford of Lancashire's county grounds. Liverpool were beaten by Rochdale on the Newton Race Ground in 1812, but it was 1824 before Rochdale were officially founded, making them one of the oldest established clubs in the county.

Among others with early beginnings were Broughton (founded in 1823 or 1824), Denton (1824), Crescent and St George's, Wellington, Everton, Waterloo and Alliance (all in Liverpool), Preston, Burnley, Ribblesdale, Cheetham, Ashton, Blackburn, Ormskirk, Eagley and Lancaster. Several found it hard to keep going, faded for a time and then returned. The *Preston Sentinel*, in its issue of 23 June 1821, reported 'Cricket was revived in Preston by the formation of the Preston Cricket Club which played on the Marsh, near Ashton.' And seven years later . . . 'The Ribblesdale Cricket Club held their second weekly meeting at Penwortham on the banks of the Ribble. The members there, about 20 in number, wore a white uniform; they took the play at 5 p.m. P. Horrocks, Esquire, of Penwortham Lodge, presented the club with a handsome cricket ball.' In 1830, the *Manchester Courier* reported that a cricket club had been established in Blackburn and already consisted of twenty-two members. 'A field near the Fox and Grapes has been selected by the club for this healthy and manly game.' The *Preston Pilot* reported that same year that 'Blackburn (28 and 21) were beaten at home (in a field near the Fox and Grapes) by Preston in an innings and two runs, playing nine a side. Over 200 spectators attended. The return was to have been played a few weeks later on the Holme, under Penwortham Wood, near Preston.'

Unfortunately, the Blackburn Club lasted only a year or two, but Preston continued and in 1832, on the Holme, beat eleven gentlemen residing in Preston who included several leading members of the Ribblesdale Club. And in 1833, according to the *Blackburn Alfred* newspaper, they lost (80 and 28) to Burnley (89 and 50) by 31 runs on the New Ground at Burnley. 'The novelty of a cricket match in this neighbourhood drew a large crowd. Burnley had been coached by Dearman of Sheffield,' reported the newspaper. The teams should have met again in August 1834 but Burnley declined to play, saying they were too weak and out of practice.

Lancaster were officially formed in 1841 yet, according to the *Lancaster Gazette* six years earlier . . . 'After playing in a field near the riverside, "for the purpose of trying their hands", a cricket club was formed at Lancaster. There was at first 17 members amongst whom, it was said, were some very good players both in batting and bowling.' Accrington were founded in 1846 when their bowling was underarm. However, the dress of the players was beyond reproach.

3

'Spotless white ducks, flannel jackets edged with blue, tight-fitting neat belts, spiked shoes, and velvet caps with gilt or coloured bands. Tall black hats were also worn although they were on their way out.'

Although cricket was generally looked upon as a manly, healthy, noble game, there were some parts of society that were not all that convinced. According to Chris Aspin in his book, *Gone Cricket Mad*, the first mention of cricket in Haslingden occurred in a set of rules published in 1832 by the Primitive Methodist Church, Deardengate. 'If any teacher be found guilty of Sabbath-breaking, frequenting public houses, card tables, dancing rooms, cricket-playing or gaming of any kind, or any other practice contrary to the Word of God, they shall be admonished for their conduct. If they repent, well; if not, they shall be expelled from the society.' He, too, pointed out that there could not have been much cricket played in those days anyway, certainly not by the men and boys who worked long hours in the textile mills.

There was a good deal of betting on the sport then, and no shortage of novelty matches, the most novel of which must have occurred on the Manchester Clifford ground in July 1863, 'one legs v one arms'. The *Manchester Courier* reported:

> An amusing match between 11 one-legged and 11 one-armed men was played on the Manchester Clifford CC ground. The novelty match drew a crowded attendance on both days, Monday and Tuesday. The men, notwithstanding their crippled condition, displayed both skill and agility. On the one-armed side a man named Longston scored 56 and 77 not out. On the one-legged side Lettford, who has no legs, stood his ground well and carried out his bat at the end of their second innings. One mishap occurred during the game. A one-legged man named Lisle, while running for a ball, fell heavily and had to be conveyed from the ground. He was unable to resume his place in the field but no serious result has apprehended from the fall.

Another curious game was played on the Manchester Cricket Club ground at Hulme in 1838 when the Catapulter, a bowling machine designed by Nicholas Felix, was chosen to play for the second team. The game, played on 3 September, was between 'Eleven first chosen, and Lea Birch with the ten next, the Catapulter bowling on the latter side.' Lea Birch was Manchester's outstanding player in those early days and was regularly chosen to support the weaker team. On this occasion, not even his skill allied to the mechanical threat of the Catapulter was enough to stop the 'Eleven first chosen' winning. They scored 158, with seven players batting against the machine which took two wickets, both bowled, before it retired, breaking down after 104 runs had been scored. Lea Birch's team, demoralized no doubt by the loss of their secret weapon, were dismissed for 47.

Manchester were among the foremost clubs of the day in Lancashire. Some said *the* foremost, although Liverpool, in particular, and Broughton, in later years, would have challenged it. According to the list of officers in the pavilion at Old Trafford, Manchester's first president, treasurer and secretary, John Rowlandson, dates from 1818, although there are references that put the founding of the club two years earlier.

Gentlemen's clubs were numerous in Manchester around this time and a cricket club was one of the few organizations where men could gather for healthy, sporting pursuits. 'Then the principal merchants and professional men lived in town and could meet every night,' said J. W. Hunter when he addressed the Manchester Literary Club in 1876. 'Living in town was not in any way objectionable. All Saints was a bowling green; the Irwell and Medlock still comparatively clear. Indeed there were no facilities for living at a distance. Travelling was slow and expensive. Southport was reached by a canal boat which took 12 hours. Liverpool was five hours away.' Cricket received no mention in 1816 in either Cowdroy's *Manchester Gazette* or the *Manchester Mercury*, whose sporting reports were of racing – which could command columns of space – cock fighting, pedestrianism and perhaps swimming. Cricket was a pastime for the wealthy and, with the problems of travelling, matches in the early part of the century were usually played between the members. At Manchester the married men would play the single, those with surnames beginning from A to J would play those from K to Z, fast bowlers would play slow bowlers.

Garrisons of infantry and cavalry were stationed nearby and Manchester Cricket Club regularly played matches against the soldiers. A scorebook for 1826, still kept at Old Trafford, detailed a match between the Garrison (1st Dragoon Guards and Queens Bays) with Carter of the Liverpool Club, and Manchester with French of the Liverpool Club. The Garrison scored 24 and 95, Carter scored 1 and 0, and Captain Murray knocked his wicket down. Manchester won by scoring 99 and 22 for two, and one batsman was given out 'foot before wicket'. Scoring rates were understandably low on the poor, under-prepared wickets of the day, and an average of 35 runs per 100 balls – about two an over by today's standard – was fairly good going. They tried to finish a game regardless of time, but often were unable to beat the weather or the light. In 1831 one match was 'Not played out, being too dark', and in 1832, in a game where scores of 77 and 42 played 60, the sad, familiar entry followed: 'Came on wet'.

5

_ holidays were always a good excuse for a game of cricket. A
_h was played in 1832 in celebration of the Passing of the Reform
_l, and more games were arranged for Coronation Day in 1838 and
_rince Albert's birthday in 1840.

Manchester Cricket Club, the father of Lancashire County Cricket
Club, was originally called the Aurora from the fact that players
used to meet at dawn in the Adelphi, at that time a green oasis
in Salford, set in the bend of the river opposite The Crescent. Its
matches attracted no public attention, not even when the _Manchester
Guardian_ came on to the scene in 1821. The new, radical newspaper
was born on Saturday 5 May, but made only one mention of cricket
that summer – and then it was of a women's match in Sussex!

The earliest mention of Manchester Cricket Club in the Manchester
newspapers came, it seems, in the early 1820s. On Monday 9 August
1824, on the ground opposite Salford Crescent, Manchester (71
and 81) beat Liverpool (69 and 81) by two runs in a game lasting
from 11 a.m. to nearly 8 p.m. In the return, in Crabtree Lane,
Liverpool, two weeks later, Liverpool (60 and 105) gained revenge
by beating Manchester (50 and 27) by 88 runs. Low scores were a
feature, certainly of the first half of the nineteenth century, and
teams would often get through two innings each in a day without
too much trouble. Manchester and Liverpool, according to Thomas
Swindells, were five hours apart in the 1820s, but that did not stop
their cricket clubs playing each other twice a year for many years,
important games in view of their size and positions of seniority
in the game in Lancashire. Consequently, the newspapers usually
managed to report their matches, if only in brief form. In July
1825, four innings were completed in six hours, and that probably
included the break for dinner (it was to be some years before the
north accepted the southern version of the midday meal as 'lunch').
Reported the _Manchester Guardian_ 'The match excited great interest
and the ground (opposite The Crescent, Salford) was crowded during
the whole of the contest.' The increasing importance of the game
between these two growing clubs might be reflected in Frederick
Lillywhite's book, _Cricket Scores and Biographies_, which listed all
the Great Matches in England. The first Great Match staged in
Lancashire was given as the game at Manchester on 10 July 1826,
when the home team (55 and 83) beat Liverpool (65 and 34) by 39
runs.

At times, the game was granted more space in the newspapers,
especially in the _Manchester Guardian_ whose attachment with Lancashire, of course, was to become deep and lasting – at least, as long
as the Manchester part of the newspaper's name was maintained.
Saturday 29 July 1831:

6

Manchester beat Liverpool. – The day, at the commencement, was very auspicious and much pleasure was anticipated by the lovers of the game, 6–4 taken in favour of Manchester who were too confident in the first innings and played carelessly. Liverpool led on the first innings by 35 which changed the betting to evens. The first two innings occupied from ten in the morning until near six in the afternoon. . . Manchester went in for the second time and succeeded in 90 notches, the Liverpool Club gained only 46, Manchester winning by a majority of nine. . . Manchester 76 and 90, Liverpool 111 and 46.

When Manchester moved to their new ground in Moss Lane, Hulme, in 1834, it was only natural that the opening game should be against Liverpool . . . 'The day being very favourable, there was a large concourse of spectators including a great number of ladies, and the fine band of the 28th added much to the enjoyment of the day.'

By the 1840s the two teams were employing professional players and in 1844 A. Girling, a bowler from Burton upon Trent, assisted Liverpool and virtually beat Manchester on his own in the ten-wicket win. By the following year he was a Manchester player when the two clubs came to a strange arrangement whereby the first innings was played in Liverpool and the second in Manchester. Liverpool had the better of things on their own ground, taking a 93–37 advantage, which Manchester easily wiped out on their own ground, scoring 117 to Liverpool's 28 for a 33-run win. An indication of the relative strengths of the clubs mighty be seen in Liverpool being assisted by two players, Nicholas Felix and William Martingell, to Manchester's one, Fuller Pilch, whose bowling returns of seven for 21 and eight for 16 were decisive.

It was around this time that Manchester cricket was immeasurably influenced from several different directions. The first came in 1842 when the Club, the players no doubt eager to test their strength, went to London to play the mighty Marylebone Club at Lord's. The *Manchester Courier* did not even mention this momentous game, but the *Manchester Guardian*, in its issue of Saturday 9 July, wrote:

Match between Eleven gentlemen of the Manchester Club and the best Eleven of the celebrated Marylebone Club, which has excited more interest in this neighbourhood, started on Thursday. The Manchester Club went in first and scored 60 [should have been 59]. . . The Marylebone Club went in about half past four but we have not heard any particulars of their play. As the members of the

Manchester Club are more celebrated for their bowling
and fielding than for their batting the score they have made
seems to show that they will cut a very respectable figure
in comparison with their highly celebrated opponents.

There were to be no more reports on the match in the *Manchester
Guardian*. Probably everybody was too ashamed to inform them that
Marylebone scored 220 and Manchester gave up the match. The
Manchester bowling, it had been reported, was very inferior, being
of the 'old underhand school' and, as *Bell's Life* put it, 'afforded the
MCC gentlemen much amusement in hitting it away.'

The Manchester gentlemen must have been severely shamed.
It looks as if they were the laughing-stock of Lord's. They did
not even bother with their second innings, but returned home, their
tails between their legs. Round-arm bowling had been practised in
the south for many years; it had been legal, in fact, since 1835, but
Manchester were still of the 'old underhand school'. Beddors Peacock, writing in the *City News* in 1896, recalled his youth in those
days in the 1840s when Manchester cricketers made the transition
from underarm to round-arm bowling, probably hastened by the
experience at Lord's. He said the old regime were reluctant to give up
underarm bowling whereas novices, however clumsily they shaped,
invariably adopted the modern style. 'It was laughable to witness the
extraordinary antics and physical contortions some of these amateur
exponents of round-arm bowling performed,' he wrote. 'They hopped
and skipped and sawed the air with a stiff arm. If, more by luck than
skill, the ball went straight to the batsman, there was neither length
nor speed in it.'

Another important step, one which affected the whole country,
came in 1846 when William Clarke, a Nottingham man, founded
the All-England XI which toured the country taking its skills to
towns and villages and awakening a new interest in the game. A
third step, introduced in 1847, was the passing in Parliament of the
Ten Hours Act, which had much wider social implications, particularly in Lancashire. The number of hours worked a week was now
limited to fifty-five and a half, making Saturday afternoons free and
proving an important factor in the movement towards the organized
sports of modern times, particularly cricket, rugby and football. As
the Rossendale cotton spinner, Moses Heap, noted in his diary 'For
a while we did not know how to pass our time away. Before, it had
been all bed and work; now, in place of 70 hours a week, we had
55½ hours. It became a practice, mostly on Saturdays, to play
games, especially football and cricket, which had never been done
before.' In the meantime, however, it continued to be the pursuit of

the wealthy, a game of high social standing. The nearest and earliest thing to a Roses match came in this same period when Manchester took on the county of York, playing them in 1845 over three days on the Manchester ground 'in the presence of a very large assemblage of the élite of the town and neighbourhood.'

Manchester, of course, provided early opposition for the travelling All-England team in 1846. It was the greatest match ever staged in the neighbourhood and started on 3 September at the Moss Lane ground at Hulme. It was said there had been very little else of local interest talked about for the previous two days. 'Attendance throughout the day was very great, including some of the most respectable merchants, manufacturers and other inhabitants of Manchester, Salford and the neighbourhood,' said the *Manchester Courier*. The newspaper went on to report that on the second day, at one time in the afternoon, the betting was as high as 10–1 against Manchester. 'We know a gentleman who, if the Manchester players should be unsuccessful, will lose between £600 and £700 through backing his townsmen,' said the *Manchester Courier*. 'Very heavy sums, we believe, are depending on the result.' The unfortunate gentleman lost his money as Manchester, all eighteen of them, went down by an innings and 31 runs.

The *Manchester Guardian* devoted over a column and a half to this important match. It pointed out:

> The Manchester Club, it is pretty well understood, do not play for money; but nothing daunted by their defeat by the Sheffield players, 20 of whom have since beaten 'Eleven of All England', challenged the latter, the crack Eleven, to a match 'for love' and undertook to pay all the travelling and other expenses of the Eleven, which we are told is about £70. The ground, which had been carefully mowed and rolled, was in fine condition and the ropes around the field were surrounded by a tolerably close triple or quadruple cordon of spectators. Within the precincts of 'the house' strangers were admitted at 2s 6d each and the number present, both of ladies and gentlemen, was very great. Thursday was a beautifully clear, bright day, exceedingly favourable for the sport and tempting to many to extend their usual promenade as far as the ground.

The wickets were pitched shortly after eleven o'clock and at six-thirty, at the close of the first day, All-England were 198 for seven, Pilch having batted four and a half hours for 61 not out. 'He was determined to give them no chance of catching his ball and he there-fore struck every ball downwards; and made his notches almost

9

wholly "ones",' said the *Manchester Guardian*. The crack team took the game extremely seriously, of course, and even forced the band to stop playing. The *Manchester Guardian* explained:

> The Eleven seemed determined not to throw a chance away; for the fine band of the 69th Regiment of Infantry, being in attendance by permission of the commanding officer, they objected to its performances during the playing, as disturbing and distracting their attention, and it was accordingly silenced during the game; playing during the dinner hour from two to three, and again after the stumps were drawn in the evening.

All-England returned to Moss Lane the following year, 1847, for a game that was to arouse rather more controversy than the quietening of the regimental band. The *Manchester Guardian*, now in its twenty-seventh year, felt confident enough to offer some fairly pompous advice to the Manchester Club: 'Whatever effect the old school of slow underhand bowling may have had in years gone by, we can assure the Club that in the present march of improvement in cricket, it savours more of the drawing room than the cricket field.'

The match was drawn, the seventeen of Manchester, with wicket-keeper given, doing well to lead All-England on first innings, and needing 61 for victory with nine wickets standing when the game ended on the Saturday evening. The *Manchester Guardian* said the All-England party had to play in Birmingham on the Monday and therefore could not continue on the Saturday. Quite so, but the *Manchester Courier* scooped its rival and came up with a much more juicy reason for not playing out the game. It seems that as the game was drawing to its climax, 'a whisper got abroad that the Eleven did not mean to finish the game . . . and at half past six Mr Mynn and his team gave up play, much to the chagrin of all on the ground. They alleged (as indeed was true) that their stipulation was to play for three days and having done so, they considered they had fulfilled their bond . . . A "cabinet council" was called which was soon brought to a close by Mr Mynn declaring "That come what would, he must see Jenny Lind." ' The famous singer was appearing that night at the Theatre Royal in Manchester, an event attracting just as much attention as the All-England team. That question settled, another one arose. What about the bets? Mr Cooke, secretary of the Manchester Club, announced they would be null and void, a hugely important decision as between £30,000 and £40,000 depended on the result.

Despite the controversial ending, it had been great entertainment, watched by several thousands. 'Although composed principally of gentlemen, there was a numerous attendance of the more humble admirers of the manly game and we also observed, at various points, the private carriages of some of our resident gentry filled with fair spectators,' said the *Manchester Courier*.

The All-England players sported tall silk hats on a Moss Lane ground which was extremely attractive, being dotted over with snow-white tents. Quaint characters added to the interest of the game, including the old Ormskirk gingerbread seller and Lillywhite's man, who printed and sold the scorecard with 'the order of going in', humorously calling 'the order of going out' when a rot set in among the batsmen. And the play itself? – 'George Parr then took the timber in hand and played on until the dinner bell was rung. After supplying themselves with creature comforts play was re-commenced.'

'George Cooke was soon bowled out by one of Mr Mynn's peculiars, which sent him to smoke his Havannah after scoring only two.'

During the following week, a member of the Manchester Club wrote to the *Manchester Guardian* on what he called a Drawback to the Great Match:

> The late cricket match was an object of interest to assembled thousands. The behaviour of the multitude was such as to call from the celebrated Felix a very warm eulogium. As a Manchester man I felt proud to hear him speak so highly of my fellow townsmen. There was, however, one drawback, which it is to be hoped will not occur again, and which was noticed with regret by several of the members, as well as by one of the gentlemen players of All-England, to myself. I allude to the separation at dinner of the professional players from the others. In the south it is customary for the noblemen to dine with the players, and, as the gentleman before alluded to said when in one of their late matches, Lord Morpeth sat down with the whole of them, 'the members of the Manchester Cricket Club might do so without compromising their dignity.' The chief advantage of cricket is that it brings different classes together, and promotes kind and good feeling. Besides this, the All-England professional players were as much gentlemen in their conduct and station as any on the ground.

It did not take long for Henry Cooke, the Manchester secretary, to reply 'I beg to say that a tent was erected in which dinner was provided at the request of the players and I have the assurance of the All-England Eleven of their approbation of the arrangements.'

In 1848 Manchester moved to the first of their two Old Trafford grounds and the first matches of consequence at the New Ground,

11

Stretford Road, were against Sheffield and Liverpool, both of which Manchester won. Land for building was apparently needed and today St Mary's Church, Hulme, occupies the site called Moss Lane which, for fourteen years from 1834–1847, was the home of Manchester Cricket Club. In this year, 1848, Manchester used only fifteen players to take on All-England and lost by only three wickets. Of the New Ground the *Manchester Guardian* wrote 'A huge roller of a ton weight is used twice or thrice a week to smoothe it down; and in the qualities of a smooth, level ground it cannot be surpassed. Indeed the crack cricketers from a distance say that it is one of the best cricket grounds in England because of it being so level.'

The first of the Roses matches – although not now universally recognized as such – came the following year in 1849, at Sheffield when Yorkshire beat Lancashire by five wickets. The return match was played the following week and the *Manchester Guardian*, po-faced as ever, said:

> We have not received a detailed account of the match, nor do we think it would have been very interesting for, from the beginning, the Yorkshire party seem to have shown a decided superiority. This was evident at the end of the first day's play. From the following return it will be seen that the Yorkshire Eleven were victorious with their first innings, having 18 runs to spare. Yorkshire 166, Lancashire 87 and 61.

This was the first time that 'Lancashire' was used in the Manchester scorebook.

Manchester, fielding twenty-two players, lost to All-England by four wickets with two minutes to spare in 1849 and drew the following comment from the *Manchester Guardian*, 'The number of clubs that have sprung up in the town within the last few years is very great; and the improvement in many of them is a proof that the game is played for its own sake. The Manchester Club does not enjoy a monopoly of the best players and it was wisely agreed that the present match should be played by the best men the district could produce.' And the conclusion:

> We must seek for a solution of the fact that Manchester, with its very great superiority in many respects, is still, in the name of cricket, inferior to many provincial towns. There are, no doubt, good players in the club; but yet it is to be confessed that no man of cricketing celebrity has yet risen up among us. So long as the Manchester club

puts its trust in paid men, it seems highly probable that this progress will be slow, if progress it makes at all, so far as the most important matches are concerned. In no town or district where cricket is carried on so extensively is there exhibited so great a lack in that main arm of a cricket club – good native bowling – as in Manchester. And this result we can only trace to a reliance upon borrowed men.

It did not take long for a country cricketer to come to the defence of the gentlemen of Manchester.

I doubt if there is a county in England which can produce 22 gentlemen players who attend daily to business and practise the game only as a recreation that can play the England Eleven. Take the ordinary occupation of a Manchester merchant or tradesman. Do you expect him to attend his warehouse day by day, snatching a few hours once or twice in the week to hurry down to Old Trafford, take a few balls, and return? No gentleman, having business engagements, can afford the time necessary to become a first-rate bowler. Neither can a gentleman in business become a wicket-keeper.

The Broughton club in nearby Salford, formed six or seven years after Manchester, made a bold move in 1851 by inviting the All-England team to their ground, All-England winning a low-scoring game by 21 runs. Beddors Peacock, writing in the *City News* forty-five years later, said that while the match, in cricketing terms, might have been deemed a failure, 'as a matter of policy it was a stroke of genius.' He went on:

From a minor suburban club, the Broughton sprang at one bound to the front rank. The annual match became for years a social function of no unimportant character. Playing and lay members joined in numbers and when the club moved to the larger and better ground the subscribers totalled up to nearly 300 making it, numerically, the strongest club in England, barring MCC. A charge for admission had to be made. It was a bright scene of gaiety. There was a maypole surmounted with a cricketer of gold armed with a bat. Beneath this pole the band of the 28th Regiment discoursed music between the intervals of the match. Marquees and tents adorned with flags and streamers studded the ground and the youth and beauty of the district assembled in great force.

Here then were the outstanding Lancashire clubs of the 1850s – Manchester, Liverpool and Broughton, all of which were highlighted in *Lillywhite's Annual*:

Liverpool cricket ground is situated close to the Terminus and is enclosed within a wall and a hedge. Its size is from 15 to 20 acres. An excellent pavilion, erected on the north side where every accommodation can be afforded. This club consists of some very fine players.

Manchester cricket ground is situated at the top of Stretford New Road and may be arrived at for twopence on the railway. The Messrs Cooke are great supporters of the game here. The ground has been made only a few years and has cost a considerable sum for drainage since it was made. A beautiful pavilion is also erected and part of the ground is thrown open to the public during a match. The club is one of the best in the north and has some very excellent players and supporters.

And in the 1853 annual:

Manchester club, established 1816. Now has 230 members. Ground hard and lively in fine weather. Property of Sir Thomas de Trafford. The club, which has existed longer than any provincial club in England, has been annually increasing in playing strength, and is now one of the strongest amateur clubs. During the past season they lost only one match out of 11. Very commodious pavilion which was erected at an immense cost.

Broughton – first established in 1823 or 1824 and continued until 1828 to meet on a small ground in Lower Broughton Lane. Since then many changes . . . The new ground has recently been enclosed, there in the centre of the splendid estate of Colonel Clowes of Higher Broughton. Very handsome pavilion now being built which will, when finished, make this one of the most complete resorts for cricketers in the Kingdom.

Two years later . . . 'More complete accommodation for the convenience of the public was never witnessed on any cricket ground, including an ample promenade for the ladies. Broughton had 300 members in 1853 with an annual subscription of one guinea. Pavilion rustic, designed by an eminent London architect. Alfred Diver of Cambridge was the professional.' In 1856, *Lillywhite's Annual* referred to Broughton as the North Marylebone Club. 'Tents and marquees are pitched for the ladies and close at hand are refreshments and a regimental band to enliven the proceedings; the pavilion enclosure is kept select and places are allotted for the numerous shilling and sixpenny lovers of the game. Nothing can be more complete than a grand cricket match at Broughton.'

The *Manchester Courier* agreed, totally. 'These matches are a great treat,' it reported in 1857 on the eve of the All-England v Broughton match. 'Tents and marquees for the comfort and accommodation of the visitors, the ladies in particular (the gallantry of the Broughton gentlemen towards the gentler sex in these matches has been quite a household word) will be erected as hitherto.'

Manchester, however, were the establishment club, and, with the help of three professionals, had again played MCC in 1852, losing this time by only three wickets. Professionals made an enormous difference in these games. When Manchester played Sheffield in the same year, the game should have been between ten gentlemen and one professional. But when it came time to leave for Manchester, Sheffield could find only five gentlemen and made up the team with six professionals. Rather than not play, Manchester went ahead – and lost by an innings and 45.

Broughton's reputation was growing through their annual games with All-England and compliments were heaped upon the 'businesslike manner of this great provincial club', providing a scene that Lillywhite once extravagantly described as 'never before equalled either in the north or south of England.' And when Manchester lost its Old Trafford ground in 1856, it looked as if Broughton would take over the role of No. 1 club, if not in the north, certainly in Lancashire.

Plans for the great Manchester Art Treasures Exhibition of 1857 fully emerged early in 1856. The site had to be decided upon fairly quickly and the newspapers were full of suggestions for the right place to hold such an event, the biggest of its kind ever held in the county, perhaps even in the north of England. One of the considerations in choosing a site was 'an atmosphere pure from smoke and dust.' The *Manchester Guardian* of 18 June first reported that Manchester's cricket ground had been chosen and that the Exhibition's executive committee were negotiating for the site, held on lease by the cricket club. Six days later the newspaper reported that the Exhibition committee were getting immediate possession of the land, estimated at over seventeen and a half acres. The *Manchester Courier* of 28 June confirmed the selection of the cricket ground, adjoining the Botanical Gardens and the Manchester South Junction and Altrincham Railway. The building was to cover three acres with the entrance in Stretford New Road. 'The Art Treasures building,'

15

said the *Manchester Courier*, 'is at Old Trafford, a pleasant suburb of Manchester two miles from the Royal Exchange. It adjoins the Botanical gardens and the Blind Asylum and Deaf and Dumb Institution.'

Manchester played several of their games at Rusholme while waiting for their new ground, but a great match organized for August, between the North and the South, was switched to Broughton. This was described as the biggest game yet in Manchester and the Broughton Club proved equal to the occasion. The wicket, it was said, looked like a billiard table and Tom Hunt, the Manchester professional, scored 102 on it, the only first-class hundred of his career. Hunt, incidentally, was killed in 1858 after playing for Twenty of Rochdale against the United All-England Eleven, run over and killed by a train as he walked from the ground to the station on the nearby railway line.

Just to underline Broughton's rising status, they took on the Gentlemen of the Town of Manchester – a team composed from various clubs in the town – and beat them by an innings. But Manchester, though deprived of the ground they had built up into one of the finest in the country, were far from finished. One of the conditions they had insisted on before giving up the ground was that a new one should be provided by the owner, Sir Humphrey de Trafford. And the land he provided, only a quarter of a mile away, was to become the Old Trafford ground that is now known throughout the cricket world. A small local club had played on these open fields, but a thorn hedge which divided the fields was removed, and accommodation was provided for players, although little was done right away for the spectators. On 25 April 1857, the Club inserted its five-line advertisement on the front pages of the *Manchester Guardian* and *Manchester Courier* to announce the opening of the new ground on Saturday 9 May.

Understandably, there was not much public interest in the opening of the cricket ground. The Exhibition was being opened on 5 May by Prince Albert and in the 142 days it was open, 1,053,538 people paid for admission, quite apart from the season-ticket holders. Queen Victoria attended on 30 June with Prince Albert, The Prince of Wales, Prince Alfred, The Princess Royal, Princess Alice and Prince Frederick William of Prussia. The excitement was intense, the crowds enormous right through to 17 October when the exhibition was closed. There was a toll-gate at Old Trafford in those days and the owners thought it necessary to insert their own advertisement three days before the exhibition began: 'To facilitate the passing of carriages through this gate on the 5th May, the public are requested to purchase pass-tickets at Greenwood's Omnibus Office, 31 Market

Street.' Stretford Road was then fringed with overhanging trees. Seymour Grove was known as Trafford Lane and there were no more than twelve houses in it. And farming was going on all around. Sam Swire, who was to play in Lancashire's first-ever county match and was secretary of the club for over thirty years, recalled an early game at Old Trafford when the next field was being mown. 'All at once,' he recalled, 'to our astonishment, a covey of partridges, disturbed by the farmers, rose from the oatfield, and setted down on the cricket crease. I picked up a couple and other players were equally fortunate.'

The next mention of Manchester Cricket Club that summer in 1857 came on Thursday 11 June, on the occasion of the Manchester v Liverpool match, played at the new ground. The *Manchester Guardian* did it proud:

> The ground which for many years was occupied by the Manchester Cricket Club, at Old Trafford, is now covered by the Art Treasures Palace. It was given up to the exhibition committee in June, 1856, and during the year that has intervened a new ground has been laid out, a new pavilion erected, and everything prepared for resuming play. The club, as we stated at the time, liberally gave up their lease to the exhibition committee for £1,000, which, considering the amount they had expended upon the land, was an exceedingly moderate demand. For the pavilion an additional £300 was given, thus making the total amount received £1,300. One of the terms upon which the land was given up was that Sir Humphrey de Trafford, the owner, should provide another field; and this condition has been carried out by the hon. baronet to the entire satisfaction of the club. The field selected is situated to the west of the Exhibition building, and consists of about seven acres of good level land. As soon as possession was obtained by the club, preparations were made for laying out the land, and for the erection of the pavilion. Of the seven acres about five were laid down for cricketing, the remaining two being reserved for a quoiting and bowling green. On the north side it is bounded by a close wooden fencing, and if this could have been continued entirely round, it would have considerably improved the appearance of the ground.
>
> The pavilion is erected on the north side, and while it is a great ornament to the ground it is well adapted for the purposes for which it will be used. It consists

of a central compartment (intended for a dining-hall), and two wings, a turret surmounting the centre. The dining-hall is 36 feet long by 22 feet wide. The western wing consists, on the ground floor, of a dressing room for the members, and above it a similar apartment for strangers, with a room for the committee. In the eastern wing are apartments for the residence of Hunt, the professional bowler, and for the accommodation of the caterer for the club (Mr. Johnson). The turret, which is raised a considerable height above the building, is a light and elegant erection, and commands a magnificent view of the surrounding country. Underneath the building is an excellent wine cellar, no unimportant acquisition in a cricket pavilion. The design for the building was drawn out by the committee, who have profited by experience; and it has been erected by Messrs David Bellhouse and Son. The roof of the dining-hall is in open rafters, which, with the door and window frames, are stained. The entire front of this room, which commands a view of the whole field, is composed of glass. The front of the pavilion, and forming the boundary between the cricket and quoiting ground, is a very neat rustic oak fencing which, in colour, corresponds with the stained wood of the building. The entire cost incurred by the club has been about £1,200. The present entrance to the field is by way of the Trafford Arms Hotel; but an arrangement has been made for opening a path leading directly from the Art Treasures platform to the ground, which will be a great convenience.

Since the old ground was given up, the club has had very little practice, and on no occasion has there been a regular match between the members. The new ground has only just been completed; and it was arranged that it should be opened with a match between this club and the Liverpool club, which was fixed to commence yesterday, at eleven o'clock. Accordingly, at that hour several members of the Manchester club assembled on the ground, and they were shortly after joined by their Liverpool friends. The weather at this time was unfortunately very threatening and in consequence of the heavy showers of rain which had fallen during the two previous days the ground was exceedingly wet though not so soft as might, the soil being composed, practically, of gravel.

*

18

Manchester fittingly won the first match on their new ground by 31 runs, scoring 152 and 46 to Liverpool's 78 and 89.

This was Manchester's fourth and last ground, finally settling only two miles from their first ground at Salford and a little over a mile from that at Moss Lane.

The surrender of the lease of the previous ground had not met with the approval of all the Manchester members and several of them had broken away to form the Western Club with a ground near Hope Hall in Eccles Old Road, Eccles. And when the county of Surrey, unbeaten that summer, came to the town to play Manchester in September it was on this ground that the game was staged. Manchester won by three runs, a great achievement that has since been hailed as a triumph and turning point for the Manchester Club. Yet this was a team composed of players from the Western and Broughton clubs as well as Manchester and included two of the great professionals of the day, John Wisden and Fred Lillywhite, plus Tom Davies of Nottingham. And as Wisden took twelve wickets and Lillywhite four in the low-scoring match, not all that much significance should be attached to the victory.

The importance of the Old Trafford ground grew quickly. When George Parr's team returned from America after their successful tour in 1859, this brilliant combination – including all the best professionals of the day – played a match at Old Trafford against Another England Eleven. As there was only a frail wire fence round the ground many people saw the game without having to pay. The gate receipts accordingly suffered and within two weeks Mr E. Whittaker, a generous supporter of cricket in its early days, had totally fenced in the ground at his own expense. All-England played United All-England there in 1861, and the North of England met the South there in 1862 with two Manchester players, E. B. Rowley and E. J. Bousfield, involved. Edmund Butler Rowley, who was to captain Lancashire through their early years, was just one of a large number of Rowleys who played prominent parts in the Manchester team.

In 1863 the North and South met again in May, and less than two weeks later sixteen of the Manchester Club and two bowlers took on the All-England team. An advertisement mentioned the trains which would stop at the Cricket Ground Station from Oxford Road. First class fares were fourpence, second class threepence-ha'penny, and third class threepence. A useful service provided by the railway was the ringing of a bell five minutes before the departure of return trains from Old Trafford Station to Manchester.

County cricket was beginning to grow. Surrey played Kent at

The Oval, Surrey scoring 192 for one in their second innings to win – 'perhaps the largest score ever recorded for the loss of one wicket.' Yorkshire played Surrey at Bramall Lane, Sheffield, and despite odds of 20–1 against them when they batted a second time needing 174 to win, they succeeded by three wickets. Interest in the counties was growing. It was time for Lancashire to become involved.

Chapter 2 1864–77

'He must indeed be an enthusiast who will encounter a nine-hour imprisonment in the bleak and comfortless Old Trafford cricket ground.'

The year of 1864 is significant in cricket history for several reasons. It was the year of the first *Wisden Almanack*, overarm bowling became legally allowed, and W. G. Grace first attracted attention on a cricket field. By this time Manchester Cricket Club was nearly fifty years old and probably the foremost club in Lancashire. So it was only fitting that it should take a prominent position in the moves to form a county club, several of its senior members being among the originators. The ground, with its fine new pavilion, was in excellent condition, and there was a wealth of amateur talent around to encourage them to think of broadening their horizons with the establishment of a county club. The formation of other county teams had become an object of interest and by the time the senior clubs of Lancashire were considering the step, there were eight leading counties – Kent, Hampshire, Surrey, Sussex, Middlesex, Nottinghamshire, Yorkshire and Cambridgeshire. Three members of the Manchester club, Alexander Rowley, Frank Glover and Sam Swire, were particularly prominent in pressing for the formation of a county club and on Saturday, 9 January 1864, the *Manchester Courier* reported that steps had been taken during the winter for forming a county club. A meeting was to be held at the Queens Hotel, Manchester, the following Tuesday.

Thirteen Lancashire cricket clubs were represented at the historic meeting at the Queens Hotel, Manchester, on 12 January 1864. Four were from the Manchester area, three from Liverpool, and the others were Ashton, Blackburn, Accrington, Wigan, Whalley

21

and Oldham. There were no representatives from anywhere further north in the county than Whalley, near Clitheroe, although several clubs like Lancaster, Barrow and Dalton had been in existence some years. The object of the meeting, it was said, was 'to consider the propriety of forming a county cricket club, with the view of spreading a thorough knowledge and appreciation of the game throughout Lancashire.' The Manchester club was most heavily represented with eleven members at the meeting, but the honour of the chairman of the meeting fell on a Liverpool Cricket Club man, Mr W. Horner. The prime mover of the meeting, Frank Glover, first addressed the group and said there seemed a general desire throughout Lancashire for a county club. Consequently, he and the gentlemen with whom he was associated had taken the preliminary steps towards it. He said the matches would be held alternately at Manchester, Liverpool, Preston, Blackburn and other places and it was hoped this way to introduce good cricket into every part of Lancashire. The nominal annual subscription would be a guinea, and . . . 'as the expenses would be very trifling, it was thought desirable that whatever surplus remained should be funded, so that at some future day they might be enabled to secure a playing ground that would do them credit and answer all the requirements of the county.'

He moved the resolution that the county club should be formed and that the gentlemen present form a committee to obtain subscriptions and enrol members. Another Manchester gentleman, T. Fothergill, seconded. Mr J. W. Allison, of Longsight, moved the next resolution which recommended that, in order to establish the club, donations or annual subscriptions be invited from clubs throughout the county. Mr H. W. Barber, from Manchester, seconded, and a sub-committee was appointed to frame rules and recommendations for the next meeting. The idea of playing matches in different parts of the county was adopted, but as Sam Swire did not approve, he would not join the committee. He felt Old Trafford should be the central ground for all matches and that Manchester should be the headquarters, as Kennington Oval was for Surrey. His view, although not supported then, was soon to be adopted. Frank Glover was elected secretary and the Earl of Sefton president. The people present at this historic meeting were: S. H. Swire, F. Glover, H. W. Barber, E. B. Rowley, A. B. Rowley, D. Bleackley, T. Fothergill, Captain Ashton, A. Birley, E. Challender, J. Holt jnr, all of the Manchester Club; R. K. Birley, J. Becton, R. Entwistle, H. Ashton of Western CC, the Manchester off-shoot; E. D. Long, H. Royle, W. Horner, Higgins of Liverpool; J. Whittington, J. B. Payne, R. Crawshaw, F. W. Wright of Broughton; E. Whittaker and E. Hobson of Ashton; J. W. Allison and E. J. Bousfield of Longsight; J. Yates and S. G. Greenwood of

Blackburn; J. Smith of Accrington; T. Wall of Wigan; J. Swailes of Oldham; Alec Eccles of Huyton; H. M. Tennent of Northern; and R. Green of Whalley.

One man who could not attend the meeting was Mark Phillips, president of Manchester Cricket Club for forty-one years and the first Member of Parliament for Manchester in 1832. He was one of the great benefactors of the game and although he could not be present at the meeting he wrote to the committee offering his full support.

> As one of the oldest members of the Manchester Cricket Club, I shall, of course, be happy to assist in promoting the formation of a county club, to encourage and maintain so fine a recreation in my native county. Will you kindly act for me on this occasion? I cannot do better than place myself in your hands, and I will thank you to enrol me as a member, and put my name down for *any* sum you think proper for launching the scheme successfully. I do not know whether I retain the honour of being President of the Manchester Cricket Club, but whether I do or not, my interest in its prosperity will terminate only with my life. I sincerely wish that every parish in the kingdom possessed a cricket club, and a good ground to play upon.

So Lancashire County Cricket Club was founded, although no county matches were arranged that season and it was to be several years before the county team was to have real appeal to the public. Even clubs in the county were slow to associate with the team and the development of pride in Lancashire cricket took time to emerge. Even so, 1864 was the first season in which any matches were played under the name of Lancashire, eight in all, in which took part such prominent players as the Rowley brothers, Joe Makinson, Edwin Bousfield, Frank Wright – who was to score the first county century at Old Trafford – Sam Swire, J. B. Payne, Edwin Whittaker, Arthur Appleby and Cornelius Coward.

Lancashire played professionals in only one of those eight matches in 1864, and that was in the return match with Birkenhead Park and Ground who had almost pulled off a surprise victory in the opening game at Warrington on 15 and 16 June. Lancashire's team for that first game after the formation of the county club was J. Fairclough, J. White, E. B. Rowley – who was to captain the county until 1879 – J. Becton, B. J. Lawrence, G. H. Grimshaw – who was to play one county game in 1868 – S. H. Swire, J. Rowley, F. H. Gussage, W. Robinson and T. T. Bellhouse. Birkenhead Park, needing 105 to win, were 90 for one when time ran out on them and for the

23

return match, at Birkenhead Park a month later, Lancashire reinforced their team with three professionals, Bill Hickton, Gideon Holgate and a player called Nicholls. Hickton scored 80 and took five wickets, but Birkenhead Park drew the match easily enough. Lancashire were represented in all the other matches by amateurs, taking on the Gentlemen of Shropshire, Warwickshire and Yorkshire twice each. They won all their home games – at Liverpool, Old Trafford and Broughton – and lost two and drew one of their away games.

The first true county game came in 1865 when Middlesex alone accepted Lancashire's challenge to 'home and home' matches. The first mention of the county team came in the form of advertisements in the *Manchester Guardian* and the *Manchester Courier* on Saturday 15 July:

> Cricket – A Grand match will be played at Old Trafford on the 20th, 21st and 22nd of July between the county of Lancaster and the county of Middlesex.

The teams were announced, Lancashire's being R. Blackstock, E. J. Bousfield, F. J. Crooke, J. F. Leese, J. Makinson, A. B. Rowley, E. Whittaker, F. Wright, R. Iddison, F. Reynolds and W. Perry. The only change in the team which actually played was the inclusion of Sam Swire, who was to serve as Lancashire's honorary secretary from 1873 until his death in 1905, due to the withdrawal of 21-year-old Oxfordshire-born Frank Wright. Swire's inclusion took the number of Lancashire-born players in that opening game up to seven. Richard Blackstock was born in Cheshire and the three professionals, Roger Iddison, Fred Reynolds and Bill Perry, were all from outside the county. Some years later Reynolds recalled that opening game when only 300 or 400 spectators were present and had to make their way to Old Trafford from Manchester by omnibus. Some wire netting was stretched round the ground and two or three canvas tents were rigged up to eke out the slender accommodation for the visitors.

The reports were tucked away at the bottom of a page and although the *Manchester Guardian* reported a large attendance, the 'gate' was only £25. This opening match is noteworthy on three counts – the first innings scores were tied, Middlesex underarm bowler Vyell Edward Walker took all ten Lancashire second innings wickets despite having bowled only a little that season, and Lancashire won by 62 runs. One of Walker's wickets, said the *Manchester Guardian*, came through 'Mr Bousfield being caught out at an extraordinary long distance by Mr Wilkinson, a splendid catch which was much applauded.' The said Mr Wilkinson, who scored 59 in the first innings, was not at the ground for the final day when Reynolds and Iddison bowled

24

Lancashire to victory. It was a great achievement but had to take its place in the newspapers well behind the elections taking place at the time when Manchester sent two Liberals to Parliament. Jem Mace and Joe Wormald were preparing for the fight for the belt and the championship of the prize ring with £200 a side, and advertisements proclaimed Grand Swimming Galas and athletic events, not to mention the attraction of the Belle Vue Gardens, Pomona Gardens and Zoological Gardens at Belle Vue. It would be some time before Lancashire cricket could overtake such events in importance in the public's eyes.

Middlesex had experienced great difficulty in getting a team together and *Bell's Life* described their fielding as not quite up to the mark at first, 'but improved on acquaintance with the ground which was in excellent order.' Play was resumed early on the final day and, said *Bell's Life*, 'It being again fine (a wonder at Manchester), a large assemblage was present.' The return match was arranged for 7 August and the newspaper commented 'We hope to see a good ring as we can assure those who have not seen much of the northern gentlemen's cricket, that they are good all-round players.' The game was played at the Cattle Market, Islington, where Middlesex gained ample revenge with a ten-wicket win in two days over a Lancashire team showing seven changes. *Lillywhite's Annual* for 1866 referred to Lancashire, the latest accession to the list of county cricket clubs. 'Not many professionals but making ample amends,' it said.

There is no mention of who captained Lancashire in those first two games but it seems probable that Alex Rowley led the team at Old Trafford and his brother Edmund in the return game.

THE ROWLEYS played significant parts in the formation and establishing of Lancashire in county cricket. Alexander Butler Rowley, a forcing middle order batsman and slow, left-hand roundarm bowler, was good enough to make his first-class debut for Manchester when he was only 16 and went on to play twelve matches for Lancashire. Edmund, who was five years younger than his brother, played an even more important role in the development of the county. He played eighty-one matches and captained the team through much of the first fifteen years, including a share of the championship with Nottinghamshire in 1879, his final year as captain, although he went on for another season under A. N. Hornby's leadership. He was a dashing, middle-order batsman and although he never scored a first-class century he did hit a remarkable 219 for the Gentlemen of Lancashire against the Yorkshire Gentlemen at Old Trafford in 1867, an innings which included five 5s and nineteen 4s. There were seven Rowley brothers who were proficient at cricket for as well as Alexander and Edmund there were James, Septimus, Arthur,

Joseph and Walter. On one occasion the Rowleys, two Swires and two Glovers played together under the title of Gentlemen of Lancashire and beat the Manchester club.

Surrey joined Middlesex as opponents for Lancashire in 1866 and after being held to a draw at The Oval, went to Liverpool's ground in Wavertree Road where they beat Lancashire by three wickets. Middlesex won both their games, by 53 runs and by six wickets, and it was only at The Oval that Lancashire could hold their head high, salvaging a draw after being 227 behind on the first innings. The first game was against Middlesex at Old Trafford where, commented *Bell's Life* 'As is always the case on the Old Trafford ground, Manchester, a beautiful wicket had been prepared.' The first bell rang at twelve thirty-five for the start of the game but it was after one o'clock before it got underway due to the late arrival of two of the Middlesex gentlemen. In the return match, again at Islington, Mr Bissett, one of the Middlesex batsmen, was awarded a six for a hit which passed over the pavilion into the cattle market. Lancashire then moved on to The Oval where Roger Iddison scored Lancashire's first century – 'as fine an innings as has been played for some time.' His 106 was made up of two 4s, five 3s, eighteen 2s and forty-seven singles and he was one of several players who were rewarded although, *Bell's Life* pointed out, 'There was no public display or time wasted on the ceremonies.'

ROGER IDDISON batted almost the whole of the final day – nearly five hours – and scored 106 of Lancashire's 321 for eight in the second innings. Iddison was one of the finest professionals of his day, a Yorkshireman who was born in Bedale on 15 September 1834, and who died in York in 1890. He went on the first tour of Australia in 1861–2, played in All-England and other representative teams, and in the days before strict qualifications had been introduced, he played for Lancashire and Yorkshire in the same season. But whenever the teams played one another Iddison was always with the county of his birth, which he captained from 1863 to 1870. He played for Lancashire up to 1870, scoring 621 runs (average 23.88) and taking 56 wickets (15.62) in his sixteen matches, and helping to steer Lancashire through those early days when the team, particularly for away games, was often desperately weak. Despite his century at The Oval – one of only two he scored in 134 first-class matches – Iddison rated his best performance being his 71 not out (out of 219) and 64 not out (143 for eight) to secure a draw against Surrey at Old Trafford in 1867.

The game against Surrey at Wavertree Road in 1866 helped convince the Liverpool club that they were not interested in taking on county matches. Liverpool had played an important part in the formation of Lancashire and for a time the club took on the expensive task of organizing and centralizing county cricket. But they lost too much money and left it to the Manchester club to take over the management of Lancashire. The idea of taking the county team to various parts of Lancashire was an admirable idea but in those early days there was still more interest in Grand cricket matches and even in ordinary club games.

Manchester took over the organization of the county team in 1867, undertaking to pay all expenses which came to £120 a year, but on condition that all home matches should be played at Old Trafford and that the selection of county teams should also rest with the Manchester club. The subscription to the club was raised to £2 2s, and the subscription to the county was reduced from £1 1s to 5s. It was not long, of course, before Manchester were accused of selecting too many of their own players for Lancashire, ignoring fine amateur talent in other parts of the county. Frequently the cry would go up to take the Lancashire matches to various parts of the county, but up until 1881, when the new Aigburth ground was opened, only Old Trafford, Whalley, Castleton and Liverpool had staged county matches.

The year of 1867 contained two notable events, one a remarkable debut innings by the 25-year-old Manchester professional Jim Ricketts, the other the start of the matches with Yorkshire.

JIM RICKETTS, the son of a barber, was one of a small number of Lancashire-born professionals to make a mark in county cricket in those early years. Born in Manchester on 9 February 1842, he played his first match from 30 May to 1 June 1867, against Surrey at The Oval where the pitch, judging by the many high scores there, must have been the best in the country. To score a century in those days was notable enough, but to open and bat through the innings for 195 not out was little short of incredible. By the end of the first day Ricketts was 153 and on the second day, according to reports, 'he played with the same unshaken patience' to carry his bat for the unprecedented score (for a colt) of 195 'which would have done credit to any veteran.' He was rewarded with £4 from the Surrey club and a collection raised another £4. Just before the Lancashire innings closed, he played several faulty strokes which prompted a former great Surrey player, who had just arrived on the ground, to remark to a friend 'Well, Fred, I have seen enough of cricket to know that that man is a rank duffer.' 'Quite so,' was the reply, 'only he has just made 180.' Ricketts, by trade a master tinsman, never again remotely approached the form of that first innings. He played thirty-three more games for Lancashire, sixty-six innings in all up to 1877, but passed 50

27

only once more when he scored 54 against Nottinghamshire in 1868. He finished his career with 1,120 runs for an average of 18.06, and died in 1894 in Sale, aged 52.

The Lancashire team stayed in London after the drawn match at The Oval in 1867 for their first match at Lord's against MCC. Ricketts, perhaps still glassy-eyed from his record innings at The Oval, was sharply reminded of cricket's fickle fortunes when he was out for a duck. Bill Hickton, a Derbyshire-born bowler who had made his debut at The Oval, took five for 69 and six for 22. Mops and pails had to be used to clear pools of water from the pitch so the match could be finished, Lancashire losing by 50 runs. Lancashire played only two counties that season, drawing both matches with Surrey and losing their first three encounters with Yorkshire. The first Roses match was at the beautiful Whalley ground where Lancashire, said by the *Manchester Guardian* to be greatly overmatched, especially in bowling power, lost by an innings and 56 runs. The *Manchester Courier* thought it only right to point out that the team were not a fair representation of the county owing to the feeling of jealousy by some leading amateurs. Yorkshire, on the other hand, were about as good as they could be.

The suggestion of jealousy on the part of some clubs and players stayed with Lancashire for many years. It was all to do with Manchester Cricket Club taking over the management and selection of the county teams and, so it was thought, favouring themselves. A newspaper called *The Sphinx* asked in 1869 if something could not be done to widen the circuit from which the players were chosen. The writer maintained that nine of the gentlemen for one particular match were local players, 'several of whom were as much out of place in a county eleven as a cab horse would be in a race for the Derby.' Sam Swire described *The Sphinx* as a nasty paper and claimed the writer of 'these so-called cricket articles' was a prominent member of the Broughton club. Several clubs arranged matches which clashed with a county fixture and Broughton even staged the still-popular festival matches, which were to include W. G. Grace in the 1870s, on the days when Lancashire were at Old Trafford in a county match.

T. T. Bellhouse, a prominent member of Manchester and Lancashire, felt compelled in a letter to the *Manchester Courier* to point out that Old Trafford was the finest ground in the North of England and that the Manchester club, being the oldest in the county, was entitled to the management of county matches. Another reader, describing himself as 'Only a Spectator', wrote to the *City News* in 1873 about the 'petty jealousies' which were hampering Lancashire's prospects. Manchester men dominated the county scene and there were frequent complaints that the management of the county club had always exclusively been in the hands of one or two Manchester members. Why, it was asked, were other good clubs, including such as Liverpool, Preston, Bolton and Broughton, seldom or never represented in the county team? There is no doubt that general dissatisfaction existed among Lancashire clubs in those early days and it took several years, and probably the appointment of A. N. Hornby as captain in 1880, to wipe it out.

Lancashire's two other matches against Yorkshire in 1867 were at Old Trafford, where they lost by 165 runs, and Middlesbrough, where defeat was by an innings and 40 runs. George Freeman, an extremely fast bowler, missed the Old Trafford match, but in the other two games he took twenty-one wickets for 149 runs.

One other important event happened in 1867. A. N. Hornby, who was to exert the greatest single influence over Lancashire cricket, made his debut. He was 20 years old when he played at Whalley where he opened the innings with Jim Ricketts, scored 2 and 3, and was out twice to Freeman.

The year of 1867 was a poor one for Lancashire. In 1868 they ventured to challenge the formidable Nottinghamshire team, and lost both matches, and were bowled out for 30 and 34 by Yorkshire. At least they managed to beat Surrey by eight wickets, their only victory over any county in three years. The *Manchester Guardian* said there was some consolation for Surrey in the fact that there were players from four different counties in the Lancashire team. In fact there were six different counties involved with George Dunlop – playing his only first-class match – coming from Edinburgh, Francis Head from London, Roger Iddison from Yorkshire, Bill Hickton (Derbyshire), Fred Reynolds (Cambridgeshire), with Lancashire represented by Jim Ricketts, Cornelius Coward, Edmund Rowley, Joe Makinson, Edwin Bousfield and Sam Swire.

The first-ever game against Nottinghamshire was staged at Trent Bridge where admission was sixpence, the wickets were pitched at eleven o'clock and a spacious marquee was provided for the ladies. Four prominent amateur members of the advertised Lancashire team, Edmund Rowley, Horatio Barber, Joe Makinson and Arthur Appleby, failed to turn up. Their places were taken by professionals, including Harry Ramsbottom from Enfield and Bill Richmond from Burnley, two batsmen who each scored 1 and 0 in the match and never played again. An unusual incident occurred when Sam Biddulph was run out after hitting a ball from Bill Hickton to square leg. The *Nottingham Journal* explained:

The ball dropped short of the tree in the Bridgford Lane fence where it was well judged and caught by Cornelius Coward. Being outside the boundary, however, the ball, it is said according to cricket laws, ought to have been considered dead, but Biddulph evidently thought himself out and as he was leaving the ground, the ball was thrown to the wicket-keeper (Mr. Bousfield) who sharply knocked down the stumps. Biddulph was thereupon given run out, an improper judgement (some cricketers say) as three runs ought to have been credited to him owing to the ball falling outside the boundary 'deed'. The umpire's verdict was not disputed, however, Biddulph, like a true cricketer, quietly leaving the ground.

Incidentally, some indication of the area around Trent Bridge may be judged from a sentence from the match report: 'Mr. Bousfield let out at a ball from Shaw, driving it to the end of the hovels by the Grantham Road for which four were marked.'

Lancashire's stock was low and in the next two years only two counties would play them. Surrey and Sussex played them in 1869 and because of the slackness in regulations covering players' qualifications, James Southerton, the great slow right-arm bowler, opposed Lancashire in all four games. He was then 41 years old but still a formidable bowler as he demonstrated by taking forty-two wickets for 489 runs. Lancashire won both Old Trafford matches and lost both away, beating Surrey by seven wickets and Sussex, who played an all-professional side, by 104 runs following the first-ever century by a Lancashire player at Old Trafford. This was 120 not out by the Reverend Frank Wright, the man who had dropped out of the first Lancashire game in 1865, and who was making only his second appearance for the county.

Five or six places were usually taken up by gentlemen in Lancashire teams of this period and one of the outstanding performances of 1869 was the eight for 68 against Surrey by a corn merchant from Enfield, Arthur Appleby.

ARTHUR APPLEBY was, for several years, the leading amateur fast bowler in England and would have made a greater mark in Lancashire and English cricket if he had felt able to leave his family business more often. His early cricket was played with Enfield, a club that would later help form the Lancashire League. He wanted to be a long stop but was told he would have to bowl, and quickly discovered that his underarm efforts were useless and he must bowl roundarm. It was unusual to have a good amateur fast bowler in those days when gentlemen preferred the gentle

art of batting, and left the donkeywork of bowling to the professionals. In fact, Appleby once said in an interview that if Enfield had had a couple of professionals, and the district had not been one in which cricket practice at night was really the only amusement, he should probably never have been known in first-class cricket as a bowler. He recalled those days when he spoke at a presentation to himself by Enfield Cricket Club:

> Although I was by no means an expert at that time [1862], having had little practice, I suppose I was an enthusiast. I knew that I, in common with other young men of this village, required some occupation in the long summer evenings, and I felt that healthy outdoor exercise was the best. Looking around, I saw no sport that seemed to me as accessible to myself, and to those in this township – none that required so little preparation, so little special training – as cricket and I therefore identified myself with the movement.

Appleby's debut for Lancashire came in 1866, when he was 23, an impressive first appearance in which he took six for 30 against Surrey at Liverpool. The Surrey secretary was sufficiently influenced to ask Appleby if he would be available to play for the Gentlemen against the Players the following season. A great honour for so inexperienced a player. His career with Lancashire stretched over twenty-two seasons, yet he played only fifty-eight times for the county, usually because of business commitments but also because of invitations to play in more attractive matches being staged at the same time. He took 245 wickets at 14.17 runs each with a best performances of nine for 25 against Sussex at Hove in 1877. He was also a more-than-useful batsman with an average of 13.31 which compared favourably with specialist batsmen in those days. His best innings came against Yorkshire at Sheffield in 1871 when he batted No. 8 and scored 99. 'I had no idea I was so near the 100,' he said later. 'On my retirement I found Mr Hornby on the steps of the pavilion ready with a new bat to present to me.' He toured Canada and America with a team of amateurs in 1872, but twice turned down the chance of touring Australia, first with W. G. Grace in 1873, then with Lord Harris in 1878, because of his corn-milling business. If he had gone with Lord Harris he would no doubt have played in the only Test match of that tour and would have joined A. N. Hornby, Sandford Schultz and Vernon Royle as Lancashire's first Test cricketers.

Appleby, bless him, kept scrapbooks which are in Lancashire's possession and are marvellous mirrors of cricket in those early days. There is even the letter written to him by Russell Walker, asking him to go to Australia that winter of 1878-9. 'I know that you are never long absent from your business as a rule. Of course as our leading amateur bowler I am obliged to ask you first of all or I should not have done my duty.'

An even more interesting letter was the one from C. J. Ottaway, dated 25 January, and starting 'My dear old Applepie', inviting him to take part in a trip to America that year. He marked the section:

> Private – the terms are *ostensibly* that we pay our own expenses. In *reality* the expense need be nothing. Patterson secured from the Allans a first-class passage for us there and back and from the railway companies private cars at our disposal. He has also arranged that the Hotel Keepers shall charge us on expenses (to them) out of pocket, and convey us free to the grounds. But as I said, to the world it is given forth that we pay our own expenses. Practically speaking it would cost more staying in England.

Appleby, however, turned that down as well.

When Appleby died in 1902 aged 59, W. G. Grace said, in tribute, that few bowlers had so easy and beautiful an action or could keep up their end for so long a time without going to pieces. He bowled a fast round left arm, took a deliberate and long run, was very straight and kept a good length. He stayed a member of the Lancashire and MCC committees up to his death and had even played for Enfield the summer before he died. Outside cricket he was a county magistrate and an alderman on Lancashire County Council, building up a popularity which was displayed on the day he was buried when work ceased and schools in the area closed.

Wisden said of Lancashire's performance in 1869, that all the good batting to be found in the county of commerce would frequently be of no avail unless the Lancashire gentlemen 'reform their fielding'. The almanack also declared: 'Better if the professional element could be strengthened and the undoubted strong amateur power more frequently played in the matches away from home.' This last comment was one that was frequently expressed through the years as prominent amateurs such as Hornby (in his first eight years), Appleby and A. G. Steel, not to mention innumerable lesser-known gentlemen, turned down requests to play for the county. Several gentlemen, of course, had business commitments and felt unable particularly to undertake long journeys with several nights away from home. Others found more attractive matches to interest them.

Edmund Rowley, the Lancashire captain, felt forced to write to Appleby and Hornby in August 1869, almost beseeching them to put the county before other considerations. In his letter to Appleby, he said:

When Lancashire have such men in the county as yourself and Hornby and they will not play, I think it is only fair to expect that the matches will be lost. At the commencement of the season I was very glad to hear that you and Hornby had arranged to play with Lancashire in all the County matches and I certainly understood that Lancashire was to have the preference – but may I ask has this arrangement been kept? My own idea is that County Cricket is the best that can be played and I really think that you should throw over any engagement you may have for the sake of playing for your county. Having such a bowler in the county as you are and not playing, it is perfectly absurd to expect that we shall ever attain that position as a County which we both for bowling and batting are clearly entitled to. As I have said before I really think that you should throw all things aside for the County's sake (even Canterbury). You have known from the commencement of the season what the county matches were and their dates, *and you also knew that you were required for all those County matches*. Therefore I think that if you found that you could not conveniently play both against Warwick and at Canterbury I think you should have given Lancashire the preference. I am sure you will not think any the worse of me in writing as above but really, I was so awfully disgusted with the exhibition of yesterday (which I am sure would not have happened had you been there) that if this state of things keeps on the County will go to —.

When I am getting up the team here to play against the Zingari on the 27th and 28th of August you will personally oblige me if you will play on those days. With your aid I think we shall be able to give the swells a good licking. And now adieu, hoping you will take my remarks in good part and that you will have lots of luck in Canterbury.

Yours affectionately,
[signed] E. B. Rowley.
P.S. Give me as early an answer as possible. I am writing Hornby.

It was a problem that was not to go away for many years. The gentlemen preferred to play at Old Trafford and avoid long journeys. Edmund Rowley, though captain, played in only seven of the first twenty-six away matches, while his brother Alex played ten of his twelve matches for the county at home. A. N. Hornby was even worse in his early years, playing in only six of a possible twenty-three

33

away matches after his debut, although staying available for more showy matches. Three of those six matches were in London and he steadfastly refused to go into Derbyshire for a game between 1871 and 1877. On average there were four or five professionals in early Old Trafford matches, but the number would rise to seven or eight, and at times nine, for away games. On one occasion, in 1871, Lancashire could not find one gentleman to go to Gravesend, and eleven professionals, seven of them colts, most of whom were hardly ever seen again, went to take on Kent with Fred Reynolds as captain, and lost by five wickets. Seven gentlemen, including Hornby, who scored 75, J. F. Leese (43), Appleby (four for 25 and four for 13), and Alex Rowley, played in the return match at Old Trafford, which Lancashire won by an innings.

By 1870, Lancashire were down to playing only two counties, Hampshire and Surrey, after Middlesex, Sussex, Nottinghamshire and Yorkshire had dropped off their fixture list. Lancashire won three of the games, including that against Surrey at Old Trafford, a game which was for Fred Reynolds' benefit and which ended in just over two days. It was a strong Lancashire team which won by eight wickets and which prompted the *Manchester Courier* to say: 'If the same team could be secured for all the county matches of the season there would be little fear of the result.'

FRED REYNOLDS was born in Cambridgeshire in 1834 and his early days, he said, went back to the time when men played in top hats and underarm lob bowling was taken seriously. In 1852 he went from his little village of Botisham to the University at Cambridge to spend his days bowling at and playing cricket with the undergraduates. He was paid a weekly wage, but before that professionals were paid by the hour or day, which was very nice when the sun shone, but not all that good in England. He spent two years at Charterhouse but in 1855 became one of the Lord's ground bowlers . . . 'to attend to the noblemen and gentlemen at the Marylebone Club,' proclaimed *Lillywhite's Annual*. He played for Suffolk and George Parr's England Eleven before joining Manchester Cricket Club in 1860, four years before Lancashire were founded. He played from Lancashire's first match until 1874, taking part in thirty-eight games and taking ninety-four wickets at 19.39 runs each.

Reynolds went on to become the Old Trafford ground manager, a job he retained until his retirement in 1908 when he was 74, a still burly figure with a rugged face and hair like driven snow. On his retirement he recalled his first days in Manchester in 1860 when club cricket was the chief sport of the amateurs and there was only one other professional besides himself. By 1908 there was a ground staff of twenty-two and the membership of under 400 in 1860 had grown to 3,000. He recalled that

34

fields were set differently in the first days of Lancashire cricket:

> We had a long stop and a short and a long leg. You see, bowlers did not at that period bang the ball down seven yards from the stumps and place a small crowd of fieldsmen in the slips. The leg break was freely resorted to and bowlers made it their business to try to hit the sticks. If I had my way I would make bowlers pitch nearer to the wickets. Batsmen have to stand inside their line and a long hop that has time to rear and is meant for a catch in the slips is not cricket. But then I'm afraid I'm of the old school.

Reynolds also recalled the days when he was given the shooting rights at Old Trafford. 'You wouldn't think we used to have plenty of shooting round here at Old Trafford,' he said. 'But we had in the 70s and every morning I could go out with the gun and be sure of some snipe before returning. The military, too, would come out to drill in the adjoining fields. Those days are gone.' Reynolds died in 1915, leaving Fred Crooke, who died in 1923, as the sole survivor from the first game.

A new bat was always presented by Lancashire for 'good displays of cricket' and Hornby got one for his innings of 132 against Hampshire in 1870. An even more unusual performance in a game watched by scarcely 500 people over the three days was that of Bill Hickton, who became the first Lancashire bowler to take all ten wickets in an innings – ten for 46. The *Manchester Guardian* reported that he received the 'Queen's Portrait' for this feat; the *Examiner* was much more straightforward, saying he had received the 'talent sovereign' which, of course, bore the head of Queen Victoria.

BILL HICKTON was born in Hardstoft in Derbyshire in 1842, a right arm, fast bowler who played in twenty-four matches for Lancashire from 1867 to 1871 before returning to his native county that same year when they entered county cricket. In those few matches he took 144 wickets at 14.05 runs each. He played for Derbyshire in their first match with Lancashire in 1871 and must have found enormous satisfaction in taking four for 16 and three for 58 in his team's surprise innings victory. He played in both games against Lancashire that year but also played for Lancashire in their four remaining games against Kent and Yorkshire. W. G. Grace spoke of Hickton as a bowler of whom the batsmen might beware.

Lancashire's opponents changed totally in 1871 when Derbyshire and Kent were played for the first time and Yorkshire again provided opposition after a two-year absence. The opening game, against the

35

newcomers to county cricket, Derbyshire, at Old Trafford, was to provide the sort of shock to the system that was to be remembered for years. Leese and Appleby chose to play for the North of England Gentlemen's team against the South, even the captain, Edmund Rowley, was absent, and four new players were blooded.

Lancashire were bowled out for 25, which still stands today as their lowest total against any county. The fall of wickets, especially the first six, makes awful reading: One for 2, two for 4, three for 4, four for 5, five for 5, six for 5, seven for 15, eight for 19, nine for 25, ten for 25. Lancashire never recovered, losing by an innings and 11 runs. The *Derby and Chesterfield Reporter* declared: 'The wickets were pitched at half past eleven. In a very short time, the Lancashire lot, not at all up to former appearances, many of their best men being at London, playing in the North v South match, were literally "mown down" by Gregory and Hickton's "shooters".'

This was the year when Lancashire played their first all-professional team, with Reynolds as captain, against Kent at Gravesend. But there were still all-Gentlemen teams representing Lancashire, such as those against Cambridge and Oxford Universities. *Bell's Life* reported from Oxford that the hit of this match was made by Mr Law (Oxford) who 'made a splendid hit to square leg for eight – the ball going down the hill, through the sheep pen, to the cowsheds.'

Lancashire's first match against Yorkshire that season produced the fifth successive win for the White Rose, this time by 222 runs at Old Trafford. The *Manchester Courier* suggested Lancashire had fought shy of encountering such formidable antagonists for some time; the *Manchester Guardian* praised them for their pluck in throwing out the challenge. The *Sheffield Daily Telegraph* described Old Trafford as one of the finest grounds in England and said the crease, though dead, was splendid, as smooth and lively as a billiard board. The newspaper said there were no more than fifty people present at the start of the first day, one hundred for the second, and only about 1,000 for the match. Reynolds, it was said, opened the bowling with lobs.

Lancashire's revenge, and first win in a Roses game, was to come at Sheffield eighteen days later when Arthur Appleby and Bill Hickton played major roles. Appleby, batting at No. 8, scored 99 and took five for 87 and three for 54; Hickton, batting at No. 11, scored 55 and took four for 62. Dicky Barlow, who was to become one of Lancashire's finest professionals and whose opening partnerships with A. N. Hornby were to be a feature of county cricket, made his debut in this game, taking the wicket of Johnnie West with his first delivery.

The *Sheffield Daily Telegraph* reported that between 2,000 and

3,000 people were there on the afternoon of the opening day. Joe Rowbotham, who had played for Yorkshire since 1861, twice refused to bowl after Lancashire had passed 300. The newspaper, in describing Hornby's fielding, said Sheffield had never seen such a fine exhibition.

Scotsman Alec Watson, another outstanding professional who was to play for Lancashire for twenty-three years, also made his debut in 1871, and recalled in 1901, when players wanted to be paid in winter as well as summer, that there was no chance of such good fortune in his early days. 'It was a hard task to keep county cricket going at all then,' he said. 'Why, the Lancashire Committee have had to leave Barlow out because they could not afford to pay him. If they could find a gentleman who could play and pay his own expenses, it was a great relief to them. How many such gentlemen do you find now?'

When ALEC WATSON first asked for a trial with Lancashire Colts he was asked by Fred Reynolds, the ground manager, where he came from. Watson told him he was born in Coatbridge in Scotland whereupon Reynolds said 'We want no Scotsmen here.' Lancashire quickly changed their minds, however, and Watson played for twenty-three seasons, taking 1,308 wickets at a cost of 13.39 runs each. Watson was born on 4 November 1844, and from boyhood worked in an iron works. He did not enjoy it and spent as much time as he could on the ground at the Drumpellier club, one of the best in Scotland. When he was 20 he played against All-England in Glasgow and four years later became professional with the Manchester club, Rusholme. Two years later he was on the groundstaff at Old Trafford and soon established himself in the side as an off spinner who was so accurate that in one game, wicket-keeper Dick Pilling said he went through the entire innings without once handling the ball.

MCC Scores and Biographies **described Watson as an artful bowler with much curl. 'An able batsman and could, when required, act as wicket-keeper or long stop, being an active little fellow.' He and Bill McIntyre used to both bowl and keep wicket at their own ends, keeping wicket alternately to each other's bowling. Watson reckoned he bowled unchanged with a partner about eighty times and had bowled 100 overs in a day. (Even with five-ball overs that is the equivalent of eighty overs today.) By 1877 he was thought to be the best slow bowler in the country and was chosen for the Players against the Gentlemen at Lord's and took five for 60 in the first innings. He was an important part of the Lancashire team which won the championship in 1881. He took 100 wickets in 1887 and it was said that in his twenty-three seasons with Lancashire he missed only two out of 285 matches and, in a career in which he sent down 71,405 balls, he never delivered a wide. There were rumblings throughout his** career that he was a thrower, but he was never no-balled. Although he played until 1893 – he was then 48 – and was considered one of the finest spin bowlers in the country, he never played for England or went on any tour. It has been suggested he was overlooked because he was a Scotsman but it was the suspicion about his bowling that probably went against him. Watson ran a sports outfitters in Manchester, and coached at public schools, including Marlborough, from where he recommended Reg Spooner. He died in Manchester in 1920, aged 75.

Lancashire played even fewer county games in 1872 than the six of the previous season. They played only Derbyshire and Yorkshire, but overcame the disappointment of a thin-looking fixture list by winning all four matches, the two against Derbyshire by an innings. The major difference in the Lancashire side was the introduction of fast bowler Bill McIntyre from Nottinghamshire, a county which was to provide Lancashire with many of their outstanding cricketers in the early years. In his first match he took eight wickets, in his second ten, his third eleven and his fourth twelve, a full bowling analysis for the season of 214.1 overs, 108 maidens, and forty-one wickets for 232 runs.

BILL McINTYRE was born in Eastwood, also the birthplace of D. H. Lawrence, on 24 May 1844, and played for his native county from 1869 to 1871 before joining Lancashire and playing for them from 1872 to 1880. For a few years he was one of the best bowlers in England and three times headed the first-class averages – in 1872 when his forty-one wickets cost him only 5.65 each, 1873 when he took sixty-three (8.38) and 1876 when eighty-nine wickets from ten games cost 11.41 each. He died at Prestwich Asylum, near Manchester, in 1892 when he was 48 years old, leaving a widow and five children.

Lancashire used only three bowlers during their four victories in 1872, Watson, a slow roundarm bowler, taking twenty wickets for 178 runs, and Arthur Appleby twelve for 130. Dicky Barlow, who had taken a wicket with his first ball in county cricket the previous season, could only stand and watch this year. Lancashire fielded strong teams for all the matches – they travelled only to Derby and Sheffield – and had eight gentlemen in the team against Derbyshire at Old Trafford. The *Manchester Examiner* also thought it worth mentioning that in Derbyshire's second innings, when the highly-rated Edward Jackson was keeping wicket, 'but four balls passed to the long stop.' This game was originally planned for Thursday, Friday and Saturday, but was altered to a two-day match (Friday and Saturday) purely so the followers of county cricket could witness a good display on the Saturday. But all Derbyshire's second innings wickets fell in an hour and a half for 51 that day and the game was over by 1.30 p.m. Another Saturday's receipts had been lost.

Cricket was booming by now. Clubs had sprung up all over the county and in an article on cricket in Manchester, the *City News* declared:

> Undoubtedly the number of lads and men who play at cricket has increased enormously during the last 20 years. Not only has there been a very large increase in the number of clubs in and about the city, but the occupation of nearly every vacant space of ground by boys engaged at cricket of an evening, with a few bricks for a wicket, proves this to demonstration. At the same time there is less play and practice on the grounds of most of the leading clubs than there used to be. The Manchester club retains its strength and power and is at the head of all the local clubs. So numerous are its players that the club can at any time raise two or three Elevens of nearly equal merit, at a very short notice.

This great Manchester club played thirty-two matches that season with what was virtually a county team and lost only once.

County cricket took its first step to proper organization and recognition in 1873 when championship regulations, and qualifications for county cricketers were formed. No more would the likes of Bill Hickton and Roger Iddison play for different counties in the same season.

McIntyre and Watson so dominated Lancashire's bowling this season that they were responsible for 635 of the 770 overs bowled and took all but ten of the 117 wickets. They bowled unchanged through both innings of both Surrey matches with McIntyre returning a match analysis of 46.3–19–70–11 at Old Trafford and 40–17–52–11 at The Oval, with Watson having figures of 45–15–79–8 at Old Trafford and 39–15–49–8 at The Oval. Lancashire, of course, won both matches handsomely. Surrey were bowled out for 33 in fifty-one minutes in their first innings at The Oval and at one time were 27 for seven in their second before recovering to reach 76. It was in this game that Hornby and Barlow opened the batting for the first time and in view of what was to follow it is interesting to read the report by the *Manchester Courier*:

> The visitors won the toss and made a start at 20 minutes after 12 o'clock, their first choice being Mr Hornby and Barlow against the 'worky' bowling of Southerton and

the fast and straight bowling of Street. The last-named batsman experienced hard lines in not having a chance to score, for the first ball delivered by Southerton, Mr Hornby drove on, and being fielded sharply by Jupp as they were running, Barlow was clean thrown out by him.

Barlow was to suffer a similar fate several times through his years with Hornby who would provide him with a sovereign each time for denying him the chance of talent money.

Lancashire, with an improved fixture list, played seven county games in 1873 with Derbyshire, Kent, Surrey and Yorkshire their opponents. They won four, against Surrey and Derbyshire, but were still not attracting crowds at Old Trafford for the matches. The *City News* said at the start of the season: 'In honesty, it cannot be said that these cricket matches are popular in Manchester. Possibly the comparative inaccessibility of the Manchester cricket ground has something to do with it. Though the ground is probably one of the best in the kingdom, it is not very easy to get at.' When Lancashire were at home to Surrey, Broughton, with a touch of bloody-mindedness it seems, staged a showpiece game involving the United South and featuring W. G. Grace. The attendance during both days at Old Trafford was wretchedly small, while crowds of 5,000 and 6,000 were reported for each day at Broughton. At the same time, All-England were playing at Rochdale, and the gingerbread man from Ormskirk, who usually favoured Old Trafford, wisely went to Broughton this time.

Hornby and Appleby were still nothing like regulars in the Lancashire team despite the appeals of their captain and the point was not lost on the Manchester public who sent their complaints to the newspapers. When Lancashire were playing Yorkshire at Sheffield, Hornby was playing for the Gentlemen against the Players at Lord's; when Lancashire played Derbyshire, Hornby and Appleby were playing in another match at Lord's.

Mr Butt wrote to the *Manchester Courier* to say he was very surprised to see Hornby and Appleby playing for the Canadian XI (the English team which had been to Canada during the winter) against a Fifteen of MCC at Lord's. 'The county club, at the commencement of this season, sent out circulars asking for support and alleging that they were in debt to a very large amount and asking all true lovers of cricket to give all the assistance in their power to encourage the game, else there would be no alternative but to allow their county matches to cease,' he wrote. 'If the county would play their best men and not such Elevens as they have done lately, there is not a shadow of a doubt in my mind but that the county matches would be much more thought about and better attended and the county would be a gainer whereas at present it is a loser as no one cares to go to a county match to watch an inferior Eleven play.'

The following day 'One Who Knows' wrote to say that Lancashire differed from nearly every other county as they played mostly professional players whereas Lancashire relied heavily on gentlemen. He pointed out that players around Lancashire turned down invitations to play and suggested that Mr Butt send to the secretary names of players good enough to play for the county who could leave their business for three days in the week.

Sam Swire, the Lancashire secretary, said the county did not rely on professional players . . . 'and although you may invite an amateur to play you cannot force him against his convenience.'

Another reader said Manchester's control over county cricket could not unite the cricketing interests of the county. 'The Manchester public are notorious for the liberality, even to lavishness, with which they support the entertainments provided by enterprising caterers; and public cricket matches form no exception to any other class of entertainment. The public must and will have their moneysworth.'

A man from Blackburn complained of the selection of the team, but said he could not blame Appleby and Hornby for going to London, and blamed the Old Trafford management – 'The Manchester club being allowed too much of its own way in the selection of players.' It was even asked if the management of the county club was in unpopular hands, which would account for the difficulty in getting gentlemen outside Manchester to play for Lancashire.

Clearly, Lancashire had to get more professionals although they were well blessed with Bill McIntyre, Alec Watson and Dicky Barlow. But if Lancashire were to have more professionals, they would have to treat them better. A reader asked 'How do men like to be thrust out of the society of gentlemen with whom they have been playing the levelling game, par excellence, immediately the dinner bell rings, into a frowsy hole to eat their bit of bread and cheese as best they can?'

Vernon Royle, the greatest cover fielder of his day, made his debut in 1873 and said in later years that when he first played there were often no more than 200 or 300 spectators. The *City News* also wrote at the end of the season that gates, which were never high, had never been so low. 'Pecuniarily and popularly, the season has been a decided failure,' it wrote. The reasons? One major obstacle was that Old Trafford was still difficult to reach. And another, which was not to be remedied for over forty years, was that games starting on Thursday, often did not reach Saturday when people had the afternoon free. The newspaper even said it knew that everything possible had been done to try to nurse the Surrey game through to reach Saturday. Games with Nottinghamshire were suggested for the following season and a plea from the heart asked 'Is it quite hopeless to suggest a match with Gloucestershire? It would certainly draw.' Unfortunately, Gloucestershire, the most attractive team in the country because of W. G. Grace, turned down Lancashire year after year.

The rumbles of discontent were still there when the 1874 season was about to start. A circular was issued by Lancashire to accompany the delivery of members' tickets. It read:

> It is the desire of the committee of the County Club that Lancashire should be able to supply a native-born eleven competent to meet any county in England, as there is no reason why they should not be. The home matches will, as in former seasons, be played on the Manchester ground, which will be generally recognized as their proper locality, both on account of the excellence of the ground, its central situation, and of the invaluable services which the Manchester Club have rendered in promoting county cricket. Since the commencement of the county matches under the auspices of the Manchester Club the receipts have been comparatively trifling, and the cost to the club has exceeded £1,000. This cannot be regarded as a healthy state of things, and an opportunity is therefore offered to all who desire to maintain the cricketing reputation of Lancashire to become members of the County Club by payment of a subscription of not less than five shillings or more than £1 1s per annum. I venture, in conclusion, to ask your assistance and co-operation with the committee in extending the numbers and influence of the county club as the best means of placing Lancashire in the rank it ought to occupy as a cricketing county.
> S. H. Swire.

A Bolton cricketer said that if the committee wanted a native-born XI, why were there so many Manchester men in the team who seldom, if ever, played for the county away from home. Such players as Dicky Barlow and Bill Burrows were rarely engaged for Old Trafford matches and were needed only when more favoured cricketers refused to travel. He was, of course, right. Only three of Barlow's first thirteen matches were at Old Trafford before he became a regular first-team player in 1875. Burrows, whose fourteen-match career was over by 1873, also played just three times at Old Trafford and eleven away from home. The Bolton cricketer also joined in the now common lament about the professionals' quarters at Old Trafford and said if the club really wished to place Lancashire in the rank it ought to occupy as a cricketing county, they would have to provide something better than a miserable hut for those who could not lay claim to the title of 'gentleman'.

Another supporter, on the same topic of division between professional and amateur, said 'Surely if professionals are considered respectable enough to associate with during play they might be deemed worthy to take their seat in the same room, if not at the same table, as the gentleman players.' William E. Hodkinson, writing in the *Manchester and Salford Gazette*, expressed the same opinion as he referred to Lancashire's game against Kent at Old Trafford in July 1874.

> The attendance was, as usual, very small. I can only account for this by the absence of a band and the distance which Old Trafford is from the centre of the city. I really believe that if the county club were to engage a band for these matches they would be better patronized. But why are these matches, I ask, always played at Old Trafford. Why are they not alternately played at Bolton, Broughton or Castleton? Each of these places can afford a band and are well patronized. Again, I cannot for the life of me understand why the gentlemen should be worshipped so much as to have the entire possession of the pavilion while the players (who are equally as much to be depended upon for winning a match) should be thrown away as 'dirt' into an old 'cow shed' on the right-hand side of the field to don their flannels, etc. Lastly, I am at a loss to know why some of the gentlemen are always playing out of the county, in other matches, when required at home.

The complaints were familiar and the club, no doubt heeding the feelings of its supporters, were soon to build a pavilion, almost immediately opposite the old one, which provided accommodation for the professionals who had a section of it to themselves.

The first game of that year of 1874 was at home to Derbyshire, on 5 June, and yet again Lancashire were let down by the amateurs with such players as Arthur Appleby, A. N. Hornby, Joe Makinson, Edward Jackson, Henry Parr and others refusing to play. Yet Lancashire continued to ask sundry gentlemen to play until finally they had a team which was the feeblest to represent the county at home. Even Joe Leese, who started the game and fielded on the opening day, was mysteriously called away and had to be replaced by Roger Walker of Bury. The opening batsmen were Walter Craig from Longsight and George Walsh from Over Darwen, both of whom were making their debuts. Between them they totalled 23 runs in four innings. Other making their debuts were Horace Mellor, who hailed from Paddington and had attended Cheltenham School, Captain William Swynfen Jervis, Roger Walker, who was an England Rugby Union footballer, and a man of whom next to nothing was known, J. Harrop. So six players made their debuts and three of them, Craig, Jervis and Harrop, were never to play again. The other three, Walsh, Mellor and Walker, were to play only once more while a seventh player, Alf Ollivant, was in his second and last match for the county. The wicket-keeper, R. Roberts, was nearing the end of a brief career and the only experience came from John Hillkirk, who probably captained the side, and the professionals, Watson and McIntyre. But there was no room for the likes of Dicky Barlow and Lancashire, not surprisingly, lost by nine wickets after being bowled out for 38 in their first innings. Lancashire had no change bowling worthy of the name and Watson bowled through Derbyshire's first innings to take nine of the ten wickets for 118 runs.

Lancashire came in for some severe criticism. The *City News* talked of the queer team and its wretched fielding. A reader of the *Manchester Courier* called the result a disgrace and said six of the eleven had no right to play in the match. Even *Wisden* referred to the strange-sounding team.

Harrop, whose only game this was for Lancashire, wrote to the *Manchester and Salford Gazette* after the game to call their attention to their omission of the prefix 'Mr' to his name in the scores of the match. He was not to be confused with a professional. Heaven forbid!

Games rarely started to the advertised time in those days. Twelve o'clock starts were often much later and on occasions it was approaching one o'clock before they got going. The *City News* reported that the unusual punctuality of the start saw three substitutes in the field for Lancashire against Derbyshire. The time for dinner seemed to be dictated by the kitchens and a bell would ring from the pavilion to summon the players from the field. The interval could also vary in time and it was usually the fielding side that decided when other breaks should be taken, perhaps for drinks or rain. In Lancashire's game with Derbyshire at Old Trafford in 1875, Hornby and Henry Parr so hammered the bowling that, said the *City News*, 'the Derbyshire men adjourned as with one accord to the refreshment room.'

Lancashire had an awful season in 1874, winning only one game out of the six, a handsome innings victory over Yorkshire at Bradford where they fielded nine amateurs and two professionals in Barlow and McIntyre. They lost three and drew the other game in a season when McIntyre, Watson and Appleby again carried the weight of the bowling, taking eighty-four of the ninety-two wickets. Kent, with only one amateur in their team due to the reluctance of several of their prominent gentlemen players to travel so far, drew at Old Trafford, but beat a severely-weakened Lancashire team by ten wickets at Maidstone. Lancashire again had a strange-sounding conglomeration of unknown players in their team and Captain Jim Fellowes of the Royal Engineers destroyed them with fast bowling that brought him thirteen wickets in the match. Two innings of the sharpest contrast were played by opening batsmen in this game. Dicky Barlow, the great stonewaller, carried his bat for 26 not out of Lancashire's 116, and Kent's Henry Renny-Tailyour, who played soccer and rugby for Scotland and played in three of the first four FA Cup Finals, hit 124 with three 6s and sixteen 4s. And each batted for 130 minutes!

One of Lancashire's major troubles, one of the most difficult to overcome, was persuading the outstanding amateurs to play regularly. Hornby played only once that year (although he played in several big games around the country), Frank Wright twice, and even the captain, Edmund Rowley, found time for only two games at Old Trafford. Counties like Nottinghamshire, Yorkshire and Surrey had settled sides, but Lancashire just could not produce a regular, permanent team and needed thirty-three players for those six games. Said the *City News* 'We do not know who will play until we see them take the field and then it is a trifle more than possible that we may be disgusted to find that a strong advertised Eleven has dwindled down to an insignificant collection of cricketing nobodies.' One advantage with Old Trafford was the abundance of alternative attractions in the vicinity. Within the space of a quarter-mile there were the Botanical Gardens, a polo match and a regiment of volunteers at shooting practice. Comparisons with Broughton, where W. G. Grace played each year and drew huge crowds, were inevitable. A newspaper called *The Critic* said the two grounds were totally different. A grand cricket match at Broughton was simply another name for a grand promenade and it offered the opinion that lady promenaders were probably more numerous than gentlemen. 'To Old Trafford ladies rarely venture,' said *The Critic*. 'There were not a dozen lady visitors during the two days play [against Yorkshire].'

Lancashire clearly had problems. They were having to rely too heavily on amateurs and were constantly being let down. They were unable to persuade other counties such as Gloucestershire, Nottinghamshire, Sussex, Middlesex and Surrey to play them, and attendances were low. Money was being lost and if it had not been for the wealthy, generous members of the Manchester club who dipped deep into their pockets every time the hat was sent round at annual meetings, then Lancashire might well have gone out of existence. Something had to be done, and the first step came in 1875 when Lancashire pulled off a remarkable win over Yorkshire at Old Trafford.

Lancashire had started the season with a draw against Derbyshire and defeat at Lord's where they renewed rivalry with MCC after five years. They broke new ground with a friendly match against Leicestershire, which was also drawn, and then took on Yorkshire at Old Trafford in a game which started on 24 June. Yorkshire were bowled out for 83 and Lancashire had moved into a strong position by the end of the first day when they were 95 for five. The pavilion, it was said, 'was alive with jovial Mancunians.' Hornby and Barlow had opened for Lancashire for the first time at Old Trafford, Hornby one of the most brilliant batsmen of the day and Barlow the safe, cautious player who was happy to play the tortoise to his partner's hare.

Lancashire took a first innings lead of 71 but Yorkshire fought back well in their second innings to leave Lancashire with a victory target of 146, a reasonably demanding total in those days. Lancashire again sent out Hornby and Barlow, from separate pavilions, of course, situated on opposite ends of the ground, and by lunch on the final day, a Saturday, they had scored 30 of the runs. Yorkshire used five bowlers, four of them quite fast, in Allen Hill, Bob Clayton, the redoubtable Tom Emmett, and the fast-developing George Ulyett, with Ephraim Lockwood supplying his slow medium-pace deliveries. But nothing disturbed the opening pair who knocked off the runs between them with Hornby scoring 78 not out and Barlow 50 not out. Hornby ran to the pavilion, Barlow ran in the opposite direction to the professionals' home, but neither could escape the attentions of the spectators. Hornby received a new cane-handled bat from Sam Swire, the secretary, and Barlow was hoisted shoulder high and presented with the handsome reward of six sovereigns. It was the first opening century partnership for Lancashire and was described as an unparalleled feat. The *City News* said it was one of the most exciting and sensational matches ever seen at Old Trafford. 'Such a sense of joyous triumph was surely never seen on a cricket ground,' proclaimed the newspaper. This triumph, completed on a Saturday, was witnessed by about 2,000 spectators, which would appear to be the highest recorded number at that time.

The victory stirred the imagination of the newspapers and the public, drawing attention to the attractions of county cricket. People talked of this match for years afterwards and there is no doubt it helped establish Lancashire as a force in the game. From then on 'gates' improved, if only slowly for a time, and Hornby and

Barlow quickly became the best-known opening pair of batsmen in England. Lancashire's strong team, plus Yorkshire's position as a foremost county, had brought in the spectators, and Lancashire finished off the season with four wins in the last five games, two of them by an innings. It was a satisfying end to a season which had started with a good deal of acrimony and suggestions that Lancashire cricket was going to the dogs. At the annual meeting, reported the *City News*, 'there was a fair and influential attendance.' Lord Sefton was president, and vice presidents were the Earl of Ellesmere, Lord Skelmersdale, R. A. Cross, MP, and Charles Turner, MP. 'At least no one will complain of a want of social standing in the nominal chiefs of our county club,' wrote the newspaper, which also felt it necessary to point out that the committee members represented a very large and wide section of Lancashire. Actually, the point was arguable when the eighteen-man committee was broken down with eight members coming from three Manchester clubs and the remaining members representing the following towns: Blackburn, Bury, Wigan, Liverpool, Preston, Bolton and Castleton, near Rochdale. Once again, as at the formation of the club in 1864, no clubs in the north of the county were represented, while Wigan stood alone for the south.

When the quality of Lancashire's opposition for 1875 was criticized, it was pointed out that the committee had tried to arrange matches with the best counties, but Sussex, Surrey, Middlesex, Gloucestershire and Nottinghamshire had all declined the challenge. One county wrote to say it had enough matches, another was in a poor way financially while a third, which relied heavily on amateurs, could not guarantee a strong team for Old Trafford. Even Gentlemen matches, which were waning, could not be arranged against Yorkshire, Shropshire, Cheshire, Warwickshire and Free Foresters. The inevitable comparisons were made between Old Trafford and Broughton, where thousands still went to watch the big game. The presence of W. G. Grace and the accessibility of the Broughton ground were referred to although another point was made in the *City News* on class and social differences. Amateurs and players, members and visitors, were all on an equal footing at Broughton. 'The social distinctions so noticeable elsewhere have at Broughton no existence,' said the writer. 'It is a mistake to look upon county matches as the goal of cricket and the summit of the cricketer's ambitions.' Nevertheless, that is just what was happening, although Hornby still could not resist the lure of other matches and once even went to play with his old Harrow companions instead of helping Lancashire take on Kent at Old Trafford.

47

It had been a good year, especially for Barlow who was now a regular in the team and had advanced his batting average from 15.4 in 1874 to a magnificent 38.8, and for Appleby, McIntyre and Watson who again dominated the bowling by taking 123 of the 138 wickets.

RICHARD GORTON BARLOW, born in Bolton in 1850, was the first great Lancashire-born professional in a career which ran from 1871 to 1891. He played through the period when the game was developing, when crowds were growing, and Lancashire were establishing themselves among the leaders in county cricket. He was an outstanding all-rounder who toured Australia three times and played seventeen Tests against Australia. His major reputation, of course, was as a stonewalling batsman and he claimed to have batted right through an innings fifty times, including an innings of five not out in two and a half hours against Nottinghamshire in 1882. It was this innings which gave birth to the term 'stonewaller' when Billy Barnes, one of the Nottinghamshire bowlers, said after the innings: 'Bowling at thee were like bowling at a stone wall.' Nobody took cricket more seriously or had a greater pride in his profession than Barlow whose devotion to the game was shown in the house he built in Raikes Parade, Blackpool. His initials were carved in stone over the front door – they are still there – a stained glass window, bearing portraits of himself, Dick Pilling and A. N. Hornby and which is now in the Executive Suite at Old Trafford, greeted the visitor at the vestibule, and a gas lamp in the hall showed the names of famous players.

The walls of the hall were covered with historic team pictures, Lord Sheffield's ground was depicted in coloured tiles in the dining room, and by the fireplace, also in tiles, were more portraits of himself, Hornby and Pilling. A profusion of cricket portraits and sketches lined the walls throughout the house and I recall his grandson, Leslie Barlow Wilson – the initials were deliberately contrived – telling me you could not get a pin between them. Cricket trophies and presents were tastefully displayed and an array of bats hung on the bathroom wall.

He was generally thought of as an unassuming man, well liked by his fellow cricketers, but he was also deeply proud of his many achievements in the game. He even designed his own headstone for his grave in Layton Cemetery, Blackpool, close to the gates. It is large and white and shows a set of stumps with the ball passing through middle and leg and at the bottom the words: 'Bowled at Last!' He had made sure the stone would do him justice, choosing the words himself:

Here lie the remains of Richard Gorton Barlow, Died 31 July 1919, aged 68 years. For 21 seasons a playing member of the Lancashire County XI, and for 21 seasons an umpire in county matches. He also made three journeys to Australia with English teams. This is a consecutive record in first-class cricket which no other cricketer has achieved.

He would have liked to have added much more, but there just was not room.

When Barlow left school at 14, he trained to be a compositor and a moulder and was 21 before he found his first regular professional cricket job with Farsley, near Leeds. That season of 1871 proved the turning point for Barlow. He played in his first big match, against George Parr's All-England team, and also made his debut for Lancashire. His debut at Sheffield was marked with success despite breaking a finger while batting on the opening day. He scored 28 not out with his hand bandaged for part of his innings and then became one of the few cricketers to take a wicket with his first ball in first-class cricket. He got to bowl only because of a stubborn, late stand and broke the partnership when he bowled Johnnie West. Yet it was 1875 before he became a regular player and 1878 before he was a recognized bowler. He headed Lancashire's batting and bowling averages in 1882 with 856 runs (average 30.57) and seventy-three wickets (9.98) and performed an outstanding all-round display in 1884 when playing for the North of England against the Australians at Nottingham. He scored a century and took ten wickets for 48 runs in the match and was rewarded with presents, including the score on satin and a collection of £16.

Barlow was an extremely fit man and played football at a high level, too, having kept goal for the North against the South at Sheffield and also representing Lancashire. As well as being a cricket umpire he also became a football referee and was in charge of the 1887 FA Cup tie when Preston North End beat Hyde 26–0. He was a teetotaller and a non-smoker . . . 'a meritorious combination rarely found among cricketers,' said one writer of the period.

At his best Barlow was probably a better bowler than batsman and certainly regarded bowling more highly. He once told Fred Root, who played for England, when he was undecided whether to concentrate on batting or bowling: 'Bowl, bowl, bowl. For goodness' sake, bowl! Batsmen are like eggs in summer – eighteen a shilling – but bowlers, real ones, are as rare as a Lord's lunch to a professional cricketer when winter has set in!'

Barlow played his last county game for Lancashire in 1891 after being left out of several matches at the end of the season and having a disagreement with the committee. He finished as he started, with a game against Yorkshire before becoming an umpire good enough to stand in Test matches.

In 1880 Barlow started business as a cricket outfitter in Stretford Road, Manchester, before taking it close to Victoria Station and then on to Blackpool. He was an inventive man. He designed wicket covers, an idea that was taken up by MCC, and also had a patent airtight valve and laceless football which he marketed.

When I traced Barlow's descendants some years ago, I discovered an illegimate son, Reginald Gorton Barlow Thompson, who lived in Southport. He told me his father had an unhappy marriage and it was on one of his regular morning walks along the cliffs at Blackpool's North Shore that he met the bookkeeper at the Imperial Hotel, a very beautiful woman who was to become his mother. Several of Barlow's possessions were left to his son when he died, including a delightful silver, mounted gong presented to Barlow by W. G. Grace 'for his fine cricket against the Australians in 1886.' Thompson also recovered the stained glass window of Barlow, Hornby and Pilling, which had been built into a summer house at the home of Barlow's daughter, his only other child. 'My half-sister, who was forty years my senior, refused to let me have anything while she was living,' he told me. 'After she died I went along to the house and offered the new owners stained glass windows throughout the house in exchange for the old vestibule window.' Thompson described his father as an autocrat. 'And a man very proud of his many achievements, and whose whole life was cricket.'

Lancashire's success of 1875, particularly the victory over Yorkshire, produced an improvement in fixtures and attendances in 1876. Nottinghamshire, the outstanding team in the country, renewed home and away matches after an interval of seven years; games were again played with Sussex after a six-year break. Gates consequently improved and the Manchester newspapers reported that the attendance for the final day of the match with Yorkshire at Old Trafford on Saturday 24 June was the best yet for a county match.

Lancashire started the season in great triumph by beating the mighty Nottinghamshire by six wickets at Trent Bridge. Wrote the *Nottingham Daily Express*: 'With such batsmen to boast of as Mr Hornby, Mr Appleby, Mr Hillkirk, the Messrs Rowley, Mr Porter and others, Lancashire need never be afraid of an opposing foe, especially when we consider what three sterling professionals they have in W. McIntyre, Barlow and Watson.' Hornby and Barlow shared in what was becoming a typical type of partnership with Hornby's wicket falling at 45, of which he had made 44, leaving Barlow still there with 0 after an hour's batting. This great match was important enough to persuade the likes of Hornby and Appleby to play in what *Wisden* described as the best Lancashire team possible. Hornby even played against Derbyshire, an event which forced the *City News* to comment 'We are glad to see that the great Blackburn amateur has grown to prefer his county games to the more fashionable and more popular great matches at the Lord's ground.'

Lancashire won four of the first five matches, but fell away so badly that they lost four of the last five, including a three-wicket defeat by Sussex at Old Trafford where they returned to their old habits and fielded a team regarded almost as the Second Eleven. Fred Greenfield, who also played with Cambridge University that year, opened the bowling for Sussex in the second innings with slow underarms and bowled Jim Ricketts and Douglas Steel with consecutive balls.

Lancashire lost both games against Yorkshire, having a particularly unhappy time at Sheffield where they lost by 18 runs after being 62 for three towards the 89 needed for victory. Allen Hill, the fast bowler, bowled Edmund Rowley and Vernon Royle at 62, Richard Howe at 64 and Arthur Appleby at 66. The last six wickets fell for 8 runs, Hill's last four overs being bowled for five wickets and 1 run. The Nottinghamshire match at Old Trafford produced the closest finish of the season, the last Nottinghamshire pair coming together with six runs needed and Fred Morley and Bill Shrewsbury seeing them home amidst great excitement. Richard Daft had one of his rare failures for Nottinghamshire, an event that was attributed in one quarter to the musketry practice of the 22nd Regiment that was taking place in the next field. Wrote the *Nottingham Daily Express*: 'Shaw arrived to Daft and amid an incessant fire of artillery – for the Manchester soldiers were holding their field day immediately outside the ground – Daft was caught at short leg.' The newspaper, in referring to Old Trafford, declared: 'The ground is situated from the centre of the city and, unless a county match runs into a Saturday afternoon, it is not often it holds out much attraction to the Manchester citizens. But the contest under notice formed an exception to the rule, inasmuch as the attendance was not only extremely large but was of a very enthusiastic turn of mind.'

For the first time since the opening Roses match in Whalley in 1867, Lancashire took a county game away from Old Trafford in 1876, Castleton, near Rochdale, staging the game against Kent which Lancashire won by ten wickets. Three Castleton players, Edmund Chadwick, John Leach and J. Schofield – the first two stood as guarantors for the match – were in the Lancashire team which forced Kent to follow on, with McIntyre taking six for 30 in the first innings and Watson seven for 61, including the first hat-trick for Lancashire in a county game, in the second. Castleton lost money staging the game, the guarantors were forced to provide, and Castleton did not stage another county fixture.

51

Although Lancashire had had a desperately poor second half to the season and had again been guilty of fielding weak teams, they were held to have had a satisfactory summer. The professionals, Watson, McIntyre and Barlow, played in every game and provided a solid backbone to the team, and Watson, McIntyre and Appleby again dominated the bowling with 160 of the 174 wickets between them. This was McIntyre's year. In the ten matches he took eighty-nine wickets for 11 runs each.

Lancashire, although in good heart from 1876, started the following season in awful style, losing four of the first five matches. And nothing was more disheartening than the first when they again sent a makeshift team to Derby and lost by 34 runs. One enthusiast wrote to the *Manchester Courier* to say that only four, at most five, of the Lancashire team were worth their place. He was probably right. In the team were Francis Melhuish, a batsman from Birkenhead making his debut in a three-match career, Manchester-born Richard Howe, playing his third and last match, Rossall-educated Campbell Hulton, a batsman who averaged 8.8 through his eight matches for Lancashire, Bill Wall from Wigan playing his only match, and Fred Stephenson, a 5 feet 2 inches tall professional fast bowler from Todmorden, who was in his second and last match. And in among the ignominy, Bill McIntyre recorded his finest match return with fifteen wickets for 47 runs. The team was a little stronger for the return match ten days later with Hornby resuming as opener and scoring 63 in the ten-wicket win. Rather more to the point was the repeat performance of McIntyre who this time took twelve wickets for 91 runs to start the season with twenty-seven wickets in his first two games at a trifling cost of a shade over 5 runs each. Yet probably the most exciting bowling of the season came from 23-year-old Bill Patterson, a Cambridge University Blue from Liverpool, who took seven for 72 and seven for 39 against Nottinghamshire and five for 90 and five for 40 against Yorkshire in the only two games he could play that season. He bowled slow right arm and Lancashire clearly looked to have made a find. Unfortunately he could not find time for first-class cricket and played only seven games for the county, taking no more than those twenty-four wickets of 1877.

This year of 1877 was the one that saw the debuts of A. G. Steel and Dick Pilling, two of the county's most illustrious players and who would have forced their way into the team at any time in Lancashire's history. Steel was still only 18 and midway between Marlborough and Cambridge University when he played his only county game of the season against Sussex at Old Trafford and scored a magnificent 87. Pilling filled a vacancy that had existed ever since the county had been formed, that of wicket-keeper. Edward Jackson had kept wicket well but was an amateur and available only on occasions, and Pilling, a professional from Church, near Accrington, was always available and after making his debut alongside Steel, stayed Lancashire's first choice for thirteen years.

Lancashire won five of their last six matches that summer, achieving the double over Yorkshire along the way. But the season still ended with the feeling that Lancashire, like the lazy scholar, could have done better. The county called on thirty-six players for their eleven games and the comment of the *City News* was unarguable:

> The constitution of our county team is in the extreme irregular and uncertain. We have almost a glut of high-class amateur cricketers but unfortunately the services of the best cannot always be depended on. The best men, like Hornby and the University representatives (Royle, Patterson, and the Steel brothers in particular) either consider it infra dig to play in the less important matches or think that a strong enough set of representatives can be assembled without them. The result is that Lancashire lose more second-rate than first-rate matches.

To be fair Hornby played in nine of the eleven matches that year and was now a regular part of the Lancashire team.

Another comment came from the *City News*:

> Good Yorkshire colts are as thick as blackberries. When one veteran disappears there is always a host of worthy rivals for his place. But not Lancashire. Professional talent, in spite of annual Colts matches, is remarkably slow in coming to the surface. On the other hand gentlemen cricketers, from the public schools or from the Universities, abound in towns like Manchester and Liverpool and the result, when our county is at full strength, is a very formidable combination.

Some indication of the size of the grounds – or perhaps it was a reflection on the standard of fielding – were the reports of a straight drive for five past the trees in the match against MCC at Lord's, and a grand drive by Dicky Barlow against Kent at Old Trafford, off which six were run. It was in this same match, with Kent, that we hear of the lordly misuse of language by Lord Harris, the Kent captain, who was not pleased at being given out caught at the wicket. Wrote the *City News*: 'Lord Harris went out palpably using strong language with reference to the umpire's decision.' The decision, whether right or wrong, gave a professional fast bowler called Harwood from Darwen his only first-class wicket. Harwood's

53

parents had christened him Baron, an inspirational choice and just the man to stand up to the Lord.

Umpires in those days were appointed by the clubs themselves and often the person to land the job was a professional player, out of the game perhaps through injury. Not surprisingly there were many disputes, many cries of bias, and players were not slow to air their disapproval of umpires' decisions. The call went out for neutral umpires and in 1883 MCC took over the duty of appointing umpires for the first-class matches.

Interest was growing in county cricket and so were the attendances. When 2,000 people attended the opening day of the game with Nottinghamshire at Old Trafford in 1877, the *Manchester Courier* was moved to comment: 'We are glad to state that the public are beginning to manifest some interest in these great matches.' And with the extra interest came more critical assessment of the facilities provided. A reader of the *City News* complained that he was unable to leave the ground at lunchtime unless he paid again for readmission. He wrote 'The accommodation at Old Trafford is notoriously meagre in the extreme; the handsome pavilion will accommodate a mere handful; and as for the refreshment – well, the less said about that the better.' He said if the rules were not changed with regard to readmission . . . 'he must indeed be an enthusiast who will encounter a nine-hour imprisonment in the bleak and comfortless Old Trafford cricket ground.' Nevertheless, the number of enthusiasts was growing. On the final day of the Nottinghamshire match the numerous assemblage numbered something around 3,500, a record for the Old Trafford ground which was surpassed five weeks later when Yorkshire were playing and the Saturday gate was about 4,500. This was an enormous improvement on the days recalled by A. N. Hornby and Vernon Royle when about 200 people watched games against Yorkshire. Yet even better days and mightier crowds were just around the corner . . . .

Chapter 3 1878–81

'Hornby has made Lancashire cricket popular with
cricketers so that now our best players are proud
to be asked to play for the county.'

By 1878 Lancashire were entering their fourteenth season of county matches. In eighty games they had called on 124 players, too many of whom had not been worth a place in the side. The major problem was that too many people were still identifying principally with their clubs; too few were prepared to put Lancashire first. Loyalty to the county was slow to develop and it is perhaps worth remembering that this was the first time in any sport that people were being asked to represent Lancashire. To many, it was just another cricket club starting up and it was taking time for players and public alike to have any feeling of allegiance to their county. It obviously did not help when the Manchester club took over the running of Lancashire's affairs for it was clear that many saw the county as nothing more than an extension of the Manchester club. Other clubs became unwilling to help, players felt a conflict of interest, and jealousy crept in on the grounds that Manchester, the premier club in the city and the county, were taking control of what should have been a county affair. It is easy to see that in some ways, those fine ideals and aims expressed at the meeting at the Queens Hotel in Manchester in 1864 looked to have been lost. The games were not going round the county and the team was too often more representative of Manchester and District than Lancashire. Yet there seems no doubt that if Manchester had not taken over the running of the Lancashire club, the Lancashire club could well have ceased to exist.

In those early years gentlemen dominated the team and while they might have been prepared to give up three afternoons of

55

business four or five times a summer to play cricket at nearby Old Trafford, it was usually asking too much of them to travel away from home for three or four days at a time. On average there were seven amateurs to four professionals in Lancashire's team for home matches in those first thirteen years; five amateurs to six professionals for away matches. Unfortunately, the quality of professionals was not high until Bill McIntyre, Alec Watson, Dicky Barlow and Dick Pilling arrived on the scene. And of those, only Barlow was a true-born Lancastrian, although Pilling's parents came from the county and he had spent nearly all his life within its boundaries.

Lancashire's struggle to find identity in the game was reflected in the quality of the opposition, which fluctuated almost from year to year. Middlesex, after providing opposition for the first two years, declined to play them over the next fifteen; there was a seven-year gap in games with Nottinghamshire; Surrey played Lancashire only twice in a nine-year period; Sussex played them twice in their first eleven years; and regular games against Yorkshire did not start until 1871, a rivalry that has since continued uninterrupted.

Despite the protests of prominent Manchester club members, Old Trafford was undoubtedly pretty inaccessible in those days. Omnibuses to Old Trafford were only few and far between and after the bus journey there was a weary tramp along Chester Road, and down the interminable lane leading to the ground. The promise of a short cut across the fields from the Old Trafford Bar to the gates made the prospect brighter. It was an effort to get to the ground and 'gates' increased only slowly through the years. The Yorkshire match of 1875 stirred new interest in the game, Hornby and Barlow were probably the first personality attractions in the team, and just when the Lancashire public was beginning gradually to associate with its county cricket team, Gloucestershire, through the mighty W. G. Grace, at last agreed to meet Lancashire's challenge in 1878. 'Mr Grace did not think our county worth the powder and shot before this summer,' wrote the *City News* at the start of the 1878 season. The Australians, making their first visit to this country, also played at Old Trafford and almost overnight, Lancashire were among the foremost counties in England. Within two years they were sharing the championship and in the following season, 1881, they won it outright for the first time.

The Gloucestershire match at Old Trafford on Thursday, Friday and Saturday, 25, 26 and 27 July 1878, was unquestionably the turning point. Lancashire's team was regarded as the best they had ever fielded with Hornby and Barlow to open, followed by A. G. Steel, D. Q. Steel, Royle, Patterson, Appleby, Edmund Rowley, Watson,

McIntyre and Pilling. The strong, attractive Gloucestershire team was headed by the Grace brothers, W. G., E. M. (who in honour of the occasion had left his duties as coroner), and G. F., with their cousin Walter Gilbert and Bill Midwinter, who had been persuaded by W. G. to leave the Australian team midway through their tour. Heavy storms of rain and a gloomy atmosphere on the opening day did not stop the crowds rolling up to make the largest attendance ever seen at Old Trafford. An attendance figure was not given but receipts of £88 7s 0d suggested something in the region of 4,500 people on the ground for that first day. Lancashire had reached 18 for three with Hornby and the Steel brothers back in the pavilion, when it rained, causing a two-hour hold-up, during which the crowd grew restless and demanded the resumption of play. W. G. Grace and Robert Miles bowled all day and only Barlow, with a little help from Royle, withstood them to take Lancashire to 88 for nine by the close of play. The *City News* commented on Grace's bowling 'His style is cumbersome, laborious and ugly, but he manages to get a very large number of wickets. Miles opened with him with left-hand slows, curiously aiming them not at the wicket but at least a yard to the off. The temptation to let out at them was irresistible and the penalty certain.'

Miles started with a wide on the second morning, Barlow, first man in and last out for 40, drove the second ball into mid off's hands and Lancashire were all out for 89. The weather was splendid on that second day, the attendance unprecedented, and it was thought about 10,000 people were on the ground, paying £269 5s for the privilege. By the time Gloucestershire were all out – for 116 for a first-innings lead of 27 – the ground was a sight to see. A solid phalanx of spectators lined the ground, six or seven deep. The front row lay down, the second sat on the grass, the third rested on forms and the rest made the most of the standing room. The *City News* wrote, prophetically, 'Friday will be quoted as one of the days in the history of the ground to be marked with a white stone.'

Large though the crowd had been on the second day, the number was to be exceeded on the Saturday, another beautiful day which attracted, according to the Manchester newspapers, anything between 10,000 and 14,000. *Wisden* went a little better, quoting 'one who ought to know all about it' . . .

Quite 16,000 were present on the Saturday; they were obliged to have four entrances that day, and the people came in such shoals that passing through the turnstiles was difficult; even with the four entrances they could not be admitted fast enough, and it is supposed that quite 2,000 went round, and got over the boards on to the ground without payment. It was estimated that more than 28,000 people witnessed the match.

About 1,500 people paid two shillings to stand on the more select pavilion side of the ground and receipts for the day of £400 5s took the grand total for the match to £757 17s 0d. Riches indeed for the county club, and bringing an end to the unseemly sight of the hat being passed round at the annual meeting to keep the club solvent.

The huge crowds, of course, brought with them huge problems. At one stage when Gloucestershire were batting on the final day, play was delayed for half an hour while the crowd was half persuaded, half forced towards the boundaries. The ring of spectators encroached so far on to the ground that out-fielding was almost impossible and some years later, recalling this overnight transformation of the crowds at Old Trafford, Vernon Royle said:

> Gloucestershire was then the champion county and had refused to play us because we were not good enough. No doubt they were quite right. But at last matches were arranged. There were no ropes round the ground so that the spectators came into the area reserved for play and sat down where they liked. When I was at cover point I was only about thirty yards from them so you can easily imagine what a small boundary there was in that match.

The crowd, described later as a ruffianly mob, even took to tearing up the ground and throwing sods at players and spectators, and arrests had to be made to quieten them down.

A disputed run out, involving Patterson and A. G. Steel, also led to a hold-up on the final morning. Steel hit a ball from Gilbert towards the top entrance gate and one of the spectators, sitting on a form, stopped the ball with his foot. The batsmen, thinking it was a boundary, were leisurely crossing to return to their creases when Jim Cranston recovered the ball which had rolled beneath the form and quickly returned it to the bowler. The wicket was put down, W. G. Grace claimed, and Patterson was given run out. Patterson returned to the pavilion, but Edmund Rowley, the Lancashire captain, went on to the field to argue the point with the Gloucestershire captain. The point was hotly contested for some time before E. M. Grace went to the point where the ball had been recovered, spoke to the spectators and then to the umpires who reversed the decision. The dispute was therefore settled amicably and Miles, amid the cheers of the crowd, conducted the batsman back to the wicket.

As for the match itself, Hornby supplied the most memorable

part of the three days by scoring 100 – he was out next ball – to lift Lancashire to 262 in their second innings and set Gloucestershire a victory target of 236 in a little over two hours. They were 125 for five at the close with W. G., helped by the short boundary, adding an unbeaten 58 to his 32 of the first innings. Wrote the *Manchester Guardian* 'All classes of the community were represented, and a good hit or a clever bit of fielding never failed of its appropriate reward in the cheer of the occupants of the pavilion or the delighted shouts from the "lower benches".'

On the face of it, it had been a great occasion. But there had been too many problems, caused by over-crowding on the popular side, leading to some unpleasantness. The Australians were due in three weeks' time and in an effort to cure the evils of the Gloucestershire match, the Lancashire committee decided to double the price of admission for the mob to a shilling. As soon as it was made public the protests poured in and the newspapers were full of it, through readers' letters, for a week leading up to the match. It was pointed out that admission to the ground side at any grand cricket match in England was sixpence, and that was also the charge for the visit of the Australians to other grounds. J. C. Later wrote to the *Manchester Courier*, saying 'If your correspondent had been present at the Gloucestershire match and seen the unseemly behaviour of the mob he would come to the same conclusion that I did, to make the admission as restrictive as possible for great matches.'

Another correspondent took the same view: 'In my opinion and that of most of my friends, the ruffianly conduct of the mob at the late Gloucestershire match quite warrants the increased charge. Anyone who is really a lover of cricket can surely afford to pay one shilling for five hours' really fine play and if not, then let them make way for those who can. The conduct of an excited Manchester crowd is hardly to be depended upon.'

Among the suggestions for controlling the crowd in the Australian match were more police officers, stout ropes all around, a person on horseback to parade up and down the edge of the crowd, and stands all round the ground.

The ground was roped for the Australian match, additional accommodation for refreshments was provided and two grandstands were specially erected. Both stands were filled and although attendance figures were not given, the receipts totalled £730, nearly as much as for the Gloucestershire match. But with the popular side admission charge having been doubled, it can be estimated that somewhere between 12,000 and 15,000 saw the match. The first day belonged entirely to the Australians. Barlow was nearly run out off the first ball of the match from the Demon bowler, Fred

Spofforth, Hornby was lbw to the second. Lancashire lost six wickets for 16 runs and it needed plucky displays from Edmund Rowley, Alec Watson, and a 20-year-old amateur batsman in his first season, Oswald Lancashire, to take them to a total of 97. By the end of the first day the Australians were 100 for one and on a showery second day they lost the remaining nine wickets for 30 runs so that they led by only 43. Their collapse might just have had something to do with their attendance the night before at a banquet in their honour at the Queens Hotel. The third day was also showery and when the game was abandoned as a draw the Australians had scored 47 without loss towards the 120 needed for victory.

It had been a fine year for Lancashire in which they had won six and lost three of their twelve matches. Their victories included their first over MCC at the sixth attempt, the double over Kent, and a marvellous innings win over Yorkshire who were bowled out twice in a day with the remarkable 19-year-old spinner, A. G. Steel, taking fourteen of the wickets.

ALLAN GIBSON STEEL was considered second only to W. G. Grace as the country's finest all-rounder in a career which ran through nineteen seasons from 1877. He played 162 first-class matches in that time, but only forty-seven of them were for Lancashire, largely because of the demands of his profession as a barrister, which took him to the position of Queen's Counsel and Recorder of Oldham, and his preference for more important, representative games. Yet people who saw him reckoned he was the county's finest all-rounder, surpassing even Johnny Briggs. He captained England four times, but was never appointed captain of Lancashire. He scored only one century for Lancashire, yet scored two for England in the thirteen Tests he played. He was 18 and had just finished at Marlborough when he made his debut for Lancashire in 1877 and failed by only 13 to score a century. He went to Cambridge University in 1878 and in that season astonished the cricket world by taking 164 first-class wickets, fifty-five of them in five matches for Lancashire. At only 19 he had walked straight into a strong University team, taking eight for 95 in his first match against an Eleven of England, the start of a phenomenal season.

He never played a full season for Lancashire and his only century for them was against Surrey at Old Trafford when he was 28 and had been just a very occasional player for some years. He was a man for the big occasion and as a batsman was at his particular best for England against Australia. He went to Australia in 1882 and scored 135 not out in a Test match in Sydney. But probably his best innings was his 148 at Lord's in 1884. He went in when England were 75 for three and scored his runs out of 238 made while he was in. He was very quick on his feet and did not wait for loose deliveries. 'Keen eyes, nerves like steel, and quickness of foot enabled him to score off balls which most batsmen would have been satisfied merely to play,' said one report.

Despite his merits as a batsman, it was his bowling which first brought him to notice and which made the greatest impression. He was described as having 'an easy, pretty, rather mincing delivery that suited very well the piquant quality of his bowling.' The *Manchester Courier* said he was the first great bowler who possessed the art of concealing from the batsman the way the ball was going to break. 'It was a totally new style of bowling and Mr Alfred Lyttelton, who kept wicket to him, said he never felt certain that he could judge which way the ball was going to turn.' Lord Hawke described Steel as slow medium pace, round arm, and breaking the ball both ways. 'You rarely get two balls alike from him,' he said. 'If there is a weak spot in your batting he seems to find it before he has finished the first over.' The Hon. R. H. Lyttelton said Steel, as far as he knew, was the first bowler who showed it was possible to break the ball both ways. He was quite slow as a rule. In batting he was a clean hitter of the ball and not nervous. Small in stature, he never slogged or hit the ball high but scored rapidly and was very quick on his feet. H. D. G. Leveson Gower even went so far as to describe Steel as a master captain and one of the greatest cricketers the world had seen.

Steel was born in Liverpool in 1858, the fourth of seven sons of a ship-owner and one of four brothers who played for Lancashire. His career as a barrister developed quickly and after being called to the Bar at the Inner Temple when still only 24, he became a QC when he was 27. He had a large Admiralty practice and became Oldham Recorder in 1904 when he was 45. He joined the Lancashire committee when he was 22 and was president of MCC in 1902.

There seems little doubt that but for the domination of A. N. Hornby and his own professional demands, Steel would have captained Lancashire and might well have played for them more. He captained England four times, three of them in one series against Australia in 1886 when England won all the matches. He said the game moulded qualities to make the real man – discipline and loyalty. When he died in 1921, aged 62, Lancashire had a history of fifty-seven years with such famous names as Hornby, MacLaren, Spooner, Briggs, Barlow and Tyldesley. Yet there were claims that Steel was the best of them all. The *Athletic News* was in no doubt. 'The greatest player Lancashire have ever produced.' And the *Manchester Guardian*: 'He will remain one of the glories of Lancashire cricket.' In his forty-seven matches he scored 1,960 runs for an average of 29.25 and took 238 wickets (13.16). In all first-class matches he finished with 7,000 runs (29.41) and 788 wickets (14.80). He was undoubtedly a formidable cricketer but the small number of matches he chose to play for Lancashire detracts from

his real value to the county. He played when it suited him and was too often prepared to play, as they say, in showier matches.

Fourteen of Steel's fifty-five victims for Lancashire in 1878 were stumped, reflecting great credit on the continuing fine wicket-keeping of the 22-year-old Dick Pilling who had thirty-two victims in the twelve matches. Barlow followed Hornby and Royle as the county's top batsmen and for the first time was allowed to develop his bowling which brought him thirty-one wickets at under 11 runs apiece. From now on, he was to be just as much a bowler as a batsman, an additional quality that took him into the England team.

By the end of the 1878 season Lancashire were looked on as one of the most brilliant and powerful teams in the country. Steel was the most deadly bowler of the day, Bill Patterson – who played only seven games – was one of the most graceful batsmen, Royle and Hornby, as well as being good batsmen, were the best pair of fielders the county had seen, Barlow, McIntyre and Watson were among the steadiest and most successful bowlers, and Pilling was one of the few thoroughly trustworthy wicket-keepers of the period. But all was not wine and roses, particularly for Fred Reynolds who was reprimanded by the committee for his impertinence in publicly insulting one of the members during the Yorkshire match, and was told he could no longer supply refreshment to the club or the public. But he was re-engaged as assistant secretary at a salary of £130 a year which would rise to £140 if his duties were carried out satisfactorily.

Following the problems at the Gloucestershire match, the committee made one far-reaching decision at their meeting in November when it was decided that the enclosure and pavilion would be reserved in future for members of the Manchester Club and Lancashire Club only. The public, even the two-shilling public, was put in its place.

The weather that winter was severely cold, right through to the middle of May 1879, and cold enough for games of cricket to be played on ice-covered lakes and ponds. Not that this bothered three of the county's amateurs, Hornby, Royle and Birkenhead-born Sandford Schultz who were with Lord Harris's team in Australia where they became the first Lancashire players to take part in Test cricket. Schultz's selection, from this distance, seems strange. He was 21, had played two years with Cambridge University without exciting attention, and in five matches for Lancashire had a top score of 42 not out in nine innings and had bowled only three overs of round-arm fast deliveries. But the choice was Lord Harris's, and qualities other than cricketing ability were required for long tours abroad in those days. The party was rich in batting, with ten amateurs and two professionals, and Schultz's only Test, which was played at Melbourne, saw him bat at No. 11, where he scored 0 not out and 20, and take one for 26. He played four more matches for Lancashire, in 1881 and 1882, and an innocuous county career ended without a wicket and with a batting average of 15.35 from nine games. Some years later when his German name 'Schultz' offended, he changed it to Storey. The same Test match was also Royle's only game as an England player, but Hornby was to play twice more, both as captain, in 1882 and 1884. Hornby's pugilistic prowess was evident during a match against New South Wales in Sydney in that winter of 1878–79 when Lord Harris was struck on the field by a spectator because of an umpire's decision over a run out. Hornby seized the offender and despite being struck himself, frog-marched him to the pavilion and the law.

All the excitement of 1878 had established Lancashire among the foremost counties and the days of small attendances and collections at annual meetings were immediately things of the past. The county positively preened itself in its new status and the *City News* greeted the new season by trumpeting:

> The days when Yorkshire could afford to send any sort of team against us, when Nottinghamshire out of mere contempt declined to meet us at all, and when the Gloucestershire champions haughtily declared that they had so many standing engagements that they could entertain no more, are over. The fame of the Graces inevitably draws thousands to the not very accessible county ground at Old Trafford. The remotest villages in far-off Fylde feel the excitement of the occasion and send contingents of country cousins to watch.

And with the growing public interest came the inevitable improvements. A new grandstand was erected on the pavilion side, ropes were put round the ground, and . . . 'thanks to the operation of the building mania, the ground can now be reached by a more direct road than was formerly available and thus the greatest fault of the ground – its inaccessibility – is partially removed.'

The Liverpool club, fired partly perhaps by the events of 1878, were themselves now thinking of greater things and there was talk of establishing a great cricket ground there where county matches could be accommodated. The *Manchester Guardian* was not impressed. 'Liverpool has not been conspicuous, we believe, for the assistance it has given to the Manchester Cricket Club who have, by judicious expenditure and careful selection and encouragement of ability, wherever it was to be found, greatly raised the Old Trafford club and ground to their present pre-eminence in the provinces,' the newspaper wrote. 'There seems no valid reason therefore why Liverpool should seek to divide the honours which Manchester has fairly earned.'

Among the early matches of 1879, as usual, was that among the county's colts, a game that should have thrown up good young players for the future. In fact, in thirteen years only one player, Jim Ricketts (famous for his 195 not out at The Oval on his debut), had won anything like a permanent place in the county team. If a player did not make an impression in his first game or two he was quickly forgotten and Lancashire's early history is full of players who made only a handful of appearances. More indulgence, it was felt at the time, was shown to amateurs with good connections.

Barlow, the only Lancashire-born professional on the county staff around this time and one who had by-passed the Colts matches on his way to the team, started the 1879 season at Old Trafford with a hat-trick on the opening day of the match against Derbyshire. 'Barlow,' said the *Manchester Evening News*, 'was rewarded with a hearty cheer on achieving the hat. Mr A. W. Cursham came in next and just escaped, amidst considerable laughter, from being bowled by Barlow's first ball.' In the next match Lord Harris resumed acquaintance with Hornby in a game which lasted only two days. The attendance on both days was of several thousands, a size that would have astonished those who formed part of the miserable attendances of the early games. More than 6,000 attended the opening day of the Yorkshire match at Old Trafford, a game in which the brothers Steel, D. Q. and A. G., played important parts in the innings win. D. Q. scored 52 – the highest in the match – and A. G. scored 31 runs and took eleven wickets, including seven for 34 in a remarkable first innings display. The editor of *Wisden* commented 'It seems the best of England's batsmen find it difficult to master the ever-varying pace, pitch and curve bowling of Mr A. G. Steel, who makes his mark in match records against the cleverest of bats, on all grounds.'

Another innings win, in which Steel took nine wickets, came against Gloucestershire, who again attracted huge crowds at Old Trafford with more than 5,000 on the first day and 10,000 on the second. This time, we are told, the utmost order prevailed throughout, and the *City News* recalled the time when it was difficult, almost impossible, to induce people to go to Old Trafford. 'Now the difficulty is to provide seeing room for the vast crowds who, six deep, line the ground,' it said.

Lancashire, having won five and drawn four of their ten inter-county matches to share the 1879 championship with Nottinghamshire, sustained their second defeat of the season in the final match when they went to Lord's and were beaten by MCC. Still, it had been a good season, both on the field and in the coffers where, despite only one of the five home games reaching Saturday, the finances were in their healthiest state ever.

One of Lancashire's all-time greats made his debut this season when Johnny Briggs, aged only 16, played against the county of his birth, Nottinghamshire, at Trent Bridge in the season's opening game. He scored 36 runs in his first innings, his highest score in the five matches he played that year, and did not take a wicket in the only match in which he bowled. His bowling was slow to develop, but he was an outstanding fielder, rivalling even Vernon Royle, and a great favourite.

Lancashire took their most momentous decision since becoming a county when they appointed A. N. Hornby captain in 1880. The letter that was sent to Hornby offering him the position is still contained in the minutes for that year.

> Dear Hornby,
> I have been instructed by the committee to ask you to accept the captaincy of the County Eleven, our friend E. B. Rowley having, as you are aware, resigned that post. Hoping this appointment may be agreeable to you and that the team may continue its successful cricket under its new captain.
> S. H. Swire, Hon. Secretary.

Hornby was now 33 years old. After an apparent reluctance to devote his energies to Lancashire in his first eight years in first-class cricket, he had now become the driving force in the county and in his years as captain and president, Lancashire were to become a great power.

ALBERT NEILSON HORNBY has proved to be the single most influential person in the history of Lancashire County Cricket Club, his attachment as player and president spreading over fifty years. He transformed Lancashire into a formidable side and was captain when they won the championship in 1881 and 1897. He was born in Blackburn into the riches of the cotton industry on 10 February 1847. His father and uncles were Members of Parliament, and they had mills in Blackburn. Hornby went to live in the heart of the Cheshire countryside where he kept a fine stud of hunters, laid a cricket field alongside his home, and outside cricket, said one newspaper after his death shortly before

Christmas 1925, lived the ordinary life of the country gentleman. He was essentially an out-of-doors man and up to a good age he regularly kept up his shooting and riding to hounds.

When he first played for Lancashire at Old Trafford, in 1868, four years after the county's formation, there were only around 200 people to watch matches against Yorkshire. He was a strong influence in changing this because there seems little doubt that his personal friendship persuaded W. G. Grace to bring his Gloucestershire team to Lancashire in 1878 and turn Old Trafford into the great ground it was to become.

When Hornby was appointed captain there was only one Boss at Old Trafford. He was a strict disciplinarian, did not like grumbling, could not understand players who got tired, and for those who were not keen he had no use. S. M. Crosfield, who himself was to become captain, once confessed to some fatigue at the end of a day's play. Hornby told him he could field next day in the long field at both ends. He was keen on players practising and once asked Arthur Paul and Jim Hallows if they had. 'No sir,' they admitted. 'Thought so,' said Hornby. 'Saw you in the bar. Get your pads on and go in first.' When he became president he still ruled Old Trafford and one famous example of his autocratic control came when Walter Brearley, originally chosen for a match, was left out at Hornby's suggestion. But there was no questioning his loyalty to Lancashire. His heart and soul were in it and when he died Lord Harris said of him: 'I suppose that what he did for Lancashire only Lancashire people know, but it was evident to everybody outside Lancashire that he was the soul of that club.' The *Manchester Guardian*, probably through Neville Cardus, talked of his blusterous play. 'Hornby was very much the squire of Lancashire cricket,' said the newspaper. 'He was, in the winter, a hearty follower of hounds and he came to the summer game with a hallooing that was gusty and challenging enough.'

Hornby first came to notice in cricket when he played for Harrow in 1864 to 1865 and was considered a 'little wonder'. He moved on to Oxford but, according to Sir Henry Leveson Gower, he went purely to play cricket and when he heard that study might be required, he returned to the family milling business in Blackburn.

He first played for Lancashire in 1867, when he was 20 and the county programme was extremely thin. In 1870 he scored his first century, 132 against Hampshire at Southampton, and also scored 163 for the Gentlemen of the North against the Gentlemen of the South. He quickly established himself as the county's foremost batsman and from 1870 to 1881, through twelve seasons, he was the only batsman to score centuries for Lancashire, seven of them in all with three in one season, 1881, when he became the first player to reach 1,000 runs for the county. This was the year Lancashire went through the season unbeaten in the championship, which they won, and he clearly was responsible for team selection and leaned on several of the outstanding amateurs to play in important matches. He headed the English batting averages that year and was spoken of as W. G. Grace's 'one superior' and is the one other cricketer who could be considered to equal him in enthusiasm and devotion to the game.

Hornby stayed a playing member at Lancashire over a span of thirty-three seasons, playing his last game in 1899 when he was aged 52, and scored 53 in his last innings. After heading Lancashire's batting averages in 1869, he was top eight times and second three in the next twelve years. He opened with Dicky Barlow and their partnerships were a feature of county cricket. In style, they were far apart, Hornby a dashing hitter, Barlow a stonewaller, but they complemented one another perfectly and their daring running reduced many opposing sides to despair. Hornby used to say that more runs were lost than were ever made in county cricket. In the course of a season he stole runs by the hundred. However, it was his captaincy which lifted Lancashire to new heights with sound judgement, an infectious example and a real gift of getting the best out of the men under him. He was a true amateur but was solicitous to the interests of his professionals. And it was typical of his loyalty that when people in high quarters objected to the delivery of one or two of his bowlers, he stood behind them and checked the movement to drive them out. He was faithful to the professionals, they were loyal to him, and if any member of the team needed a change or rest, he was sure of a hearty welcome at Hornby's home, Parkfield, at Nantwich.

As well as being a dashing batsman, Hornby was famous as a fielder who could snap up a fast-moving ball in the outfield with either hand. Nothing annoyed him more than slackness or clumsiness in the field and if any young player waited for a ball instead of running in to meet it, 'neighbouring spectators were sure to hear Mr Hornby's opinion of him in the decisive English that he commonly spoke!' He was credited with a hasty temper, and was also a good boxer, although it seems much of his talent in that direction lay outside the ring. 'He was a capital boxer,' reported *Spy* newspaper, 'as many a rowdy has found to his cost.' *Vanity Fair* described him as 'very handy with a terrible pair of fists,' although it did go on to say he was a very cheery, kind-hearted fellow whose consideration for the Lancashire professionals was a byword and his popularity quite extraordinary. 'He goes to bed early, he hates a tall hat and he always plays cricket with an uncovered head. He is gifted with much courage and is always ready to stand by a friend,' commented the magazine. In fact, he did wear a cap on the field on occasions, but it was so unusual it would be remarked on in the newspapers. His hasty temper was shown one day at Old Trafford when his son, George, was playing in the same team. George missed a catch and a cry went up:

'Oh my, what will Pa say?' Pa, in fact, shot into the crowd to look for the offender. And it was Hornby, quite early in his career, who scattered the spectators at Lord's when running for a ball, helping to persuade the MCC to arrange fixed boundaries, essential as the crowds grew larger.

Hornby played in three Tests, one in Australia in 1878–79 and two more in the 1880s, captaining England against Australia in the first Test match at Old Trafford in 1884, when he opened the batting with W. G. Grace and was stumped off the third ball he received. Hornby was also a good shot – he was captain of East Cheshire Militia – he captained the English rugby team, playing for them nine times between 1877 and 1882 (when he was 35) and he also turned out for Blackburn Rovers soccer team. He attended Old Trafford right up to his death, even going to the nets to watch the players in 1924 – the year before he died – in an invalid chair. He generally wore a soft felt hat with the Lancashire colours on it, and had a brisk, cheerful word of greeting for old friends and former players at the ground. In 1901 members of the club and several distinguished visitors gathered in front of the pavilion where Hornby was presented with his portrait which is now hanging in the pavilion.

Another important decision that was made in 1880, in addition to the appointment of Hornby as captain, was the amalgamation of Manchester and Lancashire County Cricket Clubs. A meeting was called on Wednesday 24 March, with E. B. Rowley in the chair, and it was agreed that the name of the new club should be 'The Lancashire County and Manchester Cricket Club.' Humphrey de Trafford, the landlord of the ground, was made president for the coming year, and the vice presidents were the Earls of Derby, Sefton and Ellesmere, Lord Skelmersdale, Rt Hon. R. A. Cross, R. H. Phillips MP, H. Birley MP, A. B. Rowley, O. O. Walker MP, and J. A. Bannerman. Sam Swire was elected secretary and James MacLaren treasurer. The committee, decided by ballot, consisted of T. T. Bellhouse, W. Brierley, S. Field, J. R. Hillkirk, J. R. Hay-Gordon, A. N. Hornby, C. G. Hulton, W. E. Openshaw, E. B. Rowley, Roger Walker, E. Wolff and E. Challender.

This was to be the last season for Bill McIntyre, the fast bowler, who had put in such sterling work for the county and who for the previous eight seasons had never been out of the county team. He was so unsuccessful in the first three games of 1880, taking only eight wickets at a cost of 24.37 each, that he was dropped, and after playing in one more match later in the season, he was left out for good. Lancashire have had many outstanding fast bowlers through the years. McIntyre has the distinction of being the first.

The games with Surrey were revived this season after seven years and after beating a weak-looking team at Old Trafford, Lancashire completed the double at The Oval with one of the outstanding performances of the summer. Surrey batted the whole of the first day and it was six-thirty before their last wicket fell for a total of 226, to which Lancashire replied with 113 and were forced to follow on. The captain, playing his finest innings of the season, transformed the game by scoring 126, forcing the *Manchester Examiner* to describe it as the most brilliant batting ever seen at The Oval. His century was reached out of 136 and in all he hit three 5s on the huge ground as well as thirteen 4s. After an opening stand of 98 with Barlow, who contributed 26, Hornby saw the innings defeat saved with nine wickets standing before he was out. Lancashire were 197 for three at the end of the second day – 84 ahead – and with a fast 65 from Frank Taylor and 31 from E. B. Rowley – playing in his last season – on the final day, Surrey were set to score 202 for victory. Walter Read punished the bowling of Alec Watson and George Nash – a left-arm spinner who was in his second season – and both had to be taken off before Lancashire broke through. Surrey, who scored 40 in the first fifteen minutes, were 53 for two when Read was out and after being satisfactorily placed at 96 for three, they slumped to 141 all out, giving Lancashire a famous victory by 60 runs.

Lancashire's programme of thirteen matches was their fullest since they had become a county and in the same week that they played Surrey at Old Trafford, they also played Kent in the following three days. Six days in a row was too much for the *Sporting Chronicle* who wailed 'This, I think, is a mistake as we may have too much even of a good thing.'

Pilling, now in his fourth season with Lancashire, was widely regarded as the finest wicket-keeper in the land. He stood up to the fastest bowlers, McIntyre and Jack Crossland, and scorned the customary aid of a long stop, a revolutionary move in those days. So good was his wicket-keeping against Nottinghamshire that a small presentation was made to him from the members on the pavilion side.

Umpires were still appointed by counties, but suggestions of bias were growing. Barlow, for example, was said to have handled the ball when it became lodged in his pad, but the Lancashire umpire gave him in, much to the evident disgust of the visiting team, Yorkshire. In the match against Nottinghamshire, John Selby, who was not in the side and was umpiring in the game, gave Wilf Flowers in when it was widely thought he should have been run out going for the winning run. And in the match against Kent when Ted O'Shaughnessy was also thought to have been run out, 'the Kentish umpire gave him in.' Not surprisingly there was a call for neutral umpires to be appointed, a move the MCC made three years later.

W. G. Grace rarely performed well at Old Trafford, but in a fairly quiet year for him, in 1880, he saved his first – and only – century of the summer for the game at Clifton at the end of August when Lancashire looked to be well on top on the first day. After totalling 186, with Frank Taylor scoring 66 on his old school ground, Lancashire reduced Gloucestershire to 58 for five by the end of the day. W. G., who had intended holding himself back until the following day, had to go in at the fall of the fifth wicket. By lunch on the second day Gloucestershire were 194 for seven on their way to a total of 249 of which Grace hit a magnificent 106 to help his team to their first win of the season, by seven wickets after Lancashire had collapsed for 85 in their second innings.

The Australians played a Test match against England that season, a late-arranged game at The Oval after the tourists had played only one bona fide game, against Gloucestershire. Lord Harris agreed to bury the hatchet, following the scenes in Sydney two winters earlier, and played in the inaugural Test in this country. Hornby, in common with George Ulyett, refused to play, thus missing a unique honour.

The year of 1881 proved to be the most triumphant since Lancashire's formation. Apart from a hiccup against Cambridge University on the new ground at Aigburth, Lancashire marched undefeated through the season and won ten of their thirteen games to win the championship under Hornby's inspirational leadership. They called on twenty-one amateurs and eight professionals in the summer with Dicky Barlow the only Lancashire-born professional in the side, all the others having residential qualifications. One of them, Alec Watson, was also the new ground-keeper with accommodation in the pavilion, which had grown a new wing to accommodate the professionals and obviate the invidious distinction made by the players and gentlemen having to go on the field from opposite sides of the ground. There was also a new committee room, and a telegraph office had been built to enable messages 'to be dispatched from the field.'

An interesting move by the committee this year was that ladies should not be admitted to the members' pavilion or enclosure, a recommendation that was carried unanimously. No reason was given in the minutes and none of the newspapers reported the matter so we can only speculate on the reason for the change. Cricket clubs were founded by men for men and were just as much male domains as literary or scientific clubs. The place of Victorian women was in the home and their position at important cricket matches had been little more than as attractive appendages, adornments, often with

70

their own promenades and accommodation, not as interested spectators. Now that attendances were increasing rapidly, membership was growing, and members' accommodation was becoming cramped. The ladies had been allowed in the pavilion and enclosure only as a special concession and the only ones allowed to have tickets for entry to the ground were members' wives and sisters, and then only at the discretion of the committee. In any case, the women now had their own accommodation, and perhaps it was felt the men needed rather more elbow room.

It had taken twenty-four years to move the professionals' changing room to the same side of the field as the amateurs, but they were still kept apart, of course, with separate dressing rooms, dining facilities, travelling and hotel arrangements.

Lancashire's increasingly healthy financial state was partly reflected in the fact that for the first time since the county were formed, the amateurs, who had paid all their own expenses in those early years, were now having their railway fares paid for. They were soon to have the hotel bills settled, too. As befitted their new status, Lancashire also began to partake of 'luncheon' instead of dinner and the advertisements for the games pointed out that the South Junction Company's trains would call at the Cricket Ground Platform as usual. The annual Colts game showed that Lancashire's net was still not extending far beyond the centre of the county with hardly any representatives from the far north or south of the county.

Hornby missed only one game in 1881, the first at Lord's against MCC when Rossall-educated Campbell Hulton captained the team in one of his eight games for the county, and Briggs carried Lancashire to an eight-wicket win with a fine innings of 40 not out against the best professional bowling in England in Alf Shaw, Fred Morley and Billy Barnes. Lancashire were underway, and followed up with their first county championship match, in which they beat Derbyshire by an innings and 135 runs after a marvellous innings of 188 from Hornby, the second highest ever for the county after Jim Ricketts's 195 not out in 1867. Nottinghamshire, the most formidable team in the country, should have provided Lancashire with testing opposition in the next match at Old Trafford the following week, but due to a dispute with their committee, they were without Shaw, Morley, Barnes, Selby, Shrewsbury, Scotton and Flowers and fielded a virtual second team that was no match for Lancashire who won by ten wickets, due particularly to Watson's match return of eleven for 86.

The crowds were now regularly around 5,000 or more and the gate of over 8,000 for the second day of the Kent match a week later

71

was the highest since the arrival of the Graces and the Australians. But although the accommodation was ample, it was so far short of what was required that the spectators were climbing railings and availing themselves of any vantage point in order to see the play. They were rewarded with a two-day win by an innings following a rousing start to the Lancashire innings with 100 runs in an hour for the loss of Barlow. Hornby rattled on to his second century, scored in only an hour and a half and despite Lord Harris spreading his men out like a fan. Barlow had his best bowling return with eight for 29 in the first innings and Watson did the damage in the second with seven for 37.

The only defeat in this great season came in the next match when the Aigburth ground, the home of Liverpool Cricket Club and still being used today, was opened with a game against Cambridge University. The imposing members' pavilion is still one of the finest in the country and £15,000 was spent on the enclosure, finely situated near the River Mersey on the one side and rich woods on the other. The *Manchester Evening News* of Monday, 13 June 1881 described the day:

> The morning express from Manchester brought down a large company of spectators and the grounds were well packed with people when a start was made shortly after 12 o'clock. Aigburth is halfway between Mersey Road and Cressington on the Cheshire Branch Railway from Liverpool to Garston. The ordinary train service to the headquarters of the Liverpool Cricket Club was decidedly awkward for Manchester cricket enthusiasts visiting the present match and the Cheshire Lines promptly saw the difficulty and ran extra trains to Mersey Road and a special express direct, via Garston at 10.45 in the morning, and returning at seven in the evening, a little over three quarters of an hour being the duration of the run. The Liverpool authorities have not the same facilities for reaching their ground as the M. S. J. and A. Railway provide from the Old Trafford ground, but still there is excellent train accommodation both from Liverpool and Cottonopolis.

The *Manchester Courier* wrote:

> The match was arranged as much as anything for the purpose of opening with some éclat, the new enclosure which is very prettily situated, being surrounded by trees and shrubs on every side while a handsome and picturesque

pavilion, built from the designs of Mr Harrison, architect of Liverpool, affords every comfort and convenience for the members of the head cricketing organization in the neighbourhood of Liverpool. The ground, however, being newly laid, afforded only an indifferent wicket, and the crease wore very badly indeed as the game progressed.

The *Liverpool Daily Post* said before the game that the city should consider itself favoured to see the University which had never before been so far north for a match.

G. B. Studd opened the innings for the University when the wicket was at its best and had the distinction of recording the first century on the ground in first-class cricket, carrying his bat for 106 and leading his team from 67 for five to a winning total of 187. A. G. Steel, who had arranged the match, chose to play for the University, along with two other Lancashire players in Oswald Lancashire and the Revd John Napier, and took six for 22 as Lancashire were dismissed for 71 and forced to follow on. The demolition work continued with Steel taking five for 69 and the University, needing 38 to win, won by six wickets although the going was hard with J. E. K. Studd being caught and bowled for a duck in the fifteenth maiden over of the innings!

The *Liverpool Daily Post*, who thought about 9,000 people attended during the two days, wrote after the match that great pains had been taken to prepare a perfect wicket and to all appearances it looked perfect; but it had the fault of all new grounds, it wore badly. The newspaper also referred to what it described as prejudice towards Liverpool players. The writer declared: 'One thing struck me as being very pronounced. And that was the prejudice, not to say animus, displayed by the up-country visitors towards the Liverpool men in the county team, and to account for it is a puzzler.' The *Manchester Courier* referred to 'the Liverpool contingent, who were keenly watched by hard-to-please critics.'

No doubt Lancashire were happy to get back to the less exacting demands of the championship and another innings win, this time over Surrey, a team described by one observer as scarcely being on a par with dozens of local clubs. Hornby scored 42 and was out when his bat became 'entangled in his dress' when about to play the ball. Briggs, Watson and Reg Wood, from Birkenhead Park, all scored 50s in a total of 324. Wood hit a six, a big hit to leg and a rare event at Old Trafford. Surrey totalled 69 and 130 with Watson taking ten for 64 in the match and Nash seven for 101.

REG WOOD, who was educated at Charterhouse, was a left-handed

all-rounder who made his debut for Lancashire against Kent in 1880 when he was 20. He played only six times for Lancashire between then and 1884 when his final match was against Gloucestershire, a game that was abandoned due to the death of the mother of the Grace brothers. Soon after this he emigrated to Australia and became a professional and played for Victoria. During the 1886–87 Shaw–Shrewsbury tour of Australia, Billy Barnes swung a punch at Percy McDonnell, the Australian captain, missed him and hit the wall. His hand was so badly injured that Wood was sent for to play in his place and was capped in the second Test at Sydney. He batted at No. 10, scored 6 and 0 and did not bowl, and was not required again. He died in Australia in 1915, aged 54.

A repeat innings win over Derbyshire followed the defeat of Surrey in 1881 with Hornby hitting 145, his third century, and Barlow earning his new hat by dismissing George Barrington, Harry Shaw and George Osborne with successive balls and finishing with the astonishing first innings analysis of 10.1–9–3–6. This was the second time Hornby had outscored Derbyshire all on his own, scoring 188 in his one innings to their 102 and 62 in the first match, and 145 to their combined 107 in the second!

The first real test arrived at Sheffield early in July when Lancashire and Yorkshire, who were contesting the championship, went into the game undefeated. Huge crowds of around 15,000 were present on the first two days, including a large contingent from Manchester and neighbouring towns, and the game, as usual, was keenly fought. Hornby, who was having a marvellous season, was top scorer with 46 in Lancashire's 162 and he even got a wicket with his lobs when Tom Emmett was stumped off the second delivery. The spectators, basking in the scorching sun, were highly amused, it seems, to see Hornby bowling, but the Lancashire captain had the last laugh as Yorkshire were held to a one-run advantage in the first innings. Barlow, helped by Briggs, steered Lancashire to a second innings total of 196, and when Yorkshire set off towards their victory target of 196, there was the irrepressible Hornby, taking a magnificent catch in front of the pavilion to dismiss George Ulyett. Yorkshire were 76 for two at the end of the second day, but were unlucky to have to bat on a rain-affected wicket being dried by a boisterous wind, when the game resumed at three o'clock on the final afternoon. In two hours they were all out for 145 and Lancashire, by the comfortable margin of 50 runs, had secured their sixth successive championship win.

A. G. Steel played only five matches this season, one of them in the Old Trafford encounter with Gloucestershire, still a plum fixture and which had been awarded to Bill McIntyre for his benefit. The sun beamed on McIntyre, strongly enough for Hornby to wear a cap and the newspapers to comment on it, and when W. G. Grace won the toss in front of a 10,000 crowd, a big score was expected. Every stand was full to overflowing and the spectators sat several feet deep all round the ground. Inside eighty minutes Gloucestershire were all out for 42 with Steel taking five for 34 and Watson four for 8 and when Hornby had again given Lancashire a fine start with 61 of the first 77 runs, the day ended with Lancashire in an invincible position, 194 runs ahead and two cheap Gloucestershire wickets in the bag. Only about 2,000 people turned up the following day to see Lancashire wrap up the match by an innings and 36 runs, but McIntyre, a quiet and unassuming man, still benefited handsomely by £1,000. Steel took seven for 89 for a match return of twelve for 123.

Following the Cambridge match, and Lancashire's failure on the poor Aigburth wicket, Hornby had written to the committee to ask them to transfer the Yorkshire game on 28 July to Old Trafford as 'we all think the ground is in such a dangerous state and not fit to play a bona fide county match on at present.' The committee agreed and 7,000 people turned up at Old Trafford to see Lancashire swiftly seize the initiative against Yorkshire before romping home by eight wickets with a brilliant all-round display from Steel who took seven for 59 and six for 87 as well as scoring 57 and 3 not out. Vernon Royle returned to the team and in his first appearance of the summer he was heartily welcomed by the crowd who were thrilled to see him run out Ephraim Lockwood in spectacular style. It was impossible to estimate the number of runs he saved and the *Manchester Courier* reported that his presence at cover frequently forced Tom Emmett to exclaim when called for a run, 'Nawe, policeman's theere.' A ninth-wicket stand of 70 between Emmett and Ted Peate held up Lancashire who were left needing 70 for victory, child's play to Hornby who followed up his 69 of the first innings with 50 in the second.

VERNON ROYLE played for Lancashire between 1873 and 1891 and was regarded as the finest cover-point fielder English cricket had seen. It was said he was worth his place in a team for his fielding alone. Even accounting for the poor pitches of the time, his batting figures were less than ordinary. He averaged 15.66 and did not score a century for Lancashire in seventy-four matches. And in his only Test match under Lord Harris's captaincy in Australia in 1878–79, he scored 18 and 3.

Royle's fielding, however, was something different. Lord Hawke described him as a terror at cover and Sir Henry Leveson Gower said that even when he was over 40 he was still a fine cover point. He was ambidextrous, very quick on his feet and returned the ball like lightning. He ran out a great number of batsmen in his early days before players

became wary whenever the ball was near him. Even so, he saved many, many runs as he fed uncertainty into the batsmen's minds.

Royle was born in Brooklands, Cheshire, on 29 January 1854, and first played for Lancashire in 1873 when he was 19 and before he went to Oxford. The match was against Yorkshire at Sheffield and his debut might well be unique because he was bowled first ball in each innings by Allen Hill. Royle had forgotten to put his shirt in his bag and had to play in a Harlequin shirt of many colours. The crowd remembered that when he played there again and after he had run two or three out, a shout would go up, 'Look out for the bugger in the shirt.'

Royle was a master at Elstree School from 1879 to 1899 and was ordained in 1881, becoming curate at Aldenham, near Watford. He had intended becoming involved in parish work but stayed on at Elstree where he became a partner. He leased Stanmore Park, a beautiful mansion in fifty-two acres in Middlesex, in 1901, founding one of the best-known preparatory schools in the country. Vernon Royle died on 21 May 1929, and the funeral was held the following day. It was his express wish that work should not stop at the school because of his death and while the funeral was being held, the schoolboys took part in a cricket match. He was president of Lancashire at the time, an appointment he described by saying that nothing during his whole career had given him greater pleasure.

Lancashire's next two games in 1881, following the defeat of Yorkshire, were against Nottinghamshire and Middlesex, and both were affected by rain and drawn with Lancashire in the strongest of positions. On the day the Middlesex match started – the first between the counties for fifteen years – the committee agreed that the Middlesex gentlemen should be invited to dine with them at 7.30 p.m. As Middlesex were always top-heavy with amateurs the invitation extended to ten members of the team. What happened to the solitary professional, 34-year-old Bill Clarke, is not recorded in the minutes . . .

Nothing was now going to stop Lancashire from lifting the championship outright for the first time and two more wins and a draw from the remaining games saw them safely home. But they did have problems at The Oval even before the return match with Surrey had begun. Henry Celestine Robert John, 19 years of age and born in Agra, India, the home of the Taj Mahal, an amateur opening bowler who had attended Stonyhurst College and had made his debut in the previous match, did not appear for the game and effectively reduced Lancashire to ten men for the match. A Surrey colt called Tom Bradbury, an amateur who just happened to have been born in Lancashire, at Barton-on-Irwell, was drafted into the team, batting at

76

No. 11 and not being called on to bowl. Lancashire were dismissed for 78 of which Briggs made 39, but Surrey collapsed under the fire and speed of Jack Crossland, whose most destructive piece of bowling yet brought him a return of seven for 14, including the wickets of Walter Read, Bill Game and Bill Roller in successive deliveries. By 3.45 p.m. on the opening day Lancashire were into their second innings which saw them in greatly-improved form and scoring 255, with a fine 96 from Barlow, before bowling out Surrey for 81 to achieve victory by 216 runs. Crossland finished with ten wickets in the match, seven of them bowled as he sent the stumps flying, and it was perhaps from this point that suspicions were rooted as to the legality of his action. Tom Bradbury, incidentally, had played his first and last game for Lancashire. So, too, had Henry Celestine Robert John . . .

The return match with Gloucestershire was drawn because of rain but Lancashire secured their tenth win, by an innings and 129, after bowling out Kent for 38 and 61 at Maidstone with Nash completing an impressive season by taking seven for 22 and five for 26, and Crossland bowling only three overs in the game.

This was a season without parallel in Lancashire's history, one of unchallenged triumph through the championship in which six of their ten wins were by an innings and the others by ten wickets, eight wickets, 216 runs, and – the closest of all – 50 runs against Yorkshire. The supporters had no doubts where the hosannas belonged . . . to A. N. Hornby. One writer to the *Manchester Guardian* spoke of his devotion to the game and his brilliant example in the field which had inspired his team with that spirit which had carried all before it. Another compared the score – 325 – and attendance – about 7,000 on the opening day of the match with Middlesex – with a match he attended in 1871 when Lancashire were dismissed for 25 by Derbyshire in front of about 200 people. The change was due mainly to the captain. 'For a number of years he has played in nearly all the matches,' he wrote. 'He has always played well. His presence is a guarantee for a fair attendance for there are hundreds in Lancashire who will go a day's journey to see him get 50; and more than this, he has made Lancashire cricket popular with cricketers so that now our best players are proud to be asked to play for the county.'

Another writer to the *Manchester Guardian* declared 'Those who remember the few hundreds who used to visit Old Trafford six or seven years ago, and can appreciate the universal interest now taken in Lancashire cricket all over the county, will be the first to agree that much of the popularity awakened in the game has been the result of Mr Hornby's personal influence.'

At last, Lancashire cricket had taken deep root in the minds of the county's cricketers. It was indeed an honour to be asked to play and Hornby had instilled pride into them. The team took their tone from him, particularly when it came to fielding, a part of the game in which Lancashire were acknowledged to be the finest in the country with Royle or Briggs at cover, Barlow point, Walter Robinson in the long field, Watson short slip, Pilling behind the stumps, and Hornby wherever he chose to go. Hornby scored 1,002 runs for Lancashire that summer and averaged over 50 – two firsts in Lancashire cricket, although A. G. Steel also averaged over 50 this year but from considerably fewer matches, five to Hornby's fourteen. Barlow scored over 500 runs and took sixty-eight wickets, sharing the bowling honours with Nash (fifty-one wickets), Watson (sixty-nine) and Steel, an astonishing forty-two in five games.

(Captions read from top of picture and from left to right)

1871, Gentlemen of Lancashire: Harris (umpire), John Leach, Roger Walker, R. Stubbs, A.W. Gardiner, Arthur Appleby, John Hillkirk, A.N. Hornby (on ground), William Potter, Edward Porter, John Leese, Joe Makinson.

1881, George Nash, Jack Crossland, J. Smith (umpire), Dick Pilling, Alec Watson, A.G. Steel, Revd Vernon Royle, A.N. Hornby, Arthur Appleby, Walter Robinson, Dicky Barlow, Oswald Lancashire, Johnny Briggs.

1890, George Baker, Arthur Mold, Albert Ward, Arthur Paul, George Yates, Johnny Briggs, Frank Sugg, Archie MacLaren, A.N. Hornby, Arthur Kemble, Dicky Barlow, Alec Watson, Frank Ward.

1904, Jack Sharp, Willis Cuttell, William Findlay, Alec Kermode, Leslie Poidevin, Jim Hallows, Jimmy Heap, J.T. Tyldesley, A.H. Hornby, Archie MacLaren, Reg Spooner, Harold Garnett.

1911, Lol Cook, Bill Tyldesley, Ralph Whitehead, Harry Dean, Harry Makepeace, J.T. Tyldesley, Alfred Hartley, Kenneth MacLeod, A.H. Hornby, Harold Garnett, Reg Spooner, Jack Sharp, Jimmy Heap.

1919, Jimmy Heap, Jim Tyldesley, Bill Brown, Dick Tyldesley, Ernest Tyldesley, Harry Dean, Charlie Hallows, J.T. Tyldesley, George Shelmerdine, Myles Kenyon, Alan Boddington, Vic Norbury, Jack Barnes, Harry Makepeace.

1926, Jack Iddon, Ernest Tyldesley, Harry Makepeace, Charlie Hallows, Frank Watson, Albert Nash (umpire), William E. Howard (dressing-room attendant), Dick Tyldesley, Ted McDonald, Frank Sibbles, Albert Woolley, Ernie Moore (scorer), Walter Buswell (umpire), Harry Rylance (secretary), Oswald Lancashire (chairman), Leonard Green (captain), Sir Edwin Stockton (president), Peter Eckersley, Tommy Higson (treasurer), George Duckworth, Malcolm Taylor. (*Manchester Guardian*).

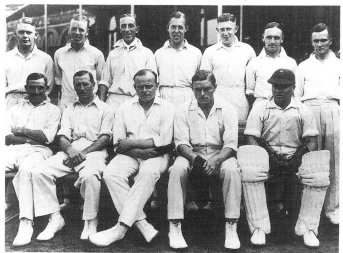

1934, Cyril Washbrook, Len Hopwood, Jack Iddon, Frank Booth, Dick Pollard, Len Parkinson, Buddy Oldfield, Eddie Paynter, Ernest Tyldesley, Peter Eckersley, Lionel Lister, George Duckworth.

1946, Bill Roberts, Eric Price, Jack Bowes, Ernie Moore (scorer), Gordon Garlick, Alan Wharton, Eric Edrich, Phil King, John Ikin, Cyril Washbrook, Jack Fallows, Eddie Phillipson, Winston Place.

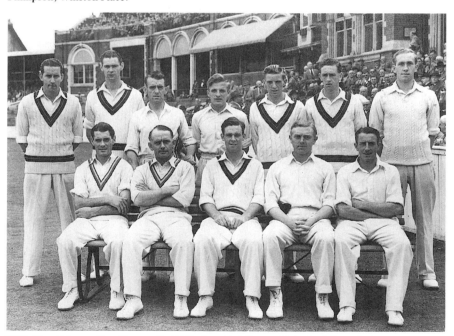

1950, Ken Grieves, Roy Tattersall, Alf Barlow, Bob Berry, Malcolm Hilton, Brian Statham, Tommy Dickinson, John Ikin, Cyril Washbrook, Nigel Howard, Winston Place, Geoff Edrich.

1957, Joe Jordan, Tommy Greenhough, Ken Grieves, Geoff Pullar, Roy Collins, Jack Dyson, Roy Tattersall, John Ikin, Cyril Washbrook, Alan Wharton, Brian Statham.

1960, Jack Bond, Ken Higgs, Geoff Pullar, Roy Collins, Peter Marner, Brian Booth, Keith Goodwin, Ken Grieves, Alan Wharton, Bob Barber, Brian Statham, Tommy Greenhough.

1964, Harry Pilling, Bob Entwistle, David Green, Duncan Worsley, Ken Higgs, Sonny Ramadhin, Geoff Clayton, Peter Marner, Tommy Greenhough, Ken Grieves, Brian Statham, Geoff Pullar.

1971, Barry Wood, Roger Tattersall, Ken Shuttleworth, Bob Ratcliffe, John Sullivan, Ken Snellgrove, Frank Hayes, Clive Lloyd, Derek Parker, Jack Simmons, Keith Goodwin, Buddy Oldfield (coach), David Lloyd, Farokh Engineer, Peter Lever, Jack Bond, Harry Pilling, John Savage, David Hughes. (*Manchester Evening News*)

1984, Jack Bond (manager), Neil Fairbrother, Steve Jefferies, Mike Watkinson, Chris Maynard, Steve O'Shaughnessy, Alan Ormrod, David Hughes, Graeme Fowler, Jack Simmons, John Abrahams, Paul Allott, Peter Lever (coach). (*Manchester Evening News*)

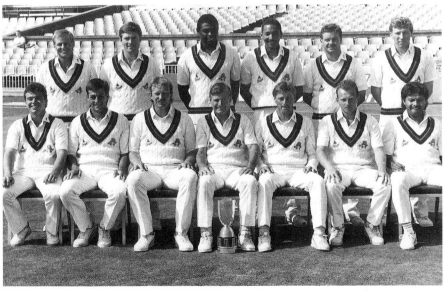

1989, Trevor Jesty, Andy Hayhurst, Patrick Patterson, Phillip DeFreitas, Dexter Fitton, Mike Atherton, Warren Hegg, Mike Watkinson, Paul Allott, David Hughes, Graeme Fowler, Neil Fairbrother, Gehan Mendis. (*Manchester Evening News*)

Chapter 4 1882–85

*'Lancashire have during the last season played in their
Eleven at least two men as to the fairness of whose bowling
there is grave doubt.'*

Jack Crossland, though playing in seven matches, took only thirteen wickets in 1881, ten of them in one match. With McIntyre gone, he was to become the county's main strike bowler the following year, taking ninety-seven wickets at 10 runs each, but at the same time fuelling the growing campaign to have him outlawed because of a suspect action. It went on for four years before he was forced out of the game, and then not for throwing, but for having failed to meet the requirements of the residential qualifications.

The first mention in the Manchester newspapers of Crossland's questionable action did not come until near the end of the 1882 season as a result of the outcry during the match with Surrey at The Oval.

Crossland was having a fine season. He had taken seven wickets against the Australians, and Fred Spofforth, the demon Aussie bowler, said Crossland was quicker than himself. He had a remarkable return of six for 7 against Somerset on an impossible Old Trafford wicket, and when he took eight Kent wickets a few days later, four of the last six came in the second innings without a run being scored off him.

One of Crossland's victims was Lord Harris, the Kent captain, who was to lead the campaign to outlaw unfair bowling, and interest was focused keenly on the fearsome Lancashire fast bowler. The *Manchester Guardian* described him as the fastest bowler seen on the ground for years.

It was in the game against Surrey at The Oval beginning on Monday, 21 August 1882, that Crossland first really stirred up the emotions of the spectators. Returning to the attack on the opening day he

79

bowled five of the six remaining wickets. The *Sporting Chronicle* reported: 'So long as the Surrey batsmen were knocking Crossland all over the field nothing was said, but immediately he began to get on the spot there was a regular disturbance.' The *City News*, after describing Crossland as being in his cruellest and most untouchable mood, said 'The spectators demonstrated against Crossland with vigour and they even carried their ill-temper into the luncheon tent and almost mobbed the stalwart Lancashire professional on the plea that his delivery was unfair. Crossland's delivery is undoubtedly peculiar but he has been passed by almost every well-known umpire in England. The whole business was disgraceful.' Crossland, it was added, seemed unaffected and took eleven wickets in the match.

Wisden reported: 'From the first, his style of bowling was greeted with marks of dissatisfaction, but with every fresh success the demonstration of disapproval became louder and louder. Cries of "Well thrown", "Take him off", and "Thrown out, Crossland", mingled with hisses and groans came from all parts of the ground and excited spectators called upon the umpires to do their duty.'

Crossland, in fact, was never in his career no-balled by a first-class umpire, a point vigorously made by Lancashire – and in particular by Hornby – through the years he was harried. The *Pall Mall Gazette* wrote after the Surrey match:

> Crossland's performances this season have been so good that it could hardly be denied that he is at present one of the best fast bowlers we have and fully entitled to a place in the England Eleven on Monday next against the Australians. Unluckily, however, his delivery is not above suspicion and The Oval people on Monday were somewhat loud in their protestations. There is a good deal of suspicious bowling to be seen just now but professional umpires, who must please to live, are not likely to stop it unless it is made worth their while.

Crossland was not chosen to play for England against Australia. He had played twice against them and it was rumoured the Australians would object to him because of his delivery. He went into the final match of the season, against Middlesex at Old Trafford, with ninety-seven wickets, but was not called on by Hornby to bowl. Steel, Nash (twelve for 99 bowling unchanged in the match) and Barlow did all the bowling as Middlesex were dismissed for 70 and 98 to lose by an innings and 271 runs.

The season ended with Crossland still under fire. Even Manchester readers in the *Manchester Guardian* wrote to say they thought his delivery was open to objection. Anybody who thought the whole issue might go away could not have been further from the truth. The annual meeting of MCC just before the start of the 1883 season brought Lord Harris to his feet again. He said Law X – which in those days stated simply: 'The ball must be bowled. If thrown or jerked the Umpire shall call "No ball" ' – was constantly being violated and throwing was making ground every year. On 12 May 1883, a Saturday, a telegram was sent from Lord's by Hornby to the Lancashire committee asking that Crossland be sent up by the first train Monday morning. The MCC committee wanted to see him and Hornby said he would see he got back all right. The Lancashire committee dug in and replied: 'Crossland plays here on Monday so he cannot leave. Shall be glad to send him when at liberty.' MCC wanted to ask him to answer charges by Nottinghamshire that he had been spending the winter in his home county, thus forfeiting his residential qualification. Ten days later the MCC threw out the Nottinghamshire objection.

One big change in 1883 was the introduction of neutral umpires and when Crossland bowled in the opening match against Derbyshire it was said his friends watched the result with eager anxiety and only breathed freely when he had completed the first over without a murmur from the umpire, Tom Brownhill, a former Yorkshire player from Sheffield who was regarded as one of the best in the country. But the great confrontation was just around the corner. The *Manchester Courier* explained: 'Monday morning last brought a scene of considerable excitement in the neighbourhood of Old Trafford. Trains heavily laden with human freight were repeatedly arriving, tram cars were crowded and cabs were dashing past in quick succession. Added to this were hundreds of pedestrians hurrying along evidently bent on pleasure. Kent were playing.'

To be more specific, Lord Harris and Crossland were playing. But the blood-thirsty were to be disappointed. Not the slightest exception could be taken to Crossland's bowling, none of the Kent representatives said a word, and Lord Harris scored 118 with fifteen boundaries, several of them off the fast bowler. Crossland did have some success when he took six of the last seven wickets as Kent tumbled from 280 for three to 309 all out, still a formidable score and one Lancashire were unable to match as they were dismissed for 206 and forced to follow on. Hornby, after scoring 88 in the first innings, followed up with 96 out of 169 for three on the same day, and with Lancashire reaching 238 in their second innings, Kent needed 136 to win.

Barlow, however, was in magnificent form, taking six for 32 as Kent were hurried out for 65, leaving Lancashire unexpected winners by 70 runs. It was a famous victory and hundreds rushed across the ground, some being knocked down in the scramble to reach the pavilion where Barlow received a warm reception. For some time the crowd assembled in front of the pavilion and loud cries for Hornby, Lord Harris and Barlow were given, but as none of them would acknowledge the shouts, the crowd quietly dispersed. In the next game against Nottinghamshire, Watson bowled 85 overs and Barlow 77, while Crossland hardly bowled at all . . . 3.2–0–3–2 and 5–2–10–0. The *Nottingham Daily Express* said that though Crossland hardly bowled there was still the usual controversy as to whether he threw. 'I offer no opinion myself – although I have one – for who is to decide when doctors disagree so extensively?' said the writer.

The game at Lord's against MCC was the biggest test yet for both Crossland and Nash, who also figured in Lord Harris's plans for ridding the game of throwers. The *Manchester Guardian* said Crossland seemed to have modified his delivery and Nash seemed fair, and as the umpires had been warned before the match to be very careful about carrying out the law on throwing, it was absurd for outsiders to question the decision of judges so competent and impartial as Farrands and Wild. The *Daily News* was not so easily swayed and thought both bowlers had put themselves on their best behaviour at Lord's. After agreeing Crossland's action was fair, the newspaper said he had modified his style for the occasion, scarcely ventured a very fast ball, and, if he always bowled like that, there would be no disputes about him – and he would not get many wickets. Nash passed muster with the umpire but his delivery was far from giving general satisfaction.

Things went quiet for a while and there was not even a suggestion of trouble in the return with Kent although Crossland proved unplayable in the second innings when he took four wickets in 26 balls, including that of Lord Harris. But The Oval was coming up, again near the end of the season, and more demonstrations were made against Crossland on the opening day as he took seven for 34 in the Surrey first innings. 'Well chucked', 'Take him off' were shouted throughout his bowling and when the innings was over spectators rushed onto the ground. As Crossland walked quietly back, he went to the accompaniment of hissing and hooting and a certain amount of jostling. The incident almost led to the game being abandoned. Hornby was unwilling to continue and it was nearly half an hour before Lancashire's first two batsmen walked out. Hornby was not one of them. He sent Frank Taylor out with Barlow while he himself continued to argue the issue with the Surrey authorities. Some uncomplimentary things were said about Crossland on the second day, particularly when he frequently hit Walter Read on the hands and legs, but there was none of the hissing and hooting of the first day. There was no need as Crossland took two for 108 and Surrey won by three wickets. Hornby was furious and said he would never play again with Lancashire on The Oval ground, although he later relented and played there several times.

The final game of the season was against Gloucestershire at Clifton, usually a fine place to finish up, with the Grace brothers hospitable hosts. Crossland's first over was a mild one but someone twice shouted from the terraces 'Why don't you bowl?' W. G., turning to that part of the ground, appealed to the shouter who was silenced for the time being. But Grahame Parker, in his book, *Gloucester Road*, wrote that Crossland soon had the ball whistling through W. G.'s beard, bowling what these days might be termed Bodyline. When a section of the crowd began barracking loudly W. G. went over to them and threatened to close the ground if they did not stop. They did and he went on to make a century.

The dispute rumbled on through the winter when Nottinghamshire announced their refusal to play Lancashire in 1884. 'Lancashire have during the last season played in their Eleven at least two men as to the fairness of whose bowling there is grave doubt,' said Nottinghamshire. Middlesex had also, for the second year, refused to play Lancashire and although a reason was not given, there was no doubt what it was. Cambridge University, too, are thought to have refused to play Lancashire. Whatever the reason, after playing in 1881 and 1882, the teams did not meet again for many years. Lancashire did agree to Surrey's invitation to play them again but said they trusted there would be no repetition of the scenes of 1883.

Crossland and Nash again went to Lord's for the MCC match early in the 1884 season and again came through unchallenged. Nothing happened in the game against Kent at Old Trafford, except that Lord Harris showed his pluck by scoring 53 in the seven-wicket win despite being repeatedly hit about the body by balls from Crossland. The issue reared its head again when the England team was being chosen to meet Australia in the first Test match ever staged at Old Trafford. The custom then was for the team to be chosen by the committee of the club at whose ground the match was being played. Lancashire, in their wisdom, named five of their own players in a twelve which included Lord Harris and Crossland, with A. N. Hornby as captain. Then a letter was read, received earlier from Lord Harris, who reiterated his feelings about Crossland. Sam Swire, the Lancashire secretary, was instructed to send the following reply:

July 7, 1884

Dear Lord Harris,
  My committee have decided to play Crossland against the
Australians, therefore we suppose under the circumstances
the English team will lose your valuable assistance which
we very much regret.

So the team, when announced, did not include Lord Harris –
who was to captain the remaining two Tests – and in his place was
a dashing young batsman from Middlesex and Oxford University,
Timothy O'Brien.
  In the end Crossland did not play. He was never to play for
England, and perhaps Hornby as captain, when coming to choose
the eleven for the first Old Trafford Test of 1884, was mindful of
the feelings about Crossland and avoided the ultimate piece of
bloody-mindedness.
  Controversy, however, was never far away. When Lancashire
played Yorkshire at Sheffield, Crossland was being barracked with
cries of 'no ball' coming from the crowd. At length, he ran to the
wicket without delivering the ball, but the cries were still repeated.
When the match was finished, Crossland went home to Sutton-in-
Ashfield where he was asked to play for Mansfield Town against
the Mansfield Woodhouse Eleven the following day. Crossland was
twice no-balled at the start of the game and was again no-balled just
as he sent the batsman's stumps flying. Crossland, though generally
regarded as a genial man, threatened the umpire in rather strong
terms and demanded he be replaced, a request which was turned
down by the Mansfield Woodhouse captain, Mr Turner. The players
then walked off in sympathy, the game was abandoned in a bitter
atmosphere, and it was suggested that the whole incident had been
premeditated, although this was denied. Crossland later sent a crier
round to inform the public that although he had been no-balled at
Mansfield they would find he would not be no-balled at Liverpool
in Lancashire's next match against Surrey.
  In another match in his home county Crossland shouted back
to the barrackers, 'You can't tell the difference between a throw
and a fair ball. Now I'll show you.' Then he sent down a perfectly
fair delivery. 'That is bowling,' he said. 'Now this is throwing,' and
threw the ball to the limits of the field, and added 'And as I'm off,
I'll leave it to you to settle who is to fetch it. Good afternoon.'
  Crossland was barracked at Derby even before he had delivered a
ball and after playing in the next match at Leicester, he was left out
of the team at Taunton, Clifton, and The Oval where the scenes of the

84

previous year were expected to be repeated and police reinforcements had been brought in. But Crossland's arm – so it was announced – was troubling him and the confrontation was avoided.

Lancashire understandably continued to support their player and, along with Gloucestershire and Sussex, refused to join with other clubs in not playing bowlers whose actions were doubtful. Lord Harris must have been getting to the end of his tether. Kent's opening match for the 1885 season was at Old Trafford in Whit week and rumour had it that if Crossland or Nash were put on to bowl, His Lordship would demonstrate. The gossip proved unfounded, although the game did lead to the abandonment of the return fixture at Tonbridge. There were 12,000 spectators on the first two days at Old Trafford and when Lord Harris walked out to bat on the opening day he was given a great ovation. Almost immediately, he was on his way back, bowled by Crossland and amid such a noise that even Old Trafford had seldom heard. The *Manchester Guardian* vividly described the scene:

> Lord Harris played the first and second balls of the over with ease, but the third completely spreadeagled his wicket. The sight was too much for the crowd and the scene which followed showed that Crossland was regarded as having had his revenge in a manner which could hardly have been calculated upon. People seemed fairly beside themselves with delight. Hats and coats were thrown up and one enthusiast actually waved his coat from the top of one of the stands.

Two days after the match Lord Harris put his feelings in a letter to the Lancashire committee:

> Gentlemen,
>   I have the honour to beg your attention on a subject which has engaged the attention of the cricketing public of late years, and which has now, in my humble opinion, arrived, owing to the action of your club, at a point requiring incisive treatment.
>   The subject is that of unfair bowling.
>   It is unnecessary to remind you that a very strong opinion has gained ground of late years that an unfair style of bowling has become too common, and that measures should be taken to check its increase.
>   In consequence, at a meeting of county secretaries, held at Lord's on December 11, 1883, it was proposed by Mr I. D. Walker and seconded by Mr C. W. Alcock, 'That the

undermentioned counties agree among themselves not to employ any bowler whose action is at all doubtful,' and this was signed by the representatives of Yorkshire, Kent, Middlesex, Derbyshire, Notts and Surrey.

Your representatives declined to agree to the resolution, contending, I presume, that the public feeling on the matter was groundless, that there were no unfair bowling actions, and that there was no necessity for any steps being taken in the matter; and with you, in not signing the agreement, were the representatives of Sussex and Gloucestershire.

Early in the following summer, however – and here, for the first time publicly permit me to observe I find it necessary to mention individuals by name, and only now, because otherwise I could not state my case – I found that, of those bowlers whose action had been particularly objectionable, Nash had disappeared from his county eleven; another, Crossland, was still in it, and, in my opinion, bowling as unfairly as in the previous season; but, personally, I was content to rest for the time being with the point I believed I had gained. I hoped that you meant, of your own free will, and without agreement with other counties, to place your eleven in an irreproachable position, and my hopes were justified by finding later on in the season that Crossland was also left out.

It was therefore with the greatest regret that, on arriving at Old Trafford on Thursday last, I found that both Crossland and Nash were to play. I acted as I thought best under the circumstances. I asked for an interview with your committee or its representatives, and I told Mr MacLaren and Mr Hornby then, before the match began, that I held myself free to take what action I thought necessary. It was impossible for me to do anything more then. For all that I knew, both bowlers might have changed their deliveries; or again, if they had not, the umpires might 'no-ball' them. In my opinion, and in that of others, after watching them carefully this year, the delivery of neither bowler is consistently fair; the umpires did not 'no-ball' them; and it remains therefore for me – pledged as I consider myself to be, to do everything in my power to discourage unfair bowling – to take the steps I told your representatives I thought it might be necessary for me to take.

First let me say that I consider your contention unanswerable – i.e., that the umpires, the sole judges, by the laws of cricket, of fair and unfair play, never have objected to the action of either of the bowlers above mentioned. I admit that it is unanswerable; and that being so, and still maintaining my opinion, in which I believe myself to be supported by a very large number of cricketers, that the action of neither bowler is consistently fair, and bearing in mind that your club has declined to pledge itself 'not to employ any bowler whose action is at all doubtful', I conceive, after careful consideration, that there is only one course open for me to adopt, and that is to advise the committee of the Kent County Cricket Club to decline any further engagement with your club – certainly for this year, and until a more satisfactory state of things obtains.

Our clubs are engaged to play the return match at Tonbridge in August. What I shall suggest to my committee is to allow you, without appearance on the ground, to take the match by our default, or, if you prefer to go by the strict letter of the law and to send your team there, to take care that there be wickets pitched, someone to toss for choice of innings, and, on our declining to go to the wickets, umpires to give you the match. Of course, it is quite possible that my committee may decline to support me. In that case, I promise you no one shall ever hear another word from me on the subject of unfair bowling. I shall consider that I have taken the last step possible, and that I may fairly leave it to some other enthusiast, with more energy, and his cricket career to look forward to rather than back upon, to take up the cudgels.

Before I conclude, let me add a few words of personal interest, certainly to myself, I think to the Kent Eleven, and perhaps to your club.

I told your representatives before the match began, and I was but repeating what I have frequently said, that if there was one county in England against which I should have a disinclination to move, that county would be Lancashire. It is fourteen years since I first played on Old Trafford for Kent v Lancashire, and I think this makes the eleventh consecutive year that I have come up as captain of the Kent Eleven. During all that time the relations between the two clubs, so far as I know, have been of the most cordial character. We always rejoiced when Lancashire was champion county. Kentish and Lancashire professionals have always been on the most friendly terms, the same amongst the amateurs; and if Mr Hornby will forgive me mentioning him last, or indeed at all, entirely divergent as are his opinions and mine, strong as they are on the question of the deliveries of these two bowlers, we have never allowed those opinions to interfere with our personal friendship, and, indeed, I believe each has no better friend on the cricket field, perhaps in a wider sphere than the other; and lastly, I had the gratification on Thursday last of meeting with such a reception from the enormous company present at Old Trafford, as I have never received on any cricket ground, in or out of England, in my life – only surpassed by the still more complimentary manifestation at my summary dismissal.

Appreciating, then, at their highest worth, that cordial reception and these friendly relations, I ask you, gentlemen, and the Lancashire cricket-loving public, to believe that, in acting as I propose to do, I am actuated solely by my anxiety to see the noble game pursued in what I conceive to be the fairest way, by no petty or jealous feelings, and with infinite regret that my action should have to be directed against two professional cricketers and against the Lancashire County Cricket Club.

I remain, gentlemen, faithfully yours,
[signed] Harris.
Huntingfield, Faversham, June 1.

The end was not far away. Kent, of course, supported their illustrious and powerful captain, and the match at Tonbridge was called off and on Monday, 29 June 1885, Lancashire replied, through secretary Sam Swire, to the points made by Lord Harris and the Kent committee.

My committee can only regret that Lord Harris has been able so far to influence your executive as to induce them to break an engagement made in all honour and good faith, without any reservations whatever as to who should or should not take part in the matches arranged for this season between our respective counties. My committee beg to remind you that since the bowling question was discussed at Lord's in 1883, when the umpires were specially instructed to carry out strictly Rule 48, the bowlers to whom you refer have appeared at Lord's and frequently elsewhere in first-class matches without having their fairness challenged by any of the most competent umpires in the country. It would appear, therefore, that you have no confidence in the body of experienced and carefully-selected men on the list of umpires of the MCC or even in the MCC committee, but you are determined to set up a standard of your own in regard to what should be considered fair bowling, and to require cricketers throughout the country to conform to it. My committee desire to refer to the amendment our representative proposed to Lord Harris's resolution at the meeting already alluded to – viz. 'That the whole question of unfair bowling be left for decision in the hands of the MCC committee.' My committee leave your executive to bear the responsibility of the action they have adopted. For our part, so long as there is a recognized authority we decline to join any particular counties in the endeavour to override cricket rules, or to make laws for themselves. But any decision of the MCC would unhesitatingly be accepted as final by the Lancashire executive.

My committee have quite as much confidence in Mr Hornby and other members of our club as you state you possess in the gentlemen of your county team, so under the circumstances are quite willing to accept your ultimatum as to the return match. In regard to the character of Crossland's bowling, we may remark that he was selected by the MCC committee, and played last year in the match North v South, at Lord's, and that the only reason why he did not play in the Kent and other matches at the close of last season was that he had injured his shoulder at Leicester and was therefore unable to bowl.

In these matches Nash was omitted because the hard state of the ground was not suited to his bowling.

A copy of the correspondence has been forwarded to the MCC committee with a request that they will pursue such a course in regard thereto as they may consider best for the future interests and welfare of cricket.

Lancashire might well have saved their breath, and the time of their secretary. Crossland had already played his last game for Lancashire, against Cheshire at the Stockport ground of Cale Park two days earlier when he took two for 19 and three for 38. On the same day that Swire was composing his letter, the MCC committee decided that Crossland no longer possessed a residential qualification for Lancashire. The committee, acting on evidence received from rate and rent collectors, a village policeman and the country squire, said Crossland had lived in his native county, Nottinghamshire, from October 1884 until April 1885.

Although the matter had been settled, albeit through a side door, the two counties still did not play at Tonbridge. Lancashire must have felt aggrieved. Yet it does seem, from a distance of over a hundred years, that Lancashire, in their commendable loyalty to their fast bowler (and Nash as well), turned a blind eye to the overwhelming mass of opinion against them. The *City News* probably hit the nail on the head at the end of the season, 'We have a feeling that though our committee could not conscientiously have thrown Crossland over, they were not wholly sorry that the matter was settled for them.' Lancashire had a fair point that the matter was in the hands of neutral umpires and Crossland had never been no-balled for unfair bowling. But the umpires, themselves nearly all former professional bowlers, were naturally reluctant to make themselves responsible for denying a fellow professional a living. After all, with Lord Harris and other prominent gentlemen at the head of a crusade, what need was there for them to interfere? This turned out to be the last year, too, for Nash as Lancashire dropped him from the team as another left-arm spinner, Johnny Briggs, at last came to the fore.

Chapter 5 1882–89

'The days when it was possible for a lazy spectator to take his ease on the greensward while watching a match are apparently over.'

At least, Lancashire's championship success of 1881 had been achieved before Crossland had really burst on the scene. Nothing could detract from that and 1882 had arrived full of enthusiasm with Old Trafford showing unmistakable signs of prosperity with new stands on both sides of the ground and with extra accommodation for the ladies and the Press. Lancashire started the season poorly but then ran into a rich winning vein with ten victories in fourteen matches to share the title with Nottinghamshire, then decided on the basis of least matches lost. Nottinghamshire lost one out of twelve, Lancashire one out of fourteen, and that to Nottinghamshire by 37 runs at Trent Bridge.

The Australians were here again in 1882 and Lancashire provided early opposition in May. The roads were crowded with pedestrians and vehicles all going to Old Trafford where the stands and platforms were filled to capacity and a deep hedge of spectators was formed around the whole circumference of the ground. The attendance for the first day, when 13,761 paid for admission, was the highest ever and, it was said, something to be wondered at. During the three days of the match, which the Australians won by four wickets, it was estimated something like 35,000 people watched the game.

Lancashire played Somerset for the first time this year and the Old Trafford game provided a piece of history when Lancashire won by an innings and 157 runs after bowling out their opponents for 29 and 51. For George Nash took four wickets in four balls, all in one over in a first innings in which seven Somerset players failed to score. It must be pointed out, though, that Nash got his wickets on the second pitch used in the match. Lancashire had scored 237 runs with a career-best 78 from Dick Pilling, but a heavy downpour on the second day so soaked the wicket that a new one was prepared – at right angles to the one used by Lancashire on the first day, running in an unusual direction, from the pavilion. Nevertheless, it is in the record books, the first of four Lancashire bowlers to dismiss four batsmen with successive balls, the others being Arthur Mold, Walter Brearley and Dick Tyldesley.

Games in those days were still liable to start only when all the players, or at least the prominent ones, had arrived, and the match at Trent Bridge did not get underway until twelve thirty due to the late arrival of A. G. Steel, who was making one of his few appearances in a championship match. He made up for some of the lost time by helping to dismiss Nottinghamshire for 116, top-scored for Lancashire in the first innings with 18 out of 52, and then took five Nottinghamshire second innings wickets to leave Lancashire with the whole of the third day, a Saturday, to score 107 to win.

The Nottinghamshire second innings had finished several minutes before the closing time of six thirty on the Friday and A. N. Hornby had asked for the wicket to be swept and rolled, the usual practice between innings. At eleven forty on the Saturday morning Hornby again asked for the roller, but the Nottinghamshire captain said, without opposing him, that it could hardly be fair to roll it night and morning. The *Nottingham Journal* said Mr Hornby insisted he was entitled to roll all the night through and assumed a very high tone. As the rule was not perfectly clear, directions were given to roll the wicket for ten minutes, and much to Nottinghamshire's delight, Hornby was out second ball. Barlow went strictly on the defensive, plodding on and on and refusing to hit even when he had a chance. Lancashire were 24 for four when Edward Porter went in and eventually, after batting an hour and a quarter, Barlow succeeded in stealing a single from Wilf Flowers amid considerable derisive cheering. Half an hour later Barlow got his second single and even managed a third before lunch which was reached with Lancashire 41 for seven. Barlow was still only 3 when Crossland came in at the fall of the ninth wicket at 47. Crossland played remarkably well in scoring 20 before he was run out, while Barlow carried his bat for 5 out of 69 in two and a half hours.

Lancashire's rise in fame was reflected that year in Ephraim Lockwood's choice of the Lancashire game, ahead of Gloucestershire, for his benefit match at Sheffield. He was the first to choose a

Roses match. Special trains brought people from various parts of Lancashire and Yorkshire and 8,000 people attended the opening day. The *Manchester Courier* said that the continued intercommunication between the counties undoubtedly rendered the interest stronger, the rivalry greater, and the contests more exciting than they could possibly be with other counties. The match was rain-affected and drawn, but Lancashire won the return at Old Trafford ten days later by seven wickets.

By the beginning of the final week of the 1882 season, Lancashire and Nottinghamshire were neck and neck for the championship and a defeat for either side would have given the title to their rivals. Neither made a mistake. Lancashire won both their closing games by an innings, against Surrey and Middlesex, with Steel scoring 99, Vernon Royle 63, Walter Robinson 101 and Frank Taylor 60 not out against Middlesex at Old Trafford. Lancashire were 344 for seven at the end of the second day and as there was no provision for closing innings, they had to keep going on the final morning when Middlesex made little attempt to bowl them out. Lancashire moved rapidly to 439 and Middlesex were bowled out twice in the afternoon for 70 and 98 with Nash taking twelve wickets. There was a crowd of close to 12,000 for the final day of the season, and when Lancashire won by an innings and 271 runs a vast crowd surged round the pavilion and cheered enthusiastically until Hornby emerged to make a speech. Then the cheering was renewed and for nearly an hour people hung about the ground, cheering the various players and making demonstrations.

It had been another great season, particularly for Barlow who headed both Lancashire's batting and bowling averages with 856 runs (30.16) and seventy-three wickets (9.68). Hornby scored 852 runs and Robinson 674, while Crossland, who did not bowl in the final match, took ninety-seven wickets (10.5) with Nash sixty-two (10.36) and Watson seventy-seven (12.25).

A good deal of money was being spent on the Old Trafford ground around this time. Drainage had been attended to, there were more comforts for the members and the public, stands, grand and otherwise, occupied almost every inch of space, BUT, said the *City News* 'The days when it was possible for a lazy spectator to take his ease on the greensward while watching a match are apparently over.' Not surprisingly, the writer recalled the days when Lancashire were at the bottom of the popularity poll and when Old Trafford was too far a pilgrimage for any but the most enthusiastic cricket follower. The ground was now among the foremost in the country and a visitor from Liverpool described it in vivid terms in 1883 in a letter to a Manchester newspaper:

> The oval green turf, nicely kept and bounded by rails and posts, outside which are seats and tiers of stands, the scoring box, the covered stands for ladies and reporters, the pavilion, new dining-hall and refreshment bar opposite, all form a unique spectacle. Great expenditure has been judiciously laid out in procuring everything that can enable a player to succeed; but there is also a serious, a businesslike air about everything, from the highest official to the white cat that trots about the ground, which never ventures a run without looking round to see if it is safe. The lunch is good and plentiful, the waiters attentive; there are telegraphs, telephones, black boards for communications received, boys to attend to the wants of members, commissionaires, and in spite of all this and the perfect regularity and smoothness with which everything works, there is nobody stalking and fussing about.

Perhaps all this high praise went to the heads of the committee members who decided, just before the start of the 1883 season, that the Lancashire professionals engaged in a county match should be provided with dinner, the charge to the club not to exceed two shillings a head. The free dinner looked to have worked wonders as Lancashire won their first seven matches of the year, including the great victory over Kent after following on.

This was the first season of neutral umpires but even the unbiased, of course, could get it wrong. Lord Harris was given not out when caught by Pilling off Crossland and later admitted he had touched the ball and added 'The umpire was mistaken.' The mistake, and the noble Lord's decision to take advantage of it, cost Lancashire quite a few runs. He was 57 at the time, but finished with 118. There were plenty of players who did not walk in those days and Barlow himself was among those who would let the umpire decide everything.

An innings of 154 against Oxford University by Walter Robinson, a Yorkshire-born batsman who had been professional with Haslingden and Littleborough, included one of the biggest blows seen at Old Trafford, a sensational hit of a full-pitched ball to square leg, over the flag post clean out of the ground and on to the railway line for six. The much-maligned Crossland organized the collection for Robinson which raised a handsome £24 2s 6d for an entertaining innings. Robinson was a vigorous driver of the ball, particularly on

94

the onside, but was also a skilful timer of the ball and an artistic player of a shot between slip and point.

Lancashire's run of seven wins, most of them by huge margins, all of them comfortable, ended, as might have been expected, at the hands of Yorkshire at Old Trafford where over 15,000 saw the first day's play. The ground had never held so many people and a large force of policemen was needed to keep the people from scrambling over the field during lunch. That opening day was dominated by a 21-year-old Yorkshire colt called George Harrison who took seven for 43 on the way to 100 wickets in this, his debut season. Harrison, a former apprentice shoemaker for seven years, bowled with grace and ease and had the speed of the fastest bowlers of the day. His performance that day was enough to secure an eight-wicket win for Yorkshire, one of five defeats in the last eight matches of the 1883 season for Lancashire.

The eight-wicket margin was repeated eleven days later at Sheffield where Yorkshire, for so long an all-professional team, fielded three amateurs in Lord Hawke, E. T. Hirst and E. Lumb. Hornby won the toss for the most important match of the year but was unfortunately without his entire professional staff who were in a delayed excursion train somewhere in the region of nearby Wharncliffe Woods. To make matters worse they had Hornby's bag and flannels with them and although the start was delayed twenty minutes, the game then had to go on without them. Hornby revised the batting order and sent in Frank Taylor and A. G. Steel, followed by Charles Haigh and Vernon Royle. Three top wickets went down for 7 runs before the professionals arrived and a breathless Barlow joined Taylor at the wicket. The rot stopped for a while but George Ulyett, the great Yorkshire player, brought it back by dismissing Hornby, Briggs and Watson, all of them bowled, for a hat-trick which produced deafening applause which went on for several minutes. It is interesting to note that Ulyett's teammates all followed a long-established custom by crowding round to tender their shillings to him for a new hat. Ulyett then went on to score 61 as Yorkshire romped on to their first double over Lancashire since 1876. It was all part of an awful end to the 1883 season for Lancashire and included a defeat at Clifton, providing Gloucestershire with their only win of the season. As *Wisden* reported 'The Lancashire season went up like a rocket and came down like a stick.'

There was no shortage of criticism. The *Manchester Evening News* put much of it down to a shortage of practice and an abundance of easy living. It said:

Professionals of Nottinghamshire and Yorkshire lose no opportunities of practice and the amateur teams do not disdain to snatch a portion of the luncheon interval or a half hour before play commences for 'a few balls'. Not so Lancashire. Our men are very rarely seen at the nets and spend the time that might be usefully occupied in practice, in sauntering round the ground with their friends. The game is not as keen as it used to be. More of the cigarette and luncheon element is being imported into it. A man cannot play cricket after a hearty lunch and continued exertion is impossible after a pipe or cigarette.

There was no shortage of other reasons, too . . . Pilling's ill health, the unavailability of the Steels, Hornby's lack of form, some players being past their best, and the shortage of new blood.

Lillywhite's Cricketers Companion pointed out how heavily Lancashire had had to rely on Nottinghamshire players and asked where they would have been without Bill McIntyre in the past and Johnny Briggs and Jack Crossland in the present. The feeling between the two counties was far from amicable and following Nottinghamshire's refusal to play Lancashire because of the presence of Crossland and Nash in the team, Lancashire sent a Christmas card to Trent Bridge that year which stated:

Cricketing Rules drawn up by the Notts CCC, 1883–84.
Rule 1. That in playing Lancashire, the Lancashire men shall not be allowed to use bats, but only broom handles.
Rule 2. That Lancashire shall not be allowed any bowlers and if so, no stumps to be used; and the Notts captain to select the bowler.
Rule 3. That both umpires shall be strictly Notts men.
Rule 4. That in case there is any fear that Notts should lose, even under these rules, the Notts men do leave the field and refuse to finish the game.

Nottinghamshire naturally replied with a New Year's card to Old Trafford:

Lancashire County Cricket.
The only rules necessary for players in the County Eleven are that they shall neither have been born in, nor reside in, Lancashire.
Sutton-in-Ashfield men (Briggs and Crossland) will have the preference.

Lord Harris, still up to his eyes at the time in trying to rid the game of its throwers, made some interesting observations about the Old Trafford spectators in an article in the *National Review*. He said the ring at Manchester was not so highly educated in cricket as it was at Lord's. 'Thirteen years ago I played in a Kent v Lancashire match at Old Trafford – perhaps, take it all round, the best in England – and I don't suppose there was £50 taken on the ground in the two days,' he wrote. 'Three years ago, in the same match, about £600 was taken. Now those spectators are as eager and excitable as Londoners but their education in cricket has only recently commenced and one hears frequent mistakes, such as cheers at the supposed fall of a wicket when a batsman plays hard on to the ground to point or to the bowler.' The total receipts at the gate for 1883 were £3,422. There was a handsome profit of £2,705 and it was reported at the annual meeting that since 1876 the club, which now had 1,237 members, had spent about £4,000 on buildings and providing accommodation for members. Nevertheless, the ground which was described by some, including Lord Harris, as perhaps the very best in the country, had its problems once more in trying to cope with the thousands who arrived for the match against the Australians in 1884 when more than 16,000 attended on the opening day and about 19,000, a record for the ground, on the second.

A new large and lofty stand was opened for the occasion, but many people who had travelled miles to see the great game, saw nothing. The committee had done their best but instead of going the whole hog and closing the gates when they thought the ground was full, they closed some of the turnstiles at three thirty on the second day but allowed people in if they took their chance of seeing anything. This led to a flood of complaints, many of them to the newspapers. One man wrote to the *Manchester Guardian* to say that thousands had left the ground disappointed and disgusted. He himself had travelled many miles on the Friday, the second day of the match, had paid a shilling, but, like thousands of others, had had to stand the whole day and did not get a glimpse of a fielder until about five o'clock. Beyond the first three or four rows of standing spectators it was almost impossible for people to see, and two writers thought a slanting footpath would be useful, such as Yorkshire had provided at Sheffield's Bramall Lane. As for the game, George Giffen, the Australian, performed the hat-trick and scored his first century in this country, but the weather helped Lancashire to a draw.

This was the year of the first Test match at Old Trafford and with the first Test at Lord's following nearly two weeks later, this made the Manchester ground second only to The Oval in Test match seniority. The team included four Lancashire players in Dick Pilling, Dicky Barlow, A. G. Steel and A. N. Hornby who, as a Lancashire committee member, had also helped select himself as captain. Nobody, I suppose, would be too surprised to learn that the first day of Test cricket at Old Trafford, 10 July 1884, was totally washed out. Rather more surprising was the performance of Hornby who opened the batting with W. G. Grace and was out to the third ball he received . . . stumped! An estimate of 12,000 was put on the crowd which saw England bowled out for 95 to which Australia replied with 141 for seven by the close of the second day. It needed some good back-to-the-wall stuff the following day, with Barlow in the thick of things, to earn England a draw.

Lancashire were in a poor spell around this time and although they finished third in the championship table they, and everybody else, were a long way behind Nottinghamshire, the great team of the period. Crossland played in eleven of the sixteen matches but took only forty-four wickets and the bowling relied heavily on Barlow and Watson. Lancashire used thirty-three players with the usual sprinkling of unfamiliar names, some of them never to be seen again and including Charles de Trafford, who was to play so heroically and for so long for Leicestershire, and Hugh McIntyre, the Blackburn Rovers goalkeeper. The four Steel brothers actually got together in one match, against Surrey on their home ground of Aigburth, which Lancashire lost by 29 runs after needing 133 for victory. D. Q. Steel scored 0 and 13, H. B. 18 and 0, E. E. 22 and 7, and A. G. 39 and 20 as well as taking one wicket. The changing fashion in cricket was displayed when Gloucestershire played at Old Trafford, a clash that only six years earlier had been responsible for the introduction of huge crowds, but which was now considered second-rate due to Gloucestershire's poor performances. The gate was low but the game had the distinction of being stopped for the most unlikely of reasons, due to the death of Mrs Grace, mother of the famous brothers. The return match was played three weeks later when Gloucestershire won by 7 runs after following on 82 behind. It was only their second win in two years, and both were against Lancashire.

Umpires were still establishing themselves and two of the decisions in the game at Derby reflected the control still exercised by the captains. Derbyshire were fighting to avoid the follow-on when Joe Marlow, their medium-paced bowler and tail-end batsman, cut a ball from Crossland for two. Charles Docker, the Derbyshire captain, immediately left the pavilion and went to Hornby to tell him it should have been four. And it was the captains, not the umpires, who went to interview the spectators on the spot before deciding that the batsman was entitled to only two. Then when Marlow was bowled by Crossland three short of avoiding the follow-on and with just over fifteen minutes of the second day remaining, the umpire raised his hand to ask Hornby whether to pull out the stumps for the day. The umpire's action led to an unseemly scene by the crowd who misinterpreted the raising of his arm as the signal for a no-ball. The crowd called the batsman back, but the players left the field to hooting and yelling.

The year of 1885 saw the finish of Jack Crossland as a Lancashire bowler and while the county waited for a new fast bowler to enter the stage, Johnny Briggs suddenly burst into prominence with the ball. In 1884 he had been little more than a mere change bowler who took seventeen wickets in sixteen matches. Now here he was with sixty-three wickets at 12.57 runs each, including a remarkable nine for 29, all nine being taken on the afternoon of the second day when Derbyshire were 87 for nine at the close. His chances of all ten wickets were quickly scotched the following morning when Watson opened the attack and bowled Bill Eadie with his first delivery.

JOHNNY BRIGGS was the most popular player Lancashire had ever had, a popularity that spread through the country. He was a comedian, a joker on the field. But he was a tragic character, too, who pulled out of a Test match with brain trouble, and who died in Cheadle Asylum after two long spells there. Briggs is the greatest all-rounder Lancashire have ever had. No other player in the county's history has scored over 10,000 runs as well as taking over 1,500 wickets. He played thirty-three times for England, toured Australia six times, and when he died, only one player had taken more Test wickets against the Aussies than he. When the Australians visited England in 1899, Briggs needed six more wickets to complete 100 against them and dearly wanted to play at least once more to try to reach the figure. Archie MacLaren, the Lancashire captain, was also England's captain, and used his influence to get a place in the team for the Leeds Test when Briggs had almost given up hope. 'It is not pleasant to think that, however indirectly, my action had a result that no one could have foreseen,' MacLaren wrote later. 'The excitement proved too much for him and sent him off his head.' Briggs had taken three of the wickets he needed on the opening day and that night was a member of the party of players who went to the Leeds music hall. During the performance his manner became strange and 'to the great distress of his friends, it was discovered that his mental facilities had become damaged.'

Briggs was admitted to hospital in July 1899, and was not discharged until 28 March the following year. He had been receiving treatment for eight months, yet he returned to play for Lancashire for one more season. That summer, of 1900, proved to be Briggs's best. He not only took over 100 wickets for Lancashire for the eleventh time, but also scored more runs than ever before, 761. He seemed to have recovered but at the end of the season he was ill again and within months, in March 1901, he was back in Cheadle Asylum where he died on 11 January 1902. Many people, including Hornby, thought that sunstroke, which Briggs had contracted in South Africa several years earlier, had caused his death. Another theory involved a match against Surrey in 1899 when Tom Hayward drove a ball which hit Briggs under the heart. 'This will kill me,' Briggs said to his wife. Briggs's epileptic fits were common knowledge in the game and only recently, Buddy Oldfield, who played for Lancashire in the 1930s, recalled being told about them by Arthur Paul, a teammate of Briggs, who became a coach at Old Trafford.

Briggs's universal popularity was reflected at the funeral at Stretford Cemetery, attended by about 4,000 people. A thousand arrived on a special train from Oxford Road station in Manchester; hundreds more came on bicycles. The great crowd was largely composed of working men who had stolen time from their dinner break. Among the impressive array of wreaths was one from the comedian, George Robey, made up of bay leaves tied with long red and white streamers. Another wreath showed stumps, bails, bat and ball, and was made up of hyacinths and violets, but it was the telegram from the Derbyshire club which most summarized people's feelings: 'Sympathize with all good Lancashire sportsmen in the death of poor little Johnny.'

Briggs was born at Sutton-in-Ashfield on 3 October 1862, and moved to Widnes when he was 14, the year after his father had first become professional with the cricket club there. His own enthusiasm for the game was fostered by his father and both were frequently seen as early as 5 a.m. practising on nearby parkland. Briggs himself was a professional cricketer when only 13, with Hornsea at Hull, and at 15 joined the Liverpool club, Northern, where he attracted Lancashire's attention. He was still only 16 when he first played for the county in 1879, when he was regarded chiefly as a batsman. He was also a brilliant fieldsman and during his first three seasons his bowling was not required. In fact, he took only twenty-six wickets in his first six years with Lancashire before he blossomed truly as a bowler in 1885. From then until 1900 he took 1,670 wickets for the county, taking more than 100 wickets in eleven of those sixteen seasons.

Briggs himself said in 1891:

> I suppose I was really played for my batting in the first instance but I have always thought myself a better bowler than bat. Then, when a cricketer has been bowling any length of time and taking a responsible position in the field as cover point, he cannot be expected to make much off the bat. I always feel satisfied if I come out first or second in the bowling analysis and have an average of 20 odd runs at the end of the season; that ought to be a satisfactory result for anybody.

Briggs the batsman averaged over 20 eleven times and topped the bowling seven times. He was only a little man, 5 feet 5 inches, but he was a hard-hitting batsman who scored nine centuries for Lancashire and one for England, against Australia in Melbourne on his first tour in 1884–85. He bowled left-arm spin and was regarded as a worthy successor to Vernon Royle as a cover point, which was high praise indeed. He finished his career with Lancashire with 10,707 runs (average 19.01) – a total exceeded by only three of his contemporaries – and took 1,696 wickets (15.60), a record for Lancashire for more than sixty years before being overtaken by Brian Statham. His Test career of thirty-three matches extended over sixteen years and he scored 815 runs (18.11) and took 118 wickets (17.74).

Lord Hawke, who ruined Briggs's benefit match by refusing to play on a pitch that had been protected from the rain, fondly recalled Briggs in later years: 'With a wicket to help him he could be a terror,' he said. 'He was a cheery, podgy soul, full of humour who perhaps played a little to the gallery, but never gave anything away.' He was also a man with an answer for most situations. When his captain, Hornby, once questioned him about his sobriety, he replied with an exhibition of trick cycling.

Briggs was involved in one of two outstanding batting performances in 1885, sharing in a record last-wicket stand of 173 with his good friend and later business partner, wicket-keeper Dick Pilling. The other was the recording of the first century for Lancashire in a Roses match, by 19-year-old George Kemp, a stylish right-hand batsman who had just completed his first year at Cambridge and was in only his second match for the county. Kemp became a Member of Parliament at the tender age of 29 and had little time for county cricket, playing only eighteen times for Lancashire up to 1892. He was created Baron Rochdale in 1913.

The record last-wicket stand was played against Surrey at Aigburth and on a wicket regarded as tricky, Surrey were all out for 117. Briggs, who had not been required to bowl, went in to bat with the score 28 for two and by the end of the first day had reached

81 of Lancashire's 186 for eight. Alec Watson was quickly out the following morning, at 193, with Briggs still on 81, and then came the partnership with Pilling which was a record for county matches at the time and has been beaten only five times since. The additional 173 runs came in 100 minutes with Briggs moving from 81 to 186 – the third highest score for the county behind Jim Ricketts's 195 not out in 1867 and A. N. Hornby's 188 against Derbyshire in 1881 – before he was stumped off Walter Read's 'underhand twisters'. He had hit brilliantly, playing all eight Surrey bowlers with ease, and hitting one 7 and eighteen 4s in his stay of 225 minutes. It was the highest score of his career and the innings he regarded as his best.

Pilling scored 61 not out, one of only two half-centuries he scored in 177 games with Lancashire. His straight drives were particularly good and it was said of him: 'The balls dead on the wicket he played correctly, and those off the line of the stumps he punished unmercifully.' The hat was sent round on behalf of the two players and the collection of £28 8s 4d was divided between them. The partnership took a good deal out of Pilling. He played in the next match against the MCC but was 'indisposed' during it and did not play again that season from the middle of July. Edward Jackson, an amateur who had kept wicket before Pilling arrived, returned to the team for the next match against Yorkshire at Huddersfield, his first game in eight years. Arthur Kemble, a 23-year-old amateur who was secretary of Liverpool for many years and who played rugby for Lancashire and England, made his debut in the next match.

The game against Surrey at Aigburth, which was washed out by rain on the final day, also produced another Lancashire chucker, less than three weeks after Crossland had finished with the game. George Jowett, a 21-year-old amateur born in Prescot, a batsman and fast bowler making his debut, was put on to bowl by Hornby, who had never before seen the player in action. He was called for throwing by umpire Jack Platts and although he played in nineteen matches for Lancashire up to 1889, he hardly ever bowled again.

Kemp's century, his only one for Lancashire, was scored at Huddersfield. It took him three hours and he scored his 109 out of 156. Yet when Yorkshire started their second innings needing 148 for victory Kemp was responsible for the dropped catch which probably cost Lancashire the game. He was fielding at long off when Willie Bates, only six at the time, skied a catch to him. Kemp missed it and Bates went on to score 82 not out in 85 minutes to bring Yorkshire victory. In all, Kemp played fifty-one first-class matches, eighteen of them for Lancashire up to 1892, but never again approached the form of that day and finished with a disappointing career average of 11.45.

Barlow's only centuries in his twenty-one-year career with Lancashire came in that summer of 1885, an innings of 117 in 3 hours 5 minutes against MCC, and 108 against Gloucestershire when he batted through the opening day for 103 not out in 5 hours 25 minutes.

With the loss of Crossland, Lancashire were again on the lookout for a fast bowler. 'We need one and we will get one,' was the cry at the 1885 annual meeting where, it seems, a few crocodile tears were shed at his going. Watson, Barlow and Briggs – only one of whom could even be described as medium paced – had done nearly all the bowling in 1885 and were to carry it for three more years until Arthur Mold appeared on the scene in 1889. It was an attack that, despite its heroics, lacked balance and pace and in three of those four years Lancashire languished in the middle of the table, a poor effort at a time when there were only eight and nine teams contesting the championship. Nevertheless, it was a time of great interest in the game; the cricket craze had got hold of people and more than 100,000 were paying at the gate for the eight or nine home matches a summer. The change that had come over first-class cricket in just a few years was remarkable. Now they were playing almost continuously through June, July and August, the audiences, once sparse when the whole thing was quite modest and unassuming, were huge and Lancashire were often having difficulty fitting people into the ground. Certainly, the days of a lounge on the grass while watching the game had gone for ever.

More alterations had been made at Old Trafford with the erection of stands, a ladies tea-room and pavilion, and a new building, directly opposite the pavilion, to accommodate reporters near the scoring box. The small though commanding stand, formerly known as the members' enclosure, had now entirely disappeared and in its place was the handsome, substantial ladies' pavilion consisting of Ruabon terracotta and red brick and built in what was known as the Cheshire style of architecture. The roof was of Welsh red tiles and the structure, two storeys high, served as a cloak and tea-room. Outside was a pavilion and forming part of it was a covered stand slightly raised above the level of the field to provide accommodation for 300 ladies.

Despite the lack of a fast bowler, hopes were high for 1886 when the Australians would play three times at Old Trafford, in a Test match, and against Lancashire and the North of England. For wasn't A. G. Steel now permanently based in Liverpool and expected to turn out more often for the county? It proved a false hope, however. Steel was to play only eleven more times in eight years for Lancashire, playing his last match for them in 1893. Three of those matches came in 1886 when he also captained England to victory in each of their three Tests with Australia. In many ways Steel must have been something of a disappointment to Lancashire. The man ranked only second to W. G. Grace as an all-rounder played just occasionally and clearly felt no need, and certainly no obligation, to play for his county. Lancashire's fortunes through those years from 1877 to 1893 might have been dramatically altered if he had played more than his forty-seven matches and given the county some of the time he was prepared to find for the big games.

The games with Kent and Nottinghamshire were resumed in 1886 now the stumbling block of Crossland had been removed and Lancashire found a specially warm welcome awaiting them, despite the exchange of tartly-worded Christmas and New Year cards, when they returned to Trent Bridge. Said the *Nottingham Journal* on the morning of the match 'The Lancashire County eleven will make a reappearance on the Trent Bridge ground today and the fact is one for congratulation. The fixtures with Mr Hornby's team supplied one of the most popular home matches and the satisfaction we have felt that our county team have held the premier position for the last two years has been just tinged with the regret that Lancashire has not been met.' The cordiality ended there. Lancashire lost sixteen wickets in less than two and a half hours on the second day and were dismissed for 42 and 48 in reply to Nottinghamshire's 173. *Wisden*, after saying it was the first match since the quarrel, also pointed out that Steel and other prominent players had stayed away. The *City News* thought five members of the team had no business at Trent Bridge, one of them no doubt being a Yorkshireman called Albert Champion who turned out anything but, with innings of 4 and 0 in what was to prove his only match. Another newcomer that year, and for that year only, was Alf Teggin, an amateur and a leg-break bowler from Salford who had a more illustrious career as an international rugby player. The team's performance, it was said, was melancholy.

Teggin's outstanding piece of bowling in his six-match career came against Kent when he took ten for 87 at Old Trafford in a match in which the start was delayed for 45 minutes because of dense fog and was then troubled by strong winds which resulted in lots of hats being blown across the field. The second match at Old Trafford that week was against a very poor Sussex team who were all out for 50 in the opening 80 minutes and then fielded slovenly as Lancashire raced to 305 for eight by the close of play. Bennett Hudson, a Longsight professional, made his debut in this match, and came within two runs of joining Jim Ricketts in scoring a century on debut. His 98 took only about two hours and he and Johnny Briggs put on 111 in an hour. Hudson had the spectators cheering madly as he drove ball after ball to the boundary and over the rails – they would have been 6s in later years and enough to have given him his hundred – before he ran out to drive Arthur Hide and was easily stumped. He hit sixteen 4s, three coming in one over from Bill Tester. Four days later, in his second innings for the county, he hit out at everything against Oxford University and scored 85. Despite this impressive beginning, the 35-year-old Yorkshire-born Hudson, who had played three times for his native county in 1880, was to play only three more matches for Lancashire and finished with the quite exceptional average, for the time, of 34.50.

Old Trafford's second Test match was staged early in July when Lancashire again had four representatives in the chosen team, Hornby, Barlow, Briggs and Pilling. Hornby's selection again drew criticism and one newspaper commented: 'The Manchester executive would do well to set an example by selecting the best men regardless of personal influence and popularity.' As it turned out Hornby dropped out of the match through injury and A. G. Steel, who played only three times for Lancashire that summer yet played in all three victorious Tests as captain, stepped up to lead the team. Barlow had a marvellous match, taking seven for 41 in the second innings and scoring 38 not out and 30 in the four-wicket win. The ladies' tent – a new and very picturesque addition to the stands – was filled with visitors and, said the *Manchester Guardian*, 'the small lawn in front contained a garden party quite as charming as that which assembled in the adjacent gardens on Saturday.'

The Yorkshire game followed hard on the heels of the Test match and Steel was again captain in a match in which he scored a magnificent 55 out of 112 and then, when 178 were needed to win, led the way with 80 not out in the victory. By now, the Yorkshire game was the outstanding one in Lancashire's calendar, and the *City News* tried to explain why: 'For downright sturdy excitement the Yorkshire match has few equals. We are such old opponents for one thing. Then we are near enough neighbours to make it possible for the visitors to bring with them a strong following of personal admirers who add a pleasing variety to the criticism and the shouting, and finally, the Yorkshire professionals are always worthy foemen whom it is as delightful as it is creditable to beat.' Steel played only four innings for Lancashire in 1886 – 83, 55, 80 not out and 14 – and it was noticeable that while Lancashire, who finished third that year, were playing Kent at Maidstone, he and his brother Harold were playing for Cambridge Past and Present against the Australians at Leyton.

Another attractive match that summer was the one against Nottinghamshire for Barlow's benefit. Alec Watson, the ground keeper, prepared a good wicket which lasted the three days, and more than 26,000 people paid for admission. The *City News* said of Barlow: 'He has in every way conducted himself in such a manner as to elevate professionalism in cricket.' And of him and Hornby . . . 'Was there ever a more distinguished pair of batters than Barlow and his captain? The wonderful things they have done between them will never be forgotten whilst Lancashire County cricket has a history.' Fittingly, they shared in an opening partnership of 109 and Hornby and Oswald Lancashire, another prominent amateur, led the way in making a collection for Barlow on the pavilion side and raising 'a nice round sum'.

All was not sweetness and light with the professionals, however. Briggs absented himself without permission on two successive days and the committee deducted two days' wages from him. But where he went nobody knew. Other committee decisions that autumn were for a former detective called Slater to be engaged as gate-keeper at the members' entrance for the coming season at the rate of £1 1s per match to include dinner and beer . . . and 'that the horse be offered to Mr Lambeth for the winter on condition that he be kept in fair working order. In the event of the horse not being disposed of in this manner, the committee resolve he be sold at once at the best price obtainable.'

The 1886 season had been disappointing for Lancashire, although they had finished third in the championship, and there were more complaints about the make-up of the team and the fact that there was no new blood about. There was no sign, either, of the fast bowler which Lancashire so badly needed and five new bowlers were added to the groundstaff for 1887. Two did not make the grade, two others, Frank Ward and George Yates, were to make modest marks, and the fifth, who was from Northamptonshire and was starting out on his two-year residential qualification, was Arthur Mold. How strange that *Wisden* that same year sounded a warning about a man who eventually was to be forced out of the game because of his bowling action. Said the Editor, after suggesting that F. A. Bishop of Essex should modify his delivery: 'Several good and unbiased players say that Mold, the fast bowler, who is now bowling for Northampton-shire, must also take care.' For the time being, however, Mold was to bowl for Manchester Cricket Club as he qualified for the county he was to serve so willingly and successfully. The county started the season with a rousing win over Sussex and included in their team, for only this game, a new amateur from Ulverston called George Bigg who turned out to be a small man who wore glasses.

Harder times, however, were just around the corner in the form of Surrey who were to crush Lancashire by an innings and

106

134 runs. Their innings was built around a marvellous partnership of 305 for the third wicket between Walter Read and Bill Roller who batted nearly all the second day in tropical heat. Read's 247 was, at the time, the second highest-ever in a first-class match in this country behind W. G. Grace's 344 for MCC against Kent at Canterbury eleven years earlier. One of the famous Barlow run-outs occurred in this match when Hornby called him for a silly single first ball of the match and Barlow was run out before he had faced a ball. Briggs was out in an unlikely way when he faced the insidious lobs of Read. The ball, it seems, did not rise more than two feet above the ground and appeared as if it might not reach the wicket. Briggs simply tried to block it, but it curled round him with just enough force to remove the bails. The *Manchester Guardian* described the delivery as the sort a boy of eight or nine would send down. 'It was absolutely ludicrous to see the daisy-cutter roll into the wicket without the astounded batsman making any attempt to prevent it,' said the newspaper.

The game against Nottinghamshire at Trent Bridge in July 1887 produced a hat-trick and, it would appear, the last reference in a Lancashire match to the collections taken on the field for an event that was still reasonably rare. The bowler who took three wickets in three balls was 26-year-old John Auger Dixon, a good batsman and a more than useful medium pace bowler who was to captain Nottinghamshire for the last eleven years of the century. His victims were Walter Robinson, Johnny Briggs and George Yates and, according to the *Manchester Guardian* 'It caused some amusement when the other members of the Eleven made the collection of shillings to present Mr Dixon with a new hat.' This clearly was an old custom, not surprisingly continued by a Nottinghamshire team which contained such long-serving players as Arthur Shrewsbury, Billy Barnes, Wilf Flowers, Billy Gunn, Bill Attewell and Mordecai Sherwin. And the collection was not restricted just to the players. The *Sporting Chronicle* wrote, 'The usual custom of collecting a shilling from everybody on the pavilion was rigidly observed.' Mr Dixon should have had enough money, then, for a quite splendid hat.

The alterations to the Old Trafford ground, which was now regarded as second only to Lord's, included spiked iron railings on the pavilion side. They probably looked rather grand but could easily have proved fatal when a Gloucestershire fielder, 21-year-old Arthur Croome, ran for a lofty hit from Dick Pilling. He missed the ball, fell over the railings, and one of the spikes entered his neck for about an inch just below the chin. He extricated himself and called for Gloucestershire's two famous doctors, E. M. and W. G. Grace, to help him. They partly carried him to the pavilion and they, assisted by Dr Royle, quickly attended to the player and stitched the wound. There was a 20-minute delay, but the railing had missed 'the vital parts' and the player was not seriously hurt. It was suggested that the game be adjourned for the day but W. G. thought the spectators would be less anxious if the match was continued. Croome took no further part in the game, which Lancashire won by an innings and 98 runs, and Hornby himself fielded as substitute for the rest of the Lancashire innings.

Lancashire played both their matches against Yorkshire that year in August and after drawing the first at Bradford, when Yorkshire scored 434 for two on the opening day with Louis Hall and Fred Lee sharing in a second wicket stand of 280, they went into the second on the crest of a victory wave and confident of winning. They did not arrive in Manchester from Brighton until the early hours and ended the first day in a hopeless position with Yorkshire 162 for two in reply to their own 129. Yorkshire won by an innings and Lancashire had to be content with second place behind Surrey in a season in which they won ten of the fourteen county matches.

The offending spikes on the pavilion railings were protected and by 1888 the railings had spread to the popular side to replace the inconvenient and unstable ropes which had marked the boundary line for many years. The substantial railing, supported by iron standards, now prevented spectators from trespassing on the field. But the cindered walks on this side of the ground were proving a great nuisance, and complaints poured out about having to stand six hours exposed to continuous whirlwinds of grimy dirt. Spectators were almost blinded by it on windy days.

The opening game of this 1888 season was against Kent and the new Old Trafford railings were immediately put to the test when spectators were standing or sitting ten or eleven deep on the popular side. The *Manchester Evening News* reported that members had arrived early that morning. 'They had settled down in various parts of the ground and judging from the provisions many had made in the way of food, ill-concealed in clean handkerchief or small basket, there is a serious intention of seeing a full day's play,' wrote the newspaper. 'Old enthusiasts, who love to linger over reminiscences of bygone days, had taken up the positions in which they are to be found with invariable regularity long before the first ball was bowled.'

The Australians were again in England in the summer of 1888 and Lancashire had the satisfaction of inflicting on them their first defeat. It was also Lancashire's first victory over them in five encounters. Right at the heart of the victory was a 29-year-old curate from Preston who was making his debut. The Revd John Russell Napier had been to Marlborough and Cambridge University at the same time as A. G. Steel, and it was Steel who was instrumental in getting Napier to play. Right from the first ball it was clear that Lancashire looked to have filled the vacancy for an outstanding fast bowler. He bowled just as fast as Jack Crossland and with only his second ball, a lightning delivery, he bowled the Australian captain, Percy McDonnell. Napier not only took three for 54 and four for 48 in the match, but also showed himself a magnificent hitter of the ball as he scored 37 in the second innings total of 154. The Aussies needed only 90 to win but Napier had Sam Jones caught in the slips off a fast ball described as 'fearful', and then got McDonnell again, caught at the wicket. The Australians were all out for 66, Lancashire won by 23 runs, and before the players had time to reach the pavilion, thousands of spectators had rushed across the ground and it took Napier and Briggs several minutes to get through the crowd and into the dressing room. An enormous crowd assembled in front of the pavilion and cheered for Hornby, Steel, Napier and Briggs who were obliged repeatedly to bow in acknowledgement. It was a great victory, one of the greatest ever, and in Napier, Lancashire looked to have solved a problem.

Yet Napier was to play only once more for the county, against Yorkshire at Bramall Lane in July. And again he sent the supporters wild with delight. He was not brought on to bowl until Yorkshire were 80 for five, and then took four wickets in fourteen balls without conceding a run in a rain-affected drawn match. He took the last two wickets in two balls . . . and never bowled for Lancashire again.

Many years later Napier, who lived to be 80, explained:

I was never a first-class cricketer. I was at Preston and I was playing a lot of club cricket on Saturday afternoons. Allan Steel, who was in the Lancashire side and had been captain of Marlborough before me, asked me to play against the Australians. I was rather a fast bowler, you see. I could not resist the invitation and the Lancashire selectors were criticized a little by the crowd. Hornby told me after the game that one of the spectators had said: 'Why are you playing that bloody parson?' He was told I could bat and bowl a bit. On the final day the supporter was asked what he thought of the bloody parson now. 'A reckon they ought to mak' him a bloody Bishop now,' he said. Australia had beaten several other counties and we were only hopeful we could put up a good show. Pilling played, as good a wicket-keeper as ever lived, as good as Duckworth, perhaps better, for it took some courage to stand close up to the wicket to fast bowling on those pitches that we had in the 80s. The Australians looked to have an easy task when they needed 90 to win, but they were a little bit funky of fast bowling. I was often asked to play for Lancashire again but I only did so once. A busy parson cannot play cricket three days a week and think about it for the remaining three weekdays. So I played just once more, against Yorkshire, and queerly enough, I put up a bit of a record again. I obtained four wickets for no runs.

Lancashire resumed matches with Middlesex in 1888 after a break of five years and won both matches. They also broke new ground by playing at Gloucester Spa on a pitch that was full of weeds. Yet on this pitch Frank Sugg, signed by Lancashire only the previous year after playing for Derbyshire and Yorkshire, scored his first century. He completed it just before the close which was just as well as rain washed out the next two days.

FRANK SUGG was born in Ilkeston in Derbyshire in 1862 and played for Yorkshire when only 21 years old. He then played for Derbyshire from 1884 to 1886 before joining Lancashire and playing thirteen seasons for them. His move to Lancashire worked wonders for him. He was immediately recognized by England and played his only two Test matches in the summer of 1888 at The Oval and Old Trafford. He was a fine outfielder, speedy, with a good return, and at Old Trafford, where the wicket was rather tricky, he was in the long field at both ends. As he trotted across at the end of one over somebody in the crowd shouted: 'Get him a bicycle.' Sugg was 6 feet tall and a fine, dashing batsman who was particularly strong on the legside and when he teamed up with the more dour Albert Ward to open the innings for Lancashire he was the county's Hornby while Ward was compared to Barlow. He was a marvellous all-round sportsman who also had football fame with Sheffield Wednesday, Derby, Burnley and Bolton. He was an outstanding long-distance swimmer, held the record for throwing the cricket ball, was a good billiards player, won prizes for rifle shooting, bowls and putting the weight, and was well-known as a weight-lifter.

Three of Sugg's fifteen centuries for Lancashire were against Gloucestershire and it was in his second, at Old Trafford in 1893, that he ran into the obduracy of W. G. Grace who usually regarded himself as infallible. Sugg went in to bat at the fall of the first wicket and as soon as he was at the crease Fred Roberts, the opening bowler, asked Grace for a fielder to be placed on the legside thirty yards behind the umpire. Grace waved the request away with the remark: 'Keep them on the offside so that he cannot hit.' Roberts again asked later for a fielder

110

before Sugg, despite rain and a slow outfield, reached his century. There were no tea intervals in those days but this did not stop Grace leaving the field to have a cup of tea by himself and leaving Gloucestershire in the charge of Octavius Radcliffe, who brought Roberts back into the attack and agreed to his request for the legside fielder. Sugg obligingly hit the first ball straight to the fielder and Roberts later treated Sugg to a brandy and soda.

Sugg regarded his best innings as his 122 against Yorkshire at Old Trafford in 1897 when he batted on a pitch that varied between hard, soft and sticky. 'When I got to three figures the public were very pleased,' Sugg recalled nearly twenty years later. 'And the locomotives on the adjoining railway whistled cock-a-doodle-do – at least as well as the drivers could make them.'

He died in 1933 aged 71.

Lancashire pulled off an extraordinary win over Oxford University in 1888 after being 93 for eight after following on 110 runs behind. Harry Barchard, an amateur who was playing in his only match, then hit 40 and he and Dick Kentfield, another amateur who was playing in one of his two games for the county, averted the innings defeat. Alec Watson, the last man, scored an unbeaten 22 and Oxford, needing 63 to win, turned their batting order upside down because they thought the result a certainty – and lost by 20 runs. Oswald Lancashire, the Lancashire captain, sent a case of champagne into the professionals' dressing room after Watson had taken five for 17 and Briggs four for 25.

Johnny Briggs had a great year as he finished third among the professionals in the national batting averages and second in the bowling. The *City News* said of him, 'The way in which he breaks his first ball from an impossible distance from the off, his second ball from an equally impossible distance from the leg, and then comes a perfectly straight one, as fast as Spofforth's fastest, must be watched to be believed. No wonder batters give him up in despair.'

The match between Lancashire and Surrey, the two top teams of the previous season, was eagerly anticipated at Old Trafford in August. Up to the day before the game started Lancashire had promises of support from the leading amateurs. Then A. G. Steel pulled out hurt, Napier was needed in Preston because of a colleague's illness, and Joseph Eccles, a fine batsman, cried off on the day because of business. But Whittam's 'K'rect card', the official scorecard of the time, included Eccles and it was some time before the public realized that the left-handed batsman actually playing was David Whittaker of Enfield, a professional who had first

111

played four years earlier. He was on the ground as a spectator when it was learned that Eccles was not coming and when play was actually about to begin, Hornby was hurriedly running about trying to locate him and rigging him up in borrowed clothes. Lancashire were all out for 35 before lunch and lost by an innings in a day in the most crucial match of the season. Poor Whittaker must have wished he had stayed a spectator for not only did he get two ducks, he also missed an easy catch which might have changed the course of the game.

Lancashire astonishingly reversed the defeat when they went to The Oval, Eccles scoring a marvellous 184 in the nine-wicket win. Surrey had been so confident of winning again that before the game started one of their officials unwisely took Hornby into the pavilion to show him where they intended putting a memento in the form of an unbroken plate to commemorate the unbeaten record of their team. Hornby was furious and immediately the game was over he took a plate from the bar, unceremoniously entered the committee room, and smashed the plate on the table, saying 'What do you think of your blasted plate now?'

The season drew to an end on a sour note when Lancashire played at Derby and the spectators jeered the former Derbyshire player, Frank Sugg. There was a noisy demonstration when he went in to bat and the mob became so abusive that Hornby, who was batting with Sugg at the time, left the field in disgust and offered to give up the match. After a delay of fifteen minutes he was finally prevailed on to continue but the incident was enough to persuade Lancashire not to play Derbyshire again for four years.

Three new players joined Lancashire in 1889 but unfortunately, all again were from outside the county. There was Albert Ward from Yorkshire, Arthur Mold from Northamptonshire and now residentially qualified, and Belfast-born Arthur Paul, whose connection with the county was to run into the 1930s. Ward and Mold were to play for England and both were to play significant parts in the re-emergence of Lancashire as a force in the game. Surrey won the title seven times in nine years between 1887 and 1895 but Lancashire at least had the satisfaction in 1889 of beating them twice and sharing the championship with them and Nottinghamshire. And at the top of their batting averages were Frank Sugg and Albert Ward while Mold took eighty wickets at 11.69 runs each in his debut season. This also was benefit year for Dick Pilling, the Prince of wicket-keepers, the first really good wicket-keeper Lancashire had had and arguably the county's best ever.

RICHARD PILLING was born in Bedford on 5 July 1855, of Lancashire parents who returned to their native county and settled in the village of

112

Church, near Accrington, when Richard was still an infant. He joined the local cricket club when quite young and showed an aptitude for wicket-keeping. But as a boy he worked a good deal with olive oil which made his hands soft. The secretary and other members of the Church club, which is now in the Lancashire League, were anxious to make the most of Pilling's talent and in order to harden his hands he became apprenticed to a mason. Lancashire badly needed a professional wicket-keeper when Pilling was given a trial against Sussex in 1877 and he seized his opportunity so quickly that his rise in the game was particularly fast. The MCC were impressed and took him on to the groundstaff the following season and as well as playing for the county he was also able to take part in MCC's principal fixtures for five seasons. Pilling was said to be the first wicket-keeper to stand up to the fastest of bowlers without the aid of a long stop and often pulled off brilliant stumpings, even when keeping wicket to such tremendously fast bowlers as Jack Crossland and Arthur Mold. He scored only two half centuries in 177 matches for Lancashire but Johnny Briggs rated his batting highly and attributed illness and delicacy of constitution to his lack of strength to use the bat effectively. Pilling was 29 when he shared in the record last-wicket stand of 173 with Briggs at Aigburth, but the runs were scored at such a fast rate that he was ill for weeks afterwards.

Pilling played in eight Tests between 1881 and 1888 and toured Australia twice. He was very highly thought of, not just as a wicket-keeper, but as a sportsman and a man. 'There was no cant or humbug about Pilling,' said *Spy* newspaper after his death. 'To know him was to like and respect him.' Another commentator said he bent to his work without ostentation or show and Briggs described him as the height of fairness and one who would never appeal without feeling certain. And nine times out of ten he was right. Pilling did not go in for any sharp practices and was always greatly respected. But he was a delicate creature, almost fragile, and was ill for three years before he died in 1891 at the age of 35. He was frequently absent from the field due to illness but would always make the effort when the situation demanded. In the winter of 1889, when aged 34, Pilling caught a cold when playing football. Inflammation of the lungs and flu followed and he was unable to play cricket in 1890. His condition deteriorated and on 25 September he set sail for Australia on the SS *Ormuz*, being sent out at Lancashire's expense for a sea voyage and sunshine, in the hope that he would regain full fitness. His health improved during the voyage and while in Australia he visited Albany, Adelaide and Sydney before 'a relapse took place and dropsy intervened.' Pilling, accompanied by a Mr James Benton of Old Trafford, left for home early, sailing from Sydney on 2 February 1891, in the Orient SS *Lusitania* which reached London on 22 March.

'Mr Benton was afraid the end was approaching and wanted to get him home to breathe his last,' said Pilling's widow later. 'It was a great comfort to me to be near him and minister to his sufferings. When Mr Pilling felt his end was near he called me to his bedside. He said he was about to leave me but that he had left me amply provided for and the income from the shop would be sufficient to keep me and the three children.' Pilling, who had arrived home on 23 March, died of consumption six days later at his home in Eastnor Street, Manchester, and was buried at Brooklands Cemetery. Alec Watson, the Lancashire off spinner who was in business with Pilling as sports outfitters, bought Mrs Pilling out soon after the wicket-keeper's death, paying £50 for her husband's name. Mrs Pilling protested, the solicitors wrangled in the newspaper columns, and she soon went into business with her husband's partner in the record stand at Aigburth, Johnny Briggs.

In his 177 games with the county, Pilling held 333 catches and made 153 stumpings, a total of 486 victims which today still stands second only to George Duckworth's 922 in 424 games. Pilling's younger brother, Will, also kept wicket for Lancashire, in just one game in 1891, the year of his brother's death.

Arthur Paul and Albert Ward played together for the Colts of the North against the South at Lord's at the beginning of May in 1889. As Lancashire were playing MCC at Lord's in the same week, both players stayed in London and made their debuts for the county. Paul was top scorer in the first innings with 36 not out, Ward batted magnificently in the second innings for an unbeaten 62 in the total of 134. The London *Star* wrote 'Paul, like Lohmann [the Surrey fast bowler], comes from a higher rank in life than most of his class. His father is Lt–Col Paul, who was till last year Chief Constable of the Isle of Man, and his brother, the Revd F. W. Paul, is the hard-working vicar of Emmanuel Church, Nottingham. Mr Paul was brought up as an architect but he failed to make a living by that profession and, being too energetic to sit down and do nothing, he enrolled himself in the honourable ranks of professional cricketers.' Paul was also a fine rugby full back with Swinton.

The opening game at Old Trafford, against Sussex, was a low-scoring match, which Lancashire won, although three of their finest batsmen, Ward, Barlow and Sugg, all fell to the lobs of Walter Humphreys. The *City News* explained lobs to the uninitiated . . . 'Slow underhand balls of the simplest and most babyish character which yet have been known many a time and oft to beat the best batters even when they seem perfectly set. He dismissed Ward, who looked as if he had never seen a lob before, and Barlow and Sugg.'

Pilling had played in all the early matches but had not been

114

well and accompanied the team to Dublin in mid-June in the hope of regaining his health. The sail was pleasant but Pilling experienced a severe attack of pleurisy and was still so unwell when the team returned to Manchester that he was left out of the game against Oxford University in view of the important matches approaching against Nottinghamshire and Surrey.

Pilling, though weak, played against Nottinghamshire, which Lancashire lost, and Surrey, which was won. When batting he almost walked, rather than ran, across the wicket and was clearly in a poor state of health. By the time of his benefit match nearly two weeks later, Pilling was feeling much better, but still could not play in the game at Old Trafford, North v South, because of a cut finger. As a measure of the high regard in which Pilling was held, no other matches were played that weekend in July 1889, so that the counties could send their best players to a match which was nursed through three days, was watched by more than 30,000 people, and which produced a record £1,500 for the wicket-keeper. It is interesting to read the letter that Pilling sent to the committee after the match:

> I beg to return you all my sincere and heartfelt thanks for having granted me a benefit match this season and also for the trouble and interest you have all taken in the matter. I especially should like to thank Mr Swire, Mr MacLaren, and Mr Hornby for the great trouble they have taken in assisting to make the match a success which it has happily turned out to be. In conclusion I can only express my deep gratitude for your kindness.
>
> With great respect, I am, Gentlemen, your obedient servant,
> [signed] R. Pilling,
> 20 August 1889.

And not surprisingly, Pilling wrote to the Manchester newspapers to thank everybody for making his benefit a success.

One of the finest of all Roses matches was held that summer, resulting in a three-run win for Lancashire at Huddersfield. Lancashire had a hard time against George Ulyett who took seven wickets, but Mold, now established as one of the country's leading bowlers, took six although defied by Lord Hawke whose unbeaten 52 helped Yorkshire to a first innings lead. Yorkshire needed only 75 for victory when they batted again but Lancashire bowled and fielded brilliantly. Yorkshire's ninth wicket fell with 4 runs needed and before he could score, last man Willie Middlebrook skied a catch to Hornby, who, although harassed by other eager fielders, safely held it. Mold had had a great game, taking thirteen wickets for 111 runs.

The Aigburth wicket, now in its ninth year, was still tending to play badly and thirty-seven wickets fell in two days for 351 runs in the match with Gloucestershire. E. M. Grace's nerve won the day for Gloucestershire in their three-wicket win and W. G. rushed on the field like an enthusiastic schoolboy. He took off his brother's cap and waved it in the air and almost carried him off the field.

Still, 1889 had been a good year for Lancashire. They had got their new fast bowler in Mold; Sugg and Ward were providing much-needed consistency in the batting, and Lancashire finished joint champions alongside Nottinghamshire and Surrey after winning ten of their fourteen matches. Lancashire's membership at the time, incidentally, numbered 1,850, with sixty life members and 600 lady subscribers.

Chapter 6 1890–96

'MacLaren's cricket belonged to the Golden Age of the game, to the spacious and opulent England of his day; it knew not the common touch.'

A. N. Hornby was 43 years old when the 1890 season started but there was no question of him retiring either as a player or as captain, a position he had held for ten years. He was held in high regard throughout the country, not least at Lord's where he had first played as a Harrow schoolboy twenty-six years earlier. Lancashire started the season by beating MCC by seven wickets. They beat Kent by an innings, but then lost to the Australians, such attractive opposition that 17,600 watched the opening day, and Oxford University. The Oxford match was one of twelve-a-side, which was not unusual in those days for University matches, but is still regarded as first-class. Lancashire scored 138 and 142, the University scored 274 and were left to get seven for victory. This they did without losing a wicket, giving Lancashire the only eleven-wicket defeat in their history, perhaps the only one in the history of the game.

One of the new rules introduced to first-class cricket in 1889 was that of allowing teams to declare an innings closed on the final day of a three-day match. It was 1890 before Lancashire were involved in a game where a closure was applied, against Nottinghamshire at Trent Bridge where John Dixon, the Nottinghamshire captain, was said to have run from the pavilion and declared the innings closed amidst general cheering.

Only a week later, Lancashire themselves declared for the first time, in a rain-affected match against Sussex at Old Trafford. Play, which had been impossible on the first day, started just before lunch on the second, and Lancashire reached 246 for two by the end of the day. There was an undefeated stand of 215 between Johnny Briggs, who reached his century in 100 minutes, and Albert Ward, which at the time was the second highest in Lancashire's history, beaten only by the partnership of 237 in 1883 against Oxford University between Frank Taylor and Walter Robinson. Play could not start on the final day until 2.50 p.m. and Arthur Kemble, who was keeping wicket in the absence of Pilling and was captaining the side for the first time, closed the innings. Sussex were dismissed for 35 in 1 hour 40 minutes and there was exactly the same amount of time left to play when they followed on. This time they were bowled out in an hour for 24 and Lancashire had won by an innings and 187 runs. Alec Watson had taken five wickets for 7 runs in the first innings and four for 6 in the second, with Johnny Briggs taking four for 25 and five for 16, the five wickets coming in seven balls. The combined Sussex total of 59 is still an aggregate record low for two innings at Old Trafford. The *City News* pointed out that the incident had no parallel, Lancashire's two wickets having beaten Sussex's twenty.

This was Lancashire's finest period in their history in Roses matches. Between 1889 and 1893 they won eight and lost only one of the ten matches, and much of their success was due to the fine bowling of Arthur Mold which was said to have frightened all the Yorkshire batsmen in 1890 except George Ulyett. He took eight for 38 in the drawn match at Old Trafford, but went one better with nine for 41 on a dangerous, rain-affected Huddersfield wicket. The last eight wickets came in 8.1 overs for 13 runs and Lancashire went on to win by an innings and 28 runs with Mold taking four more wickets. There were grumblings, it seems, about the state of the wicket and Mold's bowling. Said one unnamed Lancashire official 'We came to play cricket with men, not lawn tennis with girls.'

One of the great events of 1890 was the arrival of Archie MacLaren who attracted attention in July when he captained Harrow in the drawn match with Eton at Lord's, scoring 76 of a total of 133. The *City News* reported that Lancashire had a promising recruit in the person of Mr A. C. MacLaren, son of Mr James MacLaren, the Lancashire treasurer. A London correspondent was quoted as saying 'The chief hero of the match was the Harrovian MacLaren who is the most promising cricketing recruit of the year. It is a long time since a public school boasted so all round a cricketer.'

MacLaren lived up to those words a month later when, at the age of 18, he made his debut for the county against Sussex at Brighton, and scored a century, only the second Lancashire player after Jim Ricketts to hit a hundred on his first-class debut. Sussex had been dismissed for 86 and Lancashire had lost two important wickets, in those of Frank Sugg and Dicky Barlow, for only 9 runs when MacLaren went in to bat. Despite the dire situation and the reported poorness of the pitch, MacLaren was said to have played with the steadiness and nerve of a veteran. The *Manchester Courier* said MacLaren, whose 108 took 130 minutes, did not give a ghost of a chance and his innings throughout was a most dashing display. He hit nine 4s, six 3s, fifteen 2s, and twenty-four singles before he was out to the lob bowler, Walter Humphreys. Said the *Manchester Guardian* 'The bowling was naturally not of a very high class but on the other hand the wicket on which he had to bat was by no means so perfect as those to which cricketers are accustomed on the Brighton ground. His hits were alike for good style, clean hitting and complete confidence, his innings was a very remarkable display.' The *City News* described his arrival as the most important since that of A. G. Steel thirteen years earlier and added 'The importance to Lancashire of such a recruit who has all his life before him and who, in the ordinary course of things, will go on improving, cannot be over-estimated.' Yet perhaps even they were surprised at the heights to which MacLaren rose.

Lancashire hit the Grace brothers in form this year with large opening stands from them at Old Trafford and in the return match at Clifton two weeks later. The Old Trafford partnership was broken by Joe Hewitson, a professional slow left-arm bowler from Bolton who played in four matches that year in the absence of Johnny Briggs. He took fourteen wickets for 16.78 runs each in those four matches, the last of which was against Gloucestershire when he took two for 59. His first victim was E. M. Grace, following an appeal for lbw, and which produced this description from the *City News* 'The two Graces have a reputation amongst the initiated for the genial simplicity and innocence with which they regard an umpire who is appealed to when they are the victims of the appeal. But in this case even that resource failed and E. M. had to go.' That also marked the end of Hewitson who, despite encouraging figures, was never to play for Lancashire again.

Lancashire did not have quite so successful a year as in 1889 but even so they won seven of the fourteen matches against all the other first-class counties and finished runners-up to Surrey. The varying quality of the Eleven was again referred to and hopes were raised when the Reverend Napier, senior curate at St. Paul's, Preston, was made vicar of St. Peter's, Walsden, a living worth £250 a year with a house. Now Napier was his own master it was thought he would probably again play for Lancashire. It was vain hope.

Dick Pilling left England for Australia in September 1890, to try to recover his health, and before leaving he wrote to the committee:

I cannot leave England without writing to thank you from the bottom of my heart for the kindness you have always shown to me and particularly during my long illness. I beg also to thank you most sincerely for the handsome sum (£150) you have so generously voted towards my trip to Australia. I hope that I may be benefited by the trip and that on my return I may be able to take my place once more in the team.

With much respect I remain, Gentlemen, your grateful and obedient servant,

[signed] R. Pilling.

Pilling, alas, was to die six months later and Lancashire had lost one of her finest players. His brother Will played once that year but obviously was not up to standard and never played again. More signs that the team with which Pilling grew up in the 1870s was finally breaking up came that same year of 1891. Hornby went into partial retirement before announcing he would give up the captaincy and hand over to Sydney Crosfield in 1892. He never again played anything like a full season, although he did extend his career with Lancashire for another eight years until 1899. Dicky Barlow's distinguished career ended this year in unhappy circumstances, Alec Watson's powers showed the first real signs of failing, and Vernon Royle played his last match, against MCC at Lord's, at the age of 37.

The end of Barlow's career was most unfortunate. He played in the first sixteen matches of the 1891 season but was asked by the committee at the beginning of August to stand down for the game against Essex, then a second-class county and a match not counting in the championship. The reason given was that there were young players who deserved a trial but Barlow replied to the secretary Sam Swire, that if he did not play in that match he would not play again. Mr Swire, at the annual meeting, said the Match Committee therefore decided that Barlow should not play whether he liked it or not and had his manner been a little more courteous Mr Swire was of the opinion he might have been played again. The feeling of the meeting, and it might also illustrate the feeling towards professionals – even respected professionals – by the gentlemen of the club, was embodied in the defeat of an amendment that was put forward. The wording of the amendment was that the club 'recognized the valuable service of Barlow and regretted the severance of his connection with the team.' A harmless enough amendment, we might think, and one which would at least have observed Barlow's great service to Lancashire. But no. It was not only defeated, it was crushed, by 200 votes to four. Two weeks after the Essex match the *City News* declared 'We do not know that the Lancashire County Cricket Club committee has ever distinguished itself for tact. We suspect that it is far too high and mighty for any thing of that sort. But it is quite certain that if it permits such a cricketer as Barlow to make his final appearance with anything but the fullest honours it will never deserve loyal service at the hands of either amateur or professional again.'

Barlow, however, was never to play again in a first-class match. Hornby chose him to go on the southern tour starting at Gravesend on 17 August, but the committee overruled him. Hornby himself took part in only two of the remaining six matches after Barlow was dropped and, not unnaturally, many people connected his reluctance to play with the Barlow affair. Barlow was to play once more, in 1892, against Cheshire, a Minor County, and only then at the special request of Hornby who wrote to the secretary:

> Dear Sam,
>   I hope you will play Barlow against Cheshire. Now do to please me. Write me Lochnivar, Sutherlandshire.
>   Yours as ever.

Back came the following reply:

> My dear Hornby,
>   . . . solely out of deference to your personal desire he will be asked to play. At the same time the committee wish you to understand that they have not in any way altered their opinion as to Barlow's fitness to take part in a First Eleven of Lancashire.

Barlow, who ran a sports outfitter's shop, was later to become ground-keeper at Old Trafford for a short time, but made his mark in the game again by becoming a county and Test match umpire.

Lancashire made a poor start to the 1891 season, including a home defeat by the champions Surrey, and it was mid-June before they recorded their first victory. They played well in the second half of the summer and a late burst took them into second place again, once more behind Surrey, a quite outstanding team at the time. Arthur Mold had a great year with 112 wickets in fourteen matches against the first-class counties, including fifteen against Somerset, newly elevated from the ranks of the second-class counties. Arthur Smith, yet another Nottinghamshire-born player recruited by Lancashire, scored the first century of the season for the county in mid-July, an innings of 124 in 4 hours 40 minutes against Gloucestershire. He had first played for Lancashire five years earlier and was the son of a man who was the county's umpire for many years. He scored another century against Sussex the following year, when he topped the batting averages, but never firmly established himself in the team after that, playing forty-eight matches between 1886 and 1894.

The finest innings of the year, and one widely regarded as one of the finest ever seen at Old Trafford, was that played by A. E. Stoddart for Middlesex. He opened the innings and was 63 when Middlesex lunched at 137 for four. The total was 158 for seven when Jack West joined him and together they put on 101 of which West made 30. Stoddart was in brilliant form, driving and cutting particularly well and reaching his century in 160 minutes. The Lancashire bowlers presented a pitiable spectacle in the face of Stoddart's awful hitting and two more stubborn, steady partners in Jack Hearne and Jim Phillips, enabled him to go on to an unbeaten 215 in a total of 372.

Johnny Briggs provided Mold with great support with eighty-nine wickets in fifteen first-class county matches in 1891, but Watson, who was to play only two more years, took twenty-nine wickets in eleven games. Lancashire were clearly going to need another bowler to support Briggs and Mold if they were to win the championship. MacLaren could play only five matches this year because of business commitments but topped the batting averages with 44.2, followed by Albert Ward, who had another notable year.

By the start of the 1892 season Hornby had reconsidered his determination to retire as captain, but even so still played in only four county matches, leaving Crosfield to lead the side in one of their poorest seasons for some time when they finished fourth – and even lost to Somerset for the first time, an ignominious defeat. Lancashire's batting, although reasonably strong in appearance, collapsed too often. When asked about it at the end of the summer, Crosfield said:

> I cannot account for it, nor can anyone else. I believe we are stronger in batting than we have ever been and twice have made over 400 this year and twice over 300. But sometimes, for no particular reason, we go to pieces. The weather has been very much against us. There has been a great deal of anxiety, but the committee do all they possibly can to make things pleasant for the captain, and that makes a lot of difference. Besides, the professionals are the most agreeable fellows that one could possibly have anything to do with and are remarkable for their good humour even under the most trying circumstances.

Lancashire lost their first Roses match for four years, but gained some satisfaction in making Yorkshire struggle for the 61 needed for victory before they got home with four wickets to spare. Yorkshire were 33 for six at one stage but Ted Wainwright and Jack Tunnicliffe carried them home. It was reported by one observant newspaper that Lord Hawke, who had opened the innings, mysteriously disappeared as the game neared its climax. It is said he was finally discovered hidden away, alone and wretched, in the darkest corners of one of the back corridors of the Bramall Lane pavilion where he could hear and see nothing. The crisis was too awful even for him to watch. Lancashire's revenge at Old Trafford was convincing. F. S. Jackson, then only 21 years old, did not arrive for the game and Lord Hawke was forced to telegraph for another youngster, Joe Mounsey, to take his place. By the time Mounsey arrived Lancashire were 213 for two following a partnership of 189 between Albert Ward and Arthur Smith. The news of the exciting events of the morning spread to town, and trains and omnibuses arrived loaded with eager supporters who swelled the gate to a record 20,000 of which 18,125 paid. They, too, were treated to some fine batting with Albert Ward scoring 180 against his native county, and Johnny Briggs 115 in 150 minutes. Weary fielders, dead tired, could scarcely follow the ball and many times simply watched it roll away to the boundary. Eight bowlers were tried as Lancashire reached 437 for four on the opening day. It was a marvellous wicket and Yorkshire, though totalling 388 in their two innings, lost by an innings and 83 runs.

Punctuality was still rare enough to be remarked on. Times for starting and finishing, and for intervals, were nowhere near as rigidly enforced as they are today and no allowance was made in the regulations for adding on time at the end of either of the first two days if there was a chance of finishing the game. If the end of the game was close the captains agreed to keep going instead of returning the following morning for half an hour. So when Alec Webbe, the long-serving captain of Middlesex, refused to play on when his team were 102 for eight at the end of the second day towards the 227 needed for victory over Lancashire, a few eyebrows were raised. And when rain settled in on the final day and Middlesex escaped with a draw, Webbe's action, though strictly within rights, was considered sharp practice. Webbe himself was batting at the end of the second day when the light was poor, and though urged by the crowd to finish the game, he left the field. He maintained that though Middlesex still needed 125 for victory with only two wickets standing, it only needed a shower to ease the wicket. By the time the ground was fit for play on the final day there were only 45 minutes remaining. Webbe was dismissed after 20 minutes, but Hearne and Phillips stuck out the last 25 minutes to deny Lancashire. The *Manchester Courier* pointed out the need for punctuality which, it said, 'is equally the soul of cricket as it is in business.' It said 15 minutes were lost in starting on the first day and 10 minutes on the second.

A reader mentioned that Webbe was not alone in refusing to continue a game, that Kent in the previous match had made Lancashire go back for a third day at Tonbridge when they had no chance. Lancashire had scored 484 and Kent had replied with 47 for two when rain fell heavily for two and a half hours. Mold and Briggs then took sixteen wickets for 95 runs in 85 minutes so that Kent reached the scheduled close of play on the second day still needing 345 to avoid an innings defeat with only two wickets standing. Frank Marchant, the captain, refused to continue and play started early the following day so Lancashire could get the 3 p.m. train from St Pancras. The game was over in 20 minutes with Mold taking nine for 29 – the best return of his career – and Lancashire winning by an innings and 330 runs. George Baker, in his sixth season with Lancashire, scored the first of his four centuries in that match, 109 in just over 1 hour 30 minutes with clean and resolute hitting. Another opportunity to finish a game came against Somerset at Old Trafford when the first day was washed out by rain and the entire game was decided the following day. Somerset scored only 88 despite a good start from openers Herbert Hewett (35) and Lionel Palairet (22) and after Lancashire had replied with 116, Somerset collapsed in their second innings and were all out for 58. It was 6.15 p.m. and Lancashire needed 31 runs. But Hewett said they would play until the game was finished and Lancashire secured victory by eight wickets before 7 o'clock. 'Hewett saw that defeat was inevitable and faced it in a manly fashion instead of playing for a draw,' opined the *Sporting Chronicle*.

Lancashire, it was said, were particularly keen to beat Middlesex at Lord's after being denied at Old Trafford and Webbe again irritated the team by successfully appealing to the umpires against the light. It was thought this was possibly the first time a player had done this. The *City News* warned 'Cricket captains should carefully take note. Mr Webbe is evidently bent on winning a name for himself.' Mr Webbe, incidentally, had the satisfaction of leading his team to a nine-wicket win.

Mold again took over 100 wickets this year, twelve of them coming in the last match which was against Nottinghamshire at Old Trafford, won by an innings by Lancashire. He took seven of the wickets in the second innings, including those of Arthur Shrewsbury, first ball, and Billy Gunn. Wrote the *City News*:

Mold, who has an innocent sort of delivery which often disarms the average batter and makes him think he is a mere medium-paced bowler to cope with, gave Gunn one ball with which he was as helpless as a schoolboy. He admitted himself that he has scarcely ever before seen such a ball. Its speed was so terrific that his stroke at it might practically have been a blindfolded one, and it knocked the middle stump out of the ground in a way which certainly presents the most exhilarating view to spectators whose enemies are at the wicket. Those two balls (to Shrewsbury and Gunn) were in themselves worth a whole innings of bad ones.

Shrewsbury was adept at playing the ball with his pads and his dismissal in the first innings, by Johnny Briggs, was also interestingly described in detail by the *City News*:

Shrewsbury, amongst other things, is the inventor of a style of playing the ball with his legs. Whenever a ball puzzles him or he, for any reason, feels uncomfortable about it, if it is not pitched straight, he simply puts his leg before it and so keeps it out of the wickets. The style is, if played with discretion, wonderfully effective from the point of view of sticking in. It breaks the bowler's heart, it worries the umpire well nigh to death, and it will eventually cause a change in the rule of leg before wicket, as it most assuredly ought to do. But in this case, Briggs, who was bowling with his head as well as with his hand and arm, completely beat the great leg blocker at his own game to the unbounded joy of everybody round the field. Shrewsbury, bothered by a peculiar ball which was gyrating and twisting about in mid-air in a way which was eminently puzzling and which was apparently likely, if unstopped, to hit the off stump, quietly put his right leg in such a position that the ball could not possibly reach that point. But in doing this he left the leg stump unguarded and the ball, as if actually inspired by Briggs's cunning, shot in between the batter's legs and hit the leg wicket. The incident was one which will serve for many a bit of cricket gossip in years to come, and was worth in itself, to your true enthusiast, a year's waiting to see.

The summer of 1893 was notable for Lancashire in many respects. But it was even more noteworthy for Yorkshire who headed the championship table for the first time, winning twelve out of sixteen matches, yet losing both Roses games. The one at Old Trafford, held over the August Bank Holiday, attracted the biggest crowd ever seen at the ground, about 25,000 on the Monday when 22,554 paid. This was to prove the most exciting of Roses matches and one, which even today, will rank among the best three or four ever staged. Both teams were at the top of the championship and it was thought the title could be decided by this match. There were 5,000 on the ground an hour before the start, 11,000 had paid by noon, and the crowd doubled during the afternoon before the turnstiles were closed at 5.30 p.m. It rained during the day but in the 4 hours 20 minutes play that was possible, twenty wickets fell for 129 runs with Lancashire taking a 6-run lead on first innings. There were 11,000 people there for the second day when the game was continued on the treacherous wicket. Lancashire were bowled out for 50 and Yorkshire, needing 57 to win, were 42 for six at lunch, then 46 for nine with George Ulyett and David Hunter together needing 11 for victory. Ulyett snicked Mold for 4, Hunter got a single, and with 6 needed for victory, Johnny Briggs waved Albert Ward to the boundary rails right behind him. Ulyett, who had stood steady for some time, was fed a tempting ball which he just could not resist. He instinctively swiped, sending the ball spinning high, and Ward, who was resting on the rails, waited for it and took a brilliant catch as Ulyett and Hunter watched from the middle of the pitch.

It was regarded by most people as the most exciting finish seen at Old Trafford. When Ward caught the ball there was a great shout and a stampede, the like of which the ground had never seen before. Hats were thrown in the air and spectators raced for the pavilion shouting for all they were worth. Even the Lancashire fielders were unable to contain themselves and raced off the field almost screaming in the frenzy of the moment, pursued by a vast mob of even more lively, shouting spectators. Many members of the Manchester Exchange had been receiving telegrams telling them of the course of the game and when the result was posted up on the notice board, attention was called to it by a vigorous ringing of the call-bell. Although this was about the busiest time for the Exchange, business stopped for a time and the announcement was received by a loud cheer from the members. People who saw the game from beginning to end – the entire four innings produced only 223 runs with a top score of 64 – never forgot it. One player said the game had taken ten years off his life, another said he hoped he never took part in such a game again, and emotions ran so high in the pavilion that there were unpleasant scenes with angry rivals addressing each other violently. Ulyett said later:

I thought we were sure to win the match. I thought to myself I must try to force the fight somehow. If David Hunter had not been the last man I should have waited, but I thought it was better to make the runs if I could while I was facing Johnny Briggs. So I went for the victory, but Albert Ward was on the edge of it and we lost. I still think I adopted the right course. I thought it was 100 to one on us winning the game at one time.

As for Briggs, the hero, he sat drained in the dressing room for ages after the game was over. Neville Cardus said of the finish 'The crowd mingled with its tumult of acclamation some rich chuckles at yet another little dodge of Johnny's. But in the pavilion after the match, poor Briggs sat with a white face. Bowling his "little dodge" had well-nigh burst his heart with apprehension.'

The interest in county cricket and the crowd which attended the match was in sharp contrast to the enthusiasm – or lack of it – which greeted Test cricket about this time, certainly in Manchester. Only 6,000 paid on the opening day of the Test against Australia in August 1893, 6,000 more on the second day and 3,000 on the third. The *City News* said that the interest in the Australians was falling off and there was very little excitement at Old Trafford. The newspaper said the average spectator preferred a good county match to any in which the Australians took part, and added that the impression existed that Tests were more exhibition games than anything, producing unexciting cricket with small, listless attendances.

Lancashire played again at Tonbridge this year, losing by 67 runs. It was the fourth time the town had held the annual cricket week and it was gay with bunting. Over £200 had been subscribed by the townspeople and there was an elaborate programme of events, including amateur theatricals, a smoking concert, a ball, and a Venetian fete on the river.

Only two players have scored a century and taken ten wickets in the same match for Lancashire, Johnny Briggs and Len Hopwood. Briggs accomplished the feat three times with 129 not out and ten for 41 against Sussex at Old Trafford in 1890, 115 and thirteen for 209 against Yorkshire at Old Trafford in 1892, and 112 and eleven for 115 against Surrey at The Oval in 1893. He had rarely given a more brilliant display than his century at The Oval which took only 90 minutes. He batted 110 minutes in all for his 112 and his cutting and off-driving in one of the most dashing centuries ever seen at The Oval, were described as marvellous. He got 92 of his runs in boundaries and the other 20 runs came from one 3, three 2s, and eleven singles. His fielding at cover was said to be unequalled, and he was highly regarded as the finest all-round cricketer in the country. He and Mold again carried the Lancashire bowling, delivering nearly 1,700 overs and taking 225 wickets with no one else getting 20. Alec Watson and A. G. Steel played their last matches this year, Watson completing 283 games in twenty-three seasons, Steel forty-seven over seventeen years.

The year was also noteworthy for the Test debuts of Mold and Albert Ward, whose 1,185 runs marked only the second occasion, following A. N. Hornby in 1881, that a batsman had topped 1,000 runs for the county. He had the splendid average of 35.90 and was third only to Nottinghamshire's Arthur Shrewsbury and Billy Gunn in the country's professional batting averages. Mold played in all three Tests in 1893 but took only seven wickets for 234 runs and never played again. Ward played at The Oval and Old Trafford and scored 55, 13 and 0.

ALBERT WARD was born near Leeds on 21 November 1865, in a hamlet called Waterloo which no longer exists. He moved to Rothwell when he was 9 and practised cricket assiduously, even at the village barber's shop. The barber also sold cricket tackle, but equally interesting to the young Ward was the long mirror he had in the shop. 'I was able to stand in front of that mirror and practise all kinds of strokes in order to see that I was correct in all my movements and that they might become second nature to me,' he once recalled. When he was 18, Ward, a schoolmaster in Leeds, decided to break with school life and try to use cricket to provide something better. He wrote to clubs in Cumberland, Scotland and Lancashire for a professional engagement and secured one at Darwen in Lancashire. He played for Yorkshire at the same time, playing in four games without any success. He was asked to play for the county again in 1888 but declined. 'County cricket was not running in my mind at all,' he said. 'I had got a permanent situation and I did not care to give it up for the uncertainties of county cricket.' That finished Ward's connection with Yorkshire. He moved from Darwen to Leyland and in one week scored three centuries for them. The following year he was invited to play at Lord's for the Colts of the North against the South. He scored 25 not out and was asked to play in the following game at Lord's for Lancashire against MCC, the start of a sixteen-year career with Lancashire in which he claimed to have missed only two games.

Ward was an opening batsman with an ideal temperament, essentially patient and correct, and batted through the innings five times for Lancashire. His seven Tests all came within the space of a few months for after playing in England in 1893 he went to Australia the following year and played in all five Tests. He scored 75 and 117 in the first Test at Sydney and 93 in the last Test at Melbourne where he provided the

foundation for victory and England's 3–2 win in the series. Ward roomed with Surrey fast bowler Tom Richardson on the tour and before the final Test he bet him 100 to one in pennies he would get a century. Ward paid up with a penny which Richardson kept as a lucky coin. But Richardson was so pleased he presented Ward with an umbrella with a silver plate which read 'A. Ward b H. Trott 93. Melbourne 100 to 1. T. R.'

Ward rated as his best innings, free from flaws, his 180 against Yorkshire in 1892, a total that has been exceeded only twice in Roses matches by Lancashire players, Reg Spooner with 200 not out in 1910, and Clive Lloyd with 181 in 1972. Ward scored more than 15,000 runs for Lancashire for an average of 31 and also bowled a bit – slow, tossed-up leg breaks he called his cock-a-doodles.

Ward set up in business in Bolton as a sports outfitter in 1895, a business that still existed when he died in 1939 aged 73.

This was an exciting time for cricket. Attendances were high, money was rolling in, and Lancashire decided in 1893 on more improvements by erecting a new pavilion. Plans were submitted by six architects in February with estimates ranging from £5,985 to £6,795. The lowest, from Messrs W. Southern and Sons, had originally been for £6,723 but included a reduction of £738 if there were such modifications as concrete balconies instead of stone, half timber red deal instead of oak, and pitch pine instead of teak.

The great and continuing career of Johnny Briggs was rewarded with a benefit in 1894 and the match he chose was the Whitsuntide Bank Holiday game against the champions, Yorkshire. Briggs, argu-ably the most popular cricketer in the country, was expected to break records as the crowds rolled up to honour him. To make sure the pitch was fit for play, the Lancashire authorities took the almost unheard-of step of covering it with tarpaulins. For three weeks before the game it was specially cared for and although it rained in the days leading up to the match, the pitch was dry and ready to last three days and make Briggs's benefit a bumper. But Lord Hawke, the Yorkshire captain, refused to play on the specially-protected wicket, insisting on another one being cut, and the match was all over before lunch on the second day. Hornby had drawn attention to the fact that the pitch had been covered and had said to Lord Hawke 'If you don't like it, of course we can take another.' Lord Hawke did not like it. He said he had never heard of a great match like this being played on a wicket specially prepared like that. It was pointed out to him that on the dry wicket the game would probably go to the third day. On a wet one it would not. Lord Hawke was immovable, although he did say he would be glad to play on the wicket if he won the toss, but as a matter of principle he could not agree to it being used. So a

129

new pitch, wet and heavy from the rain, had to be prepared and it was estimated it cost Briggs £500 in gate money. Said Lord Hawke 'I'm very sorry for Briggs, but I have come here to play county cricket, and not for a benefit match.'

Much sympathy went out to Briggs. The subscription list in the pavilion was augmented because of Lord Hawke's action and each of the Yorkshire professionals handed Briggs £1. In the end he received £1,000 which was £500 less than Pilling and far from creating the expected record. It is said that when Lord Hawke tried to explain to Briggs on the field the professional said 'I do not wish to speak to you, My Lord', and also had to be persuaded to accept the Yorkshire captain's donation. A crowd of over 22,000, of which 20,011 paid, witnessed the first day when Lancashire started the match by losing their first four batsmen, Albert Ward, A. N. Hornby, Frank Sugg and Archie MacLaren, before a run had been scored. Four more failed to score and Lancashire totalled 50 with George Hirst, the Yorkshire fast bowler, taking seven for 25. Mold and Briggs bowled well but Mold tired, the Yorkshire tail got runs to take the total to 152, and Briggs must have gone home in a very bad temper. Lancashire were all out for 93 the following morning and Yorkshire had won by an innings and 9 runs, their first victory at Old Trafford for six years.

The wicket which had been carefully prepared for Briggs came into use later in the week when Kent were the visitors. The game lasted three days and Kent scored 225 for seven to win.

Hornby played three matches that year, Crosfield five, and Kemble seven, and the duties of captain fell on Archie MacLaren who was only 22 years old but was now available to play in all the matches. Lancashire had lost four of the first five championship matches when they went to Trent Bridge to take on Nottinghamshire. When the team mustered on the first morning it found itself, quite unexpectedly, with only ten men and without a captain. Hornby should have been captain but the official explanation was that he had been called away on business. A telegram was sent for George Yates to join the team, and MacLaren, one of only two amateurs in the team – the other was the inexperienced 21-year-old Bill Houldsworth – took over as captain. Lancashire lost that game by an innings, they lost the next against Kent at Tonbridge, and MacLaren was in charge of a team standing next-to-the-bottom of the table with points recorded as minus five, worked out by deducting losses from wins and ignoring draws. It is quite possible that no captain in the history of Lancashire has ever been quite as far in the red as MacLaren was by the beginning of July 1894. Happily, the plusses started to mount up, starting with another one-day win

130

over Somerset on a difficult Old Trafford wicket affected by rain. Mold bowled very fast and after doing the hat-trick, he followed up with three wickets in four balls as Somerset were all out for 31 in under an hour. Frank Sugg somehow slashed his way to 105, Somerset were bowled out again, this time for 132, and Lancashire had won by an innings and 68. Somerset, the poor things, then went to Huddersfield where they again lost in a day, to Yorkshire.

That proved a good week for Mold who went to Bristol and took twelve wickets to give himself twenty-five wickets in the week for 151 runs. Another plus arrived when Gloucestershire went to Old Trafford for the return match, a game that marked the debut of one of the great stars of the age, Gilbert Jessop, who scored 29 and 19. Cricket grounds then housed telegraph offices, an efficient form of communication, not only for the benefit of the newspaper reporters, but also for businessmen. While E. M. Grace, then aged 52, was playing in the match, he received a telegram to tell him of the birth of his seventeenth child. It was a boy who was christened Norman Vere and was to be the only one of E. M.'s children to play first-class cricket, three matches, all for the Royal Navy between 1920 and 1927.

Lancashire's only defeat in their last nine championship matches of 1894 came at Bradford when close on 50,000 people paid for admission to a match being held for Bobby Peel's benefit.

In this season, too, was recorded the first of Lancashire's three tied matches after they had been left to score 75 for victory over Surrey on a difficult pitch at The Oval. Lancashire's hopes plummeted when they lost their first five wickets for 9 runs, and then became 26 for seven. But Alf Tinsley and Charlie Smith, two more Yorkshire-born professionals, took the score to 63 before Smith hit out and was caught at cover. Gerald Bardswell, who was only 20 years old and in his first year with the county, helped Lancashire to within two of victory, but declined a fourth run off a big hit that would have tied the scores with two wickets to fall. He was caught next ball and in the next over Tinsley offered a catch which was dropped and gave the batsmen the single that tied the scores. Mold was caught at the wicket off the second ball he received – although he maintained that he neither played at the ball nor touched it – and the scores were tied.

When Johnny Briggs was injured and unable to play against Nottinghamshire in the last month of the season at Old Trafford, Tom Lancaster, yet another Yorkshire-born professional, was brought in for his debut at the age of 31. He marked it by taking a wicket with his first ball, that of opening batsman Charles Wright, and finished the innings with seven for 54. He broke down in the second innings

131

and the bulk of the workload rested again with Mold who finished a tiring season with a remarkable 144 wickets in fourteen championship matches, but 189 for Lancashire in all games. Briggs took 137 wickets, and the next highest wicket-taker in all matches was George Baker . . . with thirteen!

Surrey won the title in 1894 with eleven points, followed by Yorkshire with ten. Lancashire's late successes carried them to fifth place and at least into the black, although without any points at all from seven wins and seven defeats. Now the championship was to change radically. The nine teams making up the championship were to be joined in 1895 by Derbyshire, Essex, Leicestershire, Warwickshire and Hampshire.

One noteworthy newspaper article from that year was in the *St James's Gazette* where the writer questioned the sense in starting matches on Thursday which usually left little or no cricket for Saturday, the most convenient day for people to attend the game. 'Week after week, in London and the provinces, there is no cricket on Saturdays in county matches,' the newspaper pointed out. 'Why should first-class matches invariably begin on Mondays and Thursdays? It is not a little curious that no club has had the enterprise to ignore the conventional Mondays and Thursdays and started its matches on Wednesdays and Saturdays. We shall probably have to wait some time before the change because of counties mainly dependent on amateurs, but the experiment is sure to be tried before long.'

Lancashire themselves started one game in 1908 on a Saturday but did not think it worthwhile, and in a hotch-potch of experiments in 1914, tried starting on every weekday except Tuesday. But it was to be after the First World War before Saturday starts were adopted by all the counties.

Lancashire's inability to find more than just the occasional home-born professional cricketer who could establish himself in the county team had been a mystery since the club had been founded. The only one to have lifted himself to the rank of Test cricket up to 1895 had been Dicky Barlow, although Dick Pilling could claim to be a true Lancastrian despite being born in Bedford. Truly outstanding Lancashire-born professionals could literally be counted on the fingers of one hand, a point that was hammered home in 1895 when Lancashire came in for criticism for their reliance on players from other counties. No other county had relied so heavily as Lancashire on imported players and when they beat Yorkshire at Sheffield critics were quick to notice that while Yorkshire had only one 'foreigner' in their team (Lord Hawke was born in Gainsborough in Lincolnshire), Lancashire had ten! Only Archie MacLaren was a true Lancastrian and the remainder came from Yorkshire, Derbyshire, Nottinghamshire, Northamptonshire, Ireland and Kent. In that season alone Lancashire went into seven of their twenty-one county games without a Lancastrian on the side. Of the 231 places in the team for championship matches that summer, 203 went to players from outside the county with six from Yorkshire in Albert Ward, George Baker, Tom Lancaster, Charlie Smith, Alf Tinsley and Harry Tinsley, plus Arthur Paul (Belfast), Frank Sugg and Charles Benton (Derbyshire), Albert Hallam and Johnny Briggs (Nottinghamshire), Arthur Mold (Northamptonshire) and Sidney Tindall (Kent). The Red Rose flag was carried only by MacLaren (12 matches), Hornby (4), J. T. Tyldesley (10) and Charles Pilkington (2).

The Lancashire committee promised more thorough searching of the fields and the hedgerows, the pits and the mills, to find natives worthy of representing the county. By the time the First World War arrived they were as true as their word and twenty-two of the twenty-eight players who turned out in the championship were Lancashire born. On average, in 1914, there were eight in every team Lancashire fielded. Mind you, they did finish eleventh that year, their worst position ever . . .

Nineteen years earlier, however, it had been anything but a team representative of Lancashire that had fought for the county's honour, and it was a joy to see the emergence of a young man who was to prove perhaps the finest batsman Lancashire have ever had, J. T. Tyldesley. He was born in Roe Green, a village close to Worsley, and quickly showed his enormous promise in first-class cricket when he scored a century in only his second match. He was a dashing, entertaining batsman, a master on sticky wickets, and he created records that stood until his younger brother Ernest overtook them in the 1930s. Lancashire needed a lift after the disappointments of the previous year and were to get it in the emergence of Tyldesley and in the creation of an individual record – 424 by MacLaren at Taunton – that still stands today.

Lancashire had lost money in 1894. The treasurer blamed this on the bad weather, many of the members suggested the failures of the team, and when a point was raised at the annual meeting as to whether it was bad luck or poor play, a voice called out 'Faint heartedness'. Many agreed with him. Lancashire at this time had nearly 2,400 members, and nearly 500 lady members. Subscriptions for the year brought in £2,701, gates and stand money £2,533. Expenses for county and club matches came to £2,734, wages £1,603, rent, rates and taxes £602, cricket materials, postage, telegrams, miscellaneous £449 and donations to benefit matches £112. Still, there was a balance at the bank of more than £4,000 and a grand new pavilion, second only to the one at Lord's, and which was ready for occupation by the time of the first game against Sussex in 1895. The ground in those days was surrounded by other sports clubs. An Ordnance Survey map for 1895 shows Talbot Road ending at Warwick Road. On the left, on the way along Talbot Road towards Old Trafford, was Ashleigh Bowling Green, Old Trafford Bowling Club and a football ground, which was recently used as the car park near the office. Beyond Old Trafford, where the practice ground now is, stood Manchester City Police cricket ground, and to the left, up to the railway line, was Manchester and County Gun Club ground. Manchester polo ground stood to the right, roughly where the police headquarters are now, and up Warwick Road, from Old Trafford, was Clifford Cricket Club and Southern Cricket Club, stretching up to Chester Road. Yet another cricket ground stood partly on the land now occupied by Manchester United.

The amateur strain in the Lancashire team had died away for a while and there was only one in the side for the opening game. He was 28-year-old Sidney Tindall, playing in his ninth game and called on to captain the team which started with a seven-wicket win over Sussex. Tindall, a fast runner who used to lap his partner whenever a four was run out, won his spurs with an innings of 58 in the victory. But the match was more notable for the first appearance at Old Trafford of Prince Ranjitsinhji, who was to become the biggest attraction in the game next to W. G. Grace. The Lancashire match was only his third game for Sussex and for the whole of the three days he was the most popular figure on the Old Trafford ground. He had, it was said, the eye of a hawk and the agility of a cat.

The year of 1895 was to be Arthur Mold's greatest, but it was as a batsman that he attracted early attention when he shared in a last-wicket stand of 111 with Albert Ward against Leicestershire. Lancashire were 57 for nine when Mold went in but he played a free, confident game as he scored 57 in a partnership which lasted an hour and a half. It was the custom then, as soon as the last man was going in to bat, for a number of ground bowlers to hurry over to the popular side where the roller was kept, so as to be ready to roll the pitch. But on this day, as Mold kept them waiting, they moved into the nearby bar to get a quick drink before the innings closed. When Mold was eventually out, the rolling squad, instead of being at attention with the roller, were fixed to the bar and there was a longer delay than usual before the opposition could bat. The captain was encouraged to promote Mold to No. 10 for the next match, which was against Yorkshire at Sheffield. Mold, however, got two ducks and returned to his rightful place as last man for the rest of the summer. That half century was to prove his only one in 260 matches for Lancashire.

Just before taking part in the partnership with Mold, Ward had played for an England team against Surrey at The Oval and scored 163, which was 106 more than the next highest-scoring batsman, Yorkshire's F. S. Jackson. One newspaper was not over-impressed. 'The batting of the Lancashire professional, though steady and stylish, was by no means inspiring,' its correspondent wrote.

> Five hours is a fairly long time to be at the wickets for 163 runs but it was not the length of time altogether that made Ward's innings seem so funereal. He very rarely at any time set the spectators on a roar by a good running hit. Like most professional batsmen he refused to take any risks but simply confined himself to getting away loose balls in the safest of positions. A considerable number of his runs were made from the fast bowlers by simple glances to leg, by snicks behind the wicket, and other strokes which did not appeal to the imagination.

By the 1890s, the number of amateurs in the Lancashire team had dropped quite sharply, and on average there were usually only two, perhaps three, in any team. This contrasted sharply with the early days when in almost every year up to winning the championship for the first time in 1881 more than half the places in any summer were taken by the gentlemen. The amateurs, if not the backbone of the team, were certainly brilliant and prominent members of it, imparting an element of dash to the play which increased its entertainment value and even brought a touch of the picturesque to the game. Exclusively professional teams, such as Nottinghamshire and for a time Yorkshire, were regarded as slow and unattractive and Trent Bridge in particular reflected this at the gate. An idea of the difference the amateur was thought to make to the side came in the game against Kent when Lancashire reached the end of the first day at 341 for four. The long-serving *City News* correspondent described the scoring as not very quick. 'We have seen times when a Lancashire Eleven would easily have made 500 in the same conditions in the same time,' he said, adding 'Lancashire batting is certainly becoming slower.'

Mold was playing with a damaged finger about this time. It had been badly split during his innings against Leicestershire and was hit again in a vital match against Surrey when he was unable to bowl on the second day in a game which Surrey won by an innings. Lancashire were in the running for the championship and the next game was another tough one, against Nottinghamshire at Trent Bridge. Hornby badly wanted Mold to play and when the Surrey game finished on the Saturday he told Mold he would be taking him to Nottingham for the game starting on the Monday. In those days teams were not named before the toss and the county which batted first could send out whoever it chose without first declaring the names of the players. Once, a young amateur bowler, W. H. Pennington, was chosen to play and was changed, ready for the match. Lancashire batted and made a disastrous start and a member of the Match Committee went into the dressing room to ask Pennington to stand down as they wanted to strengthen the side with another batsman, Harry Tinsley. Pennington was never chosen again. And even when a side fielded first, a player could be replaced provided he had not bowled. If Hornby had lost the toss at Trent Bridge and Nottinghamshire had batted first, Mold would not have played and his place would have gone to the same Harry Tinsley. But Hornby, captaining the side in the prolonged absence of MacLaren who was teaching at Harrow, won the toss and Lancashire batted all day for 315 for seven. So Mold's finger was given more time to heal and he bowled on the second day on a pitch giving him little or no help.

Mold was carefully nursed through the day. Hornby took his place behind the stumps for any returns and also fielded close behind him to stop any of the hard returns. Mold was there simply to bowl, and how well he bowled. Nottinghamshire, replying to a Lancashire total of 345, were quickly in trouble and lost their first five wickets for 6 runs, all of them to Mold who dismissed four of them in four balls. He took wickets with the last two balls of one over and the first two of the next. Arthur Shrewsbury, Harry Daft and John Dixon all played but were palpably beaten and Charles Wright was caught by the wicket-keeper standing back next ball. As Mold had also dismissed Arthur Jones earlier, he had taken the first five wickets in the space of nine balls. The first innings was over in 55 minutes for 35 runs with Mold taking eight for 20, and when Nottinghamshire followed on they were dismissed again for 122. Mold this time took seven for 65 for a match analysis of fifteen for 85 as Nottinghamshire were twice bowled out in less than three hours. As this was the benefit match for Wilf Flowers and the game was over in a day and a half, the Lancashire committee trebled their subscription to the fund and sent £15.

MacLaren, although appointed captain for 1895, played in only two of the first eleven matches. He had been to Australia in the winter, a last-minute selection for the tour captained by A. E. Stoddart, and had scored a magnificent 228 in his opening first-class innings there, against Victoria at Melbourne. He did not do so well in the first four Tests and was averaging 12.5 when he went into the final Test at Melbourne, a match that was to decide the series. MacLaren scored 120 in the first innings, and his Lancashire teammate, Albert Ward, 93 in the second as England triumphed by six wickets. MacLaren returned home through Japan and missed Lancashire's first two matches of the summer. He played against Leicestershire and Yorkshire and then accepted a position as a teacher at Harrow and missed the next seven games. Lancashire had three captains during that period in which four matches were won and three lost. Tindall was captain three times, losing twice, Benton three times losing once, and Hornby once in the victory over Nottinghamshire. As Michael Down suggested, in his biography of MacLaren, the Lancashire captain was no doubt on the breadline after his tour to Australia where he had to be subbed out, and the opportunity of regular occupation at Harrow was too good to miss. MacLaren attended the Eton v Harrow match on 12 and 13 July before rejoining Lancashire for their game against Somerset at Taunton, which started on Monday 15 July. He won the toss and he and Ward opened the batting in delightful weather in front of only a few hundred spectators.

MacLaren had spent the previous six weeks bowling hard at the nets at Harrow and was extremely fit. Yet he might so easily have been out first ball, beaten by a delivery from Edwin Tyler which just missed the stumps. Ward was first to 50 but once MacLaren got going he quickly passed his partner and at lunch had scored 72 to Ward's 64 in the total of 141. The stand was broken immediately after lunch without any addition and then came the partnership with Arthur Paul which was the highest ever and is still today the third highest in Lancashire's history. Together, MacLaren and Paul put on 363 runs in 190 minutes for the second wicket before Paul was caught in the outfield for 177 off the lob bowling of Lionel Palairet. By the close of play MacLaren was 289 not out in the total of 555 for three in five and a half hours batting. The individual record was held by W. G. Grace with 344 scored for MCC v Kent at Canterbury in 1876, and as soon as he heard that MacLaren was 289 not out on the Monday night, he sent him a telegram congratulating him and hoping he would create a new record in county cricket. MacLaren himself was not aware of the record until the Monday evening and on the second day he just kept going, looking for as many runs as he could, passing Grace's record after batting 70 minutes. MacLaren was 404 not out in a total of 756 for six at lunch and when he was finally out, for 424, he had been batting 7 hours 50 minutes. He hit one 6, sixty-four 4s, ten 3s, twenty-six 2s, and eighty singles and the four centuries came in 155, 105, 90 and 94 minutes. The only chance he offered came when he was 262, a fierce drive to mid on.

Said MacLaren afterwards 'Every dog has his day, and this

was one of mine. When I had made 400 I was quite contented. I didn't try to get out, but I did not mind, and certainly I ought not to have got out to the ball off which I was caught.' Sammy Woods, the Somerset captain, wrote in *The Cricketer* magazine in 1923:

> We started what I may call a busy week in July, that is from a bowler's and fielder's point of view. Essex scored 692 in their only innings; three of their batsmen got hundreds and another 99. We lost by an innings and 317. We rested on Sunday and lost the toss on Monday against Lancashire. A. C. MacLaren kindly consented to play against us. He went in first and scored 424 in a marvellous manner. We were beaten by an innings and 450 runs. A nice week's cricket, don't you think?

Bob Porch, a middle-order batsman from Weston-super-Mare making his championship debut, recalled MacLaren's innings in *The Cricketer*:

> MacLaren's stance at the wicket as the ball was delivered was majestic. All he did was done in the grand style. The end of his bat was pointing straight at the sky above his head and his hands were about level with his right shoulder. I do not suppose that absolutely every stroke started like that, but that was the main impression . . . Let the bowler pitch the ball where he liked there would be an unhurried stroke with a full swing to counter it.

After Paul had been dismissed, MacLaren took part in two other fast-moving stands, 107 in an hour for the fourth wicket with Benton, and 95 in 45 minutes for the fifth wicket with Sugg. Benton was out when he played a ball into his mouth and gave a return catch to Gerald Fowler after scoring 43. His mouth swelled badly and he was unable to field. Once MacLaren was out it was decided to end the innings as soon as possible and as declarations could not be made until the final day, the remaining batsmen hit at everything and were out in a variety of ways. 'It is very probable that if we had gone for the record we could have made over a thousand, but we had to get Somerset out twice, which was the chief object to be aimed at, and in this we were successful,' wrote MacLaren later. 'Yorkshire beat our score the other day [887 v Warwickshire at Edgbaston in 1896] and went for the record, but they lost a victory by it.' In recognition of MacLaren's feat, Lancashire made him a life member and presented him with a gold watch and chain.

ARCHIBALD CAMPBELL MACLAREN was born in Whalley Range, Manchester on 1 December 1871, a true Lancastrian who moved out to attend Elstree School in London and then Harrow. His first match at Lord's came at the age of 15 when he played against Eton and scored 55 out of 101 in the first innings and 67 out of 204 in the second. His father, as he always did, had given Archie two weeks' practice with professionals before going to school for the summer term. In fact, Archie thought his father would have preferred him to get in the cricket team than do well academically. He made his debut and scored his first century for Lancashire when he was 18, he played for the Gentlemen against the Players when he was 21, was Lancashire's captain at 22, played his first Test at 23 when in Australia, and scored his 424 when still 23. MacLaren, in his prime, was regarded as the finest batsman in England and the Australians reckoned him the best England had ever sent to their country. In three visits he scored thirteen centuries, one of them a double and four of them in Test matches. He opened the Lancashire batting for some years with Reg Spooner and with J. T. Tyldesley coming in at No. 3, there was no finer start to an innings in England. And even today, more than eighty years on, Lancashire can have had no better start to their batting. He belonged to the Golden Age with batting that was described as kingly and majestic. He captained Lancashire for twelve seasons and led England in twenty-two Tests against Australia, a total that is still a record.

MacLaren had little success as England captain, although he was generally highly regarded as a leader. 'He had a proud scorn of caution and he sometimes gambled on hazards with magnificent disregard of the consequences,' wrote one critic. 'His skill as a captain came out best in his control over the moves of the game on the field of play; he seemed able to see the course of events hours ahead.' This high regard was not unanimous. He was stubborn to the point of near stupidity and would never acknowledge his faults. Presumably, he never accepted he had any. When things were going wrong in one match he insisted on persevering with Johnny Briggs who was being hammered. When the crowd shouted for MacLaren to change the bowling he threw the ball angrily and pointedly at Briggs at the end of each over for him to continue as if to emphasize his position as captain. He abandoned a match at Lord's after the crowd had trampled on the pitch but the wicket was fine by the following morning, by which time MacLaren had taken his bat and gone home. He was even reluctant to have Jack Hobbs in his England team in 1909. Strangely enough, Sir Henry Leveson Gower, who was chairman of the selectors then, described MacLaren as a pessimist. John Arlott wrote of him 'It was MacLaren's tragedy that all his virtues bred their own faults. He was strong but inflexible, intelligent but intolerant, single-minded but homourless, impressive on the field but often disappointingly petty off it.'

139

Neville Cardus would not hear a word against MacLaren, whom he dubbed the noblest Roman of them all. 'MacLaren could not, by nature, be inactive,' he wrote. 'His cricket belonged to the Golden Age of the game, to the spacious and opulent England of his day; it knew not the common touch.' R. C. Robertson-Glasgow said of him 'As captain and batsman MacLaren was a calculating attacker. His delight was to scatter the enemy by the strong stroke of bat or tactics.' MacLaren showed flashes of brilliance as a captain, particularly in lifting Sydney Barnes from the near obscurity of league cricket to the spotlight of Test cricket. After watching Ted McDonald and Jack Gregory in 1921, MacLaren, then in his fiftieth year, said he could find a team to beat the Australians who had thrashed England 3–0. He found his team, mostly from untried youth, and beat the Aussies in an astonishing match at Eastbourne.

MacLaren often argued that in every great match there came a turning point. 'The captain who jumps to the chance of it the quicker is the man who wins,' he said. 'From the first ball on the first day a skipper should be on the lookout for this moment.'

So sound was MacLaren's method of batting, a classical action, that at the age of 51 he played for MCC against New Zealand at Wellington in 1923 and scored 200 not out. He had played his last game for Lancashire in 1914, his previous century had been in 1910. Yet several young players who took part in that game said MacLaren's batsmanship was a revelation. Whatever his captaincy, his batting was of the highest quality and in the 1930s, when Bodyline was at its height in Australia, he stopped his taxi at the busiest crossing in Piccadilly. Ignoring the massed motor horns of London's enraged traffic, he got out and insisted on demonstrating to another old player, Gerry Weigall, exactly how he would have dealt with such bowling.

MacLaren played for Lancashire from 1890 to 1914 but effectively finished his county career in 1910 when he was 38. He had only ten innings that year, yet scored centuries at Worcester and Edgbaston. He became county coach in the 1920s after a career with the county that saw him play in 307 matches and score 15,772 runs (average 33.34) with thirty centuries. Near the end of his spell as coach he had disputes with the Lancashire committee and said to Len Hopwood, one of the rising young professionals of the time 'Just because they employ you, they must not think they own you body and soul.'

Lancashire's next match after MacLaren's great innings was against Gloucestershire at Old Trafford where W. G. Grace had the opportunity to congratulate MacLaren in person. Grace was having a marvellous season but after scoring 42 in the first innings he was out for five in the second, the first time that season he had been dismissed in single figures, and thousands who were going to Old

Trafford to see him bat were too late. Lancashire made one change to their team, 21-year-old J. T. Tyldesley making his debut in place of Alf Tinsley and starting a brilliant career that was to extend over twenty-nine seasons. He followed this by becoming the county coach, a position he held until 1929, the year before his death. He batted at No. 6 on his debut and followed 13 in the first innings with 33 not out in the second when rain on the final day denied Lancashire the chance of continuing their chase, from 148 for five, to the 193 needed for victory. The next match, a week later, was at Edgbaston, a ground that was to be Tyldesley's favourite. By hard, clean hitting, he scored 152 not out in the innings win, the first of eleven centuries he was to score on that ground. Lancashire and Yorkshire finished second and third to Surrey in the championship that summer and their match at Old Trafford, played at the beginning of the season, attracted the biggest gate seen at the ground when 25,331 people paid in an attendance of about 27,000 on the opening day of a drawn game. The ground was so packed, it was reported, that thousands could have seen nothing.

It had been an eventful and a good year for Lancashire. The programme had increased with the arrival of new counties and they had won fifteen of twenty-two matches. Ward scored 1,486 runs – a record – for an average of 44, Mold took 192 wickets – another record and one that was to stand for nearly thirty years – and Johnny Briggs 124 with the next highest being Albert Hallam (29) and Tom Lancaster (27). It is also worth pointing out that Charlie Smith, their wicket-keeper who had now established himself in the team, was the country's leading wicket-keeper with 51 catches and 25 stumpings.

Nearly 150,000 people had paid at the gate during 1895, helping towards a nice profit of £2,299, and membership continued to increase with one of the most pleasing features being the continued patronage of the ladies. Ladies' tickets – 475 were issued in 1895 – were limited to wives and sisters of members and even then were bestowed at the discretion of the committee. The ladies, of course, had their own pavilion, a comparatively new and highly attractive feature of Old Trafford, and their area was always ablaze with colour during any big match.

MacLaren was again unavailable until July in 1896 and there was Hornby, now in his fiftieth year, again captaining the team in the opening match, against Yorkshire at Old Trafford. He was as popular as ever. Said one newspaper 'It was a pleasure once again to see the veteran Hornby in the field with unimpaired activity and the same insatiable desire when batting to run out his partner.' An interesting newcomer to the Lancashire team, yet another man from Yorkshire, was 31-year-old Willis Cuttell, professional with

141

Nelson in the Lancashire League. He was given a trial and was so unimpressive that he was not chosen again that year. 'He scarcely seems equal to county work,' said the *City News*. Yet Cuttell was to become the first Lancashire player to accomplish the double of 1,000 runs and 100 wickets in a season and played twice for England in a career that took him past his fortieth birthday. The gate for the Yorkshire match was, as ever, formidable and the attendances this year were to hit a new high with more than 200,000 paying at the turnstiles. There were 22,000 for the opening day of the game against the Australians and only a few thousand less for the second day, followed by 15,000 for the first day of the Whitsuntide game with Kent and nearly 17,000 for the start of the Test match. In addition to the permanent stand accommodation, a temporary structure was erected for the Test match on the pavilion side on which it was possible to reserve seats, an innovation which, though startling to many, worked splendidly. The *Manchester Courier*, however, added a footnote 'We fear that many visitors on the side near the telegraph office experienced discomfort from the clouds of smoke which came from the tea-room.'

J. T. Tyldesley was left out of Lancashire's game against the Australians, the reason being, according to the mischief-makers, that he was a Lancastrian. But he could not be denied for long and although not as impressive as in 1895, he played in sixteen matches and scored over 500 runs for an average of 25. Hornby captained the team for the first four games but the side rarely had the same captain two games together between then and the first appearance of MacLaren in mid-July. And among the captains was Ernest Rowley, son of Edmund Rowley, Lancashire's captain in the early years. He was to play sixteen matches and acquitted himself with a batting average of 26.

There were several outstanding batting performances against Lancashire that summer of 1896. Alec Stoddart scored 109 in under 100 minutes, Richard Palairet and Sammy Woods shared in an opening stand of 110 in 45 minutes facing Mold and Briggs, Charles de Trafford, who had once played for Lancashire, scored a century in 105 minutes for Leicestershire, George Davidson and Harry Storer took part in a stand of 308 in 270 minutes for Derbyshire, and Ranji scored 165 to cast off the threat of an innings defeat for Sussex.

W. G. Grace, too, scored a century against Lancashire, carrying his bat through the innings for an unbeaten 102. But it was as an orator, or rather debator, that he attracted most attention in the match at Old Trafford when he maintained that MacLaren, while batting, had knocked off a bail while playing the ball. MacLaren

Nicholas Felix, an outstanding batsman and inventor of the Catapulter bowling machine, was also a fine artist. When touring the country with the All-England XI he sketched many of the grounds on which he played in 1852, including this one at Preston where the Northern League team still play today. (*MCC*)

This Nicholas Felix painting, from 1852, is of Broughton Cricket Club in Salford, a ground where W.G. Grace played and which is still being used today. The pavilion, with its resemblance to a church, is still in use. (*MCC*)

Another Nicholas Felix sketch from his travels with the All-England team in 1852 . . . this time the Liverpool ground at Prince's Park. (*MCC*)

This pavilion at Old Trafford, built in 1857 and later extended and modified, was pulled down at the end of the 1894 season to make way for the present building.

Dicky Barlow (left) and Dick Pilling, Lancashire's first two professionals to play for England. Barlow was an outstanding all-rounder, a right-hand stonewalling batsman and left-arm medium pace bowler; Pilling is arguably the best wicket-keeper Lancashire have had.

A.N. Hornby, one of England's foremost cricketers in the last century and the single most influential person in Lancashire's history. He, more than any other man, was responsible for Lancashire becoming one of the forces in the game.

A.G. Steel, a gifted all-round cricketer who captained England but, unfortunately, played only forty-seven times for Lancashire over seventeen seasons.

Johnny Briggs, the finest all-round cricketer in Lancashire's history with 10,707 runs and 1,696 wickets. A tragic character who suffered from epilepsy and died when only 39.

Arthur Mold, a great fast bowler who was hounded out of the game after being called for throwing. Nevertheless, his record in the 1890s is impressive. He took 1,543 wickets in thirteen years and he is one of only three Lancashire bowlers to have taken 200 wickets in a season – Ted McDonald and Cec Parkin are the others.

Opposite: Archie MacLaren . . .' his stance at the wicket as the ball was delivered was majestic. All he did was done in the grand style. The end of his bat pointing straight at the sky above his head and his hands were about level with his right shoulder. I do not suppose that absolutely every stroke started like that, but that was the main impression.' – Bob Porch of Somerset.

Five Lancashire amateurs pictured in 1908 with Reg Spooner and the hard-hitting batsman, Kenneth MacLeod, on the back row, and A.H. Hornby, Archie MacLaren and Australian Leslie Poidevin at the front.

J.T. Tyldesley, pictured during the MCC tour of Australia in 1903-4. For many years he was the only Lancashire-born professional in the team. He played from 1895 to 1923 and set up records that have been beaten only by his brother Ernest.

Walter Brearley gave it everything, even for the cameraman. He was a very fast and quite outstanding bowler, unusual among amateurs who preferred the less demanding, more artistic role of batsman. His relatively short and colourful career was punctuated with disagreements with the committee.

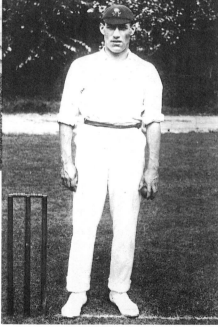

Jack Sharp, the motor-cyclist, in about 1910. He played 518 times for Lancashire, a figure surpassed only by Ernest Tyldesley, with 573. A professional up to World War I, Sharp turned amateur after the war and captained the team for three years up to his retirement.

Harry Dean, a left-arm pace bowler who took over 100 wickets eight times in the twelve seasons he played. His outstanding performance was in taking 17 wickets in a friendly match with Yorkshire at Liverpool.

LANCASHIRE COUNTY & MANCHESTER CRICKET CLUB

A·N·HORNBY
President

1881 & 1897

·1904·

S·H·SWIRE.
Hon.Sec.

J·HORNER
Hon.Treas.

A·C·MAC·LAREN
Captain

COUNTY CHAMPIONSHIP CELEBRATION DINNER

MIDLAND·HOTEL·MANCHESTER·

·WEDNESDAY·NOVEMBER·23RD·1904·

The front page of the dinner menu and toast list to celebrate winning the championship in 1904. The years under Hornby's picture, 1881 and 1897, denote the championship years under his captaincy.

TOAST LIST

1 THE KING . . . . THE PRESIDENT
"God Save The King" (Solo) Mr. FOWLER BURTON
Songs {(a) "To my first Love"—*Lohr*
      {(b) "If no one ever marries me"—*Lehmann*
                        Madame ANNIE WALKER

MUNICIPALITIES OF THE COUNTY . Sir W. H. HOLLAND, M.P.
      THE LORD MAYOR OF MANCHESTER
Humorous Selection . Mr. HUGH MONTGOMERY

3 CRICKET & CRICKETERS . Mr. J. GRIMBLE GROVES, D.L., M.P.
LORD BRACKLEY and MR. A. G. STEEL, K.C.
Songs {(a) "Son of Mine"—*Wallace*
      {(b) "The Rebel" . . . Mr. FOWLER BURTON

4 LANCASHIRE COUNTY TEAM . . Hon. F. S JACKSON
      Presentation by THE PRESIDENT
Song . "Should He Upbraid"—*Bishop*
                        Madame ANNIE WALKER
Response by Mr. A. H. HORNBY and Mr. J. T. TYLDESLEY

5 OTHER COUNTIES . Sir JOSEPH F. LEESE, K.C., M.P.
Humorous Selection . Mr. HUGH MONTGOMERY
Song . "The Border Ballad"—*Cousen*
                        Mr. FOWLER BURTON

6 THE CHAIRMAN . . . REV. VERNON ROYLE
"Here's to His Health" . Mr. A. N. HORNBY
"The Art of Chapeaugraphy" . Mr. H. ALBISTON GEE

"Auld Lang Syne"

At the Piano . . . . . . Mr. AINSWORTH

said he had knocked off the bail when setting off for the run and was therefore not out. The umpire agreed with him, but Grace, in his high-pitched but powerful voice, put his arguments forcibly and principally addressed at the umpire. The doctor declared positively that MacLaren was out, and knew he was out, and went through a demonstration showing what had happened. Several minutes were taken up with the debate and when Rowley was run out soon after, Grace took the bat from MacLaren, showed him what had happened, and then threw it to the ground. An extra ten minutes was taken for lunch, no doubt to discuss the point even further, and Grace, who was jeered by a section of the crowd, was criticized for arguing with the umpire. Lancashire, after making their opponents follow on, needed 30 to win. They started their innings at 6.15 p.m. and Tyldesley and Frank Sugg were sent out to get the runs. Grace, who was ready for a quick departure, fielded in his everyday clothes. 'He looked bulkier than ever as he stood at point in his ordinary attire,' said one report.

Lancashire won eleven of their twenty-two matches and finished second to Yorkshire this year with MacLaren averaging 54 in the half season he played and Sugg 39 while Mold (137 wickets) and Briggs (145) again carried the bowling although Hallam made a useful contribution with 58.

Chapter 7 1897–1907

*'For the first time, all the players entered the field
through the same gate.'*

Since sharing the championship in 1889, Lancashire had been runners-up five times in seven years, three times to Surrey, twice to Yorkshire. Bowlers win titles and Lancashire badly needed support for Johnny Briggs and Arthur Mold who had carried the bowling through the 1890s. Both had taken more than 100 wickets each in the years 1891 to 1896 . . . but support was needed if they were to take that extra step and clinch the championship. That support arrived in 1897, first in the unlikely form of 32-year-old Willis Cuttell who took over 100 wickets, and Albert Hallam who took ninety. Briggs was way in front with 140, Mold took eighty-eight despite being troubled by injury, and Lancashire's four bowlers all finished in the top twelve of the national averages. It was the extra cutting power Lancashire needed and gave them their first outright championship win since 1881 after a neck-and-neck race with Surrey through August. By 14 August Lancashire were on top but Surrey were closing fast so that when the two teams met at The Oval on 19 August it seemed clear that whoever won, would probably win the title as well. There were nearly 30,000 people there on the opening day and it was Surrey fast bowler Tom Richardson who turned the match on a treacherous wicket drying out under a hot sun. Lancashire, 62 behind on the first innings, ended the second day 112 for six after having no answer to the fiery bowling of Richardson who, in poor light, laid out MacLaren, broke Ward and Sugg's bats and broke Sugg's finger. Briggs was hit three times, Lees Radcliffe was lamed, Ward also suffered, and Tyldesley faced one over from the

144

fast bowler in which every ball whizzed past his head.

Lancashire lost by six wickets, and the title looked to have gone with it, especially as they could only draw their next match with Middlesex at Lord's. The title then was decided by ignoring draws, subtracting defeats from wins, and the final order being decided by the percentage of points gained from the completed games. It all meant that if a team won only one match and drew all the others it would have a percentage of 100 which would guarantee it the title – or at least a share of it. Lancashire started their final game against Nottinghamshire at Old Trafford on 26 August, the same day that Surrey were meeting Somerset at Taunton. Lancashire won by an innings to give them a percentage of 68.42 but all Surrey had to do to stay ahead of them was to avoid defeat in their last two games, against Somerset and Sussex. But in a remarkable game, Somerset beat Surrey to record only their third win of the season, and regardless of the final match at Brighton, the title was Lancashire's. Surrey, after starting the final two games with a percentage of 70, finished with 61.90 and had to be content with runners-up place . . . and that after beating Lancashire twice. MacLaren averaged 56 that season, Ward, Baker, Tyldesley and Sugg all got over 30. It was a great team effort and despite the nail-biting at the finish, Lancashire were worthy champions.

Lancashire had twenty-two professionals on the staff that year of 1897 compared with seven in 1889 and many enthusiasts expected great things from Jim Hallows, a youth from Little Lever, while other players of promise on the staff were Bill Huddleston and Lees Radcliffe. And heaven be praised, all were true blue Lancastrians. The annual meeting had heard that MacLaren would again not be available until midway through the summer and Hornby offered to take on the captaincy with occasional relief from Ernest Rowley, Sidney Tindall, and Charles Benton. Membership and gate receipts were at their highest and another sizeable profit for the year was announced despite an item in the accounts which disclosed that £216 had been misappropriated by one of the gate-keepers. Anyway, the pavilion, which had cost a total of £9,033, was now paid for and it was hoped to enlarge the ladies' pavilion. A suggestion about providing accommodation for members' bicycles, a convenient way to get to the ground, was turned down.

Lancashire's fielding had always been held in the highest regard since Hornby's early days, a point that was emphasized in the opening match of 1897 at Derby where Arthur Paul held five catches fielding at point in the second innings. Games against Hampshire were revived after twenty-seven years – Lancashire still had one player in Hornby who had played against them in 1870 –

and victory at Southampton was one of the five Lancashire forced in the first six games to put them at the head of the table. Another of their victories was the most exciting of the season, a one-wicket win over Derbyshire at Aigburth when they needed 184 for victory. The ninth wicket fell with eight still needed but Cuttell saw them to victory amid wild, uproarious cheering.

Lord Harris made his first appearance at Old Trafford in ten years in honour of Frank Sugg having chosen the Kent game for his benefit match – he made £1,000 – and nearly 24,000 people saw the first day's play, the only day on which play was possible.

Lancashire also resumed games with Essex after a ten-year gap, and the match at Leyton caused unpleasantness and involved Arthur Mold, who was batting, and Fred Bull, an off-break bowler. Lancashire were in trouble on a wearing wicket and when it looked as if they might follow on, Bull made every effort to see they did not, so that Essex would not have to bat last on a wicket that would clearly get worse. Bull bowled one ball wide to the boundary to give 4 runs away and Mold, who had kept his end up for some time, then decided to hit his own wicket and make sure Lancashire followed on. There was a heated discussion among the players during the interval and Hornby, not for the first time in his career, refused to proceed with the game. Each side accused the other of sharp practice, but in the end Bull admitted he had bowled wide on purpose, apologized for his part in the affair, and the game continued. Both players acted without any instruction from their captains and Hornby said later:

> I have been connected with first-class cricket over thirty years and have never seen such a disgraceful thing in connection with the game. Indeed, I was completely amazed when I saw Mold had knocked his wickets down and could hardly believe it, but when I heard the explanation and Bull admitted what he had done and apologized to me, I could not blame my men. But it is not my idea of playing cricket. Under the circumstances, which I hope will not occur again whilst I am playing cricket, I think Mold was justified in his action although personally I should never agree to anything of that sort being done.

Ranji again attracted enormous crowds to Old Trafford to see a Sussex team who used to be regarded as not worth the tram fare to see. But there were about 15,000 on the ground for each of the first two days of the match, and they roared with approval when Ranji stepped from the pavilion, a roar that went with him all the way to the crease. It was thought that such a reception had not been given to any player before at Old Trafford. After he was out –

146

he scored 87 – people left the ground and there were only 4,000 still there when the day's play ended. Another big crowd, again around 15,000, turned up on the final day, a Saturday, to see Ranji, who had travelled to London on the previous afternoon and had travelled all night to get back to Old Trafford. Lancashire avoided the follow-on and as it was impossible to win, Sussex decided to bat out the rest of the day. Once more Ranji was cheered all the way to the wicket, but was out to the first ball. There was an extraordinary silence and for a minute you could have heard a pin drop. Ranji shrugged his shoulders as if to apologize, then the funny side of it struck him and he started to laugh loudly. He laughed all the way to the pavilion, shaking his shoulders, and the crowd laughed with him before streaming from the ground and going home.

Hornby was still around when Lancashire took on Yorkshire in the match for David Hunter's benefit at Bradford, a game that attracted another huge crowd with spectators seven deep inside the enclosure and shortening the boundary. Hornby actually threw one intruder over the line after a heated verbal encounter, but the crowd took the matter good-humouredly and roared with delight. After all, Hornby was 50 years old and had been pushing people around for decades.

The 1897 season ended in triumph with the county on top of the table and finances in a healthy state.

This was one of the peaks in Lancashire history. By the end of the century the membership had climbed to around 3,000, there were nearly 700 ladies, and about 200,000 people were paying at the gate. Lancashire were well off and in addition to building a new pavilion they also agreed to buy the ground plus some adjoining land, an enterprise which cost them £24,732. Everything looked rosy at the start of 1898 although one member at the annual meeting did bring up the question of professionals' wages and expenses. He said he thought it unjust that players had to pay their own hotel and travelling expenses – a state of affairs that was to go on for many more years – and said they should be paid in the winter as well as summer, as they did in Yorkshire. The professionals, he insisted, were not well off. Sam Swire, the secretary, pointed out that every professional received £10 at Christmas. He thought, too, that the professionals were satisfied and said that even in Yorkshire they were not unanimous about winter payments being a good thing.

The status of professionals and the difference in treatment of amateurs had been a thorny point ever since the two classes had been brought together. Lancashire amateurs and professionals, though now at least changing in the same building after many years of being on opposite sides of the ground, still left the pavilion by separate doors and entered the field through different gates . . . and they did

147

not do that in Yorkshire either. And even A. N. Hornby, a man who had championed the players' cause through the years, still repudiated, with scorn, the idea of any professional captaining Lancashire.

George Baker, now 36 years old, was almost at the end of his career and his outstanding season in 1897, when he scored 1,444 runs, was followed by a benefit in 1898 which raised him £1,800. This was a record for the county despite his benefit match, against his native Yorkshire, ending early on the second afternoon. Hornby played in only six matches that summer, but one of them was the match for Baker's benefit. He had gone to Scotland on a shooting holiday but left his shooting box north of Inverness at 11.25 a.m. on the eve of the game to be back in time to take part. About 22,000 people watched the opening day when a collection was taken for Baker which raised £63. A collection was an innovation described by the *Manchester Guardian* as 'unusual', but drawing rather more critical comment from the *City News*, which declared 'Although the proceeding was well meant, the wisdom and dignity of such a course provoked much criticism.' Curiously, there were four Yorkshiremen in the Lancashire team, Albert Ward, Charlie Smith, Willis Cuttell and Baker, all of whom had played with Yorkshire Colts against Yorkshire in 1884, but none of whom had proved good enough for their native county.

The record for the highest individual score against Lancashire, and the only treble century that has ever been scored against them, came in 1898 from Surrey batsman Tom Hayward at The Oval. Hayward went in to bat at 81 for three, and after being dropped at 78 (a spooned catch to Briggs), at 82, at 132 in the outfield, and at 263, again a return catch to Briggs, he scored 315 not out in 6 hours 45 minutes. He hit two 5s, thirty-seven 4s, seven 3s, twenty-nine 2s, and seventy-eight singles. He and Len Braund, who played only twenty-one matches for Surrey before making his name with Somerset, put on 204 in 135 minutes for the eighth wicket. A collection taken for Hayward realized the magnificent sum of £71. Lancashire followed on 461 behind but salvaged a draw, due in part it was said, to Briggs's blunders, which had allowed Hayward to reach his great score. Another piece of high-class batting came from Essex at Old Trafford, when their largely amateur side scored what was then a record total of 336 for victory. J. T. Tyldesley, who had a magnificent season, reached his 1,000 runs in this match, without having scored a century. He had to wait until 3 August for that, an innings of 127 against Kent at Canterbury, and followed with the first of his thirteen double centuries, against Derbyshire at Old Trafford in the last match of the season.

It was a poor season for Lancashire, particularly after the heady stuff of 1897. They finished sixth in the table after winning only nine of the twenty-six county matches. Illness and injury had much to do with it. Mold missed six matches and finished with the comparatively low number of eighty-five wickets, Hallam was so ill he did not play all season, and Briggs lost form to such an extent that his seventy-nine wickets cost 24 runs each. The problem with the bowling forced the committee to ask even Alec Watson, now 51 years old, to turn out for them after an absence of five years. Watson wisely refused. Tyldesley was the outstanding batsman with 1,801 runs, Ward and Sugg each passed 1,000, but Archie MacLaren made little contribution, playing only six matches and averaging 23.30. But the outstanding performance came from Cuttell who became the first Lancashire player – there have only ever been three – to complete the double of 1,000 runs and 100 wickets in the season. He scored 952 runs and took 109 wickets for Lancashire, but lifted this to 1,003 runs and 114 wickets in all first-class matches. Only two other players accomplished the feat that year, Yorkshire's F. S. Jackson and C. L. Townsend, of Gloucestershire.

WILLIS CUTTELL was born in Sheffield on 13 September 1864, the son of William, an all-rounder who had played for Yorkshire. He had only eleven seasons in first-class cricket, but he topped 100 wickets for Lancashire four times, played in two championship-winning sides, toured South Africa, and played two Test matches. His early years were spent in league cricket, many of them in the Lancashire League where he helped Nelson win the first championship in 1892. Clubs had two professionals and Cuttell's partner was Joe Hulme from Derbyshire. In that season Cuttell and Hulme bowled 935 overs between them for Nelson and the amateurs 52. The following year they bowled 964 to the amateurs' 71. Cuttell, who became an amateur with Nelson in 1894 so he could take up the profession of a warp dresser, took 118 wickets in 1892, 104 in 1893, 106 in 1895, and 95 in 1896. It was more than enough to attract Lancashire's attention and although he was unimpressive in his first two matches in 1896 he was recalled the following year to help win the championship. *Wisden* selected him as one of their five Cricketers of the Year but that was just the start of ten good years and the continuation of a lifetime in professional cricket. He was described as combining an exceptionally good pitch with plenty of spin. Said *Wisden*:

> **He has a capital delivery and is especially clever in bowling the leg break. This he manages with no very apparent change of action, and he does not, like the majority of leg-twist bowlers, have to toss the ball high in the air. Apart from his bowling, Cuttell is a plucky, hard-hitting batsman and in the field he can stop anything.**

His performance of the double in 1898 earned him a place with C. Aubrey Smith's team in South Africa that winter. He played in both Tests – the first ever against them – and took six wickets at only 12 runs each.

Cuttell was responsible for Frank Woolley, the great Kent batsman, making an ignominious debut in 1906, Cuttell's last season when he was aged 41. Woolley, then aged 19, missed two catches, took one wicket for 103 as Lancashire totalled 531, and was then bowled by Cuttell for a duck. 'The ball would have bowled anybody,' Neville Cardus recalled. 'It was slow and it went through the air craftily curved. And when it dipped, after drawing Woolley forward, it came from the pitch at killing speed, broke from Woolley's leg stump and knocked the middle one down.' Woolley scored 64 in the second innings the following day before Cuttell again ended his innings. Cuttell's eleven seasons with Lancashire brought him over 5,000 runs (average 20.41) and 760 wickets (19.59). When he had finished playing, he became coach at Rugby School. He was there twenty years and was also a first-class umpire in 1928, the year before he died, aged 65. He continued to live in Nelson up to his death, owning a tobacconist's shop near the tramway centre.

The last summer of the nineteenth century brought the Australians, and with them Victor Trumper, to England once again, and by the time the fourth Test match at Old Trafford arrived with Australia 1–0 ahead in the series, interest was at fever pitch. No previous game in Manchester had attracted so much attention, not even the Roses matches of 1893 and 1895. Only a general election could arouse the sort of excitement that was sweeping through Manchester. Business was hurried through or thrown to the winds; special editions of the *Manchester Evening News* were produced every half an hour. People started arriving at the ground at 6.30 a.m. armed with cargoes of provisions which, said the *Manchester Courier*, 'suggested a Burton brewery trip to Blackpool', and when the gates were closed it was estimated that 26,000 to 28,000 were inside. Trips had come in very early in the morning from near and distant, from Dublin, Glasgow, Edinburgh, Dundee, Newcastle-upon-Tyne, travelling for most of the night to get there on time. Cabs, buses and trams headed for Old Trafford and even when it was clear they would not get a view of the game, people still paid to enter the ground and sit behind the crowded stand. They listened to the story of the game from the people above, cheering when they cheered. The day was hot, the atmosphere dreadful, and spectators placed handkerchiefs in their straw hats – it was said nearly everybody wore straw hats – and let the white linen cover their faces as much as possible. People were climbing on the roofs of refreshment booths and the ladies' pavilion was a symphony in bright colours with the summer dresses and the sunshades.

Long before the game began many people broke out into singing. The *Manchester Guardian* described it:

> This section of the crowd must have come from Rossendale, East Lancashire, and the district on the Yorkshire border. This is the singing country of Lancashire now as it has been for long years. Hymn tunes were sung, beginning with 'Lead me thou on' and continuing (appropriately enough) with another which contained the line 'By our captain led'.

During the sitting of the Manchester Assizes in the afternoon it was arranged by the judges that the courts, which were then engaged in the trial of civil cases, should rise at three o'clock on the second day of the match. Mr Justice Wills said they thought the Bench, the Bar and everyone else should take advantage of the unique opportunity of seeing the cricket match. But when wickets fell quickly the following day the *Manchester Guardian* said it was feared that 'My Lords the Queen's justices, who were to adjourn their courts at Strangeways, would miss all the fun.'

There was another huge crowd and the ingenuity of some of the spectators to get a good view was described by the newspaper:

> The stands, rising as they do to a great height, were packed with people. Even the space between the stands and the ordinary seats was filled up by those who made of, say four or five stone ginger-beer bottles, a raised platform for the feet, that they might see over the heads of those in front. The lower tier of stands, from which it was impossible to see the play, was artificially lifted in parts by an ingenious employment of bricks. Boxes, which at race meetings might signify what is called a 'Place', were in common use. But it was the stone ginger-beer bottle that was most closely in evidence and when it is mentioned that the groundsmen at Old Trafford secured some 50,000 examples of this sort of earthenware after Monday's play was over, it will be evident to all how great must have been the teetotal refreshment trade during the course of the match.

The amateur-professional divide was brought up in this game when Archie MacLaren led the amateurs into the field from one gate of the pavilion. It was a minute or two later before the professionals turned out although it was usual for a simultaneous entrance to be made from both gates. The *Manchester Guardian* speculated as to whether something was meant by this marked delay and mentioned that at Trent Bridge and Sheffield all players were on a level with regard to the vexed matter of entrances on to the field.

Lancashire, who had put up a new stand and a gigantic new scoreboard, were £20,000 in debt now they had bought the ground, and sought to increase the members' annual subscription from one to two guineas. It was defeated at the annual meeting.

The county were still having problems finding a captain who was there all summer and although the duties were officially shared between Liverpool-born Gerald Bardswell, a 25-year-old former Oxford Blue, and MacLaren, it was Alec Eccles who captained the team the day Jack Sharp made his debut against Surrey at Old Trafford early in June 1899. Eccles, another Oxford Blue, was 23 years old, a young but popular captain who had modestly put himself in at No. 8 in the batting order. Sharp, who was going to be good enough to score a century for England against Australia, was at No. 9, and Lancashire were 117 for seven when the two came together. Sharp, a young professional from the Leyland club, was better known at the time as a footballer with Aston Villa and was to become a double international. Together, he and Eccles put on 115 runs in 75 minutes and Sharp, batting in cavalier style, hit one ball into the covered stand near the pavilion entrance and another was sent clean over the sightscreen at the Stretford End where it knocked against the boundary wall of the practice ground. Sharp established himself in the team right from that opening game and was to play for Lancashire up to 1925, becoming one of only four players in the history of the club to take part in 500 matches or more.

Five more interesting new players in 1899 were Jerry Ainsworth, a very tall 21-year-old left-arm medium pace bowler who could break the ball either way, 24-year-old Sidney Webb, a medium pace bowler from Middlesex, 18-year-old Reg Spooner, who was to become one of Lancashire's most illustrious batsmen, 26-year-old S. F. Barnes, who never enjoyed county cricket and played only forty-six times for Lancashire, and Albert Henry Hornby, A. N.'s son who was to captain the team in the years leading up to the First World War. Ainsworth, who was born at Formby, was an amateur and, like Spooner, attended Marlborough. He played in the opening game against Warwickshire at Old Trafford and took seven wickets in the ten-wicket win. He took six for 84 against Nottinghamshire and in four matches took eighteen wickets at 16.05 each. But he was not specially interested in cricket and never played again for the county. Webb had been professional at Newport, Monmouth, before going to Manchester Cricket Club where he first played in

June 1897. While qualifying for Lancashire he played for his own county, Middlesex, nine times, taking seven for 55 on his debut at Trent Bridge. His debut for Lancashire came at Old Trafford in June when he played a significant part in the 29-run win over Sussex who were bowled out for 106 on the final day. Webb took four for 32, Tom Lancaster, of Enfield, took five for 19 and both were thanked by the committee for their efforts and each was rewarded with £2. Webb played seventy-three matches in five seasons with Lancashire with his high spot being eight for 36 against MCC at Lord's in 1902. He took 112 wickets in 1901 and when he finished in 1903, still only 28, he had taken 265 wickets (average 19.72).

An unusual dismissal happened to Albert Ward this year when he was batting against Derbyshire at Old Trafford in June. He was 72 and playing well when he on-drove a ball from Frank Davidson to the boundary. Unfortunately, the bat splintered as he hit the ball and a piece, as big as a man's palm, fell on to the wicket and knocked off the bails. Ward was out hit wicket. A similar thing apparently happened to George Wells of Sussex in 1860 when William Caffyn bowled and hit the handle of the bat, broke it, and the pod of the bat flew over Wells's shoulder and disturbed the bails. Digby Jephson, the Surrey lob bowler, had also been out in a similar way only a few years earlier. Fred Reynolds, the Old Trafford ground manager, told a much more interesting story about a match at Lord's in the 1850s when George Parr was batting and wearing a top hat, as was the style. A breeze was blowing and just as Parr hit the ball, his hat was lightly raised from his head and descended gently on to the wicket, covering it just as it had his head. The bails were not shaken, but who was to remove the hat? If he disturbed the bails Parr would be out. Umpire Caldecott decided to do it and with exquisite care removed the stovepipe, as the hat was known, without disturbing the bails.

Lancashire broke new ground this year by playing Derbyshire at Glossop, a village only a few miles over the border. The reason for going to Glossop, it was said, was that the chief magistrate and Mayor happened to be Derbyshire's captain. But seeing he had guaranteed the county club receipts to the extent of £100 it was a nice compliment to play the match there. The man was Samuel Hill Wood, later Sir Samuel Hill-Wood who was to become chairman of Arsenal Football Club. The *Sporting Chronicle* explained that Wood was a mill owner. There was a small and pretty pavilion occupied by the élite of the town, including the Mayor's wife and mother. The *Manchester Guardian* described the ground vividly:

153

Glossop ground is an amphitheatre of hills. At one end the batsman has in front of him the White Nab, the backbone of the Peak Range. The break in the mountainside shows him the path which leads to Hayfield and on to Chinley Churn. On the other side is the pleasant height of Pickness, green with meadow grass and with many a clump of trees. The ground has two drawbacks. The first and most serious is that it adjoins the railway of the Great Central Company. Shunting operations are in progress all day, disconcerting to the players. The noise is rackety and dreadful and at times the smoke from the engines obscures on one side both hill and valley. The other drawback is the ground is five or six feet higher at one side than the other.

Lancashire and Yorkshire were the two top teams when they played each other at Old Trafford in August and 20,000 people saw the opening day. The ground was aflame with the colour of the red rose which seemed to be in almost every button-hole. There were 17,000 spectators on the second day and 12–14,000 on the third when the game was drawn. Archie MacLaren and David Denton scored centuries although Denton needed help from MacLaren to get there. Denton was still only 89 with three minutes to go so MacLaren obliged by going on to bowl and sending down deliveries, described as overhand lobs, on the legside, three of which Denton hit to the boundary to reach his 100. 'A kindly act, but not cricket,' commented the *Manchester Guardian*. Up to then, only Lord Hawke had scored a century at Old Trafford for Yorkshire.

Spooner's debut came near the end of the season when he faced Middlesex at Lord's and came up against the formidable Australian, Albert Trott. J. T. Tyldesley, the kindest of Lancashire professionals, warned Spooner before the game about Trott's slower ball. 'He hides it artfully, so watch out,' said Tyldesley. Spooner scored 44 and Tyldesley, who was out to Trott's slower ball, said to him after the first innings 'You did well Sonny, but don't take Albert Trott for granted. Look out again for his slow one.' In the second innings Tyldesley was again bowled by Trott's slower one – he got 0 and 1 in the match – and the 18-year-old Spooner scored 83 out of 128 in less than two hours. Unfortunately, Spooner was unable to play for Lancashire for the following three years as he went into the Army and served in the Boer War.

The careers of two prominent players, A. N. Hornby and Frank Sugg, came to an end in 1899. Sugg, 37, was out of form and in mid-season retired as a professional but was prepared to play as

154

an amateur. Hornby, by now 52 years old – no other Lancashire player has ever played for the county at this age – took part in his last game, alongside his son Albert Henry, at Leicester. He bowed out in real style by scoring 53 out of 63 for the eighth wicket in 65 minutes.

It was during the Headingley Test of 1899 that Johnny Briggs had the epileptic fit that was to prove the beginning of the end for him. He returned to Manchester the following day and was met at Exchange Station by a representative from Cheadle Asylum. He was dazed and bewildered but managed to tell one questioner 'Tell the public I'm all right.' Briggs was admitted to hospital in July 1899, and was not discharged until 28 March the following year.

Nevertheless, Briggs was ready for the start of the 1900 season and no doubt heeding advice from the man who ran the Oxford Street Baths in Manchester, Joseph Constantine. Mr Constantine said that now the siege of Ladysmith had been raised, it was a relief to turn from the horrors of war to think about the cricket season. He pointed out that in past seasons Lancashire, in common with other counties, had not made sufficient effort to get themselves into prime health for the first match. He advocated . . . regular habits and not to neglect the usual hours of sleep. The best diet was plain, wholesome, variable and well-cooked food. A cold ablution ought to be taken on rising with a brisk rub-down and afterwards a sharp walk of twenty minutes, or exercises with dumb bells, to ensure a good reaction. Two hours brisk walking exercise in the open air at the rate of four and a half miles an hour would develop the muscles and ligaments of the legs; keeping erect and breathing through the nose would strengthen the lungs. Now and again it was worthwhile in the two hours walk to put on speed to produce free perspiration and throw off an extra quantity of waste matter, which will relieve the internal organs. When that was done a wash-over or a tepid bath and a change of underclothing should follow. After such a process a man felt at his best. He also suggested 'It is wise to avoid narcotics, as the Indian Prince does, and keep the nerves steady and strong and the eye clear. Beer and tobacco have prevented many promising young cricketers from reaching the height of their ambition – a place in the county team.'

Webb (eleven for 41) and Cuttell (eight for 46) took the early honours in the season by bowling unchanged to bring Lancashire victory by an innings over Hampshire at Old Trafford. But the big event of the year, and one of the biggest events in Johnny Briggs's career came at Old Trafford in May 1900, when he took all ten wickets in an innings for the only time in his life. The game was the first ever against Worcestershire and as the opening day, Thursday

155

24 May, coincided with the holiday for the Queen's Birthday, there was an unexpectedly large crowd there of about 7,000. By lunch Worcestershire were 70 for seven, all the wickets having fallen to Briggs. When two more immediately became his there was a good deal of excitement round the ground as to whether the popular little bowler would claim all ten. Albert Bird and Tom Straw were the batsmen and by patient, careful cricket, they kept Briggs waiting, frustrating him so much that one delivery was bowled at Straw's head in an effort to break the stand. It was hit to the boundary. The last pair had put on 32 before Bird ran out to drive Briggs and was bowled, giving the bowler a return of ten for 55. It was only the seventh time all ten had been taken in an innings and three of them had come at Old Trafford, the other two being by V. E. Walker for Middlesex in the opening county match in 1865, and Bill Hickton against Hampshire in 1870.

Lancashire must have taken notice of the man from the Oxford Street Baths because their start to the season was unusually good, not losing their first game until the end of July. It all meant large attendances and some rowdyism which caused the *City News* to make references to the stronger ale than in years past being served at the brick bar on the popular side. Lancashire and Yorkshire made the championship a two-horse race this season, and while both Roses matches were drawn, Lancashire were probably saved by rain at Bradford. 'Rain sent us on our journey home with peace in our hearts and the joy of a great deliverance,' wrote the *City News*, who went on 'Deep gloom settled on our hosts. They went home in grim and oppressive silence. It is an idiosyncrasy of theirs. When things go hardly with them, they do not grumble, they do not swear, they do not even drink, but a heavy silence comes down upon them.'

The return match, played at Old Trafford in steamy hot weather, was for the benefit of Arthur Mold, who was unfortunately injured and unable to play in the match. One report described the public arriving 'They came by rail and by tram and in buses and jiggers, and thousands of them came afoot.' Oxford Road trains were crammed and so were the buses from Deansgate and Market Street. The stands were full, the free seats occupied, there were tiers of spectators. More than 20,000 paid for admission on the Thursday, making a total gate of about 22,000, and Mold in the end collected a record £2,050.

ARTHUR MOLD was born in Middleton Cheney, a village in North-amptonshire, near Banbury, on 27 May 1863. His father died when he was a boy and when he grew up he had to provide for an infirm mother. He was never taught a trade but pursued cricket from boyhood, advancing from Middleton Cheney to Banbury where he was

professional in 1885 and 1886. One of Banbury's matches was against Free Foresters who included Lancashire's Arthur Appleby in their team. Appleby was impressed by Mold who was taken on to the Old Trafford staff in 1887, was qualified by residence to play two years later, and for the next decade, right through the 1890s, was to be among the most feared bowlers in the country. He topped 100 wickets seven times for Lancashire, his peak coming in 1894, with 189 wickets at 11.94 each, and 1895, when he took 192 (13.73). In all matches in each of those two seasons he took more than 200 wickets to become the first of only three Lancashire bowlers ever to achieve that figure. In thirteen seasons he took 1,543 wickets for Lancashire and stands third highest wicket-taker in the county's history behind only Brian Statham and Johnny Briggs. He was one of the fastest bowlers of the period and though his health was far from robust, he would bowl for hours on end. He was 5 feet 10½ inches tall and big boned and lived carefully to keep his weight below 13 stones. Being a very good shot, he tramped miles at home in Middleton Cheney with his gun. His endurance was shown against Yorkshire at Bradford when he bowled all day. During the afternoon when a wicket fell, A. N. Hornby, whose thoughtfulness towards his professionals was well-known, told Mold and Frank Sugg to go and share a small bottle of champagne.

He was regarded as a genial, gentle man, which makes it all the more a shame that he should have been forced out of the game after being no-balled for throwing. He was first no-balled in 1900 by Jim Phillips who was standing at square leg. This was the first year a square leg umpire had been authorized to no-ball a bowler for an unfair delivery. Mold bowled only one over in the first innings of that match, against Nottinghamshire at Trent Bridge, and none in the second. But it was in the following season, on 11 July 1901, against Somerset at Old Trafford, that he was finished off. It was the first time since the previous season that Mold had bowled with Phillips standing. A confrontation had deliberately been avoided in earlier games, but it was clear this was a course Lancashire could not pursue indefinitely. During the winter of 1900, in support of Phillips's action, the county captains had voted, by eleven to one, that Mold's action was unfair.

Mold opened the bowling against Somerset from the Stretford End and his first over was passed by Phillips who later said he spent that over carefully studying Mold's action. In his second over he was no-balled five times by Phillips who was standing at square leg. Mold changed ends to great cheering from the crowd but Phillips, now at the bowler's end, continued to call him. Phillips went in for lunch on that opening day heavily guarded by police, and during the interval A. N. Hornby, now club president, put on his flannels and took Mold to the nets where 'the cinematograph was applied' and pictures were

157

taken from three angles. After lunch Phillips did not call Mold at all, but such a sensation had been created that the attendance, which had been around 1,000 on the first day, swelled to 7,000 on the second. It was pointed out afterwards that twenty umpires had let Mold go on in the earlier matches and the other umpire in the Somerset game, C. E. Richardson, had passed every ball of Mold's and even said at the close of play that he had seen nothing unfair in the bowling. Another umpire, Bill West, who stood in Test matches, wrote to the *Sportsman* newspaper to say that Mold was fair and above suspicion and if he were guilty then at least four fifths of the umpires did not know the difference between bowling and throwing. 'I have asked all the umpires,' he wrote, 'and apart from Phillips and White, all think he is fair.' Mold himself said 'Throw? I can't throw half as fast as I can bowl.' He bowled through the second innings and was not no-balled.

Archie MacLaren, Lancashire's captain, said he had kept Mold on through the no-balling at Hornby's suggestion. He said they had discussed it before play started. MacLaren said of Mold:

> He had great command of the ball. He came off the pitch like lightning. He sent down at times a snorter that whipped back from the off to the leg stump. It was to this ball that his opponents took exception. But I am quite certain of this – if Mold ever threw, he threw without intent or knowledge that he was doing so. In trying to get that extra bit of work on the ball it is very easy to drop the elbow unwittingly. Mold was a really good bowler. He had one defect. He liked to see his catches held and fieldsmens' blunders upset him more than they do the man whose capacity to take such things smiling is a great asset to himself and his side.

The film that was taken of Mold bowling to Hornby during lunch of the opening day was shown at St James's Hall the following Saturday night in front of an immense gathering including Mold, MacLaren and other cricketers. Mold was 38 at the time. He had had his benefit the previous year and was obviously near the end of his career anyway. But the incident so affected him he played only three more matches, none of them at Old Trafford, and then retired. When he died, back in Middleton Cheney, on 19 April 1921, the *Manchester Guardian* wrote 'Even his critics had to admit the fine grace of his action. He was a tall, supple, genial man. He ran but a few paces to the wicket and if his action was not high, it was rhythmic in swing and exquisite in poise.'

Crowds continued to be huge at Old Trafford at the start of the century, and no wonder, with such attractions around as MacLaren and J. T. Tyldesley regularly on view, and visitors like Gilbert

Jessop and Ranjitsinhji to entertain. Jessop played a large part in Gloucestershire's win at Old Trafford and also enjoyed himself at home where he hit 82 in just over 45 minutes and 65 in 35 minutes. Ranji was an even greater attraction and Old Trafford took him deeper to its heart with a piece of sportsmanship that was appreciated by friend and foe alike. He was fielding at point when he went for a catch which he threw up by his finger tips close to the ground. There was an appeal, the umpire said out, but as the batsman, Jim Hallows, started to leave the field, Ranji called him back, told him the ball had touched the ground, and walked with him, arm in arm, back to the crease.

New visitors to Old Trafford that season of 1900 were the West Indian tourists, on their first visit to this country. The *Manchester Guardian* informed us that the amateur in the West Indies did not bowl very much because the climate forbade it. In any case, said the newspaper, there were natives willing and anxious to do the work. The *City News* was even more patronizing, but prophetic as well. It stated 'There is none of the "golly massa" Christy Minstrel element about their cricket and the tradition of the immortal Quanko Sambo has no hold upon them. With a little more experience they will have to be taken into serious account before long.'

A satisfactory season, in which Lancashire won fifteen of their twenty-eight matches to give them second place in the table behind Yorkshire, ended at Old Trafford with an innings win and a nostalgic last look over the countryside by the *City News* correspondent, who had been around a long number of years. He referred to the view from the pavilion . . . 'over the stretch of open country, with fields of wheat in the stock and patches of ruined oats.' Whatever the view, he was not to see it again for nine long months.

Soon after the end of the 1900 season, Johnny Briggs was taken ill again and was re-admitted to Cheadle Asylum in March 1901. He had played his last match for Lancashire and with Mold on his way out due to his confrontations with umpire Jim Phillips, Lancashire not surprisingly were never in the hunt for the championship, although they did manage to finish third. But nobody could touch Yorkshire around this time and the 1901 championship win proved the middle of a hat-trick of successes, three years in which they lost only two games. Despite heroic efforts from fast bowlers Jack Sharp and Sidney Webb, who both took over 100 wickets, and Johnny Tyldesley, whose 2,633 runs in a season for Lancashire is still the record today, Lancashire could not make any impression on Yorkshire.

Lancashire's weakened bowling was evident early in the season when Warwickshire's Bill Quaife and Septimus Kinneir shared in a record third-wicket stand of 327, and John Greig, an officer in the

Native Infantry, hit an unbeaten 249 in 320 minutes for Hampshire at Aigburth. By the middle of the second afternoon, Lancashire had declared at 413 for eight after bowling out Hampshire for 106. In 190 minutes to the close of play, Hampshire scored 280 for four with Greig 150 not out. Hampshire were still only 67 ahead when their captain, Charles Robson, strode out at the fall of the ninth wicket. Together, Greig and Robson put on 118 for the last wicket in a little over an hour and the match was saved. Greig, slim and slightly built, all whipcord and piano wire with tireless energy, had a limited first-class career due to being in the regular army stationed in India before the First World War.

Ranji and Jessop entertained the crowds again, Ranji all grace and majesty in an innings of 170 not out, Jessop full of power in an innings of twelve minutes in which he struck one of the biggest blows ever seen at Old Trafford. Ernest Steel, who had been living in Bombay, was having his first season in county cricket for thirteen years and was bowling his right arm slows to Jessop who advanced several yards to meet him. The *Manchester Guardian* described what happened:

> The ball flew over the heads of all the people, away out of the ground, away over the roadway, away into the railway station and on to the lines. Fortunately there was no train in the Old Trafford station at the time. A signalman, from his glass box, had carefully observed the flight of the ball. He left his box, went on the rails (one hopes that this was not against the regulations of the Cheshire Lines Committee), picked it up, sent it to an outside messenger, who in turn threw it over the boards to a fielder who returned it to Mr Steel, who seemed in no way discomfited.

The 100 wickets of Sharp and Webb were devalued a little by the repeated complaints about the Old Trafford wickets. The ground had been treated with dressings of soil, marl, etc, and some had been put on without being properly riddled, which resulted in small stones being rolled in. Batsmen were picking up pebbles and taking them back to the dressing room and MacLaren even flung a handful on the committee table, saying 'These are responsible for our batting failures.'

Ranji got his second century of the season against Lancashire in the return match at Brighton where MacLaren, after winning the toss, put Sussex in to bat and saw them reach 382 for three on the opening day with Ranji completing his double century just before the close. The *City News* later referred to a great deal of dissatisfaction being expressed at the management of the team . . .

160

'and the pious belief in MacLaren's heaven-born genius as a captain is down for revision.' The newspaper said all people were entitled to errors but some, like MacLaren, would never acknowledge one but insisted on justifying it. Reference was made to the match at Bristol the previous season when MacLaren delayed his declaration so long that Gloucestershire, set to score 450 in three hours, hung on for a draw with their last batsmen together. Despite the blunder at Brighton in putting Sussex in to bat, MacLaren insisted he would do the same thing again. The *City News* recalled the way he kept Briggs on bowling against Sussex in 1897 when his answer to the protests of the spectators was to ostentatiously pick up the ball and throw it to Briggs at the close of each over. 'A petulant obstinacy which he seems to mistake for firmness occasionally distorts his judgement,' said the newspaper.

Most of Lancashire's early games in Yorkshire had been played at Sheffield with the first game at Headingley coming in 1893, the second in 1896, and the third in 1901. The ground was described as pleasantly situated, abutting on one side on the finely-wooded park-like grounds of a large stone-built mansion of a Georgian type. It was famous for its size and in 1899 the boundary had been shortened on one side. Yet even by 1901 no sufficiently substantial barrier had been erected there and there was nothing more than a frail rope between the crowd and the field. And when 30,891 people paid to see the opening day of the 1901 match, it could have been no surprise to anybody when hundreds of spectators on the sixpenny side broke the line and scampered across the end of the field to secure vacant seats in front of the stands. Play was stopped for ten minutes while the club officials and Lord Hawke persuaded the intruders to settle themselves and sit down quietly in better places than they had paid for.

Everything was all right until the lunch interval when thousands, who had been sitting on the grass and the cycle track, strolled around the playing area, including the pitch. When it was time for the game to resume two mounted policemen were needed to help drive back the crowd and after more pleas from Yorkshire officials, from Lord Hawke and Archie MacLaren, the game resumed 35 minutes late. The whole field was strewn with paper and the Lancashire fielders sat around in knots, enjoying the sight of authority trying to get the crowd back. It was an impossible task and when play restarted the original boundaries were hidden and people were sitting in front of the sightboard. Life was not easy for the policemen in those days. They were constantly chivvied and if any stood up and obstructed the view of sitting spectators, a shower of paper bags full of dust gathered from the cinder track would descend on them. In all, 59,572 people

161

paid through the three days – giving a total gate of over 65,000 – to see a drawn match in which Frank Mitchell, Archie MacLaren and Albert Ward scored centuries.

Briggs had shown signs of recovery during the 1901 summer and had taken part in club matches arranged by the hospital. He batted and bowled well, chatted brightly with old friends, but then had another relapse, leading to his death nearly a year after his second admission, on 11 January 1902. The funeral was held four days later. Hornby, through the *Manchester Guardian*, appealed for members to attend the cemetery. He himself led a group of players, meeting at the Queens Hotel in Manchester before travelling on a special train which carried 1,000 people from Oxford Road in Manchester.

So Lancashire started the 1902 season without Briggs and Mold, the two men who had virtually carried the bowling through the 1890s and into the twentieth century. There were also doubts about the availability of MacLaren who had captained England in Australia but had resigned the positions of captain and assistant secretary at Lancashire before leaving. In a letter to Sam Swire, dated 24 September 1901, he wrote:

> It is with the greatest reluctance that a combination of circumstances causes me to resign not only the assistant secretaryship of the club but also my connection with Lancashire cricket. My wife's health is such that it is no longer possible for me to leave her for any length of time. She is very delicate, and her doctor has advised me not to leave her. She is only just able to get about after her long illness, which I hear will leave its mark. For these private reasons, and no other, do I feel bound to relinquish my position with Lancashire cricket. Last season the worry and anxiety of illness at home quite prevented me at times from concentrating my whole thoughts on the game. The kindness received at your hands, and others of the committee, will always be treasured by me, no captain ever getting better treatment than I did. Happiness of home comes before my county, and as it is my wife's wish for me to be near her I have decided to take this step, and am notifying the Hampshire committee to the effect that I will play for them next season.

Lancashire had appointed Alec Eccles captain for 1902 but in April MacLaren announced that his wife was now well enough for him to continue playing for the county. Nevertheless, Eccles captained the early games, even when MacLaren was playing, including the first match at Old Trafford, against Sussex, when another great step forward was taken in removing the gap between amateurs and professionals. For the first time, all the players entered the field through the same gate and when Albert Ward, a quiet unassuming professional, walked on to the field side by side with MacLaren, there was a good deal of applause. The change was attributed to MacLaren although it was mentioned that Eccles himself, during the previous season, had walked across to the professionals' gate to meet Ward so they could walk out together. The *Manchester Guardian* commented 'In the old days, players and amateurs met from opposite sides of the field. With the new pavilion a change for the better was made, but there were still two gates. In following the example set by Lord Hawke and treating all players as equals on the field, the Lancashire Committee have taken a step which will be widely approved.'

The *Manchester Evening Chronicle* reported 'As the men walked to the wicket in a body, there was a hearty outburst of cheering – a sure sign that the public appreciated the change. The citadel of conservatism has at last been stormed.' The newspaper also referred to pettifogging class distinction which had been suggested by two batsmen making their appearances through different gateways. C. B. Fry, the Sussex captain, had been caught unawares. As he prepared to lead his fellow amateurs on to the field in orthodox fashion, he looked towards the old spot for his professional followers. Meanwhile, the sacred precincts of the pavilion were being invaded by a strange host who went through the central exit. Then followed Ward and MacLaren to complete the revolution and pave the way for a demonstration of approval from the spectators.

Eccles soon resigned to allow MacLaren to resume as captain for the match at Sheffield which Yorkshire won by an innings. F. S. Jackson took eight for 13 despite having been out of cricket two years while away soldiering.

Victor Trumper, the great Australian batsman, was on his second tour of England in 1902 and scored his only Test century of that summer at Old Trafford, a magnificent innings in which he scored a century before lunch, reached with Australia 173 for one. Another Australian to attract attention that season was Alec Kermode who had been playing in New South Wales when MacLaren was there. With the consent of the committee, MacLaren invited Kermode, a medium-paced bowler, to qualify for Lancashire. He joined the groundstaff in June and although strictly not eligible until 1904, he was allowed by Australian captain Joe Darling to play at Aigburth against the tourists. Kermode, described as tall and strong, with a very high delivery and able to skilfully vary the pace of the ball without changing the style of his delivery, repaid Darling's generosity by bowling him as he took five for 69.

An interesting debut in 1902 was provided by 22-year-old William Findlay, an Oxford Blue who was to become secretary of MCC between the World Wars. He was a good wicket-keeper and an acceptable batsman although the *City News* thought him the ugliest bat and ungainliest hitter seen in first-class cricket for a long time. Another player to make his debut was Geoffrey MacLaren, 19 years old, and younger brother of Archie. Like Archie, he made his debut at Brighton against Sussex but was unable to emulate his brother's century on debut as he was dismissed for 0 and 3. A third debutant was Walter Brearley, then 26 years old, but who was to become one of the finest fast bowlers in England, a rare achievement in an amateur.

Sydney Barnes was Lancashire's leading wicket-taker in 1902 with eighty-four wickets, but his finest season for the county came the following year, which was also to prove his last, when he took 131 at 17.85 runs each. Those were his only full seasons in the first-class game and Barnes left county cricket having played forty-six matches for Lancashire.

SYDNEY FRANCIS BARNES, born at Smethwick in Staffordshire on 19 April 1873, was a gifted cricketer, a bowler of rare talents who displayed those talents all too rarely in the first-class arena. He preferred Minor Counties and league cricket to the more demanding first-class game which he found irksome and tiring. He was a mercenary. He played where he got the best return. The challenge of county cricket meant nothing to him. He believed himself the best bowler in the world and had no need to prove it. His record for England – 189 wickets at 16.43 each in twenty-seven matches – is clearly remarkable, but he played without the daily grind of county cricket which can so easily bring on staleness. Perhaps Barnes, like many Test cricketers, would have had to ration his energies. Maybe if he had played 400 times for Lancashire instead of forty-six, as well as playing for England, his record would not have been the formidable one it is.

Barnes played for Warwickshire four times in the mid-1890s and was professional with Burnley in the Lancashire League when he was asked to play for the county. He was not keen but reluctantly agreed when pressed by Burnley president Jimmy Sutcliffe, and made his debut in 1899. He was persuaded to join the groundstaff but stuck it for only those two years, 1902 and 1903, when he took 215 wickets. Barnes explained later that he felt Lancashire made him earn his wage, often putting him on to bowl at the start of play and keeping him there all day, unless he bowled the opposition out. He could not stand it, simply because he set himself

164

so high a standard; there was no opportunity to relax. He bowled flat out all the time and found cricket six days a week tiresome. So he returned to league cricket, although he was still good enough to tour Australia twice and South Africa and play in twenty-three more Test matches.

During his early days with Lancashire, when he was still unknown and playing just the occasional match, Barnes bowled at Archie MacLaren in the nets. MacLaren had never experienced him before but he was so impressed that he invited Barnes to join him on the tour of Australia in the winter of 1901–2. Barnes took nineteen wickets in three Test matches but was then unable to play any more because of injury. Here was a man regarded by many as the finest bowler in the world – perhaps the finest ever – and even after he had left first-class cricket he continued to play Test matches, finishing his career at 40 years old by taking forty-nine wickets at 10.93 runs each in four Tests in South Africa. In all he played in twenty-seven Tests, against Australia and South Africa, and took 189 wickets at 16.43 runs each. For Lancashire he played forty-six matches and took 225 wickets (19.81 each) before returning to league and Minor Counties cricket. He later admitted 'I was a difficult man to play with, I did my best at all times and expected the others to do the same.' And when they did not, he fumed and raged and soon became unpopular among his teammates.

Barnes was a man of uncertain temper and irascible nature. During the 1930s, when he was about 60 years old, he took part in a charity match which included a galaxy of stars including Cec Parkin and Learie Constantine. Constantine was being made to struggle for his runs and Parkin, realizing that a bit of Constantine hitting was needed to entertain the crowd, turned to Barnes. 'Chuck 'em to him, Syd,' he said. 'Let the crowd see him crack one or two.' Barnes threw the ball down, collected his sweater from the umpire and refused to finish the over or bowl again in the match. As he put on his sweater he turned to Parkin and said tersely 'I have a reputation as well as Constantine.' This was not the only time Barnes held up a match. In the second Test at Melbourne in 1911 a small section of the crowd barracked him, accusing him of wasting time. Barnes again threw the ball to the ground, folded his arms and refused to bowl again until the barracking stopped. He lived to be 94 and died on Boxing Day, 1967.

Lancashire had a likely-looking opening attack in 1903 with Walter Brearley proving an extremely fast and fiery customer to link up with the wiles of Barnes. Yet Lancashire finished fourth with ten wins and five defeats in their twenty-six matches. In his first match of the summer Brearley took seven for 43 against Worcestershire in the innings win and hit C. B. Fry several times on the body with extra fast deliveries. But the expresses which had troubled Fry were daffed away as things of no account by Ranjitsinhji who helped Sussex to their nine-wicket win.

The Lancashire team was taking on a different look about this time. The old establishment of the 1890s had gone and in its place came a new-look team, often predominantly amateur with a cluster of gentlemen, any of whom could have captained the team. In the Whitsuntide match against Yorkshire at Old Trafford, in fact, Lancashire fielded only three professionals and for the first time in twenty years there was not a Yorkshireman in the side. The amateur contingent consisted of Harold Garnett, Spooner, Findlay, MacLaren, A. H. Hornby, Eccles, Brearley, and E. E. Steel, with J. T. Tyldesley, Sharp and Barnes having the professionals' room to themselves.

New opposition was provided this summer by W. G. Grace's London County team. Grace was 48 and his huge shoulders and elephantine gait hardly recalled, said the *City News*, the slim and light-footed athlete who won hurdle races in the 1860s. W. G., it was said, failed to get a wicket 'with his archaic round-arm slows.'

Aigburth was by now having two fixtures a year and runs flowed on the ground in the games against Worcestershire and Gloucestershire. J. T. Tyldesley scored 248 against Worcestershire after nearly being out first ball, and MacLaren and Spooner shared in their record opening partnership of 368 on a soft and easy pitch against Gloucestershire. The *Manchester Guardian* said the Gloucestershire attack was not up to a county standard, yet they missed several opportunities to break the stand with MacLaren giving at least four chances and Spooner two. MacLaren's innings of 204 was regarded as chancy and below his best against a second-rate attack. Spooner's innings of 168 was regarded much more highly as he kept the ball down with unfailing certainty, driving brilliantly and hard, and showing batsmanship of a masterly quality. The partnership of 368, which lasted only 210 minutes, was the highest either for or against Lancashire and is today still the highest for the first wicket for the county. By the end of a day interrupted for half an hour by rain, Lancashire had scored 474 for three. This was only Spooner's second first-class century. After making his debut in 1899, he had spent the next three years serving in the army in the Boer War. He returned to first-class cricket in 1903 and his first century, a month before the Aigburth match, was his 247 against Nottinghamshire at Trent Bridge. It was the highest-ever score against Nottinghamshire and Spooner was only the fourth player to score a double century for Lancashire after MacLaren, J. T. Tyldesley and Sugg.

Aigburth was now highly regarded as one of the country's most attractive first-class grounds. People enjoyed going there and the *City News* summed it up in this delightful description:

The elms and poplars in their full, fresh greenery; the vista of the broad river [the Mersey] below with brown-sailed sloops and barges flitting by the wooded slopes of Bebbington on the Cheshire side, the sky-line accented by the pointed spire of a little church rising from beyond the brow of the hill. The rhododendrons in front are still a mass of purple blossom [27 June] and the ladies' lawn, with its terrace of trim turf and its rows of wicker chairs with their gaily-dressed occupants, has a pleasant, cheerful, holiday look. Old Trafford or Sheffield cricket is a serious business. Aigburth, Taunton, Canterbury cricket is still a pastime. No gravel, cinder or rubble. The absence of dust is a blessing and one is glad to escape the grittiness and the grime which make anyone who stands a day at an ordinary county match at Old Trafford or in Yorkshire seem to be the first cousin to a chimney sweep. Aigburth is one of the prettiest grounds in the north of England.

In 1903 Lancashire came up against two of their former players who were happily making good elsewhere. One was Albert Hallam who had played between 1895 and 1900 and whose career looked to have finished when he was taken ill. He had moved on to Nottinghamshire where he performed sterling service for ten seasons, playing in 194 matches for them and having an outstanding year in 1907 when he took 168 wickets at 12.69 each to play a major part in Nottingham-shire's winning the championship.

The other player was Sam Hargreave, from Rusholme, who had been on the Old Trafford groundstaff but had been released because he was not good enough. One of the Lancashire officials advised him he would never be able to make a living in first-class cricket but Hargreave decided to give it another go with Warwick-shire and joined them in 1899. He played 188 times for Warwickshire in eleven seasons, toured Australia with Lord Hawke in 1902–3, took 100 wickets in a season five times with his left-arm medium-paced deliveries, and finished his career with 919 wickets at 21.84 each. In the match against Lancashire at Old Trafford, Hargreave took five for 35 and six for 33 in the rain-affected, drawn match.

Sydney Barnes's county career ended unhappily this year when he was dressed and ready to play against Nottinghamshire at Old Trafford, only to be told his services would not be required. This followed his refusal the previous day to sign an agreement to play for Lancashire the following season. He was then 30 years old. A first-class player, it was said, could earn £5 a week or more in the league with an annual benefit of about £80. For that he would play one, at most two, days a week instead of six.

With Barnes back in league cricket, Lancashire went into the 1904 season with an attack of doubtful quality, certainly not strong enough for any team with designs on the championship. The big-hearted Walter Brearley was now among the foremost fast bowlers in the country, but who was to support him? Willis Cuttell had taken 100 wickets in three of the seasons from 1897 to 1900 but was now 39 years old; Jack Sharp had taken over 100 wickets in 1901 but was to bowl little in 1904; there was the Australian Alec Kermode who would qualify in June, and Jim Hallows from Little Lever, another fragile character whose career, like those of Dick Pilling and Johnny Briggs, was marred by ill-health. Yet everything came together, the team showed all-round efficiency, and with Cuttell and Hallows each taking over 100 wickets, the championship came to Old Trafford for the first time since 1897. It was a remarkable performance. Lancashire won sixteen of the twenty-six matches and drew ten to stay undefeated through a season in which they also drew against the South Africans and the Rest of England. They won fifteen of the first nineteen championship matches but drew the next six in August before winding up the season with a victory over Derbyshire. And in all those games they were on the receiving end only twice, against Yorkshire at Headingley and Middlesex at Lord's, where they had the worst of the drawn matches.

The outstanding, and unexpected, achievement came from Hallows, a 30-year-old all-rounder who was to become only the second player in the club's history after Willis Cuttell to achieve the double of 1,000 runs and 100 wickets in the season. And as he was the first Lancashire-born player to do it, a presentation was made to him by the club. Hallows joined the staff in 1897, made his debut the following season, but was far from robust and missed several games through ill-health. Like Briggs, he was an epileptic, and like Briggs he died young, when still only 36. He had one seizure during the Roses match at Old Trafford in 1905 and had to be carried from the field by Cuttell and Lees Radcliffe. As a bowler he closely resembled Briggs, slow in pace but full of spin and with great variety, having switched from fast bowling in 1897 on the advice of Sydney Crosfield. He scored most of his runs with hard cuts and off drives and Gilbert Jessop said his shots in the covers were the hardest he ever had to field. He scored three centuries in 1904, including 125 against Essex at Leyton when he shared in a stand of 296 for the third wicket with Reg Spooner. His two outstanding bowling performances came that year, and both were against Gloucestershire, taking nine for 37 at Gloucester and eight for 50 at Aigburth. Hallows reached his last championship innings needing 15 runs to complete the double and was given help by the Derbyshire bowlers and fielders to get there.

Among Lancashire's noteworthy wins that season was one over Kent at Old Trafford late in May. J. T. Tyldesley scored a marvellous 146 in Lancashire's total of 292, but when Kent started their first innings on the final day of a match badly affected by rain, only 4 hours 20 minutes remained. Hallows and Cuttell opened the bowling and between them took seventeen wickets as Kent were bowled out for 122 and 42 to earn victory by an innings and 128 with half an hour to spare.

One of Willis Cuttell's two centuries that summer came in a total of 580 against Somerset at Old Trafford, a total that was the highest in a county match in Lancashire at the time. MacLaren, J. T. Tyldesley and A. H. Hornby also hit hundreds, the only occasion in Lancashire's history when an innings included four separate centuries.

Brearley took seventy-seven wickets in the championship, four of them coming in one over at Derby when he took wickets with the first, second, fifth and sixth balls.

One of the most memorable games was the draw at Headingley where Lancashire struggled for a day and a half to avoid defeat after Yorkshire had scored 403. Lancashire were in a perilous position at 129 for six in their first innings when the final day of the match, for George Hirst's benefit, started. By lunch they had been dismissed for 173 and had lost one second innings wicket, that of William Findlay. The rest of the day was spent in denying Yorkshire, Tyldesley playing a leading part by scoring his first Roses century in ten years of county cricket. MacLaren batted an hour and a half for 5, Leslie Poidevin, an Australian amateur who was in his debut season, 70 minutes for 10, while Hallows played his part with a patient 21 not out. So Lancashire went home with a draw and the *City News* commented that the county had passed through the shadow of a great disaster. Certainly, if Yorkshire had won that match it would have put extra pressure on Lancashire in the closing stages of the season. The championship, in fact, became assured when Lancashire drew with Nottinghamshire at Old Trafford with two matches remaining. The all-round effort was also evident in the batting where, as well as three players topping 1,000, three more scored over 850. Tyldesley scored over 2,000 for the county for the second time, for an average of nearly 67, and Reg Spooner had his best summer yet with 1,699 runs.

An unusual feature of Lancashire's championship success was the high number of amateurs who took part. On average, each championship team contained five which contrasted sharply with the 1890s when there were usually two, at the outside three, in the team. This was the highest proportion for nearly twenty years with Spooner, MacLaren, Poidevin, Hornby, Brearley and Garnett the most regular in the side. About half the team was also made up of Lancashire-born players – again mostly the amateurs – with Tyldesley still the only constant, local-born professional. And of those from outside the county, Hornby was born in Cheshire and Sharp had played nearly all his formative cricket in Lancashire.

Yorkshire, who had won the championship four times in the six years between Lancashire's successes, reasserted themselves in 1905 when Lancashire found positions reversed and had to be content with second place. Lancashire started well enough with eight wins and a draw and held top place for much of the season. They were in second place breathing hard down Yorkshire's neck in mid-August when they went to Bristol to take on Gloucestershire without four players, Tyldesley, Spooner, MacLaren and Brearley, who were in the Test match. They lost by five wickets and with that defeat went the championship. If they had beaten Gloucestershire they would have pipped Yorkshire, who, to be fair, lost players to all five Tests that summer.

The Roses games that year again took on greater interest and importance and, fittingly enough, were shared. Lancashire won by an innings at Old Trafford when about 28,000 attended the opening day. Reg Spooner scored a century and Yorkshire, caught on an awful, rain-affected wicket, fell to Brearley and Kermode. Yorkshire took revenge at Sheffield, winning by 44 runs after being 101 behind on the first innings.

Poidevin, who came from New South Wales, played for Lancashire from 1904 to 1908, and had his best season in 1905 when he scored 1,433 runs for an average of nearly 40. His leg-break bowling, which brought him only forty-six wickets in his career, was less highly thought of. Yet he had one remarkable success when he went on at Worcester as a last expedient and took eight for 66.

Tyldesley was not quite the force he had been in 1904 but had a particularly outstanding innings against Nottinghamshire at Trent Bridge when he recorded the highest score of his career, 250. He was 156 when he was joined by the last batsman, wicket-keeper Bill Worsley, but in 85 minutes he scored 94 out of 141 before he was caught at cover after batting five and a half hours. Eleven bowlers tried to separate them as they took Lancashire from 486 to 627 with the fourth highest last-wicket stand in history. Tyldesley, who bought Worsley a new hat to celebrate his innings, spent 85 minutes over his first 50 runs, 75 for the second, 90 for the third, 50 for the fourth and little over half an hour for the fifth.

Another example of MacLaren's controversial captaincy came at Brighton where Lancashire were 587 for eight at lunch on the second day but continued to bat. To force a declaration Sussex put on

170

Charles Smith and Herbert Chaplin to bowl fast underhands, known in earlier days as 'caterpillars'. The declaration came at 601 for eight and when Sussex were bowled out for 383 – the last seven wickets having fallen in 135 minutes – MacLaren did not enforce the follow on, although there were 3 hours 45 minutes remaining. He chose to bat again and Lancashire reached 302 for six by the close.

Twenty-three-year-old Billy Cook from Preston made an impressive debut in the ten-wicket win over Gloucestershire, taking seven for 64 and four for 54. Yet, strangely, he played only eleven times for Lancashire, despite taking fifty-one wickets at 18.54 each. It was his young brother Lol who was to make more impact on county cricket in a career of 203 matches stretching from 1907 to 1923. Billy, like S. F. Barnes, said he found county cricket too tiring.

A match that produced two of the most remarkable, individual performances in the county's history came in 1905 when Somerset visited Old Trafford early in July. Somerset batted first and were shot out for 65 in 75 minutes, Brearley taking nine for 47 with his great pace and excellent length and hitting the stumps seven times. At 5.50 p.m. on that opening day Lancashire were 285 for seven in reply, but 139 runs were scored in the remaining 40 minutes, 93 of them by A. H. Hornby who was batting at No. 9. Hornby took his score to 106 the following day, hitting eighteen 4s and sharing in an astonishing ninth-wicket stand of 113 in 30 minutes with William Findlay. Judging from reports of the innings at least six of the hits would have been sixes today which would have considerably shortened the recorded time of 43 minutes for Hornby's century. At the time it stood second only to Gilbert Jessop's 40-minute century for Gloucestershire against Yorkshire at Harrogate in 1897. It was to stay Lancashire's fastest century until 1983 when Steve O'Shaughnessy equalled Percy Fender's world record of 35 minutes. Jessop again beat it in 1907 with a century in 42 minutes at Hastings but the only other person to beat it in the next seventy years was Fender in 1920. Somerset played better in the second innings but could not avoid defeat, or Brearley, who took eight for 90 to record what is still the only seventeen-wicket haul for Lancashire in championship cricket. And just to make it more memorable, he took four of the wickets in four balls!

WALTER BREARLEY was born in Bolton on 11 March 1876, and was educated at Tideswell Grammar School in Derbyshire. He played local cricket in Bolton and Bury, a fairly long apprenticeship before making his debut for Lancashire in 1902 when he was at the ripe age of 26. In a comparatively short career that finished in 1911 and was punctuated with disputes with the committee and periods out of the game, he took 690

wickets for the county at a cost of 18.70 runs each. He was an eccentric, one of the greatest characters Lancashire has known, a volatile person who had frequent brushes with authority. He was one of the outstanding fast bowlers of the early years of the century and it is surprising he did not play in more than four Tests. He himself was not backward at expressing his own surprise, perhaps even disgust, at Test team selections that did not include him. Sir Henry Leveson Gower recalled in his book, *Off and On the Field*, an occasion during his period as chairman of the Test selectors when Brearley was not chosen. 'I thought at the time and still think,' he wrote forty-four years later, 'that it was a mistake, though the captain [Archie MacLaren] disagreed with me. Brearley, however, was of my opinion. He stationed himself below the box I was occupying at Lord's, one of the clock tower boxes, and in a voice that was perfectly audible, made a running commentary on his omission, such as "I often get six wickets in an innings, and generally the leading batsmen." ' Brearley's crooning voice had caused spectators to gather and a policeman, who was parading the ground to keep the crowd in order, had to move him on.

Brearley was a great believer in keeping fit. He never smoked until cricket was over for the day, though he held that no fast bowler should be a teetotaller. He was capable of bowling, and willing to bowl, for long periods. It was said he would bowl all day on the hottest day in June and bowl with just as much pace and energy in his last over as in his first. He was a fast bowler, genuinely fast, yet he ran in from only seven yards with a body action which he himself described as being like a windmill. When he died *The Times* wrote 'As a bowler he was a model and as a man he was the most genuine human being that could be conceived.' Brearley revelled in the Roses matches and in fourteen games against Yorkshire between 1903 and 1911 he took 125 wickets – an average of nine a match – at a cost of 16 runs each.

Archie MacLaren, who was captain through most of Brearley's career, said of him:

> When playing regularly he was one of the few bowlers I should put unhesitatingly in the 'great' class. Here you had perfect length and a fizz off the pitch. Except on very rare occasions he was always turning the ball and used to swing away with his arm just enough to cause the highest in the land to make mistakes. Like Tom Richardson he could keep it up all day. He never spared himself either. Through the 1904 season when Lancashire gained the championship without losing a match, it might almost be said that he kept one end going unchanged. He was brimful of confidence and he justified in others his belief in himself. Give Brearley a wicket with a touch of fire in it and he was a man and a half to his side.

Brearley sent his son to Wrekin College near Telford – where the cricket pavilion was named after him – and often coached the boys. He was responsible for MCC sending a team to Wrekin for the first time in 1927, a team which included his old captain, Archie MacLaren, who was then 55 but still made top score in the match with 42. The following day, being Sunday, they were taken to chapel. It was a hot day and the two Lancashire veterans sat quietly side by side, their eyes closed, thinking of many things. At last, the sermon ended and the chaplain announced in a clear voice 'Hymn number 200. 200.' Those at the back heard Brearley's voice: 'Wake up Archie. This is where we take the new ball.'

Brearley also coached at Lord's where he spent many of his days in the summer. He was to be seen in the pavilion Long Room stamping in annoyance at the introduction of a new, young fast bowler. 'I could throw my hat down the wicket quicker than that,' he would declare. Brearley was at Lord's in the summer before his death, 1936. He met an old friend, C. B. Fry, on a wet day, and with their coats off, shirt sleeves rolled up, they were showing each other how to bat and bowl in the members' lunch room with the waitresses impatiently waiting to clear the tables for tea.

Brearley's batting was nothing more than an interesting diversion. He was last man and would ignore the gate and leap the fence on his way to the crease and would hurry, at times almost run, to the wicket. He frequently scorned gloves and did not always wear pads and tried hard, at least once an over, to smash the ball out of the ground.

He once bet Gilbert Jessop he would hit him to the boundary. And when Jessop rolled the ball down the pitch to the other bowler at the end of an over, Brearley seized his chance to hit the ball to the boundary. Jessop was not amused and when he batted started to hit out at Brearley who responded by bowling bouncers and head-high full tosses. Jessop was so upset that when he was out he refused to take any further part in the game and handed over the captaincy.

Brearley, however, was a genial, popular man with an attractive personality. His career was short – he took his 669 wickets in virtually seven seasons – but he left behind more impressions, more memories than many players who last three times as long. Brearley married the daughter of an hotelier in the Lake District and when he died, on 13 January 1937, aged 60, he was buried in the family grave at Bowness. He remains one of the top four or five outstanding fast bowlers Lancashire have ever had. But he should be remembered, too, just as much for his personality.

Although Old Trafford has always been a mainly male reserve, the women, as ever, have always known how to attract attention. The *City News*, just in passing, mentioned one who was quite a regular attender in the early 1900s, and if nothing else it brought a breath of fresh air into the customary cricket reports as reference was made to . . . 'A fair lady, who goes to Old Trafford in her own brougham, a sweet dream of summer drapery, exhaling fresh and pleasant odours.' What a difference such sweetness and delight would have made to the pavilion.

Lancashire broke new ground in 1906 by taking a county match to Blackpool. Festival matches had become established there, but the first championship match, against Leicestershire, started on Monday 30 July. The *Leicester Daily Mercury* described the arrangements as being of the most crude and primitive description and, judging by the shortage of covered accommodation, deduced that rain was unheard of on the Fylde coast. The *Manchester Guardian* also used the word primitive in describing the accommodation, but found compensations in the surroundings and in the spirit that pervaded the ground. It said:

> The conditions in some respect recall the happy, irre-sponsible spirit of village cricket. The spectators could sit on the grass around the ropes and occasionally exchanged ideas with an unoccupied player, or they could watch the game while strolling about on the sandhills which overlook the seats. From the hill – it is hardly less – on which the ground stands you may look down on one side upon the Blackpool Tower and Wheel; on the other, the view is across open fields in which the haymakers are at work. The playing ground is not level in any part. It is all on the slope. Boundaries are small compared to Old Trafford. The accommodation for the public – especially when the crowd runs, as it did yesterday, to close on 5,000 – strikes one as a little too primitive. For example it was curious to see leading members of the Lancashire club sitting around an empty luncheon table and being gravely informed by a waiter that the players had to lunch first and that his ability to serve other guests would depend on whether the players left anything. Their faces were a study. It is to be hoped the players were not too hungry.

The *Manchester Evening Chronicle* the following day reported that a cruiser and a torpedo flotilla had dropped anchor the previous night just off the North Pier, counter attractions which hit the gate at the start of the second day's play at the cricket match. Lancashire won the match by an innings with Jack Sharp scoring a century and a bowler called Bill Gregson, from Lancaster, performing the hat-trick. Gregson, who was playing in only his second match, took another wicket two balls later to give him four in five and in the match he had the rather impressive figures of 9.3–6–8–5 and 14.1–1–68–4. Yet Gregson, a fast bowler, played only five matches for Lancashire, all in 1906, finishing with twenty-four wickets at 17.83 runs each. Oddly enough, that was the second hat-trick of the season against the same opponents following Alec Kermode's three in three at Leicester in the first match of the season. This was one of the closest finishes in which Lancashire had been involved. Leicestershire, needing 161 for only their second win over Lancashire, were 115 for seven at the start of the final day. They got within two of victory with two wickets standing, but lost both wickets to Willis Cuttell and Kermode, and Lancashire had won by one run.

This was to be Cuttell's last season. He was 41 but age did not weary him as he showed against Somerset at Aigburth where he scored 95, batting at No. 9, and took five wickets in the first innings.

Kermode was one of several overseas players involved with counties at the time, a state of affairs that produced criticism from one newspaper which said that Nottinghamshire and Yorkshire would soon be the only counties with native-born Elevens even in the sense of belonging to Britain. Reference was made to Charles Llewellyn (Hampshire) from South Africa, Francis Tarrant (Middlesex), Jack Cuffe (Worcestershire), Jack Dwyer (Sussex) and Kermode from Australia, and Dan Reese (Essex) from New Zealand, plus several others soon to qualify. 'The championship is being reduced to an absurdity,' was the opinion.

Archie MacLaren was still captaining the side after overcoming his previous problems, not least of which often seemed to be money. As an amateur he was not to qualify for a benefit but a subscription brought in between £1,200 and £1,300 from friends in England and Australia. During lunch in the game against Warwickshire at Old Trafford A. N. Hornby, the club president, presented him with a cheque and a grandfather clock, plus a diamond and pearl necklace and pendant for Mrs MacLaren.

One man who did qualify for a benefit, and a handsome one at that, was J. T. Tyldesley who was granted the match against Yorkshire in 1906 and which helped raise him a record sum of £3,111, a figure that was not to be surpassed until Cyril Washbrook's benefit realized £14,000 in 1948. Tyldesley approached the event with the highest score of his career, an innings of 295 not out against Kent at Old Trafford, a match that also marked the debut of Frank Woolley, then 19 years old. Tyldesley went in at 12.05 p.m. with the score 1 for one and he batted 5 hours 15 minutes for a total of 531. He could do no wrong. If he mis-hit, the ball passed out of the reach of a fielder and went to the boundary. Fielders, including Woolley, dropped several easy chances, enabling Tyldesley to

175

record the highest individual score on the Old Trafford ground, and second highest only to MacLaren's 424. His innings, as described by the *City News*, was one of 'splendid cutting, vigorous driving and pretty leg placing, diversified by flukes and dropped catches.' Tyldesley hit forty-three 4s, eight 3s, twenty-six 2s, and forty-seven singles. Yet it was one of the most disappointing days of his career. He dearly wanted to reach 300 and this was the nearest he came.

Frank Woolley recalled the innings thirty-three years later in an article for *Wisden*:

> We lost the toss and I was put at third man. Tyldesley cut one very hard, but misjudging it altogether, the ball hit me on the chest. Our captain, Mr C. H. B. Marsham, feeling sorry for me, moved me to mid off and mid on; in each place I dropped a skier, although one was off a no-ball. Johnny Tyldesley was hitting us all over the place when he was joined by the last man, W. Worsley, the wicket-keeper, who was reckoned the worst batsman in the world. We all wanted to see Tyldesley get 300. I was bowling at one end and our captain called us together and said 'Who can we put on the other end to bowl a maiden over to Worsley so that Tyldesley can get his 300?' The cry went up 'Put "Punter" on' and he was told to bowl away from the stumps. His first four balls were well to the off, but to everyone's amazement, including 'Punter' Humphreys, the fifth swung in viciously and knocked down Worsley's leg stump. So Tyldesley did not realize his ambition. My analysis was one for 103 and Humphreys had one for 101. He came in for some rare 'chipping' in the dressing room for having to be satisfied with only Worsley's wicket.

Woolley scored a half century in the second innings after getting a duck in the first and as he left the field, Johnny Tyldesley, who was at long leg, said 'Wait a minute, son,' as he neared the gate. 'Well played,' he said. 'That was a good innings. You'll play for England some day.'

JOHN THOMAS TYLDESLEY was born at Roe Green, near Worsley, on 22 November 1873, and played his early cricket with those two villages before going to Little Lever, near Bolton, from where he went to Old Trafford on trial. He became known by his initials or as 'John Tommy' and was regarded as the greatest professional batsman Lancashire had ever had until his brother Ernest came along to challenge him. And even though Ernest finished up with more runs, J. T. was generally regarded by people who had the good fortune to see them both as the

superior player. Ernest certainly thought his brother the better player although that might have been modesty and brotherly love speaking. Ernest finished with more runs and a better average, but J. T. batted on poorer wickets. He was an attacking batsman, a powerful driver of the ball, and was noticed for his quickness of foot, leaping to the ball with his bat on high. He was a picture of rapid and ruthless aggression. He often used to give the advice: 'Get into the ballroom as often as you can.' When asked in 1911 if he attributed some of his success to dancing he replied: 'I have done my share of whirling buxom Lancashire lasses round a room, and that helps a man to keep light and quick on his feet.'

Tyldesley had a vast array of strokes, many of them of his own creation. He cut savagely, often from the middle stump, and was widely regarded as the best batsman of all time on a bad wicket. One of the finest innings was his 62 out of England's 103 on a terrible wicket at Melbourne in 1904. He astonished everybody by the daring way he attacked the bowling and Pelham Warner, the captain, considered it one of his greatest performances. He also scored 97 in the first innings – the last 50 on the stickiest wicket he had ever experienced – and regarded those two innings as his best ever, particularly as they paved the way for victory. Tyldesley played thirty-one Tests with a batting average of 30.75 and scored four centuries, three of them against Australia at Edgbaston, Headingley and The Oval. The other was against South Africa at Cape Town in his second Test. For Lancashire he played 507 matches – a figure exceeded only by his brother Ernest and Jack Sharp – and scored 31,949 runs, second only to Ernest.

J. T. was nearly 41 when the First World War broke out and he thought he would probably never play county cricket again. He knew he would be around 45 at best after an interval of several years and did not think he would be able to cope. When cricket resumed in 1919 he was persuaded to play although he would have preferred to retire. But Lancashire, in common with other counties, needed players of experience and Tyldesley played through 1919. He scored three more centuries, one of them a massive 272 against Derbyshire at Chesterfield, a tribute to his great skill and fitness. He averaged 43 that year and his 1,000 runs in a season were his nineteenth in succession – and not even his brother, with eighteen, could beat that. He played just once more for the first team, four years later when he was coach and was asked to captain the side in place of Jack Sharp who was injured.

One of his favourite grounds was Edgbaston. He called it his lucky ground, because as well as scoring his first three centuries there – two of them in one match – he scored ten in all there for Lancashire, plus one more for England.

Tyldesley was regarded as a gentleman, a modest man who was well loved. He was teetotal and a non-smoker, and an occasional teacher at

177

the Independent Methodist Sunday School, Roe Green, as well as a member of the chapel choir. He was generally regarded as an unselfish player who always put the team first, and when a game rested on him, Tyldesley could be electrifying. In a match against Essex at Old Trafford in 1902 Tyldesley had got his century and Lancashire needed about 15 to win with three wickets in hand. A storm was on the way and Claude Buckenham, the fast bowler, attacked as thunder and lightning arrived. In that one over Tyldesley made 16 runs and a few minutes later the ground was under water.

Tyldesley was an advocate of games of one innings played over two days. He believed that cricket stuck to three-day, two-innings matches only because the fathers and grandfathers of those in charge had played it. 'But remember then a team drove by coach and the match was not worth playing unless it was a holiday for several days,' he said in 1916. He thought, too, that players became jaded and strained over three days and that a one-innings match would make cricket livelier and put the teams on their toes.

J. T. became Lancashire's coach and also went into business as a sports outfitter in Deansgate, Manchester, a shop that still exists today as Cooke and Tyldesley. He continued to play for the second team for many years and Bill Farrimond used to recall batting with him against S. F. Barnes at Haslingden in 1926. Barnes bowled well for Staffordshire, although he took only one wicket and when Tyldesley, batting No. 7, went in to join Farrimond, he told him: 'I thought my days of scoring centuries were over, but I'm going to get one against him.' And Tyldesley, then aged 52, scored 127 in two and a half hours without a chance.

Tyldesley died on 27 November 1930, five days after his fifty-seventh birthday, as he was pulling on his boots to go to work. He left behind a rich history of the finest batsmanship played by a great professional.

Tyldesley's benefit match started on Monday, 6 August 1906, under a cloudless sky. The gates were opened at 9 a.m. and by 11 a.m. the gates were closed except for members and those who had bought three-day tickets. Three to four thousand were turned away. The crowd was estimated at over 26,000, the ladies' pavilion was ablaze with colour and the lawns were occupied by small parties of ladies and gentlemen who, finding it impossible to get seats from which to see the game, had decided to make a picnic of the occasion. The weather stayed splendid throughout the game and about 23,000 turned up for the second day. The crowd was described by the *City News* as the most orderly, soberest and best tempered ever. People had come to see the game, and the usual horseplay and prehistoric jests of Roses matches were absent. Some of that horseplay had been evident in the earlier game at Bradford where Walter Brearley had taken a return catch off David Denton but, thinking it was a bump ball, had not appealed and walked back for his next delivery. MacLaren questioned Brearley about it, said he did not agree with the bowler, and appealed to the umpire. Denton was given out and later said he had no complaint. He knew it was not a bump ball but was not going to refuse a second innings. But the crowd did not like it, the hooting started all round the ground and the noise was so great that MacLaren said he and Brearley could not hear one another. Said MacLaren 'If it had not been for the good feeling and friendship which has always existed between the teams, I would have taken the players off.'

Lancashire played Cambridge University again in 1907, their first encounter in twenty-five years, and although there was only one Blue in the University side, the county lost by the huge margin of an innings and 204 runs. This awful happening was soon forgotten when Lancashire, with a much-depleted team, pulled off a 6-run win over Kent, the 1906 champions. And a satisfactory part of the victory was the number of Lancastrians in the side with seven of them born and bred in the county and none of the others having come to the county for the purpose of playing cricket. The Lancashire-born players were Jim Hallows, J. T. Tyldesley, Jim Heap, Henry Stanning, a Leyland amateur, Alec Eccles, Bill Huddleston and Harry Dean plus Harry Makepeace (born in Middlesbrough), Jack Sharp (Hereford), Frank Harry (Torquay) and Bill Worsley (Wandsworth, Surrey). The *City News* commented 'After this striking and great success of the native born, let us hope the committee will take heart of grace and rely on the sterling material ready to hand instead of importing an inferior article from the ends of the earth' (which presumably referred to Kermode in particular and Poidevin, an amateur, in part). Another Lancastrian who would have been there if he had not fallen out with the committee was Walter Brearley who had dropped out of the team in 1906 after taking forty-nine wickets in the first five matches. He played a few representative matches in 1907 before returning to the team the following season.

The Aigburth pitch was still producing problems and two matches on tricky wickets produced results of sharp contrast for Lancashire. After Tyldesley had scored a masterly 117, Sussex were bowled out for 29 in under an hour to give Lancashire victory by 307 runs in June. They returned two months later to be bowled out for 82 and 37 by Nottinghamshire who won by an innings and 131 runs to clinch the championship. Another wicket with a problem was at Lord's, only this one was due to an angry crowd trampling all over it and forcing Archie MacLaren to abandon the match on the second day. The

179

game was played at the end of July when Middlesex were leading the championship table and play was possible for only 45 minutes on the opening day when Lancashire scored 57. There was no rain on the second day and nearly 1,000 people were allowed to pay for admission. After waiting patiently for some hours they became indignant and gathered in front of the pavilion where one of them made several speeches. Francis Lacey, the MCC secretary, told them they would be allowed in free on the final day if there was no play, but when the umpires went out for an inspection at 4.30 p.m. and decided to draw the stumps there was a demonstration described as being without parallel at Lord's. The umpires were followed by a hooting, yelling mob and had to be escorted by two policemen. Once the umpires had reached the pavilion the crowd turned and, ignoring the protecting ropes, stampeded over the pitch.

MacLaren considered the wicket so seriously damaged that after the ground was cleared he made the following statement to the Press 'Owing to the pitch having been deliberately torn up by the public, I, as captain of the Lancashire Eleven, cannot see my way to continue the game, the groundsman bearing me out that the wicket could not again be put right. The match is accordingly abandoned.' By the following day the damage done to the pitch was considered to have been overestimated and the *Manchester Guardian* correspondent who inspected the area said the wicket had rolled out without any sign of the trampling and had suffered practically no damage. The newspaper suggested that in abandoning the match MacLaren probably intended reading Lord's a much-needed lesson and it was suggested that his action had met with general approval in the cricket world. 'By his firm action he upheld the dignity of cricket and did his duty by the game and the team he captains.' It is interesting to observe that MacLaren had learned his cricket and captaincy with A. N. Hornby, another man who more than once threatened to abandon matches. Both had the same strength of character but with a tendency, perhaps, to go over the top.

MacLaren's only century in the five years from 1905 to 1909 came this year against Warwickshire at Old Trafford. But he played a marvellous innings of 92 to help secure a one-wicket win over Derbyshire at Old Trafford. However it had not been a good season. Lancashire finished sixth and were clearly weak in bowling where the improving Harry Dean, a left-arm pace bowler from Burnley, worked hard. Huddleston and Harry had their days, but there was little other support. And while Lancashire were struggling in 1907, Nottinghamshire were heading the table as undisputed champions for the first time for twenty-one years. And on top of their bowling averages, with 153 wickets at 11.78 runs each, was Albert Hallam

180

who had taken 211 wickets in six seasons for Lancashire but who had become wearied by illness and was thought not to be strong enough for the rigorous demands of county cricket.

A. N. Hornby had, by now, been president for fourteen years and at the annual meeting in December 1907, came an unexpected move to dethrone him. The suggestion was that the position should be held only for two years and that he should be 'some nobleman or gentleman whose residence in Lancashire is in a different division of the county from that of his two immediate predecessors.' It was said there was nothing personal in it but there was still a feeling that the county was mainly a Manchester affair and that it existed chiefly for South East Lancashire. This feeling had led to a lack of interest in Lancashire county cricket, and evidence was supplied in the decreasing number of spectators and members. Ten years earlier there were 2,727 members as against 2,602 then and it was felt that in order to induce the whole county to take a greater interest, it would help if the president were chosen from various parts of the county. Hornby's great service was referred to but it was also pointed out that qualities that made for success on the field were not necessarily those for the committee room or the council chamber. There were grumblings about the state of the finances, the loss of members and of some of the county's best players. The committee, however, would not support the move and the resolution was withdrawn. Nevertheless, within ten years the club had decided that presidents should stay in office for only two years.

Chapter 8 1908–18

'The years up to The First World War marked a decline
in Lancashire's fortunes and a waning of interest in
county cricket as a whole.'

Archie MacLaren was now 36. His powers were declining. He
played in fewer matches, his batting was generally well below the
high standards he had set, and after fourteen years of captaincy in
which he had missed only a couple of seasons, he handed over in
1908 to Albert Henry Hornby, the president's son. MacLaren continued to play for Lancashire up to the First World War, but made
few significant contributions once he had given up the captaincy.
Hornby had many of his father's qualities, enthusiasm, drive, love
of the game and of Lancashire cricket in particular, support of the
professionals, the sort of captaincy that inspires by unselfish example.
He captained Lancashire right through to the First World War, seven
years of moderate performances in which they finished runners-up
once, but also sank to their lowest-ever positions, particularly in 1914
when they finished 11th. Walter Brearley had two fine years in 1908
and 1909 but it was the great-hearted Harry Dean who sustained
Lancashire through this period with help from Bill Huddleston.
Finding a good spin bowler was not easy and just when Cec Parkin
burst on the scene in 1914, the War came along to interrupt cricket
for four years. The batting largely took care of itself. J. T. Tyldesley
and Jack Sharp were the backbone through the years supported by
Alfred Hartley, Harry Makepeace and, just before the war, Ernest
Tyldesley. Hornby and the fierce-hitting Kenneth MacLeod made
valuable contributions and there was also the occasional inspiration
of Reg Spooner whose best year came in 1911 when he was 30.
Hartley scored his first century for Lancashire at the start of

the 1908 season but the man who captured attention was Ralph Whitehead, the third and so far the last man to score a century for the county on his debut. Whitehead was a 24-year-old professional cricketer from Ashton-under-Lyne, a middle-order batsman who could also bowl reasonably fast. His debut was against the champions, Nottinghamshire, at Old Trafford and at the end of the first day he was 33 not out. He batted nearly three hours for his 131 not out and shared in a seventh-wicket partnership of 188 with Hornby that played such a big part in Lancashire's three-wicket win. For the most part he met the ball with the full face of the bat and played with restraint and self-possession. He was tall, which gave him a long reach, and he had a loose, relaxed style in which his three best scoring shots were the straight drive either side of the bowler, the front-foot drive in front of cover point, and a low cut either side of point. He showed good nerve and excellent defence in a fine debut which earned him a tremendous reception when he returned to the pavilion. He was warmly congratulated by his colleagues and Hornby even presented him with his county cap – a compliment indeed for a player in only his second day of first-class cricket.

At the time it must have seemed a good idea to put Whitehead on to bowl as well. After all, it just had to be his day. But four of his first five deliveries on that second day of the match were no-balled for throwing, and there was a vigorous exchange of opinion between Hornby and the umpire, Tom Brown, before Whitehead was taken off. He was put on again on the third morning, this time from the other end, but was still no-balled by Brown, this time from square leg, twice in his opening over, before Hornby again took him off. Whitehead overcame the problem and went on to take 300 wickets for Lancashire in a career that lasted until 1914.

Lancashire experimented with a Saturday start in 1908, but thought nothing was proved in the game against Yorkshire in which 13,135 paid on the opening day for a total attendance of about 16,600. The popular side was packed but there was spare room in all the stands on the pavilion side. The Monday, which was August Bank Holiday, still proved most popular with 22,493 paying at the turnstiles, which was 9,358 more than Saturday. The *City News* said the Saturday crowd was not what you would expect for the opening day of a Roses match and thought the strongest argument in favour was that many people who would like to see first-class cricket could spare the time only on Saturday. 'On Monday there was an enormous crowd, but it was not an old-time Yorkshire match crowd,' the newspaper continued. 'The rough horseplay, prehistoric humour, overflowing animal spirits, were less in evidence than on any previous occasion we can remember.' Still, the *Manchester Evening Chronicle* referred to the typical holiday crowd, 'Songs and jokes were rife all round the packed enclosure, and bursts of laughter were mingled with strains of such melodies as "Swanee River" and "Cock Robin".' Yorkshire won the match by 190 runs and Lancashire's bowling weakness was exploited in the next match by Worcestershire who scored at 100 runs an hour to get the 234 needed to win after J. T. Tyldesley had scored an unbeaten 101 in a total of 217.

Walter Brearley had two splendid seasons in 1908 and 1909 with 272 wickets at under 16 runs each. And with Harry Dean taking over 100 wickets each season all Lancashire needed was a top-class spin bowler to turn them into a championship side again. But there was not one to be found and although Lancashire made a strong challenge for the title with a flying start to the 1909 season they had to be content with runners-up place again, for the eighth time in twenty years. One of the three victories that started the season came against Somerset at Bath where Kenneth MacLeod and Harry Makepeace shared in a stand of 185 in 90 minutes. MacLeod, a Liverpool-born amateur, was only 21 and still at Cambridge University where he was also a Rugby Union player – he was to represent Scotland on the wing – a sprinter and a long jumper. He was a powerful hitter of a cricket ball and his maiden century, achieved at Bath, was an innings of 128, which lasted only an hour and a half and included eight 6s and eleven 4s. His first 25 runs came in 10 minutes and in one over from Len Braund he hit a 6, three 4s and a 2 – 20 runs in all. Most of his strokes were terrific on drives or hits to square leg. Lancashire were 81 for five when MacLeod went in and he hit lustily to reach his 50 in 38 minutes.

'Red Rose', the experienced *Manchester Evening Chronicle* writer, reported:

> MacLeod continued to thrash Braund's bowling by furious leg hitting. He was given a life on the edge of the boundary by Daniell at 77, and he repaid that favour by the longest and highest square leg hit I have seen for 25 years. I remember William Shrewsbury hitting Clayton out of the old Notts Castle ground with a flick of the wrist as it seemed, but MacLeod's fifth hit for six must have been over 120 yards from the wicket when it fell. The ball sailed through the air like a balloon. Such leg hitting exceeded even Harold Garnett when he was clouting the balls.

MacLeod completed his century by taking 14 runs off one over from Bill Greswell, two of his on drives clearing the ring for six. His century had taken him 63 minutes, the second fastest in Lancashire's history to A. H. Hornby's 43 minutes in 1905. Commented 'Red Rose':

Have we a Jessopian smiter in Lancashire? The truth must be told: we have. Need I say that MacLeod had never before made 50 for the Palatine. I hope he will make many more. We all love a hitter as much as a lord. MacLeod's hitting was positively phenomenal, and I have not seen such square-leg hitting since Jessop dropped on one knee at The Oval seven years ago and hit the Australians for 104 so that England won by one wicket. Of course, this bowling was poorer, but I have never seen any man hit so many sixes in any first-class match. Moreover, the Somerset scorer declared that it was unprecedented on this ground or any other that he had ever seen. Could we have a finer transformation a great piece of hitting can effect in one hour?

The *Manchester Guardian* said MacLeod hit with a style that not even Gilbert Jessop at his best could have improved upon; the *City News* said his batting was more a reminder of Charles Thornton than Jessop. Whoever he was like, MacLeod was to make a vigorous, lively contribution to Lancashire's batting for seventy-five matches up to 1913 in which he scored four centuries. While MacLeod was hitting his 128 and either sending the ball to the boundary or out of the ground, Harry Makepeace plodded on with his usual solid imperturbability, still looking for his first century after four seasons in first-class cricket.

Although MacLaren's form had been poor for some years, England were still choosing him for Test matches and recalled him as captain for the 1909 five-Test series which Australia won 2–1. Tyldesley played in four of the matches but even without these two and Walter Brearley for one Test, Lancashire still overcame Essex by an innings at Aigburth. Yorkshire, however, were always a different kettle of fish, especially if George Hirst was in there fighting. He destroyed Lancashire on his own several times, including his career-best of nine for 23, but at Old Trafford this year, when Lancashire needed 123 to win the low-scoring match, he removed MacLaren, Tyldesley, Hartley and Sharp for 4 runs. Lancashire were 6 for five and lost by 65 runs after Brearley had taken nine for 80 in the first innings and Huddleston eight for 24 in the second.

Harry Dean's two best bowling returns came this year when he took nine for 35 in the innings win over Warwickshire at Aigburth, and nine for 31 – after having six for 1 at one stage – against Somerset at Old Trafford. The game against Warwickshire was noteworthy for the introduction of the man who was to score more runs for Lancashire than any other player, Ernest Tyldesley,

J. T.'s younger brother, then 20 years old. He scored 61 in his first innings by steady, confident batting. Said the *City News* of him after his next match 'He shapes in excellent style with the bat and as his fielding is above the average he ought to prove a most valuable recruit to the county ranks.'

The years up to the First World War marked a decline in Lancashire's fortunes and a waning of interest in county cricket as a whole. The number of attractive players had dwindled and there were other interests like motoring, golf, bowls and lawn tennis to compete with cricket. One member at Old Trafford explained that he attended games not so much because of an intense interest in the game but because it was pleasant to be among a keenly-interested crowd and to experience a little of the prevalent interest and excitement. But latterly, he said – and he was commenting in 1912 – he had missed all that. 'The crowds are not only smaller but they are painfully quiet and undemonstrative and it becomes a little dreary sitting round the ground in a dead silence, only occasionally broken when something exceptional happens,' he said. 'Only the keenly interested go and the casual visitor, who is usually the more boisterous, stays away.' It was also pointed out that a few years earlier, whenever there was a big game, the ladies' pavilion was often a blaze of colour. Now the visitors were dotted about in twos and threes. Attendance at county matches had gone out of fashion with a large number of ladies. The popular side thought slow play was killing the game which had become more a business, less a sport.

Underhand bowling was also on the wane, but one man still practising it with some success was 34-year-old George Simpson-Hayward, a gentleman farmer who played with Worcestershire. His flicked underhand lobs had accounted for Archie MacLaren, Alfred Hartley and Kenneth MacLeod in 1909, each of them being bowled with what was described as tortuous, flighty stuff, real puzzlers with four men in the outfield. The *Liverpool Daily Post* said underhands were a sore test of patience. 'I wonder that lob bowling has gone so much out of fashion,' wrote the correspondent. 'It has always paid and it always will so long as human nature is liable to err and so long as we have so much mechanical medium pace and fast bowling.'

The start of the 1910 season was marred by the death, at the age of 36, of Jim Hallows, the best all-rounder, next to A. G. Steel, born in Lancashire. Only six years earlier he had performed the double of 100 wickets and 1,000 runs and played a major part in Lancashire winning the championship. There was no play between 2 and 3.15 p.m. on the second day of the match against Essex at Aigburth because of the funeral. The hat was taken round the ground for his widow.

George Hirst, the great Yorkshire all-rounder, was now 38 and in his twentieth season in first-class cricket, but still able to torment Lancashire, and in 1910 perform the crowning feat of his illustrious career. Hirst, bowling at something like his old pace and with fire, dismissed nine batsmen in an hour and a half – eight of them bowled – for 23 runs as Lancashire were dismissed for 61. And the following year, when Yorkshire were wobbling, he scored 156 to set up the innings win.

The coming of the motor car which, it was said, was helping to bring down the attendances at cricket matches, was seen to great advantage during the Tunbridge Wells week when Lancashire were one of Kent's opponents. The tents, as usual gay with bunting, fringed the ground, but the motor parties were something new. There were ninety-nine motors on the ground, drawn up on the opposite side to the tents. Each one was a movable grandstand. No one, apparently, suffered any inconvenience unless it was the Lancashire batsmen at the close of the day. The sun was setting and was reflected by one of the glass screens with such a crimson glare that one of them asked for the glass to be covered up. At the request of Edward Dillon, one of the fielders, a rug was thrown over it.

The 1910 season was noteworthy for two remarkable victories in which Lancashire were required to score 400 runs for victory. This had never before been achieved in a county match; in fact, the highest number of runs scored for victory before this was Leicestershire's 350 for five against Worcestershire in 1904. The record was broken at Old Trafford in June after Nottinghamshire had controlled the game for two days and had gone into the third in an apparently invincible position, 352 ahead with eight wickets standing. They had not enforced the follow-on, despite a first innings lead of 214, and in their haste for runs on the final morning they lost the remaining eight wickets for 47 runs in 45 minutes. Lancashire's target for victory was still a staggering 400 in 315 minutes, but a third-wicket partnership between J. T. Tyldesley and Jack Sharp put them well on the way. They put on 191 in 150 minutes followed by a fifth-wicket stand of 80 in 42 minutes between Ernest Tyldesley and Ralph Whitehead that maintained the right tempo. Lancashire were 327 for five with 73 more needed when Hornby, who had not been able to bat in the first innings after twisting his knee when fielding, hobbled down the pavilion steps. It was thought to be a blunder at the time because it was considered he would not be able to stand up to the strain. Short runs were no use so he hit boundaries. He lost three partners and at 364 for eight, with 36 runs needed, it looked as if Lancashire had lost. But Lol Cook stayed half an hour for three and Hornby, hitting brilliantly, carried Lancashire to a famous victory with an innings of 55 not out.

The crowd dashed across the ground and Hornby was carried shoulder high to the pavilion. Men shook hands with one another, hats were thrown in the air, there was dancing and singing on the ground. Long after the match was over people were still there. Choruses of 'For He's A Jolly Good Fellow' rang out and every time a player appeared on the balcony, the applause was deafening. To commemorate the game the committee presented each player with a solid silver matchbox. No doubt the committee thought this marvellous achievement would stay a record for many years. Yet only eight weeks later, on 13 August 1910, Lancashire did it again. This time the target was 403, the time available was about the same, 315 minutes, and the victims were Hampshire on their own ground at Southampton. Sharp again played a leading part with an innings of 150 in under three hours as he and Harry Makepeace, who scored 95, put on 242 for the fourth wicket to set up the victory by five wickets with 50 minutes to spare. Another major innings came from opener Alfred Hartley, generally regarded as a plodder but who took the bowling by the scruff of the neck to hit 81 out of 137 for three in 85 minutes.

Another spell of fast scoring came against Somerset at Old Trafford where Hartley, having the best season of his life to become one of *Wisden*'s Cricketers of the Year, and Tyldesley scored 295 in 130 minutes as they took the score from 25 for one to 320 for two.

Hornby was unable to play for a month after his heroics against Nottinghamshire at Old Trafford and among his deputies as captain was J. T. Tyldesley, the respected professional. Tyldesley led the team at Trent Bridge although there were two amateurs in the team, Alfred Hartley and Jim Jones, a Liverpool wicket-keeper who played four games in 1910 in place of Bill Worsley. Tyldesley, who scored 77 out of 88 in an hour on a sticky wicket, took the opportunity of following a custom that was often observed in earlier days, when the not out batsman of the first innings opened the second innings when they batted again. So Makepeace, 23 not out in the first innings, became Hartley's partner.

Dean had an outstanding season with 133 championship wickets, including sixteen at Bath with nine for 77 and seven for 26 against Somerset. But perhaps an even more startling display was that of Jim Heap who took fourteen wickets in a day at Northampton. Lancashire had scored 314 for five in four hours' play between showers on the first two days and won by an innings when Northamptonshire were bowled out for 114 and 88. Heap went on at the pavilion end when 21 runs had been scored and never went off as he took five for 50 and nine for 43, his career-best return. Lancashire won two matches that week and lost only ten wickets, beating Yorkshire by an innings as well.

It was immediately after these two wins that Lancashire were beaten by Sussex at Brighton in a match of fluctuating fortunes. Lancashire were 204 for two in reply to Sussex's 255 . . . and then came a remarkable collapse of wickets as thirteen fell for 68 runs. Lancashire's last eight went for 30 runs, Sussex's first five for 38, and when the second day's play ended Sussex were 68 for six, only 89 ahead. The odds on Lancashire, so one commentator said, were a guinea to a gooseberry. Yet Lancashire lost by 11 runs. They travelled to Southampton for the next match against Hampshire, a journey which, by the scheduled train service, took over four hours for 65 miles. But J. H. Maden, a Lancashire vice president, was so pleased with the way Lancashire had fought at Brighton that he chartered a special train at a cost of £22.

This was also the year of Jack Sharp's benefit, the game against Yorkshire which Lancashire won by an innings and 111 runs and in which Reg Spooner hit the only double century recorded by a Lancashire player in Roses matches. Sharp showed his appreciation by presenting Spooner with a gold matchbox. Nearly 34,000 people paid over the three days, bringing in £1,378 11s at the gate, to which was added £71 1s 5d from collections on the ground, £608 16s 4d from subscriptions, and £10 2s 4d bank interest. Payments of £221 2s 7d included £126 0s 6d insurance of gate receipts, £35 0s 6d for the gatekeepers, £25 19s amateurs' expenses, and £90 professionals' wages, leaving a profit for Sharp of £1,679 11s 1d. Among the subscribers were Gilbert Jessop, with a guinea, Albert Ward 16 shillings, Harry Makepeace 2 shillings, while the gatemen refunded £33 5s 6d.

JACK SHARP was born in Hereford on 15 February 1878, and as a young man was a clerk . . . for three weeks. 'I preferred to breathe rather than be asphyxiated, even if I was going to make nothing of games,' he said. At 17 he was on the groundstaff of Liverpool Cricket Club at Aigburth before moving to Leyland, a club which provided Lancashire with many of their players. He made his debut for Lancashire in 1899 when he was 21 and established himself as a regular in the team almost right from that game. He extended his career over twenty-seven years, playing as a professional for the first sixteen years up to the First World War, then as an amateur for the last seven years, following the War. He was more successful as a bowler early in his career and in 1901 his fast-medium deliveries earned him 113 wickets, the only time he topped 100. But it was as a batsman that he was to become more famous and he reached

189

1,000 runs in a season for Lancashire ten times, eight of them coming in his heyday between 1905 and 1912, including 2,099 in all first-class matches in 1911. He was one of the most consistently successful batsmen of the time with a sound defence, a strong off drive and excellent cut, and in 1909 he played in three Tests against Australia. He scored 103 not out at The Oval, the only English century of the series, yet was never called on to play for England again. One of his favourite jokes was to tell how he went to The Oval as a fast bowler and got a century instead.

Sharp was Lancashire's captain for three years from 1923 and when he was appointed there were some fears as to how he would handle the discipline of a side which included such diverse characters and personalities as Ted McDonald, Cec Parkin and Dick Tyldesley. But there were no problems. As one writer put it 'For a man with his genial nature and irresistible smile the other players had no alternative but to work themselves to skin and bone; like his famous comrade-in-arms, J. T. Tyldesley, Sharp had mellowed under the influence of cricket into a man of extraordinary kindliness and charm.' Although he was 47 in 1925 his skill and unquenchable spirit made him a valuable member of the side. His retirement was hastened by a piece of barracking during Cec Parkin's benefit match against Middlesex at Old Trafford. Sharp was a superb fielder, but dropped a catch first ball and was so abused he was very upset and decided to retire. He was persuaded to play again but retired at the end of the season after one of the most celebrated careers by a Lancashire player. He took part in 518 matches for Lancashire – a total which has been beaten only by Ernest Tyldesley – scored 21,815 runs for them at an average of 30.89, and took 433 wickets (27.30). He became the first former professional cricketer to become a Test selector in 1924 and used to say 'There are plenty of first-class batsmen in England. But I will never give a vote to a batsman who cannot field – that must be the first qualification of an England batsman.'

Jack Sharp was also a celebrated footballer, a right winger with Aston Villa, Everton and England, making him one of only two Lancashire cricketers to have been double internationals at cricket and soccer. Strangely enough, the other double international, Harry Makepeace, played alongside Sharp at both sports, at Lancashire and Everton. Sharp was a fast and thrustful winger with a powerful shot who helped England beat Ireland in 1903 and Scotland in 1905 and was in the Everton team which won the F.A. Cup by beating Newcastle 1–0 in 1906 and lost to Sheffield Wednesday in 1907.

Football prevented Sharp ever making a tour with MCC, and perhaps also prevented him making more Test appearances. But his sporting life was full to overflowing. He ran his own sports outfitting business in Liverpool and also became a director of Everton. He died on 28 January 1938, just short of his sixtieth birthday, and on the day he was buried

190

his beloved Everton team beat Bolton 4–1 in a First Division match.

Reference was made at Lancashire's annual meeting in 1910 to the small membership (2,500 plus 600 ladies) which was regarded as a slur on the county. One of the young members, A. P. Popplewell, tried to take the great new amateur-professional relationship another step forward by suggesting that as well as going on to the field through the same gate, they should all leave the pavilion by one door. Oswald Lancashire, the chairman, said that would be an inconvenience, but the committee would consider it.

Jack Sharp said thank you for his benefit by having a fine season in 1911, his best ever with over 2,000 runs in all first-class cricket. Reg Spooner also topped 2,000 for the only time, Harry Makepeace and Kenneth MacLeod reached 1,000 for the first time, and J. T. Tyldesley managed four figures for the fifteenth successive year. Harry Dean, like Sharp, Spooner, Makepeace – he also reached his maiden century in his sixth season – and MacLeod, had his best-ever season with 179 wickets for the county, the best since Arthur Mold in 1895. Spooner played ten times for England but, like Sharp, did not tour with MCC. Not that he never had the opportunity. He refused in 1903 and also turned down the chance to go to Australia that winter of 1911–12, a tour which was also without J. T. Tyldesley who had been to Australia in 1901 and 1903 but did not go in 1907 because the terms were not good enough. Spooner also turned down a MCC invitation to captain England in Australia in 1920–21.

REG SPOONER was born in Litherland near Liverpool on 21 October 1880, and after making his debut as a boy of 18 in 1899, he took his career over twenty-three years by playing in 1921 when he was 40 years old. He was the most beautiful of batsmen and Neville Cardus said of him 'He was fit to play before the Queen in her own drawing room.' The son of a Liverpool rector, Spooner served in the army as a subaltern in the Boer War and as a captain in the Lincolnshire Regiment in the First World War, being slightly wounded in action in October 1914. He enjoyed other sports as well as cricket, representing his country at Rugby Union and his county at soccer.

Spooner missed three years of cricket between 1900 and 1902 because of the Boer War but returned to the game in 1903 and scored 247 at Trent Bridge against Nottinghamshire and 168 against Gloucestershire at Aigburth. It was not until 1905 that he first played for England, against Australia at Old Trafford when he scored 52 in 75 minutes. In the next Test, which was played at The Oval, he was bowled for a duck. 'I never saw the ball in the bad light against the pavilion,' he said. 'It was terribly fast.' Spooner saw the ball much better in the second innings when he

scored 79 in as many minutes. He played ten times for England between 1905 and 1912, averaged 32, but scored only one century, against South Africa at Lord's. He played few full seasons, four of them between 1903 and 1906 and those of 1911 and 1912, six summers which accounted for twenty-seven of his thirty-one centuries. The demands of work were too great, restricting Spooner to a career of 170 matches for Lancashire which brought him 9,889 runs at an average of 37.17. The chairman of the England selectors around this time described Spooner as 'by far the most beautiful bat we have ever watched.'

Spooner was Lancashire's president in 1945 and 1946. At his installation in December 1944, he spoke of his readiness to help in the restoration of bomb-shattered Old Trafford . . . 'that ground which we all love so much and where we have spent so many hours with Archie [MacLaren] and the rest.' He died in 1961, aged 80, in a nursing home in Lincoln after six weeks' illness.

Neville Cardus wrote of him:

> Spooner's elegance, his apparently effortless curves and thrusts deceived many a lazy fieldsman, some of whom suffered painfully bruised palms at the end of a century by Spooner. If ever he was guilty of a crude stroke I never saw it – and I saw him play over a period of many years. He embodied the ideal public school batsman – slender, youthful, good looking in a sharp-featured way and a tuft of hair sticking up at the back of his head, was imitated by hundreds of hero-worshipping Lancashire boys of around 1905 to 1912.

Another of Lancashire's most entertaining batsmen, Kenneth Mac-Leod, hit three of his four centuries for Lancashire this summer of 1911, all of them at a fast rate, of course. His first came against Hampshire at Old Trafford when Lancashire scored 621 for six on the opening day, then the third highest in a day in a county match. The first wicket produced 81 runs in 50 minutes between Spooner and Makepeace, the second 214 in 125 minutes (Spooner and J. T. Tyldesley), the third 57 in 30 minutes (Spooner and Sharp), the fourth 136 in 70 minutes (Sharp and Hartley), the fifth 0 (Sharp and Huddleston), the sixth 110 in 40 minutes (Sharp and MacLeod). Spooner scored 102 before lunch and went on to 186, Sharp hit 135, and MacLeod was allowed to reach his hundred the following day. It had taken him 85 minutes. He also hit 95 not out in 85 minutes against Essex at Leyton with six 6s, five of them off leg-break bowler Charles McGahey who he hit for 40 runs in three overs.

Kenneth MacLeod's second century was against Yorkshire and

took 110 minutes, which must be one of the fastest, if not the fastest, in Roses matches. He went on to reach 121 in 125 minutes with three 6s and fifteen 4s. Schofield Haigh had bowled leg breaks to him with only three men on the offside, but a magnificent hit to square leg carried the ball into Bramall Lane to complete his hundred. His third century came in the closing weeks of the season against Leicestershire at Old Trafford. Lancashire were in trouble at 147 for five when MacLeod joined Ernest Tyldesley, but he hit away merrily to score 131 in 135 minutes, the 100 runs having come in under an hour. He hit two 6s and fifteen 4s and hit 80 of his runs in a half-hour partnership with Lol Cook which produced 93 runs.

MacLeod's career, like many other amateurs, was governed by the need to work and he played in only four seasons for Lancashire, 1908–9, 1911 and 1913 when he was still only 25 years old. He died in South Africa on 7 March 1967, aged 79.

A. H. Hornby played his cricket with the same sort of dash and determination that marked his father's approach and there was clearly some of his father's temperament in him when he decided to take on Old Trafford barrackers who had been jeering at fielding mistakes by the Lancashire side. After the fall of a Sussex wicket in the match in 1911 he walked over to the rails on the popular side to express his disapproval, shaking his finger at the people involved. He even threatened to have any barracker removed from the ground.

Hornby also refused an Essex offer of a substitute after Walter Brearley had been taken ill on the opening day of the match at Old Trafford. Lancashire were batting at the time and as Brearley was too ill to bat Lancashire actually went through the match with only ten men and not even a substitute fielder. It did not matter much. Harry Dean took eleven wickets, including his 150th of the season, and Peter Fairclough, a slow left-arm bowler from Bickershaw who was in his debut season, eight as Lancashire won by an innings and 64 runs.

There was a railway strike at the time which created problems, especially for one of the umpires, George Harrison, the former Yorkshire pace bowler. He left Bradford at 2.20 p.m. on the Sunday and went the whole way from Bradford to Manchester by tram car, save for two and a half miles when he had to walk to link up stages. He went from Bradford to Halifax to Hebden Bridge, on to Todmorden, through Summit, to Rochdale and Middleton to Manchester. It took him 5 hours 10 minutes and cost him 3s 1d in tram-car fares whereas an express train would have taken an hour.

The Lancashire scorer, S. Lunt, retired in 1911 after twenty-five years scoring, saying he thought county cricket was on the wane because of the rivalry of golf, motoring and other sports.

He added 'There has been a great falling off in amateur players but the professionals are a new class as compared with what they were a quarter of a century ago. In fact, in the standard of self-respect and behaviour, there is but little distinction now between the two classes.'

This was to prove Walter Brearley's last season with Lancashire. He played little during the summer due to disputes with the Committee, but was still to play again for England the following year while he played with Cheshire, who, incidentally, did not win a game and finished bottom of the table. But 1911 was an outstanding season for Harry Dean, a sergeant major of a player, a formidable fast bowler whose record for Lancashire around this time suggests he should have played more times for England than the three appearances he made against South Africa and Australia in 1912.

HARRY DEAN was born in Burnley on 13 August 1884, and made his debut for Lancashire in 1906. He played until 1921, twelve seasons in which he took over 100 wickets eight times with his left-arm pace bowling and took 1,267 wickets at 18 runs apiece. Only five other bowlers have done more for Lancashire. He took nine wickets in an innings six times, the best being his nine for 31 against Somerset at Old Trafford in 1909. He was also particularly fond of his seventeen Yorkshire wickets in the friendly Roses match at Aigburth in 1913, an extra match arranged to coincide with the visit to Liverpool of King George V. But 1911 was his finest year when he took 179 wickets for Lancashire, 183 in all. He died in Garstang in 1957 when aged 72.

The decision not to play at Blackpool in 1912 was conveyed to the members at the 1911 annual meeting in December. Commented one member, amid laughter and 'hear hears', 'Of all the places where first-class cricket is played, Blackpool is by far the worst.'

Ernest Tyldesley was still trying to establish himself in the team and at the start of the 1912 season, his fourth in the game, he hit his first century, against Sussex at Old Trafford. He reached 50 in 2 hours 15 minutes, his century in 3 hours 50 minutes which was reached with an 8, four of them coming from an overthrow, and also including seven 4s. 'His runs had been obtained by steady rather than brilliant cricket but he executed some capital strokes and never gave a chance,' said the *Manchester Evening Chronicle*. There were other Tyldesleys making their way in the game as well and on more than one occasion, J. T., Bill – who was no relation – and Ernest occupied three successive positions in the batting order. And by the following year there were at times four Tyldesleys in

194

the team when Jim, an older brother of Bill, also got into the side.

The start of the 1912 season was cold, the end of the summer was unusually wet. The *City News* described the scene at the Old Trafford ground during an early game:

> A leaden sky overhead and a pitch of putty dressed with birdlime below. Looking from the top of the pavilion, a grey curtain of haze seemed to shut down on the houses in Chorlton Road and the trees in Longford Park; no horizon was visible. Members to the number of a dozen or two kept carefully within the walls of the pavilion and the spectators on the popular side, who might be counted by the score, sought refuge in the brick bar.

And the end of the season was so wet that under six hours total play was possible in the last three matches at Old Trafford with seven of the nine days being totally washed out.

As well as the coming of the motor car about this time, there was also the arrival of the aeroplane, a sight still so novel that it twice got into the cricket reports of the 1912 season. One arrived as a much-needed diversion during the game against Nottinghamshire at Old Trafford when the natives were getting restless. Spectators, who had got fed up of waiting for play to start after rain, had charged on to the field to express their feelings, they had hooted and jeered, and abused the umpires when they went out to inspect. Then it happened. The *Manchester Evening Chronicle* reported 'At four o'clock there was an interesting diversion. An aeroplane was sighted, and as it gradually approached the ground, the spectators forgot their chagrin, cheering heartily as the airman steered within good view of them. He did not fly over the enclosure, but made a wide sweep in the direction of Manchester, afterwards turning over to Salford.' The plane, in fact, was an Avro trainer making its maiden flight. It took off from Eccles cricket ground, where an extra charge was made for the match against Horwich because of the plane. At 3.30 p.m., when the match had been going on for half an hour, play was halted as the plane took off across the ground. The second sighting came at Brighton when it was reported that 'Attention was distracted by Claude Grahame-Wright, on his biplane, flying south of the ground over the sea and circling inland, but he disappeared into cloudland, and eyes returned to the little green spot called the wicket.'

Lancashire had a marvellous time against the tourists that year, beating both the Australians (twice) and the South Africans, as well as drawing with the Springboks. The poor crowd for the match against the Australians at Old Trafford was blamed on the double

195

price of admission. 'That extra sixpence sticks in the gizzard of your Lancashire man,' wrote the *City News*.

Lancashire pulled off a particularly remarkable win at Old Trafford when they bowled Worcestershire out twice in just under two and three quarter hours for a total of 88 runs. Harry Dean, who for the second successive season was the first bowler in the country to reach 100 wickets, took thirteen for 49 on the difficult wicket, Bill Huddleston had six for 30. Play had been cut short by rain after lunch on the opening day which Lancashire had reached at 125 for two. There was no play on the second day and Lancashire took their total to 269 for eight declared on the third. Worcester started batting at 2.45 p.m. with 3 hours 45 minutes left for play and were bowled out for 47 in 90 minutes and 41 in 70 minutes, giving Lancashire victory by an innings and 181 with 50 minutes to spare.

Round about this time, Cec Parkin, who was to play for Lancashire between 1914 and 1926, was attracting attention as a professional with Church Cricket Club in the Lancashire League. But the experienced *Manchester Evening Chronicle* correspondent, 'Red Rose', said he understood the committee had refused to consider playing him because he was born in Yorkshire. 'At least,' he wrote, 'I heard that when Parkin, of Church, was first considered, the fact that he was a Tyke was against him.' How much truth there was in that is impossible to say but it is true that Lancashire were getting away from the old days when the team was primarily composed of players from outside Lancashire. Eight of the twelve regulars that year were Lancashire-born, two more came from Cheshire plus Jack Sharp (Hereford) and Harry Makepeace (Middlesbrough). In any case, Parkin was not a Yorkshireman; he was from Durham.

Ernest Tyldesley at last established himself in the team in 1913. After four years of intermittent appearances, he held on to what was usually the No. 5 position in the batting order and scored 1,306 runs for an average of 31.85 in the championship. He and his brother set up a unique record one week in June when they each scored a century in the same innings . . . twice! The first occasion was at Leicester where J. T. scored a dazzling 129 in 170 minutes after Harry Makepeace had been dismissed in the opening over on a pitch helping bowlers. The *Manchester Courier* described it as 'a display worthy of his best days, distinguished by perfect timing in driving, leg hitting and cutting alike.' Ernest reached 100 in 170 minutes and went on to 109, and the brothers shared in a stand of 101 in 80 minutes. In the following match, against Surrey at The Oval, Lancashire scored 451 for six on the opening day, of which J. T. scored 210 in 265 minutes. Ernest scored 110 and again the brothers shared in an entertaining partnership, putting on 177 in 125 minutes. Lancashire won the match by seven wickets and, fittingly, Ernest and J. T. were together at the close.

The Surrey match was also noteworthy for the 100th century scored by Tom Hayward. 'Red Rose' recorded the happy event:

> At a quarter past six the Lancashire players joined in the salvo of cheers from the crowd, and they smiled when 'Old Tom' [he was 42] doffed his cricket cap and whirled it round a head which requires the liberal use of some never-failing hair restorer. You know, Hayward scored his ninety-ninth century against Lancashire 12 months ago and this 100th celebration has, I am told, been troubling him ever since. No wonder he waved his chocolate-coloured cap.

The outstanding bowling performance in Lancashire's history came on Thursday 10 July when Lancashire and Yorkshire arranged an extra Roses match at Aigburth to coincide with the visit to Liverpool of King George V and Queen Mary. This was only a friendly match without bearing on the championship, but both counties still took it so seriously that neither was prepared to release players for the opening Gentlemen v Players match being played at The Oval at the same time. So much rain had fallen in Liverpool that the captains agreed not to play before lunch, a decision that was conveyed to the crowds waiting outside the ground. But the wicket improved so rapidly they managed to get in half an hour's play before lunch. One Lancashire player, Harry Dean, could not be found, and Yorkshire's 26-year-old Percy Holmes, who was in his debut season, deputized until after lunch. Dean went on to bowl when the score was 34 for 0 and took nine for 62. There were some exceptionally fine catches, two of them close in by Ralph Whitehead, but nothing to surpass that of Bill Tyldesley running in to meet a high drive by George Hirst in front of the pavilion. He found he had gone too far and when the ball looked to be going over his head he put up his hand and held on. Dean took eight for 29 in the second innings and the only wickets he missed in the match were those of Harry Stanley (caught low and cleverly by the bowler, Bill Huddleston) in the first innings, and Ben Wilson (bowled by Huddleston) and Roy Kilner (lbw to Huddleston) in the second. Dean's full bowling figures were 31.1–6–62–9 and 16.3–4–29–8 in a low-scoring match won by Lancashire by three wickets. His match return of seventeen for 91 is the best for Lancashire in a first-class match.

Lancashire won two of the three Roses matches in 1913, but they were rare successes in a summer in which they won seven but lost eleven championship matches to finish eighth in the table.

197

The *Manchester Evening Chronicle* described it as a most disastrous season and matters came to a head when the captain, A. H. Hornby, issued a public statement in which he accused the committee of treating the players shabbily and having acted in one instance with 'incredible meanness.' He spoke of cheese-paring economies and said their course of action had driven away young professionals of promise. He added that their proposal to cut the programme of matches in 1914 would lower the prestige and threaten the existence of county matches in Lancashire. He said the club needed more members, increased interest in cricket, and increased gate receipts. The club should have an executive committee, one prepared to take an interest in the club outside the committee room and to be in touch with the team as well as with cricket clubs in the county. The balloon was up. Special meetings were held in September and particular attention was paid to the considerable deficit that had accumulated. Oswald Lancashire, the chairman, said the club had lost £2,364 in 1910, £455 in 1911 and £800 in 1913 after a profit of £102 in 1912. So over £3,500 had been lost over the four years, and unless increased income could be obtained they would cut the programme. Lord Derby offered £200 towards the deficit and £100 a year for three years. Other offers were also read out.

There was a little more encouraging news at the annual meeting held on 12 December when the committee announced that they had decided to keep several young players they had earlier decided to sack. But they were £15,000 in debt, of which £14,000 was the mortgage from buying the land in 1898. They needed £1,500 more from subscriptions and all sorts of schemes, such as dinners, bazaars and appeals, were mentioned for raising money. Suggestions on the playing side included the committee picking the team instead of just the captain as had been the practice, and a plea was made for greater co-operation between the captain and players. And the proposal to restrict the term of presidency to two years, which had come up in 1907, went through 'in order to make the reputation of the club of as comprehensive and far-reaching a character as possible.' It was reported before the 1914 season that generous donations had been received from many leading Lancastrians and there had also been a sizeable increase in the number of members.

A Saturday start was tried again as an experiment in 1914 – every weekday but Tuesday was tried by Lancashire – and at the meeting of the county secretaries at Lord's in June it was decided that Wednesday and Saturday would become uniform in 1915 although provision would be made to start Bank Holiday games on Mondays. As it turned out, the First World War interrupted county cricket and the Saturday start did not come in until cricket was resumed. Another innovation at Old Trafford was the tea interval, which was not appreciated at all by the spectators who showed their disapproval by booing and calling on the players to return.

The opening of the season at Old Trafford was described by the *Manchester Evening Chronicle*:

> The Old Trafford ground looked most inviting, and right opposite to the Press Box, fringing the practice ground, rose the new white shelter for the people on a rainy day. Inside the pavilion there were some familiar figures – inhabitants who sit in old, high-backed chairs and look through a glass clearly at a scene which renews their youth.

Hornby was still captain, despite stirring up a hornets' nest, but missed one of the early Old Trafford matches due to being concussed when knocked unconscious by a fall of timber while repairing the hen house at his home in Nantwich. He played only half the matches that year, but was in the side for the benefit match of Bill Huddleston who raised £896 from the game against Surrey. The Lancashire committee had announced at one of the special meetings the previous September that benefits had been promised to Huddleston in 1914 and Dean in 1916. Because of the war, however, Dean was going to have to wait until 1920 for his. Huddleston, a native of Earlestown, was described as a length bowler, moderate in pace, unlaboured in delivery, always keeping the batsman playing, difficult to punish on the best of wickets, almost unplayable on a sticky pitch. He played in 183 matches for Lancashire from 1899 to 1914 and took 684 wickets at 17.55 runs each. He had a long life, living to 89 before he died in Warrington.

One of the most interesting debuts for many years came at Aigburth in July when Cec Parkin, the Church professional, played against Leicestershire. It was said the committee had been against him two years earlier because he was a Yorkshireman, but perhaps in the meantime they had discovered he was actually born in County Durham, twenty yards over the border. Parkin had been invited by Lancashire to play earlier in the season but had refused because of an injury which he thought would not stand up to three days' cricket. But he played at Aigburth and took the first five wickets up to lunch before finishing with seven for 65. The *Manchester Guardian* was absolutely ecstatic about him:

He looked from his first over to his last – he bowled right through the innings – essentially a county bowler and his good style, his accuracy, the remarkable variety of balls he has command of, his briskness and enthusiasm, and the amount of life he threw into every delivery would have picked him out in any company. He bowled half a dozen different sorts of balls, all equally good. In one over the batsman may get a slow, hanging yorker that looks at first sight an easy full toss, or a fast yorker – like the one that bowled King – that is under his bat before he can make up his mind what it is – or a good fast ball with a slight off break and very quick off the pitch, or a very well concealed ball that breaks across the wicket from leg – like the one that curled round Wood's leg and took the leg stump. And what one specially liked was the vivacity and wholeheartedness of Parkin's bowling – he puts all he has into every ball. His bowling is a pleasure to watch.

Parkin took seven for 34 in the second innings for a sensational match return of fourteen for 99 on his debut.

Lancashire had not cut the programme this summer, but they did break new ground when they took the match with Warwickshire to Lancaster. This was the seventh ground on which Lancashire had played a county match following Old Trafford, two at Liverpool, Whalley, Castleton and Blackpool. The *Manchester Evening Chronicle* was not impressed. 'Anything more unlike a county cricket ground cannot be imagined,' it wrote. 'Like The Oval, the Lancaster ground has its gasworks surrounding, and like Old Trafford it has a railway border; but with this difference – the railway shunting operations are a serious matter, as they perturb the batsmen.' The *Lancaster Guardian*, of course, was quite thrilled and said it understood the visit was a compliment to Mr J. T. Sanderson, the Lancaster captain who had been associated with the club over twenty-five years. It was just a pity he had not been asked to play. Said the *Lancaster Guardian* 'It would have given additional local interest and been some encouragement to aspiring cricketers who have too often had reason to think that the county committee are of the opinion that cricketers north of the Ribble are not worth consideration.' Like any club ground confronted with the demands of a county match, Lancaster had to make improvements and extensions. A large grandstand was loaned by the Agricultural Society, a special enclosure was provided around the pavilion, the rails on the popular side were set back halfway up the railway embankment, thus providing a natural grandstand. And lunches were served by Mrs Manners . . .

There were about 2,000 people on the Lune Road ground on the opening day, a figure that was considered satisfactory by the Lancashire authorities. Among the spectators were some of the work people of Messrs W. Thompson and Co., silk spinners of nearby Galgate, who had been given a holiday in view of the match, an evidence, claimed the *Lancaster Guardian*, 'of the keenness displayed in the healthy game by the villagers.' Lancashire replied with 128 to Warwickshire's 346 but were not made to follow on to the great satisfaction of the locals, for it ensured a third day's play. The gate on the second day was £45, and on the third day just short of £40 when 1,173 paid. Lancashire lost the match by 173 runs and were never to return to Lancaster.

Two days later, the Roses match started at Old Trafford. Lancashire were without their captain, A. H. Hornby, who had been called away to advise the War Office on the subject of remounts for the cavalry. War was declared against Germany the following day, but Lancashire, in common with most of the counties, managed to see the season through to the end of August. Lancashire had seven games remaining, two of them at Old Trafford, and decided to play on after MCC had made a statement to the effect that no good purpose could be served abandoning matches.

J. T. Tyldesley, who was now 40, had not scored a century in eighteen championship matches up to the outbreak of war. In the remaining seven games he scored four, 122 not out against Hampshire at Aigburth, 253 against Kent at Canterbury, 104 against Sussex at Eastbourne, and 144 against Northamptonshire at Old Trafford. It was as if he thought there might not be time for any more. Three of the closing matches were together in the south and because of the war two of the venues were changed with Kent being played at Canterbury instead of Dover and Hampshire at Bournemouth instead of Portsmouth. The *Kentish Gazette* said a most interesting day's play was seen by only a few hundred people at Canterbury . . . 'if we except the capital muster of Territorials.' Men in uniform were allowed free into the ground and the newspaper said most troops were appropriately seated on the side of the ground where the flags of the Allied armies were flying.

The Lancashire committee decided, that in view of the fact that many people in Manchester were working only half a day because of the war, the groundside charge would be threepence instead of sixpence . . . after lunch. This applied to two matches at Old Trafford, against Middlesex and Northamptonshire. At the request of the British Red Cross Society, the committee placed the Old Trafford pavilion at their service. It, and later all the buildings on the pavilion side of the ground, became a hospital with accommodation for eighty sick and wounded men. In the course of the war 1,800 patients were treated there.

At the end of the month, the MCC did an about turn and announced that 'it being evident that the continuance of first-class cricket is hurtful to the feelings of a section of the public,' they would not be sending teams to the Scarborough Festival.

Most of the Lancashire players joined the Forces and *The Times* of Friday, 11 December 1914, listed the following who were serving: Hornby, Brooke, Spooner, Garnett, Boddington, Musson, MacLeod, Bill Tyldesley, Harry Tyldesley, Dean, Blomley and MacLaren. J. T. Tyldesley was too old to serve and during the war he helped the Red Cross as they attended to the injured returning home. He would meet ambulance trains and in one twelve-month period travelled 5,000 miles in his own car, and 1,000 miles in the ambulance taking wounded to hospital. Jack Sharp was unable to join up because of heart trouble, a strange complaint for a sportsman who had played cricket and soccer at the highest level. He helped, through sporting events, to raise money for funds for wounded soldiers and sailors.

Another huge loss, this time of £1,308, was reported on the year, leaving Lancashire with liabilities of £12,399. The assets were said to be the ground, worth £24,000, and investments of £3,160. The annual report of 1915 mentioned that 1,667 out of the 2,300 members had paid subscriptions. Cricket did not stop altogether and one of the interesting clashes came between a Yorkshire XI and a Lancashire XI at Haslingden in August 1916. It was made all the more interesting by the fact that the top scorer, by a mile, was Kent's Frank Woolley with 116!

Letters home from the troops at the Front were a feature of newspaper coverage in the First World War. And one of special notice for cricket followers came from Harry Tyldesley who was serving with the Loyal North Lancashire Regiment. Tyldesley expressed his thanks for the materials sent out and reported details of a match played on 29 May 1915, within sound of the guns. Tyldesley chose a team of Privates to play a team of NCOs, the scores being: Privates 55 (Tyldesley 15) and 22 for one, NCOs 21 and 41 (Tyldesley six for 3 and six for 21). Wrote Tyldesley 'To speak of the battle with the Germans I might say it is rather more exciting than the battle of the Roses, but this last day or two it has been very quiet. How long do you think this awful war will last? The sooner it closes the better for everybody, the Germans more than anybody.' Harry, who had made his first-team debut in 1914 at the age of 21, lived through it all to play three more times for Lancashire before dying in Morecambe at the early age of 42. His brother Bill, who had played in eighty-seven matches between 1908 and 1914 and scored three centuries, was killed in action at Kemmel in Belgium in April 1918, aged 30. Other Lancashire players killed in action were Harold Garnett, 38, at Marcoing, Cambrai in France, in December 1917 – he played in 144 matches from 1899 to 1914 and scored five centuries – Alfred Hartley, 39, who played 112 times from 1907 to 1914 and who died near Maissemy, France, in October 1918, just before the Armistice; Egerton Wright, 32, who played four times for the county between 1905 and 1910 and was killed in Barly, France, in May 1918; and John Nelson, who played once in 1913 and died in France in August 1917, aged 25.

Chapter 9 1919–25

*'Old Trafford is becoming less conservative and a more
human institution every week. The war was not waged
for nothing.'*

The Great War ended in November 1918, and plans quickly went
ahead for the restart of county cricket in 1919. At the meeting of
the MCC Advisory Committee early in February, Lancashire moved
the confirmation of a decision taken in December that a county
championship should be held in 1919. Lancashire also moved to
confirm another December decision – that county matches, as an
experiment, should be confined to two days with extended hours of
play. This was carried 11–5 although one of those in favour, Kent's
Lord Harris, said his county were voting for it only because they
thought one season of it would finish the idea. It was agreed that
the hours of play should be from 11.30 a.m. to 7.30 p.m. on the
first day, and 11 a.m. to 7.30 p.m. on the second, and sanction was
given to taking tea intervals, to be decided by the captains and not
exceeding 15 minutes. There was a great feeling of gloom around
cricket at the time, that it would never be the same again, and one of
the reasons for two-day matches was that many in authority felt there
would not be enough interest in the game to sustain the old three-day
matches. It was pointed out that if players – and umpires – would
support the longer playing hours with less time-wasting, then there
would be almost as much time in a two-day as in a three-day game.
Umpires themselves were great time-wasters. They would follow the
slow, processional march to the wicket by indulging themselves in an
over or two just to remind everybody that they, too, had played the

game. Fielding sides strolled out, batsmen moved sightscreens, play started late, lunch intervals were often too long, and punctuality had not been a Victorian, or Edwardian, quality.

When Lancashire's committee met on 13 February 1919, among its members were Oswald Lancashire (chairman), Tommy Higson, Joseph Eccles, Edgar Hornby and Ted Roper, all former players, as well as Myles Kenyon and Edwin P. Stockton. It was reported that negotiations with members of staff who were still on active service were proceeding and also with the Red Cross Society who were vacating the pavilion that week. On Friday 4 April, it was announced that Myles Kenyon, who had captained the 2nd XI before the war, would captain the first team that year. It was quickly pointed out that this was not to imply that A. H. Hornby, who had captained the team in the seven years before the war, would not again figure in the team. Captain Hornby, it was said, was still on military service but hoped to play at intervals during the season. In the event, Hornby, who was now 41, was never to play again. He bought a farming estate of 375 acres, 16 miles from Cork in Ireland where his sporting instincts were more than satisfied by the fox-hunting and salmon fishing.

Kenyon was the youngest son of James Kenyon of Walshaw Hall, Bury, a former Member of Parliament for the Borough. He was educated at Eton and Cambridge University and held a commission during the war in the Duke of Lancaster's Own Yeomanry. He saw service in Macedonia when attached to the 9th Battalion of the South Lancashire Regiment and was one of the invalided officers returning home on the hospital ship *Dover Castle* which was torpedoed and sunk in the Mediterranean.

Among the many letters I received offering information on Lancashire cricket was one from Alan Crompton, of Gillingham, who recalled a story his mother used to tell concerning her grandfather and Myles Kenyon. Mr Crompton, his mother, grandfather and great grandfather were all born and brought up in a row of terraced factory houses in Elton, Bury, close to the Kenyon house. For some reason, Kenyon befriended Mr Crompton's great grandfather, a character known as 'Farmer' Hardman, who had been a spinner in one of Kenyon's mills and about this time was in his seventies. On match days at Old Trafford Kenyon, often chauffeur-driven, would call at the terraced house in Woodhill Street and instruct the old 'Farmer' to put on his muffler and clogs and be off to the cricket. On arrival at the ground the old man was seated in the pavilion where he was fed and watered by various members and generally treated as a sort of team mascot. But he had to wear his muffler and clogs. On one occasion when great grandmother talked him into wearing his best suit, Mister Myles insisted he was to go straight away and put his

205

proper 'togs' on. And one of Mr Crompton's mother's early child-hood memories was of having to wear her best frock and not get dirty, because Mister Myles was coming to take 'Farmer' to the cricket. An amusing story? Perhaps. But certainly one to tell us something of the time and of class distinction.

By the middle of April, a month before the opening game, arrangements for positions on the groundstaff had been entered into with Sergeant Harry Dean, Flight Sergeant Harry Makepeace, Sergeant Ernest Tyldesley, Corporal Jimmy Heap, Gunner Lol Cook, Gunner Ben Blomley, Private Charlie Hallows, and Jimmy Tyldesley. J. T. Tyldesley decided to delay his retirement and agreed to play in most matches and Jack Sharp said he would play as an amateur. The committee also received promises of support from Captain Alan Boddington, Captain George Rawstorne, Captain John Hollins, Lieutenant Frank Musson and Lieutenant C. Stowell Marriott, of the RAF, who had distinguished himself in services matches. Captain Reg Spooner had also been invited to play but had not yet fully recovered from wounds he received early in the war. Membership was £1 6s, sons of members and ladies tickets were 10s. It was also reported that although the pavilion and dining room had been given up only a few weeks previously by the Red Cross, the buildings had been thoroughly fumigated, painted and decorated. Along with other counties Lancashire were to charge a shilling for admission, double the price that had stood for fifty years since the club had been formed in 1864. The advance was to meet extra charges and to cover the entertainment tax.

Cricket was officially resumed at Old Trafford on Monday 28 April, when a heavy snowstorm swept across the ground in the morning followed by a biting north-east wind in the afternoon. Nevertheless, nets were still held and Myles Kenyon had the honour of being the first to practise batting, facing the bowling of Dean and Jimmy Tyldesley. The practice was superintended by Arthur Paul, now 54 years old. A practice match was held three days later and among the trialists was Dick Tyldesley, a younger brother of Jimmy, and described as a right-hand bowler of medium pace, but who was soon to gain recognition as one of the best leg-spinners in England.

Lancashire's opening county game after the First World War started on Monday, 19 May 1919, on a beautiful spring day but in front of only a moderate crowd. It was a day for memories, for remembering the game as it was, and for those who had given their lives. The last match in 1914 had been against Northamptonshire at Old Trafford. Lancashire's opening batsmen, Harold Garnett and Bill Tyldesley, had both died, the Northamptonshire openers, brothers Arthur and Bill Denton, had both been prisoners of war in

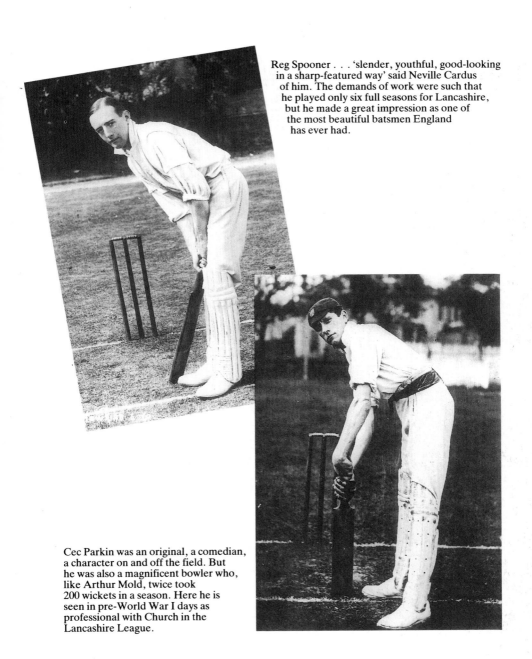

Reg Spooner . . . 'slender, youthful, good-looking in a sharp-featured way' said Neville Cardus of him. The demands of work were such that he played only six full seasons for Lancashire, but he made a great impression as one of the most beautiful batsmen England has ever had.

Cec Parkin was an original, a comedian, a character on and off the field. But he was also a magnificent bowler who, like Arthur Mold, twice took 200 wickets in a season. Here he is seen in pre-World War I days as professional with Church in the Lancashire League.

Opposite: Ernest Tyldesley played more games, and scored more centuries and runs than any other Lancashire player. As a young man, his career dragged, but from the age of 30 he scored 1,000 runs in a season sixteen times and hit thirty-four of his centuries after his fortieth birthday. Even at 45, in his last season, he scored 2,487 runs.

Left: Dick Tyldesley, a great leg-break bowler who took 1,449 wickets for Lancashire and who teamed up with Ted McDonald to play a major part in Lancashire's four championship wins from 1926 to 1930. (*Central Press*).

Right: Bill Farrimond, a wicket-keeper who was good enough to play for England, but who spent almost all his career as Lancashire's no.2 to George Duckworth in the 1920s and 1930s.

Len Hopwood (left) and Frank Watson who opened the batting many times for Lancashire in the 1930s.

Ted McDonald, an Australian who joined Lancashire while he was professional with Nelson in the Lancashire League. He was a magnificent fast bowler, probably the best Lancashire have had, and played a prominent part in Lancashire winning the championship four times in the five years from 1926 to 1930.

Eddie Paynter, a product of Lancashire League cricket, averaged nearly 60 runs an innings through twenty matches for England, a Test average surpassed only by Herbert Sutcliffe. His 322 for Lancashire against Sussex at Hove in 1937 stands next to Archie MacLaren's 424 and only one Englishman, Jack Robertson of Middlesex, has scored more runs in a day.

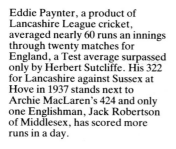

Cyril Washbrook, pictured when he was 19 and in his second season with Lancashire. He scored a century in only his second match and all that early promise blossomed into a great talent which made him one of Lancashire's finest-ever batsmen. (*City Press*)

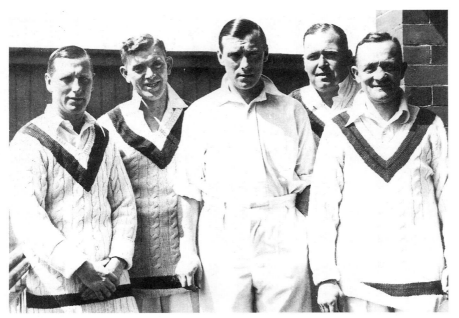

Ernest Tyldesley, Frank Watson, Charlie Hallows, Dick Tyldesley and Harry Makepeace, pictured in 1928 shortly after Hallows had completed 1,000 runs in May.

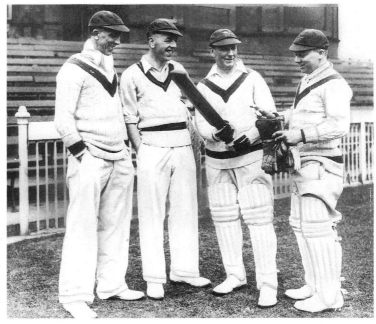

Four Test players, Jack Iddon, Len Hopwood, Ernest Tyldesley and George Duckworth.

George Duckworth pictured at Warrington Railway Station with family and friends before joining the MCC party for the 1932-3 tour of Australia.

Lancashire made history in 1935 when they became the first team to go to a match by air, from Swansea to Southampton. Two planes were chartered by the captain, Peter Eckersley, who is on the extreme right of a picture which also includes (from the left) pilot, Cyril Washbrook, Buddy Oldfield, Eddie Philiipson, Len Parkinson, Len Hopwood, Frank Sibbles, pilot and Lionel Lister.

The Old Trafford ground was seriously damaged by air raids in 1940 and in 1941 when a sentry at the main gate was killed. The top of the pavilion, the groundsman's home, the dining room and two of the stands were damaged. Craters were left on the field.

Lancashire's only defeat in the summer of 1881, when they won the championship for the first time, came against Cambridge University in a match which marked the opening of the Liverpool ground of Aigburth. This photograph of the ground was taken during the 1949 game against the New Zealanders.

Germany. Of the others who had played against Northamptonshire only J. T. Tyldesley, Sharp and Dean were in the first team of 1919. Ernest Tyldesley, Jimmy Heap, Lol Cook and Charlie Hallows, a stylish left-handed opening batsman who made his debut before the war, were soon to play, but Ralph Whitehead, now 35, and Bill Huddleston, 46, never played again. The team that played Derbyshire to launch the 1919 season included five amateurs in John Hollins, Jack Sharp, George Rawstorne, Myles Kenyon and Alan Boddington. The professionals were Harry Makepeace, J. T. Tyldesley, Vic Norbury, a former Hampshire player who was professional with East Lancashire in the Lancashire League, Cec Parkin, who was still a professional in the leagues, Harry Dean and Jack Bullough, a Bolton spin bowler. Rawstorne was in his only match for Lancashire and Norbury, despite an impressive start, Hollins and Bullough were to play little more. Ernest Tyldesley had been demobilized the previous week but Lancashire chose not to play him although he did go on the field as substitute. Heap and Jimmy Tyldesley were also available but not yet chosen.

The *Manchester Guardian* tried fleetingly to capture the emotion of the moment 'It was indeed easy to feel the sentimental aspect of the occasion. One came into the enclosure from the dusty town and there were, for many an old cricket lover, strong tugs on the heart as they again saw the soft green splashed with the spring sun and the red pavilion, and the county flag streaming in the wind.' The *Manchester Evening News* reported that Lancashire scored 200 runs in 135 minutes and added 'that the batsmen were living up to the spirit of the new times.' The *City News* said the spectators, though not much in numbers, included many old members of the Lancashire club, ministers of all denominations, and some of the giant players of old – A. N. Hornby, Albert Ward and Tom Lancaster among them. A *Manchester Guardian* picture showed Derbyshire going out to field, watched by a handful of members wearing straw hats or trilbies. Two days was long enough for Lancashire to win that opening game by ten wickets with Parkin taking seven wickets in the game, Dean and Norbury five each, with Norbury, 78, and Sharp, 84, taking the batting honours by sharing in a stand of 152 in 105 minutes for the fourth wicket.

The second game, against Essex at Leyton, saw the introduction of Lieutenant Charles Marriott, whose name was to be associated more with Kent than with the county of his birth. He was born at Heaton Moor near Stockport, was educated in Dublin and when home from school played for the Heaton Moor club. Before joining the RAF he was an officer in the Lancashire Fusiliers and was badly gassed at Nieuport, the port of Ypres in Belgium. He was a leg-break bowler of reasonable pace and although he lived in Kent, Lancashire invited him to play before he went up to Cambridge. He told Lancashire he would not be able to play much cricket away from the south of England, but would very much like to play in the Whitsuntide Roses game at Old Trafford. He was duly chosen and took only two wickets – those of Roy Kilner in both innings. He was 23 years old and swotting for Cambridge so he played in only eight games that year. When he was available he was always preferred to the rising talent of Dick Tyldesley and his best performance was his eight for 98 against Nottinghamshire at Trent Bridge in July. He played only four matches more for Lancashire, in 1920 and 1921 when he was a Cambridge University Blue, before switching allegiance to Kent in 1924. He was then a teacher at Dulwich College so, for fourteen years, up to 1937, he played only in August for Kent. Yet he took part in 101 games with them, played for England against West Indies in 1933, and toured India with MCC that same winter.

The Roses matches restored the doubters' faith in the great game and the place it clearly still held in the hearts of the English people. There were 15,000 on the opening day at Old Trafford and 20,000 on the second. The front of the pavilion and the grandstands on that side of the field were a mass of white straw hats, and white hats also predominated on the popular side. Wrote the *City News* 'With the vast expanse of close-shaven greensward, the most beautiful of cricket grounds, and the dense human throng gathered round about it, the picture was cheering and delightful under the brilliant sunshine.'

Parkin, still only a mid-week county cricketer because of his commitments to Rochdale in the Central Lancashire League, destroyed Yorkshire at Old Trafford where he took fourteen wickets for 140. Yet for three years he was to stay a part-time county cricketer, unwilling to leave Rochdale where he was highly paid and taking part, in all, in only fifteen games with Lancashire. In those fifteen games, from 1919 to 1921, he took 117 wickets, a prodigious talent which the county desperately needed in those years after the war, but which was to prefer the less arduous demands of the league until he finally joined the groundstaff in 1922.

Ernest Tyldesley had been brought into the team for the second match of the 1919 season and swiftly re-established himself to finish the summer second only to the dependable Harry Makepeace in Lancashire's batting averages with 44.18. He was just ahead of his brother, John Thomas, who was to retire at the end of the season, but not before he had recorded his thirteenth double hundred. It was a marvellous innings, showing glimpses of his old mastery with crisp, clean driving and cutting against Derbyshire at Chesterfield. His first century took him only 110 minutes and included twenty-one 4s and one 6, but he just kept going, sailing past 200 and looking as if he would at last reach his ambition of a treble hundred when he played a half-hearted stroke and was bowled. He had batted five hours, scored 272, and all that at the age of 45. There were two more Tyldesleys in the team, the brothers Jimmy and Dick from Westhoughton. Dick, in his third game, took five for 41 as Lancashire won by an innings.

J. T. knew he was not going to play any more first-class cricket after the 1919 season – he was to be persuaded to return just once more in 1923 – and played with even more freedom than in his heyday. It was doubtful whether at any time in his career he had ever been so much the hitter as he was in this, his final full season. In an innings of 170 in 160 minutes against Gloucestershire at Old Trafford, the great old batsman hit seven 6s – he hit more this season than in all his previous years – and halfway through had to have a thigh strapped. He and Ernest, who scored 96, put on 218 in 115 minutes for the third wicket.

The long-awaited return of Reg Spooner arrived on Friday 15 August, when Lancashire played Surrey at Old Trafford. The first train to the cricket ground was packed and such congestion had not been seen at the station since before the war. There were 4,000 on the ground before the game started, but before the growing crowd could experience the style and grace of Spooner again, they were first treated to a fine exhibition from Jack Hobbs, who scored a century before lunch which was reached with Surrey 192 for no wicket after two hours. But when Lancashire went in to bat Makepeace walked out with Spooner instead of his usual partner, Charlie Hallows. The crowd gave Spooner a magnificent welcome and in no time at all, we are told, he was flicking Hitch's expresses and Rushby's break-backs to the offside with the daintiness of a man using a feather duster decoratively. That, if you did not know, was the description by Neville Cardus, the *Manchester Guardian*'s new cricket writer, of one of the players he was to revere all his life.

Dick Tyldesley played in twelve of Lancashire's twenty-five matches that season and took thirty-six wickets at 21.63 runs each. Yorkshire won the championship that year with twelve wins out of twenty-six games and in a season in which nearly half of all county games were drawn, Lancashire finished joint fifth with eight wins and four defeats in twenty-four matches. Counties had seen enough of two-day matches to convince them of a quick return to the old formula, including Lancashire who had been at the forefront in introducing the experiment. The old doubts about the public's enthusiasm – or lack of it – for county cricket had been swept away, club treasurers disliked it and Lancashire's players hated the long hours right from the second game at Leyton. It had not been

209

possible to leave the London suburb until 8.10 p.m. and by the time they reached their hotel in the Strand it was 8.45 p.m. This meant that by the time dinner was over it was bedtime, which prompted one of them to observe 'Cricket is now all bed and work.'

When they played at Chesterfield, the Lancashire professionals could not find accommodation in the town and had to stay in Sheffield, leaving there at 9.30 a.m. and returning twelve hours later. It was even reported, heaven forbid, that one Middlesex amateur did not reach his home to sit down to dinner until 10 o'clock! And in one match at Old Trafford, even the members of the committee, who had voted in the longer hours, had all gone home by 7 p.m. The hours were too long and there was too much hustle and bustle which was not felt to be conducive to the highest level of play. Yet the two-day game was not without virtue. There were plenty of exciting finishes, the batsman who played for his average had largely been eliminated, there were more sporting declarations, and a good many irritatingly slack points, such as the lack of punctuality and urgency, had gone from the game.

The question of membership and subscriptions came up again and to meet rising costs, including increased payments to players, Lancashire's annual subscription was raised to £2 2s. Seven players, it was announced, would each receive £250 for the season as talent money. The *Manchester Guardian* was moved to write a leading article in which it said that while cricket had come to a standstill during the war there were big standing expenses to be met all the time. Pre-war expenses of cricket had doubled, prices were rocketing, and counties also had to compete with league clubs who were able to offer professionals better terms. County cricket, said the *Manchester Guardian*, had now become, through a host of inevitable social causes, dependent on professionalism.

Membership was still only about 2,200. Again the cry went out for more members, a cry that was met by an observation by the *Manchester Evening News*' experienced cricket writer, J. R. Clegg, which demands re-printing:

> Probably there are not a few enthusiastic ladies who would gladly pay a guinea provided they could have the privilege of entering the pavilion now sacred to the mere males. Is the time at hand, I wonder, when wives and sweethearts will be able to take their seats in front of the pavilion? I doubt it. Still, Old Trafford is becoming less conservative and a more human institution every week. The war was not waged for nothing.

The crowds continued to grow in 1920 and the Roses match

at Old Trafford, this time being held in August, attracted 67,000 people over the three days, a record for a championship match at the ground. All Lancashire's home games were now starting on Wednesdays and Saturdays and the crowd for the opening day, a Saturday, numbered more than 25,000 and was the largest since J. T. Tyldesley's benefit game in 1906. But the Bank Holiday crowd on the Monday exceeded even this. There were 20,000 present when the game started and hundreds of people were left stranded on the railway stations, tramcars were packed, and taxi-cabs were at a premium. The roofs of several buildings at the ground were deeply lined, there was a thick ring of people inside the rails, and for the first time for thirty-nine years, ladies were allowed in the members' pavilion. The gates were closed with about 32,000 people inside, and 10,000 witnessed the third day's play.

The 32,000 beat the 1906 record by more than 5,000, and the 67,000 total, though far behind the 78,792 for the Roses match at Headingley when George Hirst had his benefit in 1904, and the 80,000 for the Surrey-Yorkshire match at The Oval in 1906, was only 11,000 fewer than for the whole of the 1919 season. Ten thousand schoolboys were there, which was also the highest ever.

It was now seventeen years since S. F. Barnes had played county cricket but he was still considered good enough, though 47 years old, to be asked go to to Australia with Johnny Douglas's team. But Barnes refused. The MCC would not pay for his wife and child to go and he said he would therefore not let cricket interfere with business. This opened the way for Cec Parkin, still basically a Saturday-afternoon cricketer, but who willingly agreed to go to Australia for what turned out to be his only tour. The 1920-21 tour of Australia should have been captained by Reg Spooner who agreed to take the team, then withdrew, mainly through fitness but partly because of business.

With Parkin playing in only five matches and Dick Tyldesley still learning county cricket, the weight of the bowling in 1920 fell on Lol Cook and Harry Dean, who were now both 35. Cook played in all twenty-eight matches, Dean missed only one, and between them they bowled nearly 2,000 overs with Cook taking 150 wickets and Dean 124. That was to be Dean's eighth and last season of taking over 100 wickets, but Cook, one of the greatest-hearted workers in Lancashire's history, stayed to achieve it in the next two seasons as well. In the match against Derbyshire at Chesterfield in 1920 he took seven wickets for 8 runs with one of the finest pieces of skilled bowling in Lancashire cricket for many years. He took seven for 22 against Hampshire and in one week had taken twenty wickets for 151 runs so that he had completed 100 wickets before the middle of July.

211

The match against Hampshire proved a thrilling finish after Hampshire had needed only 66 for victory. They had got 6 runs the previous evening but play could not begin on the final afternoon until 2 p.m. because of heavy rain. The ground was not even fit then with patches of mud on the pitch, but Hampshire wanted to get an early train and agreed to play. It all looked so easy for Hampshire when they were 53 for three with only 13 more needed to win. Four wickets fell for the addition of one run and when Cook bowled John Greig – the same man who had scored 249 not out against Lancashire in 1901 – Hampshire were 57 for eight with 9 runs wanted. The ninth wicket fell at 60 and after taking a single, Frank Ryan hit Harry Dean to leg. The batsmen ran three but could not manage the fourth which would have levelled the scores. The next ball lifted sharply and took the edge of the bat as Alex Kennedy tried to protect himself. Alan Boddington, the wicket-keeper, ran at full speed for several yards to take the catch and give Lancashire victory by one run.

Dean, who had had to wait four years for his benefit because of the war, earned £2,217 from the match against Kent. It lasted only two days, the weather was poor on the second, but Dean's popularity earned him a sum that was second only to J. T. Tyldesley's £3,111 in 1906. Perhaps the occasion was too much for him for although Kent were bowled out for 104 and 88, he took only two wickets. Cook had ten and Parkin eight. The *City News*, looking for one word to describe Dean, settled on 'grit'. The newspaper described him as genial with a homely countenance. 'He goes back a few paces from the wicket, takes several short running steps and sends down the ball with his left hand by an action of peculiar grace and skill.'

The Australians came to England in 1921, their first visit for nine years, and with them came one of the several fine pairs of opening bowlers they have produced, Ted McDonald and Jack Gregory. They destroyed the cream of English batting that year and the first sight Lancashire supporters had of them came in July when they beat Lancashire by an innings in two days. Gregory took ten wickets but McDonald only two. McDonald also failed in the drawn Test match but showed his true talents at Aigburth the following week when he took eight for 62 in the second match against Lancashire. Nobody knew it then but here was the man who was to provide that extra pace that would turn Lancashire into a championship-winning team.

The Old Trafford pavilion was gay with bunting when the Prince of Wales, later King Edward VIII, honoured the ground with his presence during the match against the Australians. Lancashire could not cope with the fast bowling and nine of the batsmen in the first innings were out to catches to the slips or the wicket-keeper. The

212

crowd cried 'Pitch 'em up, Gregory', and the *Manchester Guardian* cried 'Has English batsmanship fallen so low that the fast, short ball, aye, the fast long hop, is becoming deadly.' The Test match turned into one of cricket's curiosities when Lionel Tennyson tried to declare at 341 for four, 40 minutes before the close of the second day. He was an hour too late under the rules that existed then and when Australia took the field again Warwick Armstrong, their captain, was barracked so much he sat on the ground in protest until it stopped. Then followed another breach in the laws as Armstrong, who had bowled the last over before the 'declaration', also bowled the first after it. Cec Parkin, who had played in the previous two Tests, was called up for this one only the day before the start. Charlie Hallows made his debut and Charles Marriott, in his last season as a Lancashire player, was in the party, although not chosen.

Australia won that series 3–0 and were undefeated when they went to Eastbourne on 27 August to play a team chosen by Archie MacLaren, who had maintained all summer that he could pick a side to defeat the Aussies. Every member of his team was an amateur and MacLaren himself, then aged 49, batted at No. 9, as his side were bowled out for 43 in 75 minutes on a perfect wicket. The Australians took a first-innings lead of 131 but MacLaren's team pulled themselves together to score 326 in their second innings with G. A. Faulkner opening and scoring 153. The Australians, needing 196 to win, were bowled out for 167 to provide the sensation of the season. One other former Lancashire player was in the team, Walter Brearley, who was aged 45 but did not bowl in the match after hurting himself as he vaulted the fence.

A fine new player looked to have arrived at Old Trafford when 26-year-old Walker Ellis, son of Jerry who had played for Lancashire in the 1890s, hit a sparkling century against Kent in only his third game. He went in when Lancashire were 229 for three and batted 10 minutes before lunch on Trinity Monday without scoring. In 95 minutes after lunch he raced to his century and went on to 138 not out in under two and a half hours. He treated Frank Woolley as if he were a Saturday afternoon bowler and went from 89 to his hundred with five hits – 2, 4, 2, 2, 4. 'Lancashire,' said *Wisden*, 'played their winning game sedately, taking six and a half hours to score 462.' Ellis, unfortunately, was never to approach the form of this fine innings again. He played thirty-three times more for the county but scored only two 50s to finish with a batting average under 17.

Another player to score an entertaining century that year, and again it was to prove the only one of his career, was George Shelmerdine. It, too, came against Kent, but this time at Maidstone,

213

and Woolley came in for more punishment as Shelmerdine reached his 50 with two 6s over the sightscreen off him. He hit two more 6s by some quick, decisive, upstanding, thrashing strokes, and completed his century in under two hours. He hit four 6s and ten 4s in his 105 and shared in a stand of 88 in 55 minutes with Dick Tyldesley.

Parkin, who had been to Australia the previous winter although still effectively a league cricketer, played only six matches for Lancashire in 1921, yet took fifty wickets. His best performance came at Aigburth, a ground he seemed to like, where Hampshire were set to score 211 for victory. The last ball of the last over, delivered by Parkin, hit Todmorden-born Walter Livsey on the pad and with the appeal still ringing round the ground Parkin, without waiting for the umpire's decision, raced jubilantly for the pavilion, followed by the rest of the team. Lancashire had won by 27 runs and Parkin had taken eight for 90. Twenty of those runs had come in one over against Lionel Tennyson who, two weeks later, hit a magnificent century against Lancashire at Southampton. He reached his hundred in 110 minutes with four 4s in two overs off Dick Tyldesley and went on to 131 not out in 135 minutes, an innings of ferocious hitting. Lancashire, 74 behind on the first innings, needed 322 to win, a target that was beginning to look remote when Charlie Hallows was out at 196 for five. But a seventh-wicket stand of 105, with Dick Tyldesley hitting sixteen 4s in a remarkable innings of 75, brought Lancashire a famous three-wicket win.

Jimmy Heap was given a benefit in 1921, a fitting reward for a man who had served Lancashire well for twenty years. Heap, a left-arm bowler, was often kept out of the team by the superior bowling of Harry Dean but still took 412 wickets at 23 each with his rhythmic, relaxed bowling. This must have been the year for the honest labourer for Lol Cook was chosen for the Players against the Gentlemen at Lord's after taking ninety-one wickets by 12 July on hard pitches. He went on to take 148 wickets that year for Lancashire to follow his 150 the year before. And the year after that, he took 142.

ERNEST TYLDESLEY, slightly-built and ever-so-stylish, played the first of his fourteen matches for England in 1921, the start of a Test career that looks decidedly curious from nearly seventy years on. He started by being bowled first ball by Jack Gregory at Trent Bridge, and in the second innings was struck on the head trying to hook the same bowler. Tyldesley had to be helped from the field and to add insult to injury he was out bowled again as the ball had fallen on to the stumps. He was not chosen for the second or third Tests but returned at Old Trafford to give a dazzling display with an innings of

78 not out, which was more than enough to keep him in the side for the final Test at The Oval where he scored 39. Yet in the next four years he played in only one of the fifteen Tests in which England engaged and was not chosen to tour either Australia or South Africa. Tyldesley, it seemed, had to do something extraordinary to get into the England team and he produced it in 1926 when he hit seven hundreds in seven consecutive matches. The last came at Taunton two days before the Old Trafford Test and provided him with his 2,000th run on 22 July. The selectors had been unable to ignore such consistent brilliance and he played in the fourth Test and top-scored with 81. Yet out he went again to make way for Percy Chapman to lead the team in place of Arthur Carr. He went on the next two tours, of Australia and South Africa – where he scored two Test hundreds – scored the first ever Test century against the West Indies at Lord's in 1928, played in the two other Tests in that maiden series, but then never played again. It all left him with 990 runs and three centuries from fourteen Tests, and a startlingly good average of 55.

It might all seem silly now but it has to be remembered that competition for places was fierce in those days with Tyldesley having to compete mainly with Frank Woolley and Patsy Hendren. At least it helped him to concentrate his enormous talents on Lancashire and enabled him to set up several records for the county which still stand today. He had played in most games, 573, scored most runs with 34,222, and hit most centuries, ninety. His record in all first-class cricket was 648 matches, 38,874 runs (average 45.46), and 102 centuries. He played in all five championship-winning teams of 1926, 1927, 1928, 1930 and 1934 and was top of the batting averages in four of those seasons.

It does seem remarkable that he and his brother John Thomas, who both came from the humble beginnings of village cricket with Roe Green, near Worsley, should be the two players with the highest total of runs in Lancashire's history. Ernest played sixty-six games more for Lancashire than his brother, scored 273 more runs, seventeen more centuries and averaged nearly 4 runs an innings more. J. T. used to say that Ernest would be a better player than he ever was, Ernest used to say that J. T. was the superior of the two. On balance, it seems that Ernest was right, regardless of the figures. J. T. was the better batsman.

While J. T. burst on the scene and swiftly established himself, Ernest developed much more slowly in a career that dragged in its early years but blossomed right after the First World War to become the stylish backbone of Lancashire cricket for almost two decades. R. C. Robertson-Glasgow wrote of him 'After military service he came back with a new power on the offside though, to the end, his hooking and strokes between mid on and mid wicket remained his special glory.' Tyldesley was 30 when the 1919 season started. Effectively, he was just beginning his career but he was to reach 1,000 runs in a season sixteen more times to add to the two immediately before the War. In all first-class matches he topped 2,000 six times and once, in 1928, his exceptional year, he reached 3,000. Thirty-four of his centuries came after his fortieth birthday and his last glorious year, that of 1934 when he scored 2,487 runs and averaged 57.83, was achieved at the grand age of 45. He hit seven double hundreds in his career and the finest would have to be the one against Surrey at The Oval in 1923 when he saved Lancashire from what looked like certain defeat at the start of the final day, 117 behind with four wickets down. When Peter Eckersley resigned the captaincy after the 1935 season, there were suggestions that Ernest Tyldesley would take over the position. But the committee resisted the temptation to break with tradition to appoint a professional captain, and turned to Lionel Lister instead. Tyldesley retired soon after but later became the first former professional player to serve on Lancashire's committee. He became partially blind in his later years before dying in Rhos-on-Sea in 1962, aged 73.

Early in the 1922 season another new player made an immediate impression with a debut that left supporters full of hope for his future. His name was Rupert Howard, a Preston cricketer whose first day in county cricket ended with him 88 not out after only 80 minutes batting. 'On Monday let us hope Howard will achieve the distinction of a century in his first match,' wrote the *Manchester Guardian*, a sentiment that must have been echoed throughout Lancashire, and especially in Preston. But although there were still two days to play, Myles Kenyon declared first thing on the Monday morning and Lancashire, who had scored 460 for two, went on to victory by an innings and 75 runs. Howard was never to get that hundred, nor even another 50. He was 32 years old, there was work to do, and he played only seven more times for Lancashire up to 1933, by which time he was the club secretary, a position he held until 1948. His sons, Barry and Nigel, also played for Lancashire, Nigel going on to captain England in India.

Lancashire, it seemed, needed more of the Howard spirit in their batting. They were getting a reputation for being an over-serious team, a collection of cricketers who, it was said, had taken the pursuit of efficiency to an extreme. Neville Cardus said the Lancashire players had been playing like men under an unreasonable strain. Lancashire had become defensive and showed little style in batting; they played too much for safety. Was the trouble due to the lack of amateur batting?

The 1922 Roses match at Old Trafford provided one of those finishes that belong in the history books. So here it is. At the end of the first day, Yorkshire had reached 108 for six after bowling out Lancashire for 118 on a dubious wicket. On that Saturday evening Geoffrey Wilson, the Yorkshire captain, who had been the sixth batsman out, was taken ill and had to be operated on for appendicitis. There was no play on the second day and the players went to see *Charley's Aunt* at The Prince's. Yorkshire, after taking a first innings lead of four and then bowling Lancashire out again for 135 on the final day, were left needing 132 to win with ample time to get them, and with 10,000 spectators on the edges of their seats. With half an hour to go Yorkshire needed 24 for victory with only one wicket standing and Wilfred Rhodes and Rockley Wilson together. They reached the final over, bowled by Parkin, who was in his first full season, and taken by Rhodes, needing five to win. Rhodes blocked the first four balls and the fifth was a no ball, leaving Yorkshire within one good hit of victory. But Rhodes scorned the chance, took just a single from the last ball and Yorkshire, who were top of the table and were to become champions, were happy with first innings points. In addition, of course, they had denied Lancashire any. So an exciting match was left drawn with Yorkshire needing 3 runs and Lancashire one wicket for victory. Neville Cardus stopped shaking long enough to point out that Yorkshire had scored only 3 runs in the last five overs, and Lancashire had had nearly half an hour in which to take that last wicket.

Myles Kenyon gave up the captaincy after the 1922 season. He had led the team since the war and in four seasons had played in eighty-five of the 116 matches and seen Lancashire finish runners-up once and fifth three times. He was to play just six more games, all against the Universities over the next three years when Lancashire needed a captain, and finished with a batting average under 15. Jack Sharp, an amateur since the war, was appointed captain. It was a revolutionary step to appoint a former professional, even one who had since turned amateur, and many members were not entirely in favour, despite Sharp's popularity. Lionel Tennyson, when asked about it, said:

> With regard to the distinction between amateurs and professionals, I cannot see how it will affect the matter. He is now an amateur and when a professional player becomes an amateur he automatically receives the privileges of amateurs and is, of course, styled 'Mr'. This trifling matter merely indicates the distinction which will continue to exist between men who play cricket for pleasure and those who make it their honourable means of livelihood.

Support also arrived from A. N. Hornby, who wrote a short note, still contained in the Sharp scrapbooks in the possession of his son Geoffrey:

Parkfield, Nantwich.
May 14th.

Dear Sharp,
Wishing you all the very best this coming season. No good my saying play up Lancashire because they always did and always will do.
    Yours ever,
    [signed] A. N. Hornby.

Sharp, unfortunately, was not well enough to play in several of the opening games in 1923 and in the Whitsuntide match against Yorkshire, the committee, instead of following the usual policy of appointing an amateur, persuaded J. T. Tyldesley to lead the side. Tyldesley, now 49 years old, forsook his coaching and second-team duties to make his first appearance since 1919, and for the only time in his life, played in the team as an amateur. The game was ruined by rain and Tyldesley, batting at No. 6, was out for nine in what turned out to be his last innings. Lancashire played Kent at Old Trafford in the same week, but Tyldesley did not play. He had been brought back for the big one and was not going to play again. Leonard Green, who was to captain Lancashire through their hat-trick of championships starting in 1926, took over until Sharp was fit again. Sharp, now 45 years old, had a decent season, scoring 693 runs for an average of 33 and hitting a marvellous century at Lord's, one that was described as one of the best seen on the ground all season. His century took him just over two hours and was cited as an example of the difference between batsmanship before and after the War. One regular at Lord's said it was a treat to see again a batsman who kept his legs clear of the wicket, who cut and drove in front of the wicket, and never poked.

The slower scoring rates continued to bug many people and Dick Young, the Sussex and England player, came to the defence of modern batsmen by arguing that batting was more difficult than twenty years earlier. He pointed to the swerving character of the bowling, to the inswings and outswings, to the break from the leg, to the ball which came in abruptly from the off, and to the massing of fielders on the onside. He urged that the old methods, the old strokes, and even the old stance, were not possible if a batsman were to make runs.

The year had started sadly with the death of Jimmy Tyldesley, one of the four cricketing brothers from Westhoughton, all of whom

218

died relatively young. Bill was killed in the War aged 30, Jimmy was only 33, Harry was to die aged 42, while Dick, the most famous member of the family, was only 46 when he died. Jimmy, a fast bowler, had helped the county through those uncertain years after the war and was the leading wicket-taker in 1919 with seventy-two. In 116 matches for Lancashire between 1910 and 1922 he took 309 wickets.

The MCC had been to South Africa in the winter of 1922–23 and although they had won the series 2–1 they had run into problems with a 27-year-old left-arm pace bowler called Alf Hall, who had taken twenty-seven wickets at 18.55 runs each. Hall's father wrote to Old Trafford from Johannesburg to point out that his son was born in Bolton, he was coming to England, and would like to help Lancashire. Lancashire needed a pace bowler and were interested, but MCC ruled against his playing in the championship in 1923 because he had already played for South Africa in the same calendar year. He did play against the Universities and with success, having a match return of eight for 149 at Cambridge and eight for 96 at Oxford. He also played for Lancashire against West Indies and the Rest of England and in 1924 was fully qualified to play in the championship, too. One of the early games of that season was against the South Africans who said they would not have recognized their former teammate, who was not bowling anything like as well as he had done at home. In five matches Hall took three wickets for 199 runs . . . and that was the end of his career with Lancashire. He returned home and played three more Tests, all against England.

The 1923 season was also notable for the arrival on the first-class scene of George Duckworth, who was quickly to be recognized as Lancashire's finest wicket-keeper since Dick Pilling.

GEORGE DUCKWORTH, born on 9 May 1901, was the eldest of ten children of Arthur Duckworth who kept wicket for Warrington for twenty years. And just because his father was a wicket-keeper, George was told to keep wicket for the Grammar School second team when he was a scholar of 12. He obeyed though he had never kept wicket before and also played in that position for Warrington 2nd, stepping up into the first team at the age of 15 when his father injured a finger. After seeing the 22-year-old Duckworth's first two matches, J. R. Clegg, the *Manchester Evening News* cricket writer, said he thought he would turn out to be Lancashire's best wicket-keeper for some years. This was a prophecy that turned out to be true. He stayed Lancashire's first-choice wicket-keeper for fifteen years, ahead of Bill Farrimond who was also good enough to play for England around the same time. Duckworth had to be a fine keeper when Lancashire played such magnificent, but

219

different bowlers as Ted McDonald, Cec Parkin and Dick Tyldesley in his early years. He was short and square, rather like an Oxo cube or a tank, and had a belligerent, demanding appeal which must have intimidated all but the strongest umpires. He played in twenty-four tests between 1924 and 1936 and would have played many more if Les Ames, with his accomplished batting, had not been around.

Duckworth's best year was Lancashire's best, that of 1928 when both were invincible. Duckworth claimed 107 victims with seventy-seven catches and thirty stumpings, including some breathtaking catches off leg glances against McDonald. Only Les Ames and Hugo Yarnold have taken more in a season and he is comfortably Lancashire's outstanding wicket-keeper in numbers of batsmen dismissed with 1,095. He toured Australia three times, twice as reserve to Ames when he did not play in any of the Tests, including the Bodyline tour of 1932–33. He retired in 1937 but played once more for Lancashire in 1938 when Farrimond was absent, taking his number of matches for the county to 424 in fifteen seasons. He later became a baggage master for touring teams, he broadcast on cricket and Rugby League and as well as being a director with Warrington Rugby League team, he served on Lancashire's committee, surviving the 1964 upheaval before dying on 5 January 1966, when he was aged 64.

Lancashire took a county match to Blackpool in 1923 for the first time since 1911, but had to travel from London the previous evening after playing at Lord's. They were still in Crewe refreshment room at midnight, it was well after 2 a.m. when most got to Manchester, and a few hours later they were on the early train to the coast. Cec Parkin made it all worth the effort when he took fifteen wickets in the defeat of Glamorgan, giving him twenty-five wickets in the week. By the end of June Parkin had taken 100 wickets, yet was beaten to the mark by Maurice Tate who was playing at Headingley and got there two hours ahead of him. Parkin, in only his second full season in first-class cricket, had another great year with 186 wickets for Lancashire, 209 in all, to follow the 181 of 1922.

Ernest Tyldesley was also having another superb year and his best innings was unquestionably his 236 against Surrey at The Oval which saved the day. Lancashire had followed on 251 behind and were still 117 adrift with six wickets standing when the second day ended. Tyldesley, 81 not out overnight, batted in all for five hours to earn a draw for his team in what is still the record score at The Oval by a Lancashire player.

People were queueing at 7 a.m. for the Roses match at Bradford. By 11 a.m. the ground was full but when the gates were closed the crowd rushed them and broke them down, several being hurt in the process. There were 30,000 people inside the ground and 10,000 outside, some of them perching on telegraph poles to try to get a glimpse of the play. Yorkshire won again and Lancashire had now gone nine Roses games without a win.

For the first time in his career Harry Makepeace scored 2,000 runs in the 1923 season, his average of just under 50 giving him third place in the English batting averages behind only Patsy Hendren and Phil Mead. Yet he could not get into the Players' team for the match against the Gentlemen, nor was he chosen for either of the Test trials. The second trial was held at Lord's in mid-August and when other players cried off, the selectors sent for Makepeace who was so indignant he refused to go. The committee persuaded him and he, Ernest and Dick Tyldesley were in the Rest of England side which lost to England.

HARRY MAKEPEACE, like his captain, Jack Sharp, was an international at cricket and soccer. Both played cricket either side of the First World War and both played in the same Everton team which played in two successive F. A. Cup finals in 1906 and 1907. Makepeace had the edge over Sharp in number of appearances for England, 4–2 at football and 4–3 at cricket. He toured Australia, which Sharp did not, and scored a Test century at Melbourne, and when his playing days were over after twenty-five years, he coached Lancashire for twenty years more. He followed in the great stonewalling traditions of Dicky Barlow and Albert Ward, a continuity that provided Lancashire with a stiff backbone over nearly sixty years. He was born in Middlesbrough on 22 August 1881, but moved with his family to Liverpool when he was only 10. It was here he learned both sports with Merseyside junior clubs. He was signed by Everton in 1901 as a forward but developed into a wing-half, winning his first cap against Scotland in 1906, the year he first played for Lancashire. Makepeace was then 23 and opened the innings with Archie MacLaren against Essex at Leyton. His development was slow. He was in his sixth season before he scored his first century although he was unfortunate in his second summer when MacLaren declared at lunch with Makepeace 99 not out. Lancashire were in their second innings against Sussex at Eastbourne and 100 appeared on the scoreboard for Makepeace when the players went for lunch. MacLaren declared and it was later discovered the man on the machine had made a mistake. Makepeace was a run short.

It was in 1911, when he was 28 years old and five years after his debut, that he really burst into prominence. He scored centuries at Stourbridge and Leyton and topped 1,000 runs for the first time. That was the first of twelve successive seasons in which he scored 1,000 runs. Twice he got over 2,000, the best season being 1926 when he scored 2,340 runs and averaged nearly 49 in the first of Lancashire's three successive championship wins. His tour of Australia came in 1920–21 and his finest performance was at Melbourne in the fourth Test when he scored 117 and 54. He played in four Tests in Australia, averaged nearly 35 against an attack spearheaded by Jack Gregory and Ted McDonald and in the face of a depressing 5–0 series defeat – yet never played again. The *Sydney Referee* said of Makepeace's century 'He was typical of the proverbial bull-dog pluck, a stern, determined battler, giving no points away and losing none. Watching the ball right up to the handle, Makepeace clipped everything that came along loosely.'

When he finished playing in 1930, Makepeace had played 487 times for Lancashire and scored 25,207 runs at an average over 36. The last of his forty-two centuries came on his forty-eighth birthday, the year before his retirement. He had coached Everton for a while and now coached Lancashire until after the Second World War, another twenty years of service before he died in 1952 aged 71.

Makepeace was a highly-respected, well-loved man. Everybody who came into contact with him spoke fondly about his courtesy, understanding and willingness to help. The *Liverpool Echo* writer, 'Ranger', said: 'His death removes one of the finest sportsmen it has been my good fortune to know. The name of Harry Makepeace was always synonymous with the highest standards of skill and clean sportsmanship at both cricket and football.'

The really quick bowler Lancashire had been looking for since the days of Walter Brearley arrived at Old Trafford in 1924. He was Ted McDonald, the Australian who had destroyed England in 1921 and who had returned to this country the following year to become professional with Nelson in the Lancashire League. Douglas McDonald, one of Ted's two sons who are still living in Lancashire, thought his father had been approached by Lancashire when he was here with the Australians in 1921. He joined Nelson purely to qualify for Lancashire, probably preferring the life of the professional cricketer in England to his life with the Co-op in Melbourne where he was an accountant. The facts would not quite support this for McDonald was still attached to Nelson when he qualified for Lancashire in 1924, and even went so far as to sign another two-year contract binding him to Nelson in 1925 and 1926. His commitment to Nelson, where it was said he was paid £600 a year, meant he could play only mid-week county cricket in 1924. Lancashire took care of the new contract with Nelson by buying it out for £500, plus the promise to play a county match at Nelson over the following two years.

Lancashire were also waiting for another Australian to qualify. But Frank O'Keefe, who came to this country with McDonald in 1922 and was playing with Church, another Lancashire League club, died in March, aged 27, following an operation for peritonitis.

McDonald made his debut on Wednesday, 28 May 1924, against Kent who questioned his residential qualification to play for Lancashire. The MCC declared everything in order and McDonald started his English county career by bowling non-stop for thirty-five overs and taking six for 73. Jack Sharp was captaining a side deprived of the services of his two main bowlers, Cec Parkin and Dick Tyldesley, who were in the Test trial at Trent Bridge. He made up for it by leaving McDonald on at the Station End. McDonald started at a great pace and Duckworth, standing well back, had to jump to take the ball. After ten fast overs, McDonald alternated between medium and fast as he took six of the first seven wickets. McDonald played twelve more matches that summer and finished with sixty-four wickets at 18 runs apiece. With McDonald in full support of Parkin and Dick Tyldesley, what might Lancashire achieve in 1925?

Tyldesley and Parkin had a great time in 1924. Tyldesley took 167 wickets in thirty matches for Lancashire (average 13.32) and Parkin 194 in thirty-two (13.38). Each took five wickets or more in an innings eighteen times and some of their returns were quite remarkable.

Parkin took eight for 20 in the opening match, against Derbyshire, and then produced some phenomenal bowling in the game against Glamorgan at Aigburth. Lancashire themselves had been bowled out for 49 and even as the telegrams of congratulation were winging their way from South Wales, Parkin was picking his way through their batting. He conceded only one run as he took the first six wickets, two of them caught in the deep, two snaffled by Dick Tyldesley at short leg, one bowled, and one a return catch when he threw the ball high in the air and caught it behind his back. He finished with six for 6, Tyldesley took four for 16 and Glamorgan were all out for 22 as they headed towards defeat by 128 runs.

CEC PARKIN was born in County Durham, not far over the Yorkshire border, on 18 February 1886. He played once for Yorkshire in 1906 before being barred, and was in league cricket when Lancashire asked him to play in 1914, the year that saw the start of the First World War.

Parkin was a character, an original, a comedian on and off the field who was loved by the crowds who flocked to see him in the early 1920s when he became a full-time county cricketer. Jack Hobbs described him as the best bowler in England at the time. Charlie Hallows, who played alongside him, said after fifty years playing and coaching, that Parkin was the best he had ever come across. Neville Cardus was a shade more cautious in his assessment but still described him, after a lifetime in the

game, as one of the greatest off-breakers he had seen anywhere. Not that Parkin could be described solely as an off spinner. Hallows said he was four bowlers in one who could open the attack with the new ball, bowl off breaks, leg breaks and wrong 'uns. He was unplayable on a sticky wicket and throughout a career that was relatively short in the first-class game, he produced many remarkable bowling returns.

When the war finished in 1918 Parkin was lured to Rochdale, the Central Lancashire League club, where he was the highest-paid professional in the country. Jimmy White, a powerful London financier and former Rochdale bricklayer, was president of the club and told the committee to get the best professional money could buy for the 1919 season. They went to Parkin, prepared to pay him £8 a week, which was big money then. The player asked for £10 and a deputation went to London to discuss the matter with Mr White who made a quick decision. 'Give it him,' he said. 'They pay street sweepers that down here.' He was the highest-paid professional in England but he needed a lot of money – he had seven children. Somebody once said to him 'It says here, Cec, you're the best bowler in England.' He replied 'Ay, but that doesn't feed these young devils.'

Parkin continued to play for Lancashire, but still only on odd occasions, and in the first three years after the war, he played only fifteen times for the county as he maintained his allegiance to Rochdale. But he was so impressive, he was chosen to tour Australia in 1920–21 and played in four of the five Tests against Australia in this country in 1921. He was 36 when he finally became a full-time first-class cricketer with Lancashire in 1922 and in his first full season he reached 100 wickets ahead of any bowler and finished with 181. In 1923 he took 209 wickets in all matches, 186 of them for Lancashire, and again reached 200 in 1924, 196 of them for Lancashire. He played for England against South Africa in 1924 but this proved to be his last Test match following his public criticism of the captain, Arthur Gilligan. Parkin's decline was noticeable almost from that game. He took 150 wickets the following year but the spring, it was said, had gone from his stride.

926 Parkin took thirty-nine wickets and did not play after the fourteenth match. So he played four full and five part-time seasons with Lancashire, but still finished with 901 wickets from 157 games. Cec Parkin was an outstanding bowler. If he had spent all his playing life with Lancashire – or any other county – he could have created records that would still be standing today. His flirtation with the first-class game, similar though longer than that of Sydney Barnes, was not enough to establish him among the greats.

Parkin was a popular man, a favourite with the people and the players. When teammates had benefits Parkin was always at the heart of them, whether taking a collecting box into the crowd or organizing

224

auctions in the pavilion during breaks in play. He enjoyed short runs and in one game found himself at the same end as his fellow batsman. The ball went flying for overthrows and instead of scampering back to his crease, Parkin shouldered his bat like a rifle, and marched down the pitch singing 'The British Grenadiers'. He returned to the leagues after finishing with Lancashire, he became a publican, put on weight so that he was around 18 stones, and for a time returned to Old Trafford as a bowling coach. Parkin died in a Manchester hospital of cancer of the throat in 1943 when he was 57. His ashes were scattered at Old Trafford.

Two weeks after the Glamorgan match, Parkin took five for 6 against Derbyshire, a return which Tyldesley improved on in the game against Leicestershire at Old Trafford in July. Parkin and McDonald opened the bowling and Tyldesley, two days after playing in his first Test match, was not introduced until Leicestershire were 78 for three. In five overs, he took five wickets without giving away a run and Leicestershire were all out for 89 with seven of their players failing to score. The fourth wicket gave Tyldesley his 100th of the season – it was 3 July – and was greeted with a great outburst of applause from the popular side which was renewed again and again. Tyldesley's five overs went as follows: . . . . . . w . . . . . w . . . . w . . . . w . w . Not to be outdone, Parkin took the first seven wickets in the second innings against Leicestershire before heavy rain forced the players off at 12.45 p.m. on the third day. Play resumed at 1.15 p.m. without any inspections of the wicket and on the stroke of lunch Lancashire got the ninth wicket when Charlie Hallows took a fine, diving catch. The players were going in to lunch, but Major Fowke, the Leicestershire captain, had already sportingly sent Alec Skelding out to bat, and the game continued. Skelding arrived to the accompaniment of thunder and lightning and it was 1.40 p.m. before Tyldesley got the last wicket. Five minutes later the heavens opened, and a deluge swept the ground.

Dick Tyldesley and Cec Parkin's greatest double act came on the Headingley stage on Tuesday, 10 June 1924, when Yorkshire, needing only 58 in their second innings to win, were bowled out for 33. It had been a low-scoring match on a rain-affected wicket but even so, Yorkshire, fielding an all-professional side captained by Wilfred Rhodes, were confidently expected to win easily enough. The ball was shooting, jumping and turning and every delivery was watched in anxious silence by the 3,000 spectators, nearly all of them Yorkshire supporters waiting to acclaim another victory. Yet the innings had been going only 80 minutes when George Duckworth stumped the last man, wicket-keeper Arthur Dolphin, and Lancashire had won a Roses game for the first time since 1919. Dolphin was so far out of his ground that Duckworth did not appeal but simply shouted 'Hurray', and Dick Tyldesley stood in the midst of his own team with a red, perspiring face, laughing like a schoolboy. Tyldesley had taken six for 18 (ten for 87 in the match) and Parkin three for 15 (eight for 61).

DICK TYLDESLEY was born on 11 March 1897, one of four brothers who played for Lancashire between 1908 and 1931. The boys were the sons of 'Old Jim' Tyldesley, a cricketer of massive build and immense local prestige in the Westhoughton area, a spin bowler and a captain who believed in terrorizing umpires and opponents. Dick, it seems, was the apple of his father's eye and came in for a little extra attention than that afforded to his brothers. In the evenings a page of Dick's homework book would be pegged down on a practice ground at what father reckoned to be a perfect length for a slow bowler. Dick bowled hour after hour with varying speeds, flights and spins until he could drop the ball at will on the paper. Old Jim, meanwhile, rested and smoked his pipe and grunted approval when necessary. Dick left the coalfield for a trial at Old Trafford in 1919 and his portly figure and broad, honest face quickly made him a favourite. At first he tended to pitch his leg breaks too far outside the batsman's legs, but as soon as he began to drop them to the line of the wickets with top spinners and off breaks thrown in, he became outstanding. He was in his fourth season, in 1922, before he took 100 wickets in a season, but from then on he reached 100 every season until 1931, the year he left Old Trafford after being unable to come to agreement over terms. His best year was 1924 when he took 167 wickets for the county, 184 in all matches and at the ridiculously low cost of under 14 runs each.

Neville Cardus said of him that year:

> He found that blind length which is a rare quality – among leg-break bowlers he alone has been able to exploit such a length. The price of a good leg-break bowler is a wavering length. Tyldesley is accurate and quick off the pitch, unusual in a leg-break bowler. Tyldesley did not get all his wickets with breaking balls – there is where the guile of this bland Lancashire lad comes in. Tyldesley's straight ball, alive and kicking with what is called top spin, is getting notorious on all cricket fields.

He was a true Lancashire lad, as broad in accent as in girth, a man of the soil. He had a simple, dry wit, an often unconscious humour that people loved. Cardus used to enjoy telling the story of Tyldesley taking a short-leg catch close to the ground and calling back the batsman – a Yorkshireman – as he left the crease. The ball, it seemed, had touched

226

the grass. Cardus complimented him later on his sportsmanship and Tyldesley replied 'Thanks Mr Cardus. Westhoughton Sunday School, tha knows.' And when the players were boarding the train for one of their many long journeys, it was Tyldesley who would cry out 'Is t' beer loaded up?'

Tyldesley made his Test debut in 1924, playing in four of the five Tests against South Africa and taking twelve wickets for 249 runs. He went on his only tour that winter, to Australia where he played in only one Test and did not take a wicket. It was to be six years before England asked him to play again, in two of the 1930 Tests with Australia when he took seven more wickets to finish his seven-Test career with nineteen wickets.

Tyldesley weighed about 16 stones in his playing days but was a wonderful fielder at short leg where his agility was amazing for a man of his bulk. He was a fighter with a cheery disposition and an outstanding personality who refused to accept defeat until the last ball had been bowled. His batting was an odd mixture of dainty pattings and cow shots with a heavy bat and in 374 matches for Lancashire he scored one century, against Nottinghamshire at Old Trafford in 1922, and fifteen 50s. He was a stubborn man. He dug in when he could not come to agreement with Lancashire at the end of the 1931 season and passed out of the first-class game when still only 34 and with a few hundred more wickets at his finger-tips. He then played with Accrington in the Lancashire League and Nantwich in the North Staffordshire League before dying on 17 September 1943, aged 46.

The day after Lancashire's memorable win over Yorkshire in 1924 marked the start of the Kent match set apart for Ernest Tyldesley's benefit and the celebration of Lancashire's Diamond Jubilee. There was no play on the opening day but 6,129 paid admission, a tribute to the popularity of the unlucky Tyldesley. During the morning the committee congratulated Parkin and Dick Tyldesley on their fine bowling against Yorkshire, while Parkin enlivened the weary hours of waiting in the pavilion by repeatedly auctioning the ball with which the damage was done. The proceeds went to Ernest's benefit, and the ball was later returned to Dick. On the second day the rain eased enough to allow the game to start, a good crowd assembled with more than 12,000 paying for admission, the 3rd Old Cheshires made merry music and the tea tables stood invitingly on the lawn. Dick Tyldesley took a huge collecting box round the ladies' pavilion and he and Parkin later collected money on the popular side where they were warmly greeted after their great performance at Headingley, and raised £129 towards the final figure of £2,458 for Ernest's benefit.

227

Many celebrated people attended the Diamond Jubilee dinner, among them Lord Harris who referred to his considerable part in ridding cricket of its throwers forty years earlier. He also spoke on covered wickets, saying he thought they would have a detrimental effect on the game and would lessen public interest. 'Let nature have its way and give the bowler his day,' he said.

George Duckworth, who had made his debut in June the previous year, scored his first 50 for Lancashire on 1 July 1924, and was progressing so rapidly that that same evening he learned he had been chosen to play for the Players at Lord's two weeks later. It must have been marvellous experience for so young a player to have kept wicket to such extremes as the express deliveries of McDonald, the leg-breaks and googlies of Dick Tyldesley, and the mysteries of Parkin.

After all the thrills of Headingley, where Yorkshire were bowled out for 33, it was not surprising that feelings were running high when the return match was staged at Old Trafford in August. There were 35,000 people present on the Bank Holiday Monday, a record for the ground, taking the gate receipts for the first two days to £2,450 and persuading the police to remove it in a prison van under special guard. Commented the *Manchester Evening Chronicle* 'Is it so very long ago when the county club was in financial distress with sore need of money and of practical businessmen? In recent summers the county club has gained new life and never has it been more prosperous or more happy than in its great Diamond Jubilee year.' Unfortunately, the weather again could not match the occasion although there was time enough for Maurice Leyland to score his first century for Yorkshire.

Train journeys were proving something of a problem about this time. Although Lancashire's match with Essex at Blackpool finished at 3.10 p.m. on the final day, the team did not arrive at Swansea for the match with Glamorgan until 8.15 a.m. the following morning. They left London Road Station in Manchester at 11.45 p.m. and had to make do with pillows and rugs in their reserved coach. Jack Sharp, who was now a Test selector, was unable to play and Alf Pewtress, an amateur batsman from Rawtenstall, captained the side for the first time. He lost the toss, Lancashire fielded, and the side went on to taste defeat for the first time that season in their twenty-third match. Malcolm Taylor, a stylish left-hand batsman from Heywood, made his debut and did not score a run in either innings as Glamorgan sensationally snatched victory by 38 runs. Glamorgan had entered the championship only three years earlier and their victory over the mighty, invincible Lancashire was hailed as a miracle. Pewtress sent his congratulations to Glamorgan through the *South*

Wales Daily Post who quoted Cec Parkin as saying 'We were fairly beaten and we have not any excuses to make at all. To put it bluntly, we came down to Swansea this week expecting to knock hell out of Glamorgan and I'm afraid we were a bit over-confident.' Harry Makepeace said he thought Lancashire threw the game away. 'We never expected Glamorgan to reach 100 in either innings. We ought to have got their people out much more cheaply – oh, much more cheaply.'

The Welsh papers were in ecstasies over the victory. The *South Wales Daily News* waxed lyrical:

> Lancashire, proud County Palatine, with all its tradition and prowess, unbeaten by the best of the English counties, has yielded to parvenu Glamorgan, the butt of short-sighted English critics. The scene which followed must be mirrored for ever in the memories of those who were present. It was a demonstration of proud amazement of heartfelt gratitude to those who had brought glory to Wales.

Six thousand joyous souls clustered round the eleven players and Frank Ryan, who had taken three wickets in an over, was carried back to the pavilion.

Ted McDonald joined Lancashire full time in 1925 and Jack Sharp, entering his third year as captain, must have been reasonably confident of winning the championship after finishing third and fourth in his first two years. Certainly, he could have asked little more of his bowlers. McDonald (198 wickets), Parkin (150) and Tyldesley (137) took 485 wickets between them, Charlie Hallows scored over 2,000 runs for the first time, Frank Watson, Harry Makepeace and Ernest Tyldesley all got over 1,000, and George Duckworth kept wicket immaculately, whether to McDonald or to Parkin and Tyldesley. For two weeks in June, Lancashire stood at the head of the table, but once Yorkshire had displaced them there was no stopping the White Rose taking the title for the fourth successive year with Surrey the runners-up and Lancashire third.

For the fifth time in their history Lancashire were involved in a game which was all over in a day in 1925. Once again it was Somerset, and, as in 1892 and 1894, the match was played at Old Trafford and Lancashire walked away with an easy win, this time by nine wickets.

The Whitsuntide Roses match was at Old Trafford this year and a record crowd of 36,000 – 31,975 paid - attended the second day. Often they sat and stood in a silence like that of the grave. They cheered every hit, every successful piece of fielding and stayed right to the end of a long day, closing at 6.45 p.m. Motor cars of all sorts, shapes and sizes rolled up in ceaseless procession into the spacious and well-equipped motor park now possessed by Lancashire, said to be the finest in the country and a big boon to the members. The game, however, was tedious and Lancashire had to be satisfied with first innings points.

Old Trafford staged three county matches in succession between 30 May and 9 June, that 1925 Whitsuntide, and the gates and receipts were as follows:

			£	s	d
v Yorkshire	1st day	12,474	728	5	3
	2nd	31,975	1959	16	1
	3rd	13,595	828	10	2
Total		58,044	3516	11	6
v Kent	1st	7,787	445	15	6
	2nd	13,263	779	18	0
	3rd	327	14	7	1
Total		21,377	1240	0	7
v Surrey	1st	20,112	1191	19	2
	2nd	20,176	1235	19	0
	3rd	618	31	0	7
Total		40,906	2458	18	9
Grand total		120,327	7215	10	10

The attendance figures represented only those who had paid and with the numbers of members added, there were about 65,000 spectators for the Yorkshire match, 24,000 for Kent, and 46,000 for Surrey, a grand total of 135,000 spectators for the three games.

Cec Parkin, who in 1924 had offended cricket with criticisms of the England captain, Arthur Gilligan, had his benefit match against Middlesex in 1925. He did all right, collecting £1,880, but the game was marked by a sad incident which led to Jack Sharp resigning the captaincy after saying he would never again play at Old Trafford. Sharp fielded at short leg and dropped a sitter off Harry Lee to the first ball of the match bowled by, of all people, Cec Parkin. The captain came in for abuse from the spectators throughout the match and there were even suggestions that he had dropped the catch to make sure of prolonging Parkin's benefit match. The *Liverpool Echo* correspondent, who went under the name of 'Bee' and knew Sharp especially well, interviewed the player who told him the Old Trafford crowd were known as wolves. He said they did not give a player a chance and said there had been cases where barracking had so upset some of the best batsmen in the side that they had delib-

230

erately thrown away their wickets rather than suffer further scorn. He said it was the popular side and not the members who were the problem. The barracking had continued for three days and he did not want to play again at Old Trafford because the crowd was too unkind.

There were three matches remaining at Old Trafford and Sharp missed the first two, against Glamorgan and Nottinghamshire. But he did captain at Blackpool and Nelson before relenting under pressure and agreeing to captain Lancashire in their last match at Old Trafford, against Gloucestershire. He received a great reception when he led the team out, the applause and cheering lasting for several minutes. He said later 'The appreciation of the attitude of my many friends and a large majority of the club has induced me to change my mind. I altered my decision because I did not want to leave Old Trafford, which has pleasant memories for me, with any ill feeling.' Nevertheless, he did resign the captaincy in November although he said it had nothing to do with the incident and was purely because of business. 'After twenty-five years of cricket I was beginning to get tired,' he said. He was 47.

The game against Gloucestershire marked the highest partnership against Lancashire at Old Trafford, a record that still stands today. It was for the third wicket and was between 39-year-old Alf Dipper and 22-year-old Walter Hammond who came together at 20 for two and in 3 hours 45 minutes shared in a partnership of 330. It was a long time since the Lancashire bowling had been made to look so cheap. Dipper scored 144 but it was Hammond, even at that age, who caught the imagination with his 250 not out. He reached 100 in 125 minutes, 200 in 250 minutes and reached his 250 in 350 minutes, by a drive for 6 off a ball offered in the most thoughtful manner by the kind Dick Tyldesley.

It was during the closing weeks of the season that Lancashire played at Nelson for the first time, a game which had been promised as part of the payment for the Lancashire League club agreeing to release Ted McDonald. The match was against Derbyshire and was on a Lancashire League ground for the first time. Nelson became the eighth ground in Lancashire to stage the county's matches and to make doubly sure, they prepared two wickets, one of them with marl dressing, under the supervision of one of Lancashire's former players, Willis Cuttell. The game started on a Saturday and the Lancashire League avoided clashes with the county match by having no fixtures at the neighbouring grounds of Colne, Burnley and Lowerhouse. There were 10,000 spectators on the opening day and 6,000 on the Monday despite the mills refusing to close for the half day as they did when Nelson Football Club, then a Third Division side, staged important Cup-ties. The match receipts were nearly £1,000 and Lancashire were more than happy with their arrangement over McDonald. Nelson, perhaps feeling a little full of themselves, asked for more attractive opposition than Derbyshire for 1926; a team with one or two personalities. They were given Essex.

The *Manchester Guardian*, through Neville Cardus, enjoyed the trip to a new ground:

> The Nelson cricket field rests in a valley; around there are hills and trees and fields. To approach the ground you must walk through narrow streets that wind up and down. Authentic Lancashire? The crowd on Saturday was Lancashire in its homeliness; everybody was acquainted with everybody else and all used the Lancashire and not the Manchester speech. I found it pleasant to see Lancashire cricket in a setting so full of 'county' flavour; here could we enjoy more than ever the rough and jolly shape of Richard Tyldesley and here we could understand such 'Lancashire lads' as Iddon, Duckworth and Hallows. The crowd watched the match with the interest and enthusiasm of true lovers of the game. Lancashire cricket springs out of the soil that is as honest and as rich as any in Yorkshire; let us cultivate it like any conscientious gardeners.

Lancashire won the match by 97 runs. Charlie Hallows opened the innings and scored 65 not out and 68 and McDonald, back on 'home' ground, took one for 12, and four for 47.

The signing of McDonald, however good he might have been, did not meet with universal approval. He was a Colonial. Many thought the Lancashire team was for Lancashire players and a resolution to that effect was presented to the annual meeting on Monday, 7 December 1925, when an unusually large number of members attended for the important vote. The resolution, proposed by Mr T. O'Gorman was 'That in future no player shall be put on the county team unless he has a birth qualification for the county, this resolution not to affect any player who is at present engaged by the county.' The committee opposed the resolution and Sir Edwin Stockton, the president and former treasurer, said it was the standard of play that mattered and not accidental birthplaces. He said people would not support indifferent sides; they came to see good cricket, not to look into birth certificates. Such a policy would have deprived first-class cricket of many great players of the past. The feeling of the meeting on Mr O'Gorman's motion was never tested because a watered-down amendment was carried. It read 'That this meeting is of opinion that, while the committee should as far as possible only include Lancashire-born men in the county team, it is undesirable that men who have settled and whose interests are in the county, should be excluded from county cricket.'

It was announced that in seven years the membership of the club had grown from 1,080 to 3,831 which represented a growth of income from £1,475 to £9,338.

Less than three weeks after the 1925 annual meeting, A. N. Hornby, who had fashioned the course of Lancashire cricket, died at his home in Nantwich. Here was a man who had played in the first match against Yorkshire and who had seen Old Trafford gates for Roses matches grow from 200 to 36,000. His funeral was held just before Christmas and an almost continuous stream of motor cars moved through the narrow, tortuous streets of Acton in Cheshire, a cortège that passed between avenues formed by the public. The large crowd stood in the rain while the Reverend F. O. Poole, another rugby international and personal friend of Hornby, conducted the graveside service. There were wreaths of red roses from Lancashire and white ones from Yorkshire. The Lancashire wreath was placed on the coffin along with the family one and Albert Henry, his son, plucked a red rose and threw it into the grave. Said the *City News* 'Many of his acts would not appeal to our more democratic age today. But Lancashire will never forget what they owe him. In the history of Lancashire cricket A. N. Hornby will be honoured for all time.' He was 78.

Chapter 10 1926–30

'This was the most glorious period in Lancashire's history.'

With the retirement of Jack Sharp in 1925, the committee made every effort to get 29-year-old Ormskirk-born Jack Barnes to become captain. He had played for Lancashire when business allowed since 1919, a fine, stylish batsman who had scored three centuries and captained the side on occasions. But he was a Liverpool cotton merchant and did not want to give an entire summer to playing cricket. So he refused. Alf Pewtress, who had been chosen by the committee to lead Lancashire at the end of the 1925 season whenever Sharp was away, had, like Sharp, played his last match that year. So the committee turned to 36-year-old Major Leonard Green from Whalley, a middle-order batsman who had been playing since 1922 and had scored one century, at Gloucester in 1923. It was an inspired choice. He captained Lancashire for only three years, and they won the championship in each of them. This was the most glorious period in Lancashire's history. After the hat-trick of championships, they won the title again in 1930 and then, for the eighth time in their history, were champions in 1934. And that is the last time they have won the title outright although they did share with Surrey in 1950. The man at the heart of Lancashire's resurgence from 1926 was their Australian fast bowler, Ted McDonald, who took 484 championship wickets at 20.50 runs each through those hat-trick years.

EDGAR ARTHUR McDONALD was born in Launceston, Tasmania, on 6 January 1891, and first played cricket for the island when he was 18. Two years later he was on the mainland playing for Victoria. His first game was against New South Wales when he took two wickets for 116

234

runs; his second was against MCC when his only first innings wicket, that of George Gunn, cost him 106 runs. It was a poor start and he was not chosen again for three years, until the season following the outbreak of war. When the war finished he went straight into the Victoria side and made an immediate impact so that when Test cricket was resumed in 1920–21, against England, McDonald played in three of the five Tests. Although he was disappointing with six wickets costing 65 runs each, he was in the team for England in the summer of 1921, teaming up with Jack Gregory to form one of the most magnificent pairs of opening bowlers the world has seen. *Wisden* thought McDonald the finer bowler, Gregory by far the most alarming. Australia won the series 3–0 with McDonald taking twenty-seven wickets at 24.74 runs each and Gregory nineteen at 29.05 each.

Frank Woolley, who played in every Test in the 1921 series, once said he respected Gregory more than McDonald. 'Gregory bowled fair,' he said. 'He could slip one when he wanted to. He was tall, you see. Used to jump in the air. If he dropped it a yard or two short it always came up pretty high.' Of McDonald he said:

> Some, like the Australian McDonald, sometimes bowled at you deliberately. Once, after hitting him over square leg for six twice, I walked down almost to the bowler's end and began patting down the pitch – near his toes. He looked straight at me and said 'Keep your eyes open!' In the next over he hit the peak of my cap! But he never was cross. He was a good sport. He'd chat afterwards and he'd say 'You know I'm not trying to hit you' and I'd say 'Well, why on earth do you bowl like that, Mac?' 'I get more wickets that way, that's why,' he'd say, bursting out laughing.

Douglas Jardine, who led England on the Bodyline tour of 1932–33, wrote in the *Nottingham Evening News* on Monday, 22 May 1933, that the first time he saw leg theory bowled – and well bowled – was by McDonald.

McDonald was back in England the following year (1922) to play for Nelson in the Lancashire League. It was a great coup for Nelson and created enormous interest, not just in the small cotton town, but throughout the league. He played for Nelson from 1922 to 1924 and after also playing part of the season for Lancashire in 1924, he became a full-time county cricketer in 1925, when he was 34. Lots of fast bowlers are nearing the end of their careers at 34 and if not, have usually passed their best. But McDonald played for Lancashire until he was 40 years old, bowling his heart out and helping them win four championships in five years. In eight summers with Lancashire, of which only six were full ones, McDonald took 1,053 wickets at 20.96 each. In those six full seasons, he took more than 100 wickets five times and 200 once for a total of 963 . . . an average of 160 wickets a season for six years from the age of 34.

McDonald was a beautiful, graceful fast bowler who ran up to the stumps silently and stealthily, rather like the West Indian, Michael Holding, in recent years. But there were times when he had to be goaded, prodded or beseeched into real action. At times, such as at Dover in 1926, he would forsake his fast bowling to experiment with off spinners. Kent had had all day in which to get 400 to win and McDonald started sending down his spinners from round the wicket before lunch. The game dragged on and during the tea interval the players begged him to get into action and Leonard Green ordered a large whisky for him. He went on to the field and took a hat-trick at a great pace.

Reg Parkin, son of Cec, joined the Lancashire staff in the 1920s and was often 12th man because of his fine fielding. 'He was a great bowler and a fine man,' said Reg of McDonald. 'And his lunch always consisted of a fish sandwich and a large whisky.'

It became noticeable in 1929 and particularly in 1930 that McDonald seemed to have lost some of his skill and had developed a marked tendency to pitch short to try to demoralize batsmen. He had a serious loss of form in 1931 and though he took various spells of rest he could not produce his old pace and at the end of the summer had taken only twenty-six wickets at 38.65 runs each. His contract had another year to run but it was ended by mutual agreement and McDonald, now turned 40, returned to the leagues where he played with Bacup and then with Blackpool as an amateur. He managed the Raikes Park Hotel in Blackpool and was returning home in the small hours of Thursday, 22 July 1937, after playing in a benefit match at Manchester, when his car was in collision with another vehicle on the Blackrod by-pass near Bolton and crashed through a fence and into a field. McDonald was unhurt and went back to the road and was discussing the incident with the other driver and the occupants of his car and a policeman when a third car came along, struck McDonald and killed him. He was 46.

The 1926 season marked the start of the finest period in Lancashire's history with four championships in five years, the only 'failure' coming in 1929 when they were runners-up. Eight players provided the backbone of the team through those championship years – Charlie Hallows, Ernest Tyldesley, Frank Watson, Jack Iddon, Frank Sibbles, Dick Tyldesley, George Duckworth and Ted McDonald. Harry Makepeace and Leonard Green played in the 1926–7–8 winning years but had effectively finished by 1930. Others who made significant contributions were Peter Eckersley, Malcolm Taylor, Len

Hopwood and Eddie Paynter. Seven members of the hat-trick winning team were Test players, although only Duckworth and perhaps Ernest Tyldesley could ever be said to have established themselves in the England team. And only three of them played Test cricket during those hat-trick years – Hallows (one game), Ernest Tyldesley (four) and Duckworth (one) – which must have considerably helped Lancashire's cause. Yet the really important contributor, and the one – if one man can ever be thought to be so important – to win the championship for Lancashire through those years was McDonald.

Lancashire were slow to get moving in 1926. On the morning of 1 June they were standing in seventh position in the championship with only two victories. But on that day they pulled off a most unlikely win over Surrey at Old Trafford to take the first real step towards the title. As one writer put it 'This game will surely make a new team of Lancashire; the inspiration of it can hardly be forgotten in a hurry.' Surrey, who had led by 95 on the first innings, needed to score only 159 in 150 minutes to win. By tea, with an hour left, they wanted 58 with seven wickets standing. But soon after the interval Jack Hobbs was stumped and Bert Peach bowled in one over from Sibbles and Surrey, after slumping to 122 for nine with 13 minutes remaining, lost by 34 runs when Dick Tyldesley had Stan Fenley lbw with the last ball of the match.

There is a photograph of the 1926 team which includes Cec Parkin, dressed in his suit with waistcoat and tie. It was a nice thought but Parkin really played very little part in winning the championship, taking only thirty-six wickets in eleven matches. His last game for the county was their fourteenth of the season, against Leicestershire at Ashby-de-la-Zouch when he was hit out of the ground four times in seven balls by a tail-end batsman, Haydn Smith. That finished Parkin and also looked to have ended any thoughts of Lancashire winning the championship as they went down by 144 runs to one of the weakest counties.

Yorkshire won the first Roses match at Bradford by an innings, but by the time the return had arrived at the start of August, Yorkshire, the Champions, were being hard-pressed by Lancashire, the Pretenders. The championship was decided at this time by percentage of points obtained to maximum points possible. And as three points were awarded to a county winning first innings in a drawn match as against five for winning the match, strong teams facing one another played first for the three points . . . then looked for the win. Lancashire and Yorkshire did not even get to the second innings at Old Trafford, Lancashire taking three points to Yorkshire's one after scoring 509 for nine declared to Yorkshire's total of 352, the last wicket falling ten minutes from the end of the final day. There were no hold-ups in this tense tussle, not a shower, not a drop of rain, and 375 overs were bowled, an average of 125 overs and 287 runs a day. The crowd on Bank Holiday Monday was estimated at 45,000 after 38,955 had paid, the largest ever seen on a county ground anywhere in the country. And the aggregate attendance for the three days, including members, was around 71,000. There was one unfortunate incident in the match when Edgar Oldroyd was struck on the head by a ball from Ted McDonald and had to be carried semi-conscious from the field by Malcolm Taylor and Dick Tyldesley. He did not come round properly and was taken to Manchester Royal Infirmary vomiting and bleeding from the nose. Happily, he recovered but he did not play again that season.

Yorkshire stayed top of the championship that year right up to the home straight. But they could not hold off the strong run by Lancashire who won nine of the last twelve matches. Ten days from the end Yorkshire were top, but Lancashire stepped up the pace, winning the last three games by eight, ten and ten wickets, while Yorkshire won only two of their last five games. The Yorkshiremen, whose team had gone through the season undefeated, were none too pleased. They pointed to Lancashire's two defeats in the championship, one by an innings and 94 to Yorkshire, and added, in *Wisden*, 'In face of these facts it may reasonably be urged that the present system of deciding the championship is unsatisfactory – and with that opinion most people will agree.'

Lancashire went into the last match needing to beat Nottinghamshire to win the title and without their captain, Leonard Green, who had hurt his wrist. Peter Eckersley, who was to become captain in his own right in 1929, led the team to a famous victory in which Harry Makepeace scored 180 in what many regarded as the best innings of his life. Nottinghamshire, 234 for four at tea on the first day, were all out for 292. By the end of the following day they were 46 for four in their second innings after trailing by 162 on the first. They managed to avoid the innings defeat – just – and it was left to the senior professionals, Ernest Tyldesley and Harry Makepeace, who had done so much for Lancashire that season, to have the honour of getting the 33 runs needed for a ten-wicket win.

The crowd surged over the railings almost before the ball had been fielded and a cordon of police who rushed to hold them back were helpless. The spectators scrambled for souvenirs and the umpires had a few tussles with people who tried to take from their pockets the coppers which they had used for counting the number of deliveries. Arthur Carr succeeded, after a struggle, in getting the ball and he and Peter Eckersley autographed it and presented it to Sir Edwin Stockton, the Lancashire president. McDonald took eleven wickets in this match, part of his haul of 163 for the season. He had a great summer which also provided him with his only first-class century, by courtesy of Middlesex captain Frank Mann who agreed to play on into the lunch interval for one over so McDonald could complete it. It took him 100 minutes, achieved mainly by good batting before he began to slog towards the end.

The year of 1926 marked the second visit to England since the War of the Australians, an attractive side led by Herbie Collins who were to lose the Test series 1–0 after starting with four draws. The Old Trafford Test was played towards the end of July and with the outcome of the Ashes, of course, still open. The interest was tremendous; cricketers were celebrities, and crowds flocked to Old Trafford from all over the country to witness the Fourth Test. The *Manchester Evening Chronicle*, more than any other newspaper, conveyed the feeling of the ordinary spectator to this great clash. This report tells us not only of the attraction of cricket at this time, but tells us much about the working man, especially the Lancashire working man, of his feelings, his habits, his humanity.

The *Evening Chronicle* sent a reporter to Old Trafford shortly before midnight on the eve of the opening day. A policeman pointed out the queue which had already formed, consisting of about twenty men, lounging about or sitting against the wall, arguing the toss with heat and animation. 'There was but one argument,' reported the *Evening Chronicle* on the first day of the match, Saturday 24 July:

> Tyldesley. Would he be played or would he not? 'Played be blowed,' said the explosive member of this little parliament, 'he's got to be played, and him with that record what would knock them all into a cocked hat.' The small man with a clay pipe thought not. At this there was a chorus of dissent. There was a scuffle, heavy blows, a crash, and the onlooker staggered up the road, spitting. A man quietly walked back to the queue and sat down. There was a moment's silence. 'Quite right, Bill,' said a quiet voice. 'Ah've been working all day, but a mint o' gold wouldn't keep me from the Test match. Ah'm proud o' staying out all night, tired though I be.' 'Same here, same here,' the other men cried in chorus.
>
> The first to arrive at the queue, I found, was Bernard Linguack, a 15-year-old schoolboy of Southport. He had arranged with two other schoolboys to leave Southport early yesterday (Friday) for the walk to Manchester. His companions, one gathered, were prevented from joining in the adventure. Their purpose was discovered and they

239

were thrashed soundly and sent back to bed. Undaunted, Bernard made the journey alone, arriving at 7 p.m. last night. He was dead beat and lay on his back near the entrance. The men, with rough kindliness, threw a coat over him. 'Yon's the reet spirit,' they said.

A young man, Henry Rust, of Linton Street, Salford, chanced to be passing. Seeing the plight of the boy, he offered him a bed for the night. 'I can't risk it,' replied the lad. 'Don't bother lad,' said the men. 'Tha shalt be th' first to go in the morrow.' And the lad went away with his kind Samaritan. There was a stout man who had walked on crutches all the way from Warrington; clogged miners from Leigh; men and lads from the mills in thin overcoats, wearing scarves round their necks. And occasionally an escorted woman came long, and turned away again when she realized there was no hurry as yet to take her place. It was a loosely-formed queue in which each man bagged his place by setting down his can of milk, his sandwiches and provisions for the day. Now and again, two or three would get up and go to drink a cup of tea under the flaring naphtha lamps of the neighbouring stall. The remarkable thing is that the crowd did not increase from midnight until nearly six o'clock in the morning, and from that time until eight it grew but slowly. At six there were only seventy-five people at the gates. At half past seven there were from 450 to 500. The first train that came into the station had two people in it, and a number of others arrived which were nearly as empty. The early Corporation cars carried very few people, and it was not until eight that traffic became brisk.

Montague Wesley was there, the one-legged man who does marvels in the way of jumping. William Thorne, of Pendlebury, he announced, had accepted his challenge to a high jumping and 100 yards hurdle race. Israel Joseph also made it known to the public that Hobbs had promised him a new pair of legs if he made a century in this Test and the match was won. But the great attraction for the queue was a miner, one of those born natural humorists whose every word and gesture go straight to the heart of a crowd. His witty comments kept it in an uproar, especially when an unlucky padre became the butt of his wit.

The first woman arrived at five o'clock and the men – even those who had waited all night and were chagrined to find that it had not been necessary – gallantly offered

240

to move her up to the head of the queue. But she blushingly declined, and pleaded equal rights and equal opportunities. From an early hour those entertainers who were well known to Test match followers were busily at it, reaping a meagre harvest from the small crowd. About eight o'clock the crowd began to get impatient. 'Come on; what about these doors?' they yelled. 'Hurry up, we'll have th' Aussies missing their boat back.' Early arrivals last night were six Leigh miners who dredged two tons of coal out of the Bridgewater Canal yesterday to pay their admission to the ground. They walked to Old Trafford and prepared an al fresco meal about midnight.

Very few of the waiters had omitted to bring food, with which they were generously supplied. All were lost in admiration of Percy Brown and A. Russel of Ancoats, the self-styled 'Cowheel eating champions of Lancashire.' Between eight o'clock last night and eight o'clock this morning these two mighty eaters had disposed of six large cowheels. All their available cash had been spent on cowheels. They relied upon their wit and entertaining powers to provide the rest. 'They have been as lively as crickets all night,' said an elderly man. 'They have sung and danced and kept us all awake. We have managed to scrape enough together to pay for their admission – and another cowheel.' A party of miners from Swinton spent the night on the banks of the neighbouring canal [near United's football ground] as affording better shelter. This morning alongside the queue, there was an impromptu rugby match between miners from Swinton and Leigh, and Swinton carried off the honours.

At 8.15 mounted police arrived and marshalled the queue. In the last 15 minutes it had increased by some 800 more. There were not more than a score of women in the early-morning arrivals. The gates opened promptly at 8.30 and there was an orderly entrance. The queue numbered about 3,000 and stretched the length of the ground with an overflow along Talbot Road. Just prior to opening, several men who had kept an all-night vigil, bargained their places in the queue. The first latecomer to accept the invitation roused the ire of the majority and there were no further acceptances.

Despite an all-night wait, the majority were spick and span, particularly the miners and other unemployed who had remained out all night. They brought their army

241

experience to bear, and many of them had a 'wash and brush up' in the canal. One towel and a piece of soap did duty for the lot. It transpired that many of the miners had brought army mess tins with the intention of 'drumming up' in the roadway. They were unable to prepare tea, however, as there was no drinking water available and they were loth to use that out of the canal. Just before the gates opened the news spread along the crowd that fresh crabs were on sale. An enterprising merchant had set up a booth crammed with hundreds of crabs. Several clubbed together to purchase crabs for a second breakfast which was eaten on the ground.

Half an hour after the gates opened, there was a crowd of 10,000 to 15,000 assembled. Both of the covered stands on the popular side were filled. To make sure of having a good view of the game there was a rush for the portion surrounding the playing pitch which had been allocated specially for today. Mackintoshes were spread on the damp grass and the front-seat spectators sat down to await 11.30. Considerable indignation was expressed when the police on duty prevented men from playing cards. 'We're not gambling,' it was said. 'It doesn't matter,' was the reply. 'It isn't allowed on this ground.' Men in plus fours and women with cushions arrived on the popular side and paid the additional fee for accommodation on the stand. Most of the crowd carried mackintoshes and lunch cases.

When the flag lent by Mr Plum Warner, that has never known defeat in a rubber of Test matches, was hoisted, it brought the first cheer from the waiting thousands. Charabanc parties from towns all over Lancashire and Yorkshire made their appearance. One party from Blackburn marched in two by two, each pair carrying in the crook of the arm a bottle of beer.

Another reporter was at London Road Station:

From everywhere within a radius of 80 miles of Manchester there were special rates by all trains for Test match devotees. 'What's the wicket like, mate?' was the password as they landed, clutching brown paper parcels of sandwiches, or worse, and stowed the empties under the seats. Another group, their faces hidden under large cloth caps, solemnly mounted on a trolley at the end of the platform. 'Silence for the choir,' commanded a sepulchral voice. Two others hitched themselves to the shaft and slowly paraded the

242

trolley and its load up the platform. A little faltering on the higher register, the choir sang this little song:

'We want Tyldesley,
'We want Tyldesley,
'We want Tyldesley,
'Tyldesley for the Test.'

Reader, it is a simple song. It was rendered with more vigour than harmony, rising to a yell of command on the last noble phrase. A simple song, but there were many wet eyes when it was over, and large, strong men coughed with suspicious vigour into their handkerchiefs.

Several thousands of visitors had arrived at the various stations of the city by nine o'clock this morning. A large number of women and girls were mixed in the crowd for Old Trafford. They also took the match very seriously. In the place of the usual feminine conversation they grimly discussed the relative advantages of 'sticky wickets' and the necessity of 'Ernest' being included in the team. They were prepared for a long wait. As they settled on the corner seats and opened their attaché cases, a hasty glance disclosed bags of buns and bottles of milk and, whisper it gently, knitting . . . Charabancs brought other bands from the outlying Lancashire villages.

The *Daily Dispatch* identified the first man in the queue that Friday night as Mr A. Turner of Hulme and said the miners from Leigh, who were wearing clogs, had set off before 6 p.m. A coffee stall was set up, some sang songs, others tried to sleep. The *City News* said eighty special tramcars had been laid on, the first tram leaving the city at 7.30 a.m. In addition to the ordinary service, 100 trams an hour plied between the city and Old Trafford for the first hour or two. The Australian team motored from Edinburgh the day before the match started and stayed at the Midland Hotel. Sir Edwin Stockton's guests, who had travelled from London on a special train driven by one of the latest oil-burning machines, were also staying at the Midland.

Several thousand enthusiasts gathered outside the Queens Hotel on the Saturday morning to watch the English team depart. Four motor cars drew up and when the players appeared there were three cheers for England and three more for their captain, Arthur Carr. With the team was a huge Teddy Lion mascot wearing a cricketer's cap and the English badge, while Frank Woolley carried a large blue golly sent to the team for luck.

Similar scenes at the ground were witnessed on Sunday night and

243

Monday morning. The *Daily Dispatch* said the first spectator on the Sunday night was a schoolboy, William J. Whiteside from Ducie Avenue, Clayton. He arrived at the ground shortly before midnight and just ahead of four colliers who had walked from Oldham. They warmed themselves on coffee and then played football on the nearby spare land. The *Manchester Evening Chronicle* of Monday 26 July, reported that from as far back as Friday night, regardless of the weather, a number of people – principally colliers and schoolboys – had never left the immediate area of Old Trafford. They had slept on ground sheets under hedges, under carts and umbrellas, sometimes finding their pitches covered with water and sometimes wakening to pitiless rain beating on their faces.

The Maharajah Kumar of Vizianagram, who was then only 20 years old and who was to captain India in England ten years later, stayed at the Midland and drove to the ground in his Rolls Royce. When asked about the weather, which restricted play in the drawn match to ten deliveries on the Saturday, he said 'You people ought to do something about it. In India we don't let the weather get the better of us. In India when it shows signs of getting out of hand, we turn our enchanters and sorcerers on to it and it is brought to its senses in no time.'

Sir Edwin and Lady Stockton entertained the teams and their guests to a dinner at the Midland Hotel where the Banqueting Hall was a blaze of splendour. The central portion of the top table was a miniature cricket pitch, the vivid green complete with wickets, bat and ball. A kangaroo carved out of a huge block of Norwegian ice was wheeled triumphantly around the room. Salmon was served with sauce Collins, the potatoes were associated with Bardsley, patties were given a Macartney savour, chicken was garnished with a Carr salad. Tim O'Brien, now 64 years old and the only survivor from the first Test at Old Trafford in 1884, was among the guests. The Stocktons also laid on a boat trip along the Ship Canal on the Sunday.

The title was Lancashire's again in 1927. Ted McDonald again led the attack with 150 wickets followed by Dick Tyldesley with 100 and Frank Sibbles eighty-nine. Charlie Hallows cleared 2,000 runs for the second time for an average of 73, Ernest Tyldesley and Frank Watson both scored more than 1,500. Lancashire won seven of their first ten championship matches but rain through July and August restricted them to three wins in the remaining twenty-two matches. Their only defeat came in the penultimate championship match, a thrashing by Sussex by an innings and 196 runs at Eastbourne which looked to have cost them the title. Slow batting on the second day cost Lancashire the chance of beating Leicestershire in the final match and Nottinghamshire, who had decisively beaten Glamorgan and Derbyshire in the same period, looked to have made sure of their first championship for twenty years. Nottinghamshire went to Swansea for the final match needing only to avoid defeat to take the title. How could they possibly lose? Glamorgan had not won a match all season and had just lost to Nottinghamshire at Trent Bridge five days earlier. Nottinghamshire scored 233 and Glamorgan replied with a record opening partnership of 158 in 135 minutes to give them the foundation for a total of 375. Opener Bill Bates, 43 years old and Yorkshire-born, scored 163 and with Nottinghamshire sensationally dismissed for 61 in their second innings, Glamorgan had won by an innings and 81 runs and given the title to Lancashire by the narrowest of margins. The miracle had happened and arrangements in Nottingham for a civic welcome and reception had to be cancelled. Leonard Green was at Scarborough at the time. When told of the result, he said 'Is that true? Well, I am glad, but I am sorry for Notts.'

Three of the best centuries of the summer were played against Lancashire in the first half of the season. Walter Hammond, who seemed to thrive on the Lancashire bowling, scored a marvellous 187 in three hours at Old Trafford, Percy Chapman hit 260 in little over three hours at Maidstone, and Henry Enthoven scored 139 for Middlesex at Lord's, the last 89 coming in 55 minutes. Hammond had scored 99 and rescued Gloucestershire from 11 for three in the first innings. In the second, he reached his 50 in 40 minutes, his century in 85. He took on McDonald and was largely responsible for the fast bowler's second innings analysis of 36–1–165–2. In one over he hit five successive balls for 4, he hit three more 4s in an over and hit Jack Iddon for three 6s. One short delivery from McDonald which was aimed at Hammond's heart, was met with a horizontal bat which sent the ball hurtling back past the bowler to the boundary. Chapman's 100 took 95 minutes, his 200 came in 170, a blood-stirring double hundred that took Kent to 441 after being 70 for five. He and Geoffrey Legge shared in a stand of 284 in 130 minutes, which is still a record today for the county's sixth wicket. And McDonald? – 25–3–118–3. Enthoven had taken nearly two and a half hours to score his first 50 runs, then spent 25 minutes over his second 50. McDonald, with the new ball, was hit for 37 runs in three overs by Enthoven who scored 97 of the 110 made by the last two wickets to save the follow-on and earn Middlesex a draw.

Hammond that year became only the third player after W. G. Grace and Tom Hayward to score 1,000 runs by the end of May. And Charlie Hallows came desperately close to joining him as he scored 850 runs in his first ten innings. He had matches against Glamorgan and Worcestershire to get the 150 needed and was going well with 30 at Swansea when one half-appeal from the wicket-keeper resulted in him being given out lbw by umpire Jack Cuffe, who was living in Little Lever, the same village as Hallows! Lancashire needed only a few runs for victory in the second innings and when Hallows failed with his only knock at Dudley against Worcestershire, his chance had gone. He totalled 921 by the end of May and completed his 1,000 on 7 June. Remarkably, Hallows was to achieve the feat of 1,000 in May the following year, 1928. Hallows finished second in the national averages that summer of 1927 with an average of 75.58, he scored a century for England against The Rest, but was not chosen for the MCC tour of South Africa that winter of 1927–28.

CHARLIE HALLOWS was born in Little Lever on 4 April 1895, the nephew of Jim Hallows who had performed the double of 1,000 runs and 100 wickets for Lancashire in 1904. Charlie made his debut in 1914 and immediately established himself as a stylish left-handed opening batsman after the First World War, first with Harry Makepeace as his partner and then with Frank Watson. He is the only Lancashire player ever to have scored 1,000 runs in May, achieved in 1928, his benefit year, when he scored 2,564 runs for the county at an average of 65.74. This followed his outstanding batting the previous year and although clearly one of the foremost batsmen of the time, he played only two Tests and never toured with MCC. This was the peak of his career, yet two years later he had effectively finished. His runs and his average were halved in 1929, he never again even reached 1,000 runs in a season, and played his last match for Lancashire in 1932.

Hallows did not play in the opening match of the 1928 season, against Oxford University, so his first game was not until 5 May. But by 15 May he had scored four centuries and totalled 476 runs. A bit of a lean spell followed – comparatively speaking – and with two games to play, against Yorkshire at Sheffield and Sussex at Old Trafford, he required 324 more for the 1,000 in May. Clearly, it was a much stiffer task than the previous year when he had approached the last two games requiring 150 more. He did not really think he had much chance and when he hit only 58 and 34 not out in the drawn game at Sheffield, he was sure his chance had gone.

When the game against Sussex began at Old Trafford on Wednesday 30 May, Hallows still needed 232 runs. The captain, Leonard Green, was unfit and Peter Higson was brought in to lead the team, one of only three appearances he ever made for Lancashire. Higson played his part in Hallows's achievement by winning the toss and choosing to bat. Sussex were no pushovers with formidable opening bowlers in Maurice Tate and Arthur Gilligan, but by the end of the day Lancashire were 376 for three with Hallows 190 not out. He needed 42 more. Hallows hardly slept that night. The tension was tremendous and all he wanted to do was get down

to Old Trafford and get on with it. He was a bag of nerves when he walked out again to continue his innings. He said later he felt sure Sussex gave him the last 10 runs. 'I wish they hadn't,' he said. 'I was confident enough but playing carefully to make sure I did not miss.' He also badly wanted to get there because his benefit match was starting the following day. The Sussex bowlers bowled everything down the legside for the last 10 runs, and the final run from the nervous Hallows almost produced a catch for square leg. For a split second he thought he was out. Then everybody in the field gathered round to congratulate him. Next ball he was out when Jim Parks snapped up a beautiful catch. But it did not matter. Charlie Hallows was in history. The next match was for Hallows's benefit and, not surprisingly, he received nearly £3,000 which beat Ernest Tyldesley's and was second only to J. T. Tyldesley's £3,111 in 1906.

In the years from 1914 to 1932, Hallows scored 20,142 runs with fifty-two centuries for Lancashire; he scored 20,926 and fifty-five centuries in all first-class matches, and more than 1,000 runs in all eleven seasons from 1919 to 1929. Opening the innings with Makepeace in his early years played a large part in Hallows's success. But his partnerships with Watson were more prolific and in 1928 they shared in twelve stands worth more than 100 runs, five of them double centuries. These were the days when Jack Hobbs and Herbert Sutcliffe were England's established opening batsmen and Hallows played only twice for England. He took part in the 1921 game against Australia at Old Trafford after virtually only two years in first-class cricket, and his second appearance did not arrive until 1927 when Hobbs was injured and he played against the West Indies. When his county career was over Hallows went into the leagues before becoming a coach, first with Worcestershire, before finishing his career as he began it, at Old Trafford with the Lancashire team, more than fifty years after his debut! He died in 1972, aged 77.

Whatever reservations there might have been about Lancashire's championship wins in 1926 and 1927, they were swept aside in 1928 when they were unquestionably the finest team in the land. In 1926 they had been beaten twice, once by Yorkshire who stayed undefeated and were runners-up; in 1927 they won by a fraction of a point after Nottinghamshire slipped up against Glamorgan in the final match; but in 1928 there was no question – and here was the finest team in Lancashire's history.

The Lancashire batting in 1928 was the strongest it has ever been. For the first time in the club's history, three players, Hallows, Watson and Ernest Tyldesley scored more than 2,000 runs, and two more, Iddon and Makepeace, exceeded 1,000. Hallows scored eleven centuries that summer – a record for Lancashire – and Watson and Ernest Tyldesley nine each for the county. The Hallows-Watson opening partnerships were the best ever with twelve over 100, five of them double centuries. And the summer also produced the highest-ever partnership for Lancashire, one of 371 in 315 minutes between Tyldesley and Watson for the second wicket in Hallows's benefit match against Surrey at Old Trafford. Watson scored 300 not out in that match, only the second Lancashire player after Archie MacLaren to reach that figure, and the only treble hundred ever scored at Old Trafford.

FRANK WATSON was born on 17 September 1898 in Nottingham and was one of the very few 'foreigners' in a team whose players were mostly Lancashire-born. He was a stubborn, largely unattractive batsman whose name was usually linked with that of Charlie Hallows in lengthy opening partnerships. There was nothing extravagant or spectacular about him; he was down-to-earth, solid and dependable. To some he was unmemorable although he scored nearly 23,000 runs for Lancashire and hit fifty centuries, three of which were double-hundreds, one a treble-hundred. Watson was a heavy and consistent scorer but never played for England. Like Hallows, he suffered by playing at the same time as Jack Hobbs and Herbert Sutcliffe.

Watson went on one MCC tour, to West Indies in 1925–26 when he averaged over 40 in ten representative games and scored his only century from the unlikely, and apparently unexplained, batting position of No. 10. Watson first played for Lancashire when he was 21 years old in 1920, but it was 1923 before he got his first century and totalled 1,000 runs for the first time. He reached 1,000 twelve seasons out of thirteen – he was ill and missed most of the 1931 season – and went on to 2,000 in three successive years. He took part in seven double-hundred opening partnerships with Hallows – five of them in 1928, the year when he and Ernest Tyldesley put on 371 for the second wicket against Surrey at Old Trafford, which is a record for any wicket for the county. His unattractiveness was perhaps best summed up, though in a convoluted way, in his obituary notice in *Wisden*, which read 'Watson was a batsman whom spectators of 50 years ago will, unless they were fervent Lancashire supporters, remember as one of whom they wished to see as little as possible.' Still, Watson played an important part in Lancashire's five championship successes, allying his sheet-anchor batting with medium-paced or slow bowling which brought him over 400 wickets and earned him a reputation for breaking troublesome partnerships. His best season as a bowler was in 1925 when he bowled nearly 700 overs and took sixty-two wickets. His career was shortened by a ball from Bill Bowes which hit him in the eye and affected his confidence, forcing his retirement in 1937 at the relatively young age of 38. He died on 1 February 1976 aged 77.

Lancashire's bowling in 1928 relied heavily on McDonald in particular and Dick Tyldesley in support. McDonald bowled 1,254 overs and took 190 wickets for the county, Tyldesley 104 wickets, and the nearest to them were Iddon with sixty-three, Hopwood forty-three and Sibbles thirty-nine.

The batting asserted itself right from the opening match against Northamptonshire at Old Trafford when a total of 528 for four was reached in just under six hours with runs coming at 100 an hour after lunch. Watson scored 233 in 245 minutes and shared in stands of 200 with Hallows for the first wicket and 179, in 90 minutes, with Tyldesley for the second.

The most important and memorable match was the one against Kent at Old Trafford in mid-August. Kent were second in the championship table to Lancashire and if they were to have any realistic chance of overhauling them, they had to win. Frank Woolley, whose debut for Kent had been at Old Trafford twenty years earlier, certainly tried hard to provide it, and Len Hopwood, who was twice hit for six by Woolley, recalled the innings in some detail in later years:

> McDonald decided he could get Woolley out with a bouncer on the legside. So Jack Iddon was put halfway between the wicket and the boundary and 'Mac' began to bounce them. Woolley started to hit them, and we were all playing merry hell at this. Eventually Woolley did hook and Iddon took the catch and 'Mac' was full of glee. 'It's worked' he shouted. Yes, and Woolley had scored 151.

His runs came in just over three hours out of Kent's total of 277. Lancashire replied with an opening stand of 155 in 125 minutes from Hallows and Watson, the prelude to a total of 478 for five declared in six hours. Kent had no answer to the fire and pace of McDonald in the second innings and were all out for 113 to lose by an innings and 88. McDonald followed his seven for 101 of the first innings with eight for 53, a match return of fifteen for 154 which was the best of his career.

A week later, at Brighton, the championship was Lancashire's. Their first aim was to secure first innings points, and after Sussex had scored 300, Watson and Ernest Tyldesley shared in a stand of 306 in 225 minutes. Lancashire led by 242 before declaring and bowling out Sussex for 282 to secure victory by eight wickets with 15 minutes to spare. Lancashire had gone through 1928 undefeated, winning fifteen of their thirty matches and taking first innings points in nine others. Ten players formed the foundation of the team – Hallows, Watson, Ernest Tyldesley, Makepeace, Iddon, Hopwood, Green, McDonald,

Dick Tyldesley and Duckworth. Sibbles and Taylor played the most regular supporting roles.

One interesting game occurred at Colchester where Lancashire ended the Essex second innings at 6.25 p.m. on the second day. Lancashire needed two to win but there was no time to restart and the players had to return the following morning for what turned out to be two balls. The wicket-keeper, George Eastman, did not bother about pads, Johnny Douglas wore a sweater and plus fours, while others appeared shirt-sleeved in ordinary clothes. The following year, a rule was introduced, allowing extra time on the second day if there was a chance of finishing the match.

Leonard Green resigned the captaincy after completing the remarkable record of three championships in three years, and handed over to 24-year-old Peter Eckersley who led the team for seven years. It could not have been easy following a record like Green's and Eckersley had to be content with joint second place behind Nottinghamshire in his first season in 1929. Lancashire never really looked like winning the title after losing three of the first twelve matches, although they came along with a successful run of seven wins out of the remaining sixteen to finish joint second with Yorkshire. Only Frank Watson topped 2,000 runs this year, Hallows's form deteriorated alarmingly and the bowling again relied too heavily on McDonald (142 wickets) and Dick Tyldesley (154). The nearest bowler to them was Hopwood with forty-five wickets, which emphasized how reliant Lancashire were – and had been since Cec Parkin retired – on just two big-hearted men.

Two outstanding performances that year came against Lancashire with Gubby Allen, the Middlesex amateur fast bowler, and Tich Freeman, Kent's mighty leg-spinner, each taking all ten wickets in an innings. Allen achieved the feat at Lord's on his return to the Middlesex team. Ernest Tyldesley stood like a rock to score 101 but when he was out, the remaining six wickets fell in 50 minutes after tea. Four fell in five balls to Allen who finished with ten for 40, eight of which were bowled. Kent were leading the championship when Lancashire faced them at Maidstone late in July and although Freeman took ten for 131, Lancashire won comfortably by 189 runs. Watson and Hallows scored centuries, Ernest Tyldesley hit 66 and 97 and the wickets were shared between six bowlers.

Lancashire ran into another formidable bowler when they played the Minor Counties at Old Trafford. In the opposition, still going strong, was 53-year-old Sydney Barnes who bowled Hopwood with his sixth ball, took a slip catch, and despite bowling for an hour, took so little out of himself he was as intimidating at the end as at the beginning. He finished with two for 98 but extolled the virtues of a length on a wicket designed for batsmen. He persuaded Makepeace

250

to hit in the air when he had scored 70 – 'the fowler snaring the old and crafty bird,' said the *Manchester Guardian*.

Lancashire made a marvellous start to the 1930 season, winning four of the first five matches to take top position in the championship table, a place they held for all but about six weeks of the season. Dick Tyldesley and Ted McDonald were again mainly responsible for Lancashire's fourth championship win in five years, although there was more support this year, from Len Hopwood, with eighty wickets, and Frank Sibbles (fifty-five). Tyldesley took more than 100 for the ninth year in a row and played a major part in Lancashire's successful start to the season with four for 36 and five for 49 against Northamptonshire, six for 30 against Gloucestershire, and seven for 30 against Glamorgan. There were only 3 hours 15 minutes left on the final day for Lancashire to bowl out Glamorgan and when McDonald was hit for 23 runs in two overs, prospects did not look too bright. Tyldesley, however, bowled superbly with a marvellous final spell of 6.2–6–0–5 which brought Lancashire victory after 20 minutes of the extra half hour.

Tyldesley was the second player in the country to reach 100 wickets that season. He got there near the end of July, long after Tich Freeman, who at this time was approaching 200! His best performance of the season soon followed, at Leicester where he took eight for 35 in the second innings to give him twelve for 64 in the match. This was the only game in which Jack Barnes played that season. It was also his last for the county. He was called up to captain the side when Eckersley pulled out with a finger injury. He was late arriving so Ernest Tyldesley captained until he got there with George Duckworth, who was standing down, fielding substitute.

McDonald took 108 wickets to Tyldesley's 133 that year, a creditable enough season but one in which it was evident that he was no longer quite the force of the hat-trick years. After all, he was nearly 40. He was bowling short and relying on the bumper much more than in previous years and one man who punished him for it was Frank Woolley who scored a century at Dover. McDonald bowled very short length balls to five slips and a gully but after taking five for 97 in the first innings, it was Tyldesley who brought victory by 101 runs with an immaculate six for 29 in the second. McDonald's best bowling was probably at Edgbaston where he took six for 72 and five for 135 in the defeat of Warwickshire. He took the last four wickets in six balls, including the hat-trick.

The best game of the season was played at Old Trafford at the end of June against Kent, who were at the top of the table at the time, eleven points ahead of Lancashire. McDonald took eleven wickets and Tyldesley seven in the innings win, but both were outshone by reserve wicket-keeper Bill Farrimond, stand-in for George Duckworth, who was playing in the Test match against Australia at Lord's. As well as scoring 46 not out, Farrimond had seven victims in an innings with six catches – all off McDonald – and a stumping to equal the world record held by Warwickshire's 'Tiger' Smith. The committee showed their appreciation by presenting Farrimond with a cheque, the ball mounted and inscribed, and the scorecard mounted on vellum and enclosed in a silver frame. It did not stop Farrimond from being dropped for the next match against Worcestershire at Old Trafford, however, when Duckworth returned to the side. This was not the first time such a thing had happened to Farrimond. In 1927, when Duckworth was engaged in the Players v Gentlemen match at Lord's, Farrimond deputized in the Lancashire team at Taunton. He held seven catches in the match against Somerset, but then had to make way for Duckworth in the next match against Surrey at The Oval.

BILL FARRIMOND was Lancashire's reserve wicket-keeper for fourteen years and their No. 1 choice for two. He had the unusual distinction of playing for England while he was Lancashire's reserve, winning four caps with two matches in South Africa when Duckworth was ill, once in the West Indies in 1935, and again later that year against South Africa at Lord's. Farrimond regularly deputized in the Lancashire team for Duckworth who played a good deal of representative cricket and who was also on occasions persuaded to stand down to allow Farrimond the chance of more first-class opportunities.

Loyalty is steadfastness in allegiance, regardless of circumstance. Duckworth's loyalty was probably never tested all the time he played from 1923 to 1938. Farrimond's was, year after year as he stayed with Lancashire, knowing from the moment he arrived at Old Trafford – the year after Duckworth – that he was destined to be No. 2, almost for ever. He could have moved, but he stuck it out. After all, Lancashire were a great side, winning five championships in nine years. It was non-stop champagne stuff and perhaps it was better being No. 2 with Lancashire his home county, than No. 1 with almost any other county.

Farrimond contrasted sharply with Duckworth who was all noise and aggression, ebullience and belligerence. Farrimond was polite and quiet. He became No. 1 wicket-keeper for just two seasons, 1938 and 1939, after Duckworth's retirement. He made eighty-five dismissals in 1938 – a figure beaten only by Duckworth, Geoff Clayton and Farokh Engineer – and seventy-two in 1939 when his benefit brought him a modest £1,000, the lowest for twenty-five years. Farrimond was then 36 and destined

not to play county cricket again. He died at his Westhoughton home in November 1979, aged 76.

Lancashire held top place until the middle of June, regained it for three days in mid-July, and then stayed on top again from the beginning of August right through to the end of the 1930 championship programme. The day after bowling out Kent for 89 in 105 minutes at Dover, they were hit for 415 for six by Sussex at Eastbourne and in the end were more than happy to take part in a game that did not even produce a result on the first innings and provided both teams with four points. Exactly the same thing happened in the following match at Trent Bridge, which sent Lancashire into the last match at Blackpool, against Essex, needing first innings points to be sure of at least sharing the championship. They did more than that. They won by 178 runs and the championship was theirs yet again. Yet for all their success, and the inclusion of such accomplished players as McDonald, Duckworth and Dick Tyldesley, Lancashire were not considered an attractive side. Mr R. S. Young, a Member of Parliament, even wrote to the newspapers, describing the team as unpopular in the south because of their safety-first methods of playing. Their reputation for interesting cricket was at a low ebb and poor crowds attended most of their games. Perhaps the most damning evidence on their style of play was provided by Neville Cardus, a champion of Lancashire cricket. On the opening day of the final match at Blackpool he wrote in the *Manchester Guardian* 'Frankly, I have little interest in the match between Lancashire and Essex, being heretical in the extreme about Lancashire cricket of the present day. I hope Gloucestershire win the title.' Heresy indeed, but it speaks volumes about Lancashire's cricket of that period.

Nevertheless, when McDonald knocked the off stump of Ken Farnes flat to the ground on the final afternoon of their championship season, Lancashire had become champions for the fourth time in five years. The crowd rushed to the pavilion and Eckersley responded by saying to them 'Thank you very much. I hope you are all as pleased as I am.' The crowd called repeatedly for individual members of the team but none would respond. They were busy celebrating with champagne provided by Sir Lindsay Pilkington, the president of Blackpool Cricket Club.

Chapter 11 1931–34

'Unless somebody spoils Washbrook, he will go a long way.'

After five great years, Lancashire found themselves amongst the also-rans between 1931 and 1933, finishing sixth twice and fifth. They lost Ted McDonald in 1931. The great Australian fast bowler was 40 years old and although he had taken over 100 wickets the previous season, when he had again helped Lancashire win the championship, the cracks were beginning to show. The rhythm, the menace, the greatness had gone and although he was rested and coaxed through the 1931 season he could manage only twenty-six wickets at 38.65 runs each in twelve matches. It was very sad, but a great career ended and Lancashire were all the poorer for his loss. Dick Tyldesley again took over 100 wickets, Sibbles took ninety and Hopwood seventy-four, but the batting lacked Frank Watson, who was ill nearly all season, while Charlie Hallows was still struggling to find a form that, like McDonald's, was never to return. There was an opening for a batsman and Eddie Paynter was the one who galloped in to establish himself in the side with 1,200 runs. But the tell-tale signs that Lancashire were not the force of the previous five years came early in the season when they lost by four wickets to Sussex and by 126 runs to Worcestershire. Tich Freeman repeated his feat of two years earlier at Maidstone when he again took all ten wickets in an innings, this time at Old Trafford. Lancashire's last pair were McDonald and Duckworth, and Kent conspired that no one else but Freeman would get that last wicket. McDonald was deliberately dropped at long on, Aidan Crawley, fielding on the boundary edge, allowed a 4 so that Freeman could attack his more likely victim, McDonald, and the last wicket

254

added 25 before Freeman got the tenth wicket at a cost of 79 runs.

Lancashire's unpopularity in the south surfaced at Eastbourne in 1931 when the Mayor, Lieutenant-Colonel Roland Gwynne, made a speech at the annual meeting of Eastbourne Cricket Club in February when he said Eastbourne was tired of always seeing 'a certain county from the north.' The Lancashire professionals interpreted this as a derisive reference to themselves and declined to attend the Mayor's lunch at the ground on the opening day of the match that summer. Sir Edwin Stockton was present and visited the players at their hotel before the game to get them to change their minds, but they refused. Ernest Tyldesley, the senior professional, told the *Eastbourne Chronicle* 'We felt we could not accept the hospitality of the Mayor after the speech he made.' The Mayor said he was simply voicing the wishes of the club in wanting a change after having had Lancashire several times when only two county matches a year were held in the town. 'I very much regret if any offence has been given to the Lancashire players,' he said. The players attended the lunch on the second day but the Mayor did not – so that no possible aggravation should occur, explained the *Eastbourne Chronicle*.

By the time the 1932 season started Lancashire had lost Dick Tyldesley as well as Ted McDonald. Tyldesley, no doubt feeling the weight of supporting the Lancashire attack for so long, fell out with the club over terms and left county cricket, never to return. He was only 34 when he finished and while no longer quite at the height of his powers, he was still a force Lancashire could ill do without. So now Lancashire were without the two men mainly responsible for them having won the championship four times in five years. In addition, Charlie Hallows was on the brink of finishing – he played only seven times and averaged under 10 – and Lancashire were looking for new blood. Eddie Paynter had an outstanding year with 1,830 runs with five centuries and selection for the tour of Australia. Sibbles took over the role of No. 1 bowler, sending down 1,160 overs in twenty-eight matches and taking 131 wickets with the best performance of his career coming against Yorkshire in the Whitsuntide match when he took seven for 10 and five for 58 in the innings win.

Lancashire broke new ground in 1932 by taking a match to Alexandra Meadows, Blackburn, the home of East Lancashire, the Lancashire League club. It started raining at tea time on the opening day and continued for the next two days. One of Lancashire's greatest players, A. N. Hornby, was born at Blackburn and played on this ground. It is said that in one game, about 1870, he stopped playing to take a barracking spectator by the slack of his garment and run him out of the ground.

255

Frank Watson had the doubtful honour in 1932 of having the first benefit match to be totally washed out and had to be content with £1,268, the lowest since before the First World War.

Lancashire ran into that great double act, Harold Larwood and Bill Voce, at Trent Bridge that year when, after sharing in a century partnership in 70 minutes, they bowled Nottinghamshire to a 124-run victory with Larwood taking nine for 128 in the match and Voce seven for 84. Another face that was becoming all too familiar was that of Walter Hammond who scored 164 against them at Cheltenham and 264 at Aigburth, the highest score of his career and the highest ever – it still is – at the Liverpool ground.

The year of 1933 saw the arrival of a man who was to become one of Lancashire's greatest batsmen, Cyril Washbrook. He was only 18 when he went to Old Trafford and while the first team were losing by an innings to Yorkshire after being bowled out twice in a day for 93 and 92, he was scoring 202 not out for the second team at Bradford. He scored his runs on Monday 5 June and two days later he was making his debut with the first team against Sussex at Old Trafford, off-driving the first ball he received in county cricket, from Robert Scott, to the boundary before being lbw for seven in Scott's next over. Wrote Neville Cardus 'Washbrook's first ball was a half volley on the offside and needed but a simple swing of the bat to send it to the boundary. He lost his wicket by means of an indiscreet stroke, clean across the line of a good-length ball. It was the kind of stroke we shall expect to see Washbrook make some day when he is 156 not out and 30 years old.' Washbrook scored 40 not out in the second innings and Cardus, cynically, had another go, 'He is a boy of considerable promise. No doubt in time he will have all his strokes painlessly extracted and then he will be ready for county cricket and innumerable innings of 50 achieved in three or four hours each.'

The following match was also at Old Trafford, against Surrey, and the 18-year-old Washbrook had the enormous pleasure of scoring a century in only his second game. Surrey had scored 478 with centuries from Bob Gregory, Harry Squires and Freddie Brown. Washbrook opened the innings with Len Hopwood and scored 152 with eighteen boundaries after 5 hours 20 minutes of bright, confident batting. He shared in a partnership of 191 in 165 minutes with Ernest Tyldesley. Cardus was there again 'Washbrook does not cramp his style with the "push"; his hits are positive enough and vital at the finish of them. His faults are not inherent in his style; they are merely those of inexperience. Time will discover all his gifts and gladly nourish them, if he does not listen to false counsel.' Remembering Reg Spooner's debut at Lord's thirty-four years earlier, Cardus said 'Maybe another intimation of immortality was given to Lancashire cricket. For a lad of 18, this was cricket radiant with promise. Unless somebody spoils Washbrook, he will go a long way.'

Lancashire started the 1934 season with the reputation of having stolid bats and no bowlers. There was probably a good deal of truth in this. They lacked a good, quick bowler, an Arthur Mold or a Ted McDonald. And there was no evidence to suggest that a top-class spinner was around to succeed Dick Tyldesley. Yet despite winning only one of the first nine matches that season – that included Oxford University and the Australians – they won the championship again, their fifth success in nine years.

One of the earliest delights for Lancashire followers was the sight of Jack Hobbs scoring his 197th, and last, century. He batted four hours for his 116 and hit forty-eight singles, at the age of 51. As he walked back up the Old Trafford steps, members sang 'Auld Lang Syne' to him, a moving piece of sportsmanship. Perhaps he played in honour of George Duckworth's benefit, a match that needed all the support it could get as Lancashire were standing in tenth place in the table with that solitary victory, over Somerset. A big white sheet was carried round the ground for people to throw money into it and a card went with it which read 'What is a Duck worth?' It turned out to be worth only £1,257, which was lower even than that for Frank Watson, whose match was a total washout. Benefits at Lancashire had passed their peak and from then until the season before the Second World War, 1939, they gradually declined with Jack Iddon getting £1,266, Frank Sibbles £1,229, Len Hopwood £1,105, and Bill Farrimond £1,000.

Ernest Tyldesley made a piece of history in 1934 by scoring the first century for Lancashire against the Australians – Alan Wharton, Geoff Pullar, David Green and Frank Hayes have since joined him – in a game which saw a Scottish amateur fast bowler called Arthur Baxter take the first three wickets by bowling Bill Woodfull, Bill Brown and Len Darling. The wickets cost him 38 runs before strained ankle tendons forced him out of the match. He was in business in Southport and the previous year had played twice against the West Indians and taken thirteen wickets for 170 runs. Yet those three matches were all he played, giving him sixteen wickets, all of them Test cricketers and including George Headley and Learie Constantine as well as the Australians, for 208 runs. He batted only once and did not score. It was thought he was qualifying for Lancashire but his only other county appearances were for Middlesex, twice, in 1938.

Lancashire were into their eighth championship match before they produced their second win. Cardus had written before it 'None of us cares twopence about the championship, certainly not this year, when it is obvious Lancashire cannot possibly win it!' They won comfortably at Bristol, Worcester and Southampton before going to Trent Bridge for a match which, probably more than any other, proved their spirit and their right for another championship.

Nottinghamshire's two opening bowlers, Harold Larwood and Bill Voce, had been at the forefront of England's attack on the Bodyline tour of Australia in 1932–33. They had used the same leg theory bowling in county matches and several counties were reported to have taken exception to it. The *Nottingham Guardian* reported that it had even been said that some of the county captains would refuse to play against Nottinghamshire unless that type of bowling was dropped and the rumour was that Lancashire would walk off the field if it was used. Arthur Carr, the Nottinghamshire captain, said the Lancashire professionals all denied it and the *Nottingham Evening Post* said it was superb length and demoralizing pace, rather than leg theory, which were responsible for Lancashire being dismissed for 119. Cardus said Larwood did not use a Bodyline field but that Voce was more intimidating with three legside fielders close to the wicket, a mid on and a fielder on the boundary edge. Ernest Tyldesley hooked three successive short balls from Larwood before being bowled by a ball which kept low, the first of six batsmen who fell to Larwood for one run, three of them bowled, three caught in the slips. Larwood took six for 51 – Voce had four for 49 – and then scored 80 in 45 minutes on the second morning, pulling Hopwood for four 4s in one over and taking 16 off one over from Iddon which included two 6s. Larwood also hit Hopwood and Frank Booth for two 6s each to reach his 80 out of 105 with six 6s, eight 4s, two 2s and eight singles.

Nottinghamshire led by 147 but Larwood was tired and Voce was ineffective on a wicket more suited to spinners. Suddenly, the Nottinghamshire bowling looked feeble and Lancashire took advantage to score 394 for seven declared. Ernest Tyldesley scored 109, his ninety-ninth century, and he and Lionel Lister, a 22-year-old amateur batsman who had scored a century in his second match the previous year, shared in an exhilarating stand of 182 in 130 minutes. Lister had been hit on the chest by a ball from Larwood and had fallen to the ground in the first innings. He recovered on the field but was soon out, caught in the slips. In the second innings he went in when Lancashire still needed 35 to avoid an innings defeat and with Watson, Hopwood, Iddon and Paynter out. He scored a fine 86 and Nottinghamshire went in to bat a second time with 2 hours 45 minutes remaining and 248 wanted for victory. They had seven wickets standing with an hour to play, but Hopwood was spinning the ball and the eighth wicket fell with 15 minutes remaining. Larwood walked in, hit 4, 4 and 6 and eight minutes from the end was caught on the boundary edge. When Ben Lilley hit a boundary, the crowd refused to return the ball and let a fielder go for it. But with three minutes to go Harold Butler was lbw and Lancashire had won a remarkable victory by 101 runs with Hopwood the hero with six for 58 (ten for 157 in the match). George Duckworth, whose body was badly bruised by the blows he had taken batting against Larwood and Voce, hurled the three stumps in the air, sending them spinning like catherine wheels. Ernest Tyldesley, usually the most composed and subdued of players, threw his cap in the air in recognition of the sweet revenge for Saturday morning's humiliation.

Just over two weeks later, Lancashire issued a statement that they would not play Nottinghamshire in 1935, a reminder of the rift in the mid 1880s when the teams did not meet for two seasons because of the dispute over Jack Crossland. Yet the teams had still to play the return match in 1934, at Old Trafford starting on Saturday 21 July when Frank Watson and Eddie Paynter were unfit and Washbrook, now 19, and a 24-year-old batsman from Nelson, Cliff Hawkwood, opened the batting. And as the two inexperienced players walked out to face the mighty Nottinghamshire pair, Voce told them it was not them they were after, 'but them up there' he said, motioning to the senior players' balcony. The two openers were dismissed relatively cheaply by Voce who also struck Iddon under the heart, knocking him to the ground. The *Nottingham Evening Post* reported 'The crowd sat in silence while umpire Parry administered first aid and a relay of Lancashire players dashed out of the pavilion with restoratives. A few minutes massage brought Iddon round and the shock of a loud appeal for lbw by Harris, which the umpire ignored, helped him to recover.' By the end of the day Iddon was 144 out of Lancashire's 387 for six. He went to Manchester Infirmary that evening for an X-ray which showed nothing was broken and on Monday completed his double hundred before the declaration. Nottinghamshire were forced to follow on but managed to save the game with four wickets standing.

Larwood wrote some years later that Carr had said to him and Voce before the match 'Well boys, I don't know what's going to happen in this match but there is going to be a protest against you and Bill.' Larwood said he refused to play, Carr said he would have to, and Larwood said he would bowl at half pace. He said the wicket was easy, he bowled nowhere near his usual pace, but several players ducked and drew away. Larwood said that Duckworth told him the following day he had protested about the bowling. 'Later that day George Duckworth came to see me and said the president of his

259

club (Dr H. H. I. Hitchon) wanted to see me. "Look George," I said, "if he wants to see me let him come and ask me and not send a little cock like you to tell me." That day the crowd cheered me as I bowled. They wanted to let me know I had their sympathies.'

JACK IDDON's double-century was the high spot of a season in which he scored 2,381 runs for Lancashire at an average of 52.91. That season he and Ernest Tyldesley scored 4,868 runs between them – and did not play in one representative match. He was an outstanding all-round cricketer, a right-handed batsman who scored 21,975 runs (average 37.05) for the county, a left-arm spinner who took 533 wickets (26.66). He is one of only three players – Johnny Briggs and Len Hopwood are the others – to have scored 10,000 runs and taken 500 wickets for Lancashire.

Iddon was born at Mawdesley on 8 January 1902, and made his debut in 1924 when he had the very modest record of 339 runs and two wickets from twenty-two matches. Improvement was slow but regular and Lancashire must have had great faith in him as he played in twenty-five matches in 1925 but still scored only one half century in thirty-six innings and took fifteen wickets. He was a regular player by 1926 and two more moderate seasons in the first two years of the championship hat-trick were followed by his best in 1928 when he scored 1,353 runs (average 52) and took sixty-three wickets (average 25). That was the start of twelve successive seasons, right up to the war, when he scored 1,000 runs in each with the 2,381 of 1934 being by far the best and earning him a place in the MCC team in the West Indies where he played in four Tests. He played once more for England, against South Africa in 1935, completing his Test career with two half centuries and an average of 28.33, and no wickets. He was a hard-hitting batsman, an attractive and valuable player who took part in all five championship-winning teams. His best bowling was a rather special nine for 42 in 1937 on a wearing pitch at Bramall Lane which Hedley Verity had not been able to exploit. Although he had made his debut as long ago as 1924, Iddon, at the age of 44, was ready to resume his career with Lancashire after the war when he was tragically killed in a road accident in Staffordshire just before the start of the 1946 season.

Tropical heat hit Old Trafford during the 1934 Test match against Australia in July and hundreds of spectators collapsed from exhaustion. I remember Len Darling, the Australian batsman, telling me nearly forty years later that he had never experienced heat like it. Lancashire had played at Blackburn a few days earlier and spectators were disappointed when Ernest Tyldesley was dismissed only 27 short of his 100th century. Iddon and Paynter, however, did score centuries in the innings win over Northamptonshire, whose players, according to the *Blackburn Times*, were full of praise for the Blackburn hospitality and the delightful setting of the cricket field. 'A background of trees and pleasant green countryside, when they had expected an aspect of mill chimneys, was a surprise that impressed the Northants players,' the newspaper reported.

The 100th century arrived for Tyldesley in the following match, the return with Northamptonshire at Peterborough when Lancashire repeated the Blackburn result – victory by an innings.

Lancashire won five matches in July to move into second place behind Sussex. Two weeks later, after beating Derbyshire and Middlesex and despite losing first innings points to Yorkshire at Old Trafford, they were on top – and they stayed there. The two top teams clashed at Eastbourne in the penultimate match and first innings points was enough for Lancashire. They decided to freeze out the match two hours before the end of the second day with five points in the bag. They did not look for victory but batted on until only 2 hours 45 minutes were left and Sussex needed 375 to win. So Lancashire went into the final match at The Oval needing only to avoid defeat against Surrey to win the championship. This they did by scoring 453 for eight declared and bowling out Surrey for 294 early on the final day. The follow-on was enforced, and Peter Eckersley, the captain, was asked at lunch how he felt about winning the title. 'No, I'm sorry,' he said. 'It is not yet won. I would rather not say anything until today's play is finished. In fact, I have refused to allow the team to be photographed as the champion team of 1934. We are superstitious.' It was just a pity that they were not at Old Trafford. For when the match was over, and they were champions, they returned to the pavilion amidst silence.

Lancashire's success had come as a surprise. They did not look to have the all-round strength or the enterprise to win the championship. But players rose to the occasion. Several of them put in the best performances of their career, including Ernest Tyldesley who, at the age of 45, scored more runs than ever before in a season for Lancashire with 2,487 (average 57.83). Jack Iddon scored more than 2,000 runs for the only time in his career, Len Hopwood took 100 wickets for the first time and became only the third player in the club's history to score 1,000 runs as well, while Frank Booth took over 100 wickets for the only time in his life. Booth had first played in 1927 but was in only his second full season in 1934 and reached 100 wickets in the final match, the extra one played between the champions and the Rest of England.

Another satisfying point for Lancashire in 1934 was that out of eighteen players who took part in the championship, only Frank Watson (Nottinghamshire) and Len Hopwood (Cheshire) were not born in Lancashire. Both were absent in the match against Nottinghamshire at Old Trafford, allowing Lancashire to field their first-ever team of Lancashire-born players. It was Cyril Washbrook (Barrow, near Clitheroe), Clifford Hawkwood (Nelson), Jack Iddon (Mawdesley), Ernest Tyldesley (Roe Green), Lionel Lister (Formby), Harry Butterworth (Rochdale), Len Parkinson (Salford), Peter Eckersley (Newton-le-Willows), George Duckworth (Warrington), Frank Booth (Manchester), and Frank Sibbles (Oldham).

Chapter 12 1935–39

'The thought of a black man taking the place of a white man in our side was anathema.'

Lancashire were unable to sustain another challenge for the championship in the five years remaining before the outbreak of the Second World War. They slipped to fourth in 1935 when Ernest Tyldesley and Jack Iddon were kept out of the side for long periods because of illness or injury. Tyldesley played in only eleven of the thirty-two matches and Iddon twenty-one and their combined total of 1,859 runs was far behind their formidable collection of 4,868 in 1934. Frank Watson had trouble maintaining form and it all enabled Cyril Washbrook to burst forth with 1,724 runs and an average of 45.36. And into the side for the first time came 'Buddy' Oldfield, an exciting, brilliant 24-year-old batsman from Dukinfield who scored 1,000 runs in his debut season. Len Hopwood was the only bowler to take 100 wickets as he completed the double for the second successive year, but Dick Pollard was denied the honour only by an attack of tonsillitis at the end of the season. Frank Booth again bowled admirably and Eddie Phillipson had his best season with seventy-one wickets.

LEN HOPWOOD was born in Newton Hyde, Cheshire, on 30 October 1903. He was 18 when he joined the Old Trafford staff in 1922 when Archie MacLaren was coach. MacLaren made no secret of the fact that he considered Hopwood rich in promise and offered him what was then the top wage for a youngster on the groundstaff.

Hopwood, a left-arm spin bowler and right-hand batsman, made his debut the following year, but the money was not good for a young player making his way in the game and a disagreement over terms in 1925 forced Hopwood into a temporary break with the club. He played

with Wallasey and Cheshire, and did not make any appearances for Lancashire until he returned in 1928 to help them complete the hat-trick of championship wins. Hopwood was at his best in the 1930s and was an important member of the side which again won the title in 1930 and 1934. As several outstanding players of the 1920s left, Hopwood seized the opportunity to become one of the three best all-rounders Lancashire have ever had. He was a batsman of some obduracy and an accurate spinner and when his career came to an end up against the Second World War he had scored 15,519 runs (average 30) and taken 672 wickets at 22 each. Between 1930 and 1939 he missed getting 1,000 runs only once, in 1932. That particularly lean season was followed by his best as a batsman as he hit seven centuries and 1,972 runs.

Hopwood played his only two Tests in 1934, close to home at Headingley and Old Trafford, but they brought him only 12 runs in two innings – he was dismissed by another left-arm spinner in Bill O'Reilly in both – and did not take a wicket. He used to recall the match at Headingley where he was on the receiving end of the fantastic loyalty of the Yorkshire spectators. 'Whenever Hedley Verity, Yorkshire's left-arm spinner, bowled a maiden over, 30,000 pairs of hands applauded the feat in enthusiastic fashion,' he said. 'I went on to bowl. My first over was a maiden. Instead of the generous applause expected, a Yorkshire voice roared out a sarcastic 'Put a bowler on.' Hopwood had his benefit in 1938 when it rained and rained and gate receipts of £136 compared with expenses of £373. But members rallied round, more donations arrived and in the end the fund totalled £1,105. Hopwood never went on a tour, MCC or unofficial, was not chosen for the Players and did not take part in a Festival match. So all but three of his 400 first-class matches were for Lancashire, the others being the Tests and a Test trial. He had the distinction of becoming the first former professional cricketer to become president of Lancashire when he was appointed for 1981–82. He died on 15 June 1985, aged 81.

Lancashire won twelve of their twenty-eight championship matches in 1935 with the finest probably being their display against Kent at Dover near the end of the season. Instead of enforcing the follow on when Lancashire were 165 behind, Percy Chapman chose to bat again and set Lancashire a victory target of 396 in 300 minutes on a crumbling wicket. Watson and Hopwood started them off with 103 in 90 minutes, Hopwood and Iddon put on 149 in 105 minutes, and when Iddon was out at 327 he had scored 141 in 150 minutes with some colossal driving. Lancashire won by five wickets with 18 minutes to spare.

Lancashire looked to have victory in the bag at Weston-super-Mare where Somerset, needing 206 to avoid an innings defeat, were 176 for five. But Norman Mitchell-Innes, a 20-year-old Oxford University Blue who played his only Test match for England that year, against South Africa, scored 139 and enabled Somerset to draw. It was his second century against Lancashire that summer following one for the University. Somerset provided more excitement in the final match at Old Trafford. Or to be more exact that great hitter, Arthur Wellard, did after going in to bat at 3.40 p.m. with the score 109 for five. He hit a ball from Iddon over the former ladies' stand, he hit him straight and nearly cleared the Hornby stand, and in 35 minutes had reached 50. Hopwood was hit straight out of the ground into Warwick Road near the railway station and Wellard was 93 out of 243 for nine when Horace Hazell joined him. Wellard reached his century in 82 minutes with another 6 and to the accompaniment of frenzied roars and cheers from the pavilion. He finished with 112 in 90 minutes with ten 4s and five 6s, one of which hit one of the pavilion towers.

Peter Eckersley resigned the captaincy in 1935 when he became a Member of Parliament for Manchester Exchange and although he was only 31 he did not play again for the county. He had been captain seven years, the longest period of captaincy since the start of the First World War when A. H. Hornby was in charge. He played 256 times for Lancashire, scored only one century and averaged 18.50. But he captained Lancashire through a transitional period when the great 1920s side was breaking up, and had the satisfaction of twice leading the county to the championship. He was a wealthy man and made a piece of history when he hired aircraft to take the players from Swansea to Southampton in 1935, the first time a county team had travelled to a match by air. The choice of his successor rested between 47-year-old Ernest Tyldesley, who was prepared to become an amateur to take the position, Harry Butterworth, a Rochdale amateur, and Lionel Lister, the Formby amateur who had played only eleven times in 1935. Lister was chosen with the future in mind and Tyldesley retired after playing in two matches more. The team immediately sank to 11th in the championship table, equalling their lowest position ever, in 1914. Eddie Paynter scored over 2,000 runs, Iddon 1,722 and Hopwood 1,602. Oldfield and Washbrook also reached 1,000 and Lancashire's batting at least had an attractive look about it. Pollard was the only bowler to take 100 wickets, Sibbles, Hopwood and leg-spinner Len Parkinson took over fifty but there was not enough penetration to make Lancashire a threat. They were missing a really fast bowler.

During the year of 1936 Leslie Warburton, a 26-year-old Haslingden-born all-rounder who was professional with Littleborough in the Central Lancashire League, was chosen to play in a Test trial at Lord's. Warburton, who was an outstanding cricketer, played only six times for Lancashire between 1929 and 1938, resisting several tempting offers and preferring the security of his position as a bank clerk to the uncertainties of first-class cricket. One of his matches was against Yorkshire at Headingley in 1936 when he took three for 47 with his medium-fast bowling and attracted the attention of the England selectors who were looking for bowlers to go to Australia that winter. Still Warburton was not impressed. 'I am not long married,' he told a reporter. 'I am fairly comfortably settled in the bank and for the little extra which comes to me as professional with Littleborough.' Mrs Warburton was asked if she would 'permit' Leslie to go to Australia if he were chosen. 'Certainly not,' she declared. 'He has his work to attend to and he has his hobbies.' She disclosed that the hobbies were varied. 'He knits,' she said, 'when he is not playing the piano or violin.' In the event, Warburton got a duck and failed to impress with his bowling in the North v South match. He went back to Littleborough and achieved the double the following year, scoring 1,311 runs at 100.84 and taking 118 wickets at 8.25.

Lancashire went to another new ground in 1936, Preston becoming the tenth ground in the county to stage first-class cricket. The opposition were Gloucestershire, an attractive side with Walter Hammond who, announced the *Lancashire Daily Post* the day before, would definitely be playing. There was a new scoreboard for the occasion on the West Cliff ground which had a playing area larger than Old Trafford or Aigburth and on which, more than eighty years earlier, All-England matches had been staged. Joe Wormald, the groundsman, stayed up all night in the pavilion, occasionally walking out to the wicket to make sure everything was all right. Hammond and Charles Barnett scored half centuries for Gloucestershire, off-spinner Tom Goddard enjoyed himself on the responsive pitch, and Lancashire's first experience of Preston ended in defeat. A representative of the *Preston Herald* went to the match on the opening day and was impressed. 'There was none of the yelling, shouting, and the vulgarity you unfortunately get at most football matches,' he wrote. 'I am speaking quite seriously when I say that anyone troubled with nerves – and I'm afraid most of us in these days of noise, speed, wireless and gramophones are – will be well advised to pay a visit to West Cliff.' Another feature of the season was the century scored before lunch at Lord's by Lister, who was dropped by Ian Peebles in the gully before he had scored. He scored 104 not out and one drive for six was said to have almost posted itself in the telegraph office in the clock tower.

The criticism of Lancashire batting as slow, stodgy and unattractive persisted and on the morning of Saturday, 22 May 1937, the Lancashire committee demanded brighter cricket. The players were indignant and maintained that too many of the wickets did not allow brighter cricket. In any case, they said 'We have done no worse than follow the usual policy of Lancashire cricket for many years past.' The committee said that although Lancashire batsmen of the past may have been bores, it was unwise for the present players to assume they could be both bores and failures. On that day Lancashire scored 358 for six against Warwickshire at Old Trafford.

Cyril Washbrook scored four centuries that summer and three of them came in successive matches. In five innings his top score had been four, which he followed with 72, 2 and 121 not out – out of 211 for four and a six-wicket win at Northampton – 106 and 52 not out against Surrey at Old Trafford, and 145 and 2 against Sussex at Aigburth. The fourth century came at Hove in one of the most memorable of matches when Lancashire scored 640 for eight in 136.2 overs on the opening day. That is the highest number of runs achieved by Lancashire in a day and the second highest in county cricket. Eddie Paynter scored 322 of them, still the second highest innings to Archie MacLaren's 424, with three 6s and thirty-nine 4s. Only one Englishman, Jack Robertson of Middlesex, has scored more runs in a day than Paynter and oddly enough, the third highest, 316 by Richard Moore of Hampshire, was scored on the same day as Paynter's, 28 July 1937, about 80 miles down the coast at Bournemouth.

Paynter had been at Old Trafford playing in a Test match and had travelled all night in a sleeper on the train to London. He arrived at Hove at eight o'clock, and just had time for breakfast and a shower before walking to the ground and starting on his historic innings. He and Washbrook opened with a stand of 268 in 155 minutes, his first century arriving 15 minutes before lunch, taken with the total 175 for 0. The remaining 93 runs of the stand came in 35 minutes before Washbrook was out for 108 after sharing in the third highest opening stand in the county's history. Jack Iddon was out cheaply but Buddy Oldfield matched Paynter's mood and together they put on 271 runs at 120 an hour. Paynter reached his 200 in 205 minutes and another century had been claimed between lunch and tea when Lancashire were 411 for two with Paynter past 250. His first mistake came at 260 when he was missed in the slips and Paynter went on to 322 out of 546 before he was third out, lbw to Jim Parks, a dismissal he put down to his all-night train journey! Hopwood, who went in to bat when Paynter was out, said in later years:

We always said of Eddie that he'd scored over 300, had a shower, dressed and had a drink by six o'clock! George Duckworth and I put on 50 in the last half hour and we were given the bird for slow scoring. There was nothing anybody could do with Eddie in that mood. I just wouldn't bowl to him in the nets. He never tried to play cricket properly, but would just sling his bat at it and hit it all over Old Trafford.

Lancashire won that match by an innings and 5 runs after a valiant fight by Sussex to make them bat again.

EDDIE PAYNTER was born on Guy Fawkes Day in 1901 which perhaps accounts for the fireworks he produced in his batting. He started work when he was 12, dividing his day between school and the cotton mill, a natural stepping-stone for an Oswaldtwistle working-class lad. He finished school at 13 and went to the brickworks where he lost the ends of the first and second fingers of his right hand in a brick press. It was an injury which forced him to pull out of a Test match twenty-three years later when one of the fingers was so badly bruised and swollen he could not hold the bat. Paynter was brought up on Lancashire League cricket with Enfield, the same club that was to produce Jack Simmons. He had a trial with Lancashire at 18 immediately after the First World War, played in the second team at 19, but did not get on to the staff and into the first team until he was 24. Another five years passed before he got a regular place in the Lancashire team and in that same season, 1931, when he was 29 years old, he scored his first century and made his Test debut. The following year he played the innings he regarded as his best, 152 out of Lancashire's total of 263 against Yorkshire at Bradford when he twice hit the left-arm spin of Hedley Verity into the stand and twice over the stand. He hit five 6s and seventeen 4s and his last 50 runs came in half an hour.

Paynter went on the Bodyline tour of Australia in 1932–3 and became a hero when he rose from his sick-bed in Brisbane to win a Test match for England. He spent four days in hospital with tonsillitis but returned to the game to hit the winning runs with a six. He played three Tests in Australia and two in New Zealand and although he averaged 61.33 in Australia, he did not play Test cricket again until 1937. He was one of *Wisden*'s Cricketers of the Year in 1937 but got into the first Test against Australia at Trent Bridge in 1938 only because Joe Hardstaff was injured. He scored 216 not out, a record in England against Australia at the time. He averaged more than 100 from six Test innings that summer and went to South Africa that winter where he averaged 81 in Tests. Despite these great figures, Paynter was dropped

for the third and final Test against West Indies in 1939. Lancashire were playing at Trent Bridge when the team was announced and one of the batsmen brought into the England team was Nottinghamshire's Walter Keeton. Paynter made up his mind to show the selectors they were wrong, which he did with an innings of 154. That turned out to be Paynter's last century for Lancashire. The Second World War was just around the corner and when it was over, Paynter was 44 and no longer in Lancashire's plans.

Paynter played 293 times for Lancashire and scored 16,555 runs at an average of 41.45, one of only six batsmen to have averaged over 40 for the county. He played in twenty Test matches, scored 1,540 runs and averaged 59.23, a Test average beaten only by Herbert Sutcliffe. In all, he scored forty-five centuries, seven of which became double hundreds.

Lancashire were on the receiving end that season of what Bill Edrich described as the biggest hit he had ever seen at Lord's. 'Big Jim' Smith was the batsman and he lost the ball by hitting it over the grandstand, a hit that Edrich thought was worth 12 as it flew, he reckoned without exaggeration, at least twice as high as the statue of Father Time. Lancashire were also on the receiving end of Walter Hammond's bat yet again when he scored 121 in two hours at Old Trafford.

Frank Sibbles, a quiet, modest, unobtrusive man, took his benefit in 1937. He had first played in 1925 and had his best season in 1932 when his 131 wickets cost him 17.54 runs each. He was steady and reliable, hardly ever spectacular, but a settled member of every championship-winning side. He was a medium-paced swing bowler who could open the attack or turn to off spin when the situation demanded as it did in 1932 when he took seven for 10 against Yorkshire. It was said he was mechanical without change in pace or flight, but he was also regarded as a worker who pulled his weight. Fittingly, he topped 100 wickets in his benefit year which also proved to be his last year as he retired with an arm injury. He finished with 932 wickets at 22 runs each and a modest batting average under 15 from 308 matches.

The annual meeting in 1937 produced praise from Myles Kenyon, the former captain who was now president, for the captain and his young team of triers who had provided bright cricket. 'Last season saw a rebirth of county cricket,' he said.

This year also marked the last season of Frank Watson, leaving Lancashire with only Jack Iddon who had played regularly in all the championship-winning teams. The young side was in the process of rebuilding again and in the two years before the war they finished in

269

a creditable fourth and sixth positions. They started the 1938 season well enough with seven wins in nine matches to hold second position in the table to Middlesex. And while Paynter was at Trent Bridge scoring 216 not out in the Test match against Australia, Lancashire were scoring 564 for nine against Glamorgan at Old Trafford. There were centuries for Washbrook, who reached his hundred in 93 minutes and scored all his 124 runs before lunch, Oldfield, who took 127 minutes and went on to 122, and Hopwood, whose 100 took 165 minutes on the way to his 127. Paynter's activities in the Test match kept a member of the Lancashire staff on a nearly non-stop circuit of the Old Trafford ground with a board carrying the news.

The Australians visited Old Trafford in June and Eddie Phillipson had the satisfaction of dismissing Don Bradman for 12, caught in the slips in the first innings. Teams rarely did that sort of thing twice to Bradman and in the second innings he scored a century in 73 minutes, which at the time was probably the fastest ever against Lancashire.

Happily for Lancashire, Hammond was in the final Test when Gloucestershire played at Old Trafford. But it only opened the way for Charles Barnett to open the bowling and take five for 63 and six for 40 and score 168 runs in the ten-wicket win inside two days. Reg Parkin, the 29-year-old son of Cec, had a good match with 60 runs in 75 minutes and three wickets for 67 runs with his off spin. But Reg was unable to establish himself in the team and played only twenty matches between 1931 and 1939. The 1938 season was notable for the remarkable progress made by a 21-year-old leg-spinner called Len Wilkinson who took 145 wickets and was selected for MCC's tour of South Africa that winter.

LEN WILKINSON was born in Northwich, Cheshire, in 1916 and, like Eddie Paynter, arrived on Guy Fawkes Day. The family moved into Lancashire and Wilkinson's early cricket was spent with Heaton in the Bolton League where he started as a fast bowler. He turned to leg spin when he was 14 or 15 and after trials at Old Trafford when he was 18, he finished his job as a little piecer in a cotton mill and joined the staff the following season, 1936. His first-team debut came in 1937 when he dismissed the New Zealand captain, Milford Page, in his first over. He was in the first team from the start of the 1938 season and after eight matches, up to the beginning of June, he had taken only sixteen wickets at 40 runs each. But he was to play in every game and, more through consistency than flashes of brilliance, he approached the twenty-sixth game at Canterbury at the beginning of August with eighty-seven wickets. This game, against Kent, was to be his best with five for 72 and seven for 53 in the 125-run win. He finished the season with a burst of fifty-eight wickets in fourteen innings through August to finish with 145 wickets, a figure

World War II is over, but the Battle of the Roses goes on for ever. It is 1946 at Old Trafford and Brian Sellers, the Yorkshire captain (left) and Jack Fallows, in his only season as Lancashire's captain, return to the pavilion after tossing.

Ken Cranston, dashing and debonair, took over from Jack Fallows as Lancashire's captain, a position he held for only two years before returning to his dental practice. Yet in those two years he played eight times for England, toured the West Indies with MCC, captained England, and scored 3,099 runs and took 178 wickets.

The Hilton brothers . . . Malcolm (left) took over 1,000 wickets with his left-arm spin, his finest season coming in 1956 when he took 158 wickets at under 14 runs each. Jim, who was two years younger, played only eight times for Lancashire before spending four years with Somerset. (*P.A.-Reuter Photos Ltd*)

Alan Wharton, an outstanding all-round cricketer who was a left-handed batsman good enough to play for England and a right-arm medium-paced bowler good enough to share Lancashire's opening attack many times with Brian Statham. When he left for Leicestershire in 1960 he had scored 17,921 runs, taken 225 wickets and held 223 catches.

Brian Statham, Lancashire's foremost bowler since World War II with a record 1,816 wickets at an average of 15.12 each for the County.

Geoff Pullar was one of England's leading left-handed batsmen in the late 1950s and early 1960s when he played twenty-eight Tests. He twice exceeded 2,000 runs in a season for Lancashire before finishing his career with Gloucestershire. (*Hallawell Photos*)

Tommy Greenhough, the last leg-spinner to hold down a regular place in the Lancashire team. His peak was in 1959 and 1960 when he took more than 100 wickets each season, played in four Tests, and toured the West Indies with MCC. (*Daily Express*)

The Gillette Cup belonged to Lancashire when they pulled off a hat-trick of wins between 1970 and 1972. Pictured here after the 1972 success are chairman Cedric Rhoades with Farokh Engineer, Jack Simmons and Jack Bond. (*Sport & General*)

Peter Lever was 30 years old when he went on his first England tour – to Australia in 1970-1. But he was still good enough to go again four years later, a selection that had him laughing all the way to the other side of the world. (*Daily Express*)

Farokh Engineer, the Indian wicket-keeper who was Lancashire's first signing when immediate registrations for overseas players were introduced in 1968. His wicket-keeping was world-class and he contributed many dashing batting displays, particularly in the one-day games. (*The Guardian*)

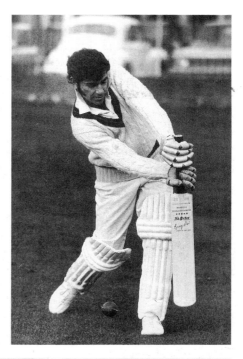

David Lloyd had an unenviable task following Jack Bond as captain from 1973. He held the position for five years and took Lancashire to three more Gillette Cup finals. He played nine times for England in this period and scored a double century against India. (*George Herringshaw*)

Jack Simmons was 27 before he made his debut for Lancashire. But he played on until he was 48, took 1,000 first-class wickets and played a prominent part in Lancashire's triumphs in the one-day game. He also had the distinction of captaining Tasmania to Gillette Cup success in Australia.

Clive Lloyd was a great joy to watch. He was an electrifying fielder following in the great Lancashire tradition of cover fielders, and a brilliant batsman. He had two spells as Lancashire captain and his record with the West Indies is unmatched by any captain in Test history. (*Patrick Eagar*)

Steve O'Shaughnessy, the Lancashire batsman, pictured with
Percy Fender two days after equalling, in 1983, Fender's world
record of a century in 35 minutes. (*Manchester Evening News*)

One of the greatest delights of Cyril Washbrook's first summer
as club president in 1989, was to present a county cap to
Mike Atherton shortly after the 21-year-old former Cambridge
University captain had been chosen to make his debut for England.

Test players old and new. Present-day Lancashire players Neil Fairbrother, Paul Allott and Graeme Fowler are pictured with two of Lancashire's greats, Brian Statham and Cyril Washbrook. (*Manchester Evening News*)

Time to celebrate again. Lancashire, winners of the new Sunday afternoon competition in 1969 and 1970, had to wait until 1989 before they won it again. Seen here are Andy Hayhurst, Gehan Mendis, Wasim Akram, Neil Fairbrother, Phillip DeFreitas, Warren Hegg and Paul Allott. (*Manchester Evening News*)

that has since been beaten only by Malcolm Hilton and Roy Tattersall. Wilkinson went to South Africa with MCC that winter, very much the junior spinner as he accompanied Doug Wright, Hedley Verity and Tom Goddard. But he still played in three Tests where he took seven wickets at a cost of 38.71 runs each. He topped the averages in all matches with forty-four wickets (18.86).

The following English season of 1939 turned out to be an anti-climax. Wilkinson took sixty-three wickets for Lancashire at 30.85 runs each, eighty-eight in all matches. 'That season really was a disaster,' he recalled.

> Nothing went right. I don't know why. I have thought about it over the years because I wasn't anywhere near as good that year as in 1938. The only thing I can think is that I tried to be too perfect, particularly with the googly. That is the only logical conclusion I can come to. I had an England cap on my head and as an England player I had to be good.

Wilkinson was not to get another chance to regain his ability until 1946. He played for the army during the war and on returning to Lancashire, when he was still only 29, he was injured during his first match and had to have a cartilage operation. He played in two more championship matches in 1947, took one wicket, and never played again. He was 30 years old.

Lancashire, although now being well served by Dick Pollard and Eddie Phillipson, were still in search of that elusive quick bowler and for a time there was a suggestion that Learie Constantine, the great West Indian all-rounder who was established in league cricket in the county, might join them.

It is interesting now to hear the views of players then as recalled by Len Hopwood in a series of articles in the *Manchester Evening News* in 1975. 'In those days the thought of a coloured chap playing for Lancashire was ludicrous,' wrote Hopwood. 'We Lancastrians were clannish in those less-enlightened days.' But word got out that Lancashire were negotiating with Constantine and the atmosphere in the dressing room was electric. 'We wanted none of Constantine,' said Hopwood. 'We would refuse to play.' Constantine never did become a Lancashire player. 'In all fairness I must say we had nothing against Learie Constantine personally,' wrote Hopwood. 'He was, in fact, very popular with us. There was no personal vendetta. But the thought of a black man taking the place of a white man in our side was anathema. It was as simple as that.'

Two players who made their debuts in 1939 were professionals in the Lancashire League, Syd Hird, an Australian with Ramsbottom,

271

and John Ikin, at Accrington. Ikin played four matches that year and established himself in the Lancashire and England sides after the war. Hird played one game against Gloucestershire at Old Trafford, did not bat and did not bowl in a game restricted by rain to half an hour. Another debutant was John Brocklebank, a 23-year-old leg-spinner from the Wirral, a Cambridge Blue in 1936. He had toured Canada with MCC in 1937 and before playing for Lancashire, had represented the Gentlemen against the Players and been chosen for the MCC tour to India that winter of 1939–40, a tour that was cancelled when war broke out. He played only four times for Lancashire, making his debut against Yorkshire when he bowled nine overs and did not take a wicket, and completing his brief career with five wickets at 55.80 runs each. He later became Sir John Montague Brocklebank, Bart, chairman of the Cunard shipping line when the order was placed for the *QE2*.

The enormous advances being made by Oldfield were reflected in his selection for the final Test against West Indies that year, the last Test match to be played in England for seven years and which ended twelve days before war broke out. Oldfield batted at No. 3, a high position which surprised him, especially with batsmen like Walter Hammond, Denis Compton and Joe Hardstaff in the team. But Oldfield impressed, scoring 80 and 19, in what turned out to be his only match for England.

NORMAN OLDFIELD was born in Dukinfield, Cheshire, on 5 May 1911, and was taken on to the Lancashire staff in 1929. It was here he got the nickname of Buddy which has stayed with him all his life. Jack Latchford, another junior player, was known as 'Bud' after the rose buds on the sweaters and blazers of young professionals. 'We can't have two "Buds",' said coach Harry Makepeace, 'so you'll be Buddy,' he said to Oldfield. It was not easy to get into the Lancashire team in those championship-winning days and it is a measure of Lancashire's faith in Oldfield that he was on the staff six years before making his debut. But he scored 1,000 runs, the first of five successive years up to the war in which he reached 1,000. His impact was immediate – he was compared to J. T. Tyldesley – and Neville Cardus enthused 'O, none so rich in natural gifts has been found by Lancashire since the days which saw the blossoming of the Tyldesleys. If this young man does not go to the top of his calling there will be a scandalous interference with destiny.'

Oldfield, only 5 feet 2½ inches tall and a shade shorter than Eddie Paynter, soon had a reputation as a fearless batsman, one who actually relished taking on the fast bowlers. When the war finished Oldfield refused the terms offered by Lancashire which were, he said, exactly the same as in 1939. By then he had a family and needed more security

so he, along with Albert Nutter, went into the leagues before going to Northamptonshire. An autocratic Lancashire banned the two players from the ground and only recently Oldfield's son, Clifford, wrote to the *Sunday Times* from his home in Australia, recalling his father taking him to Old Trafford for a Test match and having to hand him over to George Duckworth at the gates. But as a Northamptonshire player, of course, Oldfield had to go into Old Trafford to play and one of the most satisfying moments of his career was the century he scored there against Lancashire. But Buddy lived to regret his move. 'I should never have left Lancashire,' he recalled. 'Really, it was the only team I wanted to play for and I missed Old Trafford. The money at Old Trafford soon caught up and if I had stayed with Lancashire I think I would have been chosen for England again. Northants were too unfashionable. I deemed it an honour to play at Old Trafford and for Lancashire. At Northants, it was a job of work.' When his playing days were over, Oldfield became an umpire and then coach . . . at Old Trafford.

Lancashire ran across 'Big Jim' Smith again in 1939 and in under half an hour, as a result of much swishing and swinging, he scored a half century at Old Trafford. He also did the hat-trick and took seven for 55 in Middlesex's win and the *Manchester Guardian* was moved to comment 'What with his first innings punching and second innings bowling, the next visit of this friendly giant to Old Trafford will be watched with fearful joy.' Unfortunately, Smith was never to play against Lancashire again. The war was almost upon us. Lionel Lister was actually padded up ready to bat at Northampton when he was summoned to join his regiment a week before war was declared. Tommy Higson, junior, was called up to captain the team in the next match at Dover, from where the players travelled back to Old Trafford for the final match against Surrey. This game should have been played at The Oval, but as the ground was not available because of the situation, it was switched to Old Trafford and started on Wednesday 30 August. Lancashire players had arrived at the ground from Dover at 4 a.m. and some slept in the pavilion before fielding later in the day. The game continued on the Thursday but the final day was cancelled. War was declared two days later.

Chapter 13 1939–53

'We in Lancashire are determined that cricket shall again flourish in the land.'

The Old Trafford ground was again turned over to the war effort . . . or to be more exact it was taken over by the army who requisitioned it as soon as war broke out. It became home for a unit of Royal Engineers, a transit camp for troops who had escaped from Dunkirk, and a storage area for the Ministry of Supply. Old Trafford was seriously damaged by air raids in 1940 and 1941 when a sentry at the main gate was killed. The top of the pavilion, the groundsman's home, the dining room and two of the stands were damaged, and craters were left on the field itself. Cricket, of course, was impossible at the ground but charity matches, in which Lancashire and former Lancashire players took part, were held all over the county. In 1941 for example, a Lancashire team played West Indies in a twelve-a-side one-day match at Fazakerley where about 10,000 spectators watched a game played for the Lord Mayor of Liverpool's Charity Fund. The West Indies included 'Manny' Martindale, Learie Constantine and Ellis Achong, while Lancashire's team was mainly made up of the outstanding players from the 1920s and 1930s, the senior of whom was 46-year-old Charlie Hallows. Tournaments of matches were held between the Army and the Royal Air Force, one of which was held at Liverpool and which included five Lancashire players, namely Lance Corporal Frank Sibbles and Bombardier Len Wilkinson in the Army side, and Sergeant Cyril Washbrook, Corporal Eddie Phillipson, and Leading Aircraftsman Albert Nutter with the RAF.

Among other prominent players who had represented Lancashire and joined the Forces were Frank Booth, Dick Pollard, Tommy Higson, Peter Eckersley and Lionel Lister, as well as some like

Ken Cranston, Eric Price, John Ikin, and Bill Roberts who were to make their names after the war. The only one to lose his life was Eckersley who was killed in a flying accident at the age of 36 while serving with the RNVR.

Three services matches were held on the ground in 1944, and in 1945 services personnel and German prisoners of war, who were paid three-farthings an hour, helped tidy the ground. Several matches were staged that year, including two against Yorkshire, one of which was first-class and staged at Bradford for the benefit of the widow and children of Hedley Verity, the Yorkshire and England left-arm spinner who had died while serving in Italy. A three-day 'Victory' Test was held at Old Trafford where England, helped by Pollard and Phillipson who took fifteen wickets between them, beat Australia by six wickets. The public, thirsty for entertainment after six years of war, rolled up in great numbers, 72,463 watching over the three days.

A £100,000 appeal was launched 'to men of goodwill' to re-build Old Trafford. In its appeal the club stated:

> The destruction by enemy action of cricket facilities at Old Trafford, the heart of cricket in Lancashire, was one of Hitler's early achievements. We in Lancashire, however, are determined that cricket shall again flourish in the land. The Committee, with your help, intend to raise on the ashes of the old pavilion an edifice of which not only we in Lancashire, but the country at large may well feel proud: a centre for our great National Pastime, which will rank as a worthy heritage of the sacrifices made by so many lovers of the game throughout the country. War in Europe has been victoriously concluded, and our thoughts can again dwell upon the resumption of peaceful pursuits. Let, therefore, your response to this appeal be the measure of your gratitude. It is no ordinary appeal, but a great rallying cry for the restoration of that spirit inherent in all true Britishers – the spirit of cricket. We want £100,000 because that is the sum necessary to build a pavilion with all essential amenities and facilities, with grandstands of a level of comfort worthy of a modern home for a great National Asset – the Game of Games – cricket. Eminent Lancashire architects have already prepared plans which can be examined by those interested, and as soon as the release of the necessary labour and materials, in relation to National circumstances, can be ethically justified – the work will begin immediately. For those splendid men who

275

will come back to play and enjoy the game, no less than for those who have joined the immortal company, the fulfilment of our plans will be a symbol of our deliverance and a golden memory of our achievements.

Unfortunately, this figure was not reached and the fund closed with a total of £42,236, which did not allow for the total rebuilding of the pavilion. Among the donations was one of £500 from Hanson Carter, the Halifax-born cricketer who kept wicket for Australia and who toured England three times. It was Carter who pointed out at Old Trafford in 1921 that Lionel Tennyson, England's captain, had broken the laws in declaring the innings closed.

County cricket resumed in 1946 after a break of six years and as in 1919, in common with most other counties, Lancashire found several holes in their team. Of those who had played in 1939, Jack Iddon, the captain-elect, was killed in a car crash seventeen days before the great new season started, while Eddie Paynter, Buddy Oldfield, Albert Nutter, Bill Farrimond, Len Hopwood, and Lionel Lister were never to play for Lancashire again. Oldfield and Nutter could not agree terms and went into league cricket before returning to first-class cricket with Northamptonshire, Farrimond retired at the age of almost 43, Hopwood finished through ill health, and Lister was not available. Paynter was 44 and as the season approached he was asked to go to Old Trafford. Paynter wrote later:

> As I drove over the moors, I wondered what the committee had in mind for me. The record showed that I was a consistent run-scorer in league cricket and had been since the county programme ended, but on the debit side my 44 years of age had to be entered. Conversation with the committee soon made it evident I had not been called to discuss any playing association with the club, but purely the question of recognition of past service.

Paynter had missed a normal benefit because of the war and was asked what he thought a reasonable sum in lieu. He said £1,000, expecting to be given more in recognition of eighteen years with the club. The committee, however, granted him £1,078 and Paynter was bitterly disappointed, particularly when Cyril Washbrook collected £14,000 two years later.

Those from 1939 who were available were Cyril Washbrook, Winston Place, Eddie Phillipson, John Ikin, Bill Roberts, Dick Pollard, Gordon Garlick and Len Wilkinson. Recruitment was needed and the newcomers were Phil King, a Yorkshireman who had played for Worcestershire, Alan Wharton and Eric Price from the leagues, Geoff and Eric Edrich from Norfolk, Tom Brierley, who had kept wicket for Glamorgan in the 1930s, and the new captain, Jack Fallows.

Following Iddon's death and the refusal of Tommy Higson to captain the team, the county turned to the 38-year-old Fallows, son of the club's treasurer, who had no first-class experience and whose appointment was not greeted with universal support. But he did a difficult job well and Lancashire led the way for two months before winning only three of their last ten games and finishing third in the championship. Travel and accommodation were utilitarian, food was still rationed, but there was a lot of fun and excitement in the return of cricket. Fallows leaned heavily on the field on his senior professionals, Washbrook and Pollard, but his experience as an officer in the Forces proved useful off the field. He tried to look after his team, to look to their comforts, and showed his wisdom one morning in a London hotel when there were only four eggs for breakfast between twelve players and a scorer. 'We are in the field this morning,' declared Fallows. 'Let the bowlers have the eggs . . . the batsmen can have them tomorrow.'

These were Washbrook's finest years. In 1946 only Walter Hammond finished above him in the national batting averages and only Denis Compton scored more centuries. And nobody in England scored more than his 2,400 runs, which included nine centuries and gave him an average of 68.57. Winston Place scored nearly 1,900 runs for an average of 41.51 and Lancashire had the finest pair of opening batsmen in the country. King and Ikin also exceeded 1,000 but only one bowler, left-arm spinner Bill Roberts, took 100 wickets.

King, a hard-hitting batsman who could open the innings but usually batted in the middle order, stayed only two seasons with Lancashire. When cricket resumed in 1946 King offered to play without payment for his pre-war county, Worcestershire, for the first 1,000 runs and then to receive £1 for every run after that. King was a gambler, but Worcestershire were not and refused the kind offer. So King went to Lancashire where he averaged 28 in his two seasons and scored just two centuries, one of them a triumphant 121 against the county of his birth, Yorkshire, the other included a century before lunch. Poor Bill Roberts played only four years before he died in 1951, aged 37. In 114 matches he took 382 wickets at 20.86 runs each and often shared the attack with another left-arm spinner, Eric Price, who played in the first two years after the war and took 115 wickets at 20.63 runs each before moving to Essex where he played two more years. Washbrook, Ikin and Pollard all played Test cricket that year – Ikin was in his first full season as a county cricketer at

277

the age of 28 – and all went with the first MCC tour after the war to Australia.

DICK POLLARD, born in Westhoughton on 19 June 1912, was flame-haired with a temper to match and was known at Old Trafford as 'Th' Owd Chain-horse'. The nickname came because of his ability – at times his insistence – to bowl for long periods. The war took perhaps the best years of a career which stretched from 1933 to 1950 and although he was nearly 34 when county cricket resumed in 1946, he was still good enough to play for England four times and tour Australia. His number of wickets for Lancashire exceeded 1,000, but only just. Although some of the life had gone from his bowling at the end of his career, he was allowed to go on and reach the thousand. And once safely past the landmark, he dressed himself in his best cricket togs and blazer and informed the chairman that time for retirement had arrived.

Pollard joined the Old Trafford staff on the same day in 1933 as Albert Nutter and Cyril Washbrook and two years later had established his place in the side when he took 100 wickets in all first-class matches. That was the start of a run in which he took 100 wickets in each of the seasons up to the war, a period when he was at his best. His most productive season came in 1938 when he bowled more than 1,200 overs and took 149 wickets. He bowled more than 1,200 overs twice more after the war and was reluctant to be taken off. 'He did not like being taken off and you don't get many bowlers like that,' recalled Cyril Washbrook. 'He was an honest, plain-speaking Lancastrian and a darn good trier.'

Pollard was chosen to play for England for the first time against India at Old Trafford in 1946 and took five for 24 – off twenty-seven overs – and two for 63. It was enough to get him on the MCC tour of Australia, but he was unable to get into any of the five Tests. He went on to New Zealand where he played his second Test, but did not get into the England side again until 1948 when the Australians were in England. He was remembered by many people for being the batsman responsible for the nasty accident that happened to Sid Barnes who was fielding at short leg during the Old Trafford Test. Pollard swung mightily, Barnes was hit in the kidney area and badly hurt. Pollard then took three for 53, followed by two for 104 and none for 55 at Headingley – he twice dismissed Don Bradman, flattening his off stump at Headingley – to finish his Test career with fifteen wickets at 25.20 runs each. His career was nearly over. He had his benefit in 1949, when he made £8,035, and played five more matches in 1950. He finished with 1,015 wickets for Lancashire at 22.15 each, the seventh bowler after Watson, Briggs, Mold, Dean, McDonald and Dick Tyldesley to take a thousand for the county.

Lancashire had a good year in 1946. They played enterprising

278

cricket and gave supporters a good run for their money in the championship. Yet Fallows was sacked, either because of his habit of losing the toss at a vital stage of the season, or for averaging 5.39 as a batsman. Either way, Lancashire replaced him with a man who has one of the most remarkable, if not unique, records in the game, Ken Cranston.

KEN CRANSTON spent only two years in first-class cricket yet he played in eight Test matches, toured West Indies with MCC, captained England in a Test, took four wickets in six balls against South Africa, and in all, scored 3,099 first-class runs and took 178 wickets.

Cranston was born in Aigburth, about a mile from the ground where Lancashire have been playing since 1881, on 20 October 1917. He left club cricket with Neston to captain Lancashire in 1947 and 1948, and then turned his back on cricket and returned to work as a dentist. 'I wanted to prove myself,' he said forty years later. 'I knew I was a reasonable player and it is only by playing first-class cricket that you find just how good you are. I did enough in that short time to satisfy myself. I went to the West Indies at the end of my first season and it was all an anti-climax after that. I had a family growing up and I wanted to establish myself in dentistry.' Cranston had played a lot of good-class cricket before the war, mainly public schools and universities with several appearances at Lord's. He had also played for Lancashire 2nd and had scored a century against Yorkshire 2nd before playing for the navy and a British Empire team during the war. His father, who had kept the dentistry practice going during the war, looked after it through the years that Cranston captained Lancashire.

Lancashire finished third and fifth and won twenty-one championship matches during Cranston's captaincy. 'Our only weakness was the lack of a really quick bowler,' he said. He batted No. 6 or 7 for Lancashire and scored 1,928 runs for an average of 40.16; he bowled just above medium pace off the seam, opened the attack several times, and took 142 wickets (23 average) for them. He was pressed to stay on as captain after the 1948 season but his mind was made up. He did not play for Lancashire again but was happy to play the occasional game for the Free Foresters and MCC.

Cyril Washbrook, of course, was again Lancashire's leading batsman through those two years with 4,630 runs at an average just short of 70 in all matches for the county. And Washbrook was also Cranston's counsel, his right hand, and Cranston was always grateful to him for the advice he gave and weight he carried. 'He was such an experienced player and could have made me look a fool', Cranston once said. But he never did. For Washbrook's loyalty was always to Lancashire, no matter who was appointed captain. Winston Place and Washbrook both exceeded 2,500 runs in the sunny summer of 1947 and each scored two centuries in a match. They shared in six stands over 100, one of them a double hundred, another a treble hundred when they put on an undefeated 350 against Sussex at Old Trafford. After a close struggle for first innings lead, the openers scored at 90 runs an hour to reach 350 by the end of the second day. They were only 18 short of the record set up by Archie MacLaren and Reg Spooner in 1903 but Cranston declared first thing the following morning so the bowlers could get whatever help the moist wicket would give them. In the end he was right because Lancashire won with only 45 minutes left and just ahead of a thunderstorm. Washbrook scored nine centuries for Lancashire – eleven in all games – and Place ten and their foundations enabled Lancashire to average around 385 per innings throughout all matches.

Washbrook scored double centuries against Sussex and Surrey in the space of six days at Old Trafford, the start to four centuries in successive matches on the ground. They were followed by 122 against Essex and 103 against Cambridge University, making only their second-ever appearance at Old Trafford. Another outstanding Washbrook-Place partnership, this time of 183, produced a remarkable ten-wicket win over Gloucestershire, who must have left Old Trafford wondering how they came to lose after scoring 415 in their first innings. Not even this matched the openers' undefeated 233 in 113 minutes at Eastbourne to bring about a ten-wicket win with only ten minutes to spare. Washbrook scored 176 and 121 not out in the match and I cannot help wondering if the former Mayor of Eastbourne, who was responsible for the Lancashire professionals boycotting his lunch after a few ill-chosen words in 1931, had been able to witness the great Lancashire performance. Lancashire were certainly an exciting team to watch in those days and nothing could have been more thrilling than the tied match – the second in Lancashire's history – against Hampshire at Bournemouth in the following match. Washbrook and Place scored 142 in 90 minutes towards the 221 needed for victory but last man, Alf Barlow, was run out in the final over going for the run that would have brought victory. Lancashire then moved on to Lord's for their sixth win in the last seven matches – and the one that gave most satisfaction as they beat Middlesex, who had already won the championship. Denis Compton scored his sixteenth century of the season to equal Jack Hobbs's record but could not save Middlesex from their 64-run beating.

John Ikin and Geoff Edrich, who had become regular and reliable Nos. 3 and 4 in the batting order, also topped 1,000 runs in 1947, but only Dick Pollard, who bowled over 1,200 overs, exceeded 100 wickets. He took 144 and carried the bowling with Cranston claiming eighty-three, Roberts fifty-one and Ikin fifty.

JOHN IKIN, born at Bignall End, Staffordshire, on 7 March 1918, was only 16 when he first played for his home county and among his teammates was Sydney Barnes, then aged 61. He made his debut for Lancashire in 1939 before going into the army. He served as a 'Desert Rat' and when the war was over immediately established himself in the Lancashire team and won a place with England in the Test series against India in 1946. He became an England player with only eighteen first-class matches behind him and followed his debut by going to Australia with MCC that winter. He was regarded as the ideal team man, enthusiastic and unselfish, and was widely respected throughout the cricket world. He batted left-handed, bowled right-handed leg breaks, and took catches as well, and it was more as a utility player than as a specialist that he took part in eighteen Test matches. His Test record was less than ordinary. He scored 606 runs for an average of 20.89 and took three wickets at 118 each. But he was steady, reliable, and adaptable, a brilliant fielder, and he filled a need in the decade after the war. He could open the innings or bat in the middle of the order, and his willingness, courage and soundness lifted him above the ordinariness his figures suggest.

Ikin's career with Lancashire extended to 1957 and consisted of 288 matches in which he scored 14,327 runs – average 37.70 and including 1,000 runs in a season ten times – and took 278 wickets at 28.79 each. He also held 419 catches in 365 first-class matches, most of them while fielding at short-leg for Lancashire and forming a hungry trio of close-in catchers with Ken Grieves and Geoff Edrich. He died on 15 September 1984, aged 66.

Cyril Washbrook's benefit was taken in August 1948, the first Lancashire player to have been given the Australian match. Nearly 50,000 people paid for admission, the largest of the season, and Washbrook received a colossal £14,000, which beat the previous record of £3,111 by J. T. Tyldesley in 1906, and which stayed a record until beaten by Farokh Engineer in 1976. Don Bradman, the Australian captain, did not enforce the follow-on and scored a fine 133 not out on his last appearance at the ground. Lancashire comfortably played out time, although Bradman took the new ball five minutes from the end and Ray Lindwall bowled Ikin and Pollard with successive deliveries. Poor Ikin. For the second time in successive games, following Essex at Blackpool, he was out for 99. It was a strange decision by Bradman and one which did not meet with the approval of Keith Miller, who refused to bowl with the new ball. 'He should have let Ikin get his hundred,' he said later.

281

Lancashire had also played the Australians at Old Trafford in May when Malcolm Hilton, a 19-year-old left-arm spinner, earned everlasting fame by dismissing Bradman twice. A similar sort of fame must have been in Hilton's mind when he went for the winning hit at The Oval and was caught by Laurie Fishlock, leaving Surrey winners by one run.

MALCOLM HILTON, born in Oldham on 2 August 1928, was just turned 18 when he made his debut in the last match of the 1946 season. He played until 1961, sixteen seasons in which he had to hold off the challenge of another Lancashire left-arm spinner good enough to play for England, Bob Berry, and in which he took over 100 wickets in a season four times. He played in fourteen matches in that triumphant year of 1948 when he twice saw off Don Bradman, but it was 1950 before he became a regular first-team player and took 135 wickets at 16.79 runs each and played in the first of his four Test matches. His second Test came the following year against South Africa and in two Tests in India that winter, under Nigel Howard's captaincy and when he had the unusual experience of opening the English attack with Lancashire teammate Roy Tattersall, he took eleven wickets at only 17 runs each. But he was never to play for England again although his finest season was yet to come, in 1956 when he took 158 wickets at under 14 runs apiece. His career-best championship performances came that summer with eight for 39, and a match return of fourteen for 88, against Somerset at Weston-super-Mare.

Hilton's only century came in 1955 when, batting at No. 9, he reached his hundred in exactly two hours on a Northampton wicket so perfect that when he bowled he took only George Tribe's wicket for 137 runs in sixty-one overs. Hilton did not reach 100 wickets again after that marvellous season of 1956 and after taking only twenty wickets in 1959 – the season he reached his 1,000th – and not playing in 1960, he retired after playing in three matches in 1961. He captained the second team in his last two years and when he had finished playing he had taken 926 wickets for Lancashire (average 18.81) and 1,006 in all. Yet he was still only 33.

Lancashire pulled off an unlikely win at Leicester in 1948 when Leicestershire, needing only 124 to win, were almost there with 26 wanted and six wickets standing. Then Pollard and Roberts each took two wickets in three balls and Percy Corrall, attempting a six off the last ball of the match, was brilliantly caught by Nigel Howard on the boundary edge to give Lancashire victory by 4 runs. It was Corrall who was keeping wicket in 1933 when Washbrook, in his first season, swung round in hitting the ball and struck him on the ear. He was taken to hospital in a semi-conscious state and did not play again that season. For a time it was feared the injury would end his career but he recovered and resumed in 1934.

Ken Cranston ended his county career in the grand manner by scoring 82 in the first innings of the final match with Kent at Old Trafford before making the winning hit in the seven-wicket win. It had been known for some time that Cranston would leave county cricket at the end of the 1948 season. He had enjoyed himself, had proved himself a cricketer of considerable talents, and knew he would soon become bored with the endless, at times repetitive, drudgeries of the game. In any case, he had to get back to his dentistry and earn himself a living. Lancashire had two alternatives as his successor. There was the natural choice, that of 34-year-old Cyril Washbrook, a respected, solid, knowledgeable professional. And there was 23-year-old Nigel Howard, a batsman who was averaging 32, son of the secretary Rupert Howard, inexperienced, but more importantly, an amateur. The time was not quite right for the introduction of a professional and Lancashire went for Howard.

NIGEL HOWARD was born at Preston on 18 May 1925, and became the most distinguished member of a cricketing family which included his father, Major Rupert Howard, who had played for Lancashire between the wars and had scored 88 not out on his debut, and his brother Barry who played thirty-two matches between 1947 and 1951. Howard, educated at Rossall, made his debut in 1946 but did not attain anything like a regular place until 1948. He was a stylish, aggressive batsman who averaged 24.70 through 198 matches up to his retirement in 1953. He reached 1,000 runs only once, in 1950, but went close on three other occasions. He scored only three centuries, one of them coming at Maidstone where he went in just before tea and was 138 not out at the close. He played four Tests for England, all of them in India in 1950–51 when he captained a team which also included three other Lancashire players in Brian Statham, Roy Tattersall and Malcolm Hilton. He was an enterprising captain who would accept any reasonable challenge and would join Washbrook to open the innings and force the pace. Said Washbrook of him 'His own personal success mattered very little to him, but the success of the team was of paramount importance.' He retired from the game in 1953, when he was 28, to concentrate on the family textile business, and in 1976 moved to the Isle of Man where he died three years later, aged 54.

In the five years that Howard was captain, he achieved something that three captains before him and many more after him could not – he led his team to the top of the championship, even if they did have to share it with Surrey in 1950. But 1949, his first season, was not a happy one. Lancashire finished eleventh and Howard came in for a good deal of criticism which clearly affected his batting and must have undermined his confidence. There was no shortage of runs in the team. Ikin had his best season yet in volume of runs, Wharton reached 1,000 for the first time in company with Washbrook, Place, Edrich, and a newcomer from Australia who had been playing in the Lancashire League, Ken Grieves.

KEN GRIEVES was from Sydney, a 23-year-old batsman, leg-break bowler and brilliant fieldsman, particularly close to the wicket. In only his second match, batting at No. 7, he scored 68 and 91 and took eight wickets. Two matches later, at Oxford, he scored the first of the twenty-six centuries he was to get in fourteen seasons with Lancashire. He went on to score 1,407 runs and become the fourth player after Buddy Oldfield, Phil King and Ken Cranston to score 1,000 runs in his first season. He also took sixty-three wickets as well as holding thirty-two catches and it seems such a pity that his bowling talent was allowed to languish through the years.

Ken Grieves had played for New South Wales in the two years after the war and came to England only because Keith Miller had decided at the last minute not to join Rawtenstall, the Lancashire League club, in 1947. Grieves took his place and after two successful seasons in league cricket, joined Lancashire in 1949. He played until 1961 and returned in 1963 to captain the team for two years, giving him fifteen seasons with the county in which he played 452 matches, scored 20,802 runs (average 33.39) and took 235 wickets (28.80). He failed to reach 1,000 runs in a season only twice and his outstanding year was 1959 when he scored over 2,000 runs for the only time in his career. He was one of the most brilliant close-to-the-wicket catchers Lancashire have ever had and holds the record for most in a season for the county with sixty-three in 1950. He also holds the record for most catches in a match with eight against Sussex at Old Trafford in 1951 when he also equalled Dick Tyldesley's record of six in a single innings.

Lancashire's bowling in 1949 had lacked penetration. Eddie Phillipson had retired, Dick Pollard was nearing the end and Lancashire were searching desperately for the man who could spearhead their attack and their challenge for the championship.

The change in Lancashire's – and Nigel Howard's – fortunes was immediate. From out of a clear blue sky came Roy Tattersall and Malcolm Hilton to take nearly 300 wickets between them and drive Lancashire to their best season for sixteen years. Tattersall took 171 wickets for the county at 13.29 runs each and Hilton, still only 21 years old, took 127 at 15.32. And, of even more lasting significance was the emergence of the fast bowler Lancashire had been looking for, Brian Statham, who, within twelve months, was to establish himself in the Lancashire team and play for England. Grieves again took sixty-three wickets, left-arm spinner Bob Berry fifty-three and Lancashire at last had an attack that was to bring them sixteen championship wins and a share of the championship in 1950.

ROY TATTERSALL was born in Bolton on 17 August 1922, and was already 25 when he made his debut for Lancashire as a medium-paced bowler after playing with Tonge and Bradshaw in the Bolton League. He shared the opening attack with Pollard in 1948 and took a Glamorgan wicket with his fourth ball. But he was persuaded by coach Harry Makepeace to try off spin and 1950 was his first full year as a spinner, his 171 wickets being the highest for the county since Ted McDonald's 198 in 1925 and a total that has not been touched since. In all matches that year he took 193 wickets and could have got 200 if he could just have got into the attack in the one-day win over Sussex at Old Trafford. Hilton and Peter Greenwood, another off spinner, opened the bowling and the first delivery, to John Langridge, turned square. Tattersall was told to get ready to bowl, but Greenwood got a wicket the same over and Tattersall, his fingers twitching, did not send down a ball.

Tattersall finished top of the national averages but did not play for England who used eight other spinners that summer in the Test series with the West Indies. He was not chosen for the tour of Australia although he and Statham were flown out later when Doug Wright and Trevor Bailey were injured. Between 1950 and 1954 Tattersall played in sixteen Tests and took fifty-eight wickets at 26.18 runs each. He would have played more if he had not to face such fierce competition as that provided at the time by Jim Laker. Tattersall took 100 wickets for Lancashire seven times in eight seasons from 1950 to 1957 and finished his career with 1,168 wickets at a cost of 17.39 for Lancashire, 1,369 at 18.04 in all. In 1956 Tattersall and Glamorgan off spinner Don Shepherd were leading the race to 100 wickets. Tattersall had taken ninety-one, was third in the national averages, and was dropped for seven championship matches. When he asked the coach Stan Worthington for the reason, he was told 'Ours is not to reason why.' Tattersall said it knocked the stuffing out of him. 'I understand they wanted to play all-rounders to strengthen the batting,' he said. 'From then on I didn't have a full season and when I was left out of the team in 1959 and 1960, I couldn't continue. I couldn't live off second-team money. I was 38 when I finished, but I could easily have gone on for three or four years more.' Tattersall took more than 100 wickets in 1956 and 1957, took ninety-four at less than

18 runs each in 1958, played in only one championship match in 1959, and left the club at the end of 1960. He moved to Kidderminster to play league cricket and to work for a carpet manufacturer.

Malcolm Hilton and Bob Berry, Lancashire's two left-arm spinners, both played for England in the summer of 1950. Berry's only two Test matches came that season against West Indies and his nine wickets at 25.33 encouraged MCC to pick him to go to Australia and New Zealand with Freddie Brown's team that winter.

BOB BERRY, born in West Gorton, Manchester, on 29 January 1926, played for Lancashire between 1948 and 1956. A left-arm spinner, he took part in ninety-three matches and would have played many more but for the competition provided by Malcolm Hilton. He outshone Hilton in a couple of seasons, particularly 1953 when he took ninety-eight wickets at 18.97 each, including all ten for 102 against Worcestershire at Blackpool, only the third time in Lancashire's history that this feat had been achieved. But in the end he moved to Worcestershire, where he played from 1955 to 1958 and Derbyshire (1959–62). His ninety-three games for Lancashire brought him 259 wickets at 22.77 each.

Cyril Washbrook was injured early in 1950 and in his absence Lancashire won three out of five championship matches, including the Roses clash at Sheffield where the spinners took thirty-three of the thirty-eight wickets to fall and which ended in a thrilling 14-run win. He returned for the game at Lord's and Lancashire promptly lost for the first time as they failed by 124 runs to get the 300 needed for victory in 200 minutes. Statham's debut came two matches later, on his twentieth birthday on 17 June when Lancashire beat Kent by an innings and 73 in two days at Old Trafford. Statham could have been forgiven in his debut season if he had thought county cricket was easy. He took part in six innings wins, some in two days, one in one day, and Lancashire shared the championship.

The one-day win came at Old Trafford on 12 July, giving Lancashire victory by an innings and 87 runs ten minutes into the extra half hour. Sussex won the toss but were dismissed in 95 minutes for 101, John Langridge carrying his bat for 48. Lancashire replied with 239 of which Geoff Edrich and Alf Barlow scored 67 for the seventh wicket in just over half an hour. Sussex were dismissed a second time for 51 in 75 minutes to give Lancashire the sixth one-day win of their history, the fifth at Old Trafford. Peter Greenwood bowled twenty-six overs in the two innings and took nine for 67. Malcolm Hilton, celebrating the award of his county cap, opened the attack with him, was never taken off, and finished with eleven for 50. The only other bowler to get on, for three overs in the first innings, was Bob Berry, while Roy Tattersall, with eighty-nine wickets behind him, could only stand and watch and twitch. The game lasted six and a half hours and consisted of 123 overs.

Lancashire had won seven successive matches and were top of the table when the August Bank Holiday Roses match arrived at Old Trafford, where 66,647 paid to watch the game, 31,679 of them on the Monday when Lancashire's last pair, Berry and Statham, scrambled the 7 runs needed for first innings points. Lancashire won three of the next four games and only rain deprived them of the chance of beating Warwickshire at Old Trafford in the penultimate match, when victory would have secured the championship for them.

Lancashire went into the last game at The Oval against Surrey, their nearest challengers, needing only 4 points for first-innings lead to take the title. There was a dramatic start when Lancashire, after winning the toss, lost Washbrook and Place in three balls to Stuart Surridge. They never really recovered although the middle-order batsmen all made useful contributions to give them a working total of 221. Peter May batted stubbornly to score 92 in five hours to make sure Surrey took first-innings points and with the game ending in a draw, Lancashire had completed their programme and were 12 points ahead of Surrey, who had one game to play, against Leicestershire. Twelve points were awarded for wins then and although rain took away some of the playing time, Surrey won the last match by ten wickets – their eighth win in their last nine matches – to share the title. Still, it had been a good year and Lancashire, now with a membership around 10,000 and a waiting list, also recorded a paying attendance of more than 252,000 in the year, compared with 246,000 in 1948.

Lancashire were to finish third in each of Howard's remaining years as captain, 80 points behind Warwickshire in 1951, 68 behind Surrey in 1952, but only 28 behind Surrey in 1953. Geoff Edrich had his best years in 1951 – 1,693 runs (average 43.41) – and 1952, when he failed by only 23 runs to reach 2,000 for the season as he averaged 41.18.

GEOFF EDRICH, one of four first-class cricketing brothers, was born in Norfolk on 13 August 1918, and had played for his home county before the outbreak of war. He fought against the Japanese and was held prisoner of war for three and a half years before being liberated in August 1945, by which time he weighed 6½ stones. In 1939 he had been approached to play for Hampshire the following year. In 1946 he was recommended to Lancashire who signed him and his brother Eric on their pre-war reputations with Norfolk. Eric played only until 1948 but

Geoff went on until 1958, reaching 1,000 runs eight times and averaging 34.74 through his 322 matches for the county.

Tattersall was away a lot in 1951, on Test and other representative calls, and took only eighty-two wickets for Lancashire, 121 in all matches. Hilton had another fine year with 120, Statham took ninety-two, and five players scored over 1,000 runs. Lancashire had to dig deep into their reserve strength for one match against Hampshire at Aigburth when Howard, Tattersall, Statham, Ikin and Hilton were playing in the Gentlemen-Players match at Lord's. Lancashire still won that one, by an innings, with Edrich scoring 155, and Peter Greenwood, who had problems competing as a spinner with Hilton, Tattersall and Berry, taking three for 42 and five for 10. Greenwood, who also scored his only century that summer with 113 in 140 minutes against Kent, played in only three of Lancashire's remaining twelve matches after the defeat of Hampshire, eleven of which were drawn and the other lost.

Buddy Oldfield had one of his most satisfying moments when he scored a century for Northamptonshire at Old Trafford, one of three in successive years he was to score against his former county. Harry Makepeace retired as coach in 1951 after forty-five years' association with the club, was granted a pension of £150 a year, and died the following year. Tattersall, Ikin, Statham and Hilton were chosen to tour India that winter under Nigel Howard's captaincy and with new secretary Geoffrey Howard – no relation – as manager. Ikin later pulled out due to injury.

Winston Place had his benefit in 1952, fifteen years after his first match, and received £6,297, a figure that was as high as players were getting twenty years later. He scored only one century that year, but also hit 99 against Essex on the eve of his benefit match before he was stumped.

WINSTON PLACE was born in Rawtenstall on 7 December 1914, a sound opening batsman who later moved into the middle order. He made his debut in 1937 and had only three seasons with the county before war broke out. When it was over he was 31 but he had ten more good years during which he teamed up with Cyril Washbrook to form one of the finest opening partnerships Lancashire have ever had. He scored 1,000 runs in each of the eight years after the war, his best by far coming in 1947 when he scored 2,408 runs for Lancashire at an average of 68.80 to earn his place in the MCC team for the West Indies where he played all his three Tests and scored a century. He played in 298 matches for Lancashire, scored thirty-four centuries and 14,605 runs at an average of 36.69.

Lancashire's third, and to date the last, tied match came in 1952 against Essex at Brentwood. The first innings was not decided until the third morning, but the rest of the day's play produced 457 runs in 116.4 overs. Essex, set to score 232 to win, reached the final over with 9 runs wanted and the last pair together. One of the batsmen was Trevor Bailey who hit the first ball of the over, from Hilton, for six, ran two off the second ball when he was missed in the deep, and fell to an excellent catch by Howard off the fourth to leave the scores tied. Another exciting finish came in the Roses match at Old Trafford in August – again more than 40,000 people paid for admission – when Lancashire's last two batsmen, Frank Parr, who shared the wicket-keeping that year with Alan Wilson, and Bob Berry resisted all Yorkshire's efforts to separate them. The Northamptonshire match at Old Trafford also provided great excitement on the final day after three declarations had left Lancashire needing 176 to win in 110 minutes. The last ball of the match was bowled with Lancashire 174 for eight and was delivered to Berry from a former Lancashire player, Albert Nutter. Berry took a simple single but the fieldsman's return was dropped by the wicket-keeper and the batsmen scrambled home for the second run and victory. The penultimate match of the season, against Sussex at Hove, saw the debut of Peter Marner, aged only 16, and three months younger than Lancashire's youngest ever, Johnny Briggs, who had held the record since 1879.

Tattersall continued to be Lancashire's leading wicket-taker with 146 in 1952 and 135 in 1953 and had one of his finest days when he took nine for 40 against Nottinghamshire at Old Trafford in 1953. He took seven of the wickets, including the hat-trick, in nineteen balls without conceding a run. Statham reached 100 for the first time in 1952 and just missed out the following year, Hilton took sixty-nine wickets in 1952, Berry took ninety-eight in 1953. Lancashire had found the bowlers to take wickets, the fast bowler they had been searching for had come along, the first five or six batsmen were regularly getting 1,000 runs, but they could not quite press for the title.

Lancashire were involved in another one-day match in 1953 when they bowled out Somerset for 55 and 79 at Bath with Tattersall opening the attack in both innings and bowling unchanged to take thirteen of the wickets for 69 runs. Lancashire themselves were in trouble at 46 for five but along came Marner, now 17 years old, to hit four 6s and a 4 in a half-hour stay which brought him 44 runs and enabled Lancashire to total 158. The match, of eighty-two overs, was over by 5.30 p.m. on a wicket unsuitable for first-class cricket. Bertie Buse, the 42-year-old Somerset medium pace bowler, had his team's best return with six for 41, but he was a sad man at the end of the day. For this had been his benefit match . . .

Bob Berry became only the third Lancashire player after Bill Hickton (in 1870) and Johnny Briggs (1900) to take all ten wickets in an innings when he bowled out Worcestershire at Blackpool in 1953. Lancashire, with a first innings lead of 74, had closed their second innings at 262 for eight declared, and Worcestershire looked beaten when they were 153 for five with all the wickets having fallen to Berry. But Bob Broadbent and Richard Devereux put on 104 in 85 minutes before Berry separated them. The next four wickets fell to Berry and Lancashire had won a great match by only 18 runs after seven minutes of the extra half hour. Ikin, with four catches, made an important contribution to Berry's piece of history-making. Another thrilling finish came at Old Trafford where Northamptonshire won a low-scoring match on a difficult pitch by one wicket with George Tribe steering his team home with two masterly, unbeaten innings of 73 and 37. Edrich played one of his finest innings for Lancashire when he scored 81 not out in a second innings total of 141.

Chapter 14 1954–59

'Meek submissiveness had gone and bodies, like cricket clubs, that tried to run their organizations on pre-war lines invariably ran headlong into trouble.'

With the retirement of Nigel Howard as captain after the 1953 season, Lancashire had no alternative to Cyril Washbrook as his successor. And it would have looked silly if they had tried to find one. The only amateur other than Howard to have played in the 1953 season had been 20-year-old Colin Smith, who was to win a Blue in the following four years at Cambridge University. Lancashire could have gone outside the club as they did in 1962 when Joe Blackledge was appointed, but with a player of the stature of Washbrook on hand, it would not only have been folly to have looked outside, it would have been insulting. Washbrook's appointment met with general acclaim and he was to continue to hold the position for six years, until he was 44 years old. When he took over Lancashire, the team was still in such capable hands as those of Alan Wharton, Geoff Edrich, John Ikin, Ken Grieves, Winston Place, Malcolm Hilton, Brian Statham and Roy Tattersall. A year after he had handed over the captaincy to Bob Barber, only Grieves and Statham of those stalwarts remained and Lancashire were looking to a new, young breed which included such talented players as Barber, Geoff Pullar, Peter Marner, Jack Dyson, Ken Higgs, Tommy Greenhough – all of whom were brought along and capped during Washbrook's captaincy – and Geoff Clayton, capped in 1960. Lancashire finished tenth, ninth, second, sixth, seventh and fifth under Washbrook.

Washbrook was one of the most respected players in the game, a loyal, honest man who believed in the game's customs and disciplines. He had been brought up on stern control and believed in

291

it and it would seem that he had problems bridging the gap with the young players bursting with life and ambition. Life in England had changed dramatically since the war. Men had given their lives for their country and were no longer prepared to be subject to the grave, and often unfair, disciplines of pre-war England. The meek submissiveness had gone and bodies, like cricket clubs, that tried to run their organizations on pre-war lines invariably ran headlong into trouble. Lancashire, unfortunately, continued to run along in this fashion until the committee was overthrown in 1964. Two fine examples of change in outlook were provided by Alan Wharton and Geoff Edrich, who had served in the war. If one word had to be found to sum up the feelings of men such as these, it would be equality.

Wharton came from a strong socialist background and found difficulties adjusting to the conservative world of a members' club in first-class cricket. He had also served in the Royal Navy and it was probably inevitable that he would take on authority when he felt authority was wrong. He became a barrack-room lawyer, capable of standing up for himself . . . and for other people. An incident early in his career illustrates perfectly the change that came over cricket – and life – after the war. He was in a game at Gloucester early in 1946 when he fielded as 12th man through a long, exhausting Walter Hammond innings. He left the field feeling shattered and as he walked into the dressing room, Dick Pollard called out 'Get me a bloody cup of water, Wharton.' Wharton told Pollard he could get his own cup of water and was probably not surprised when he was later called before a three-man committee for showing insubordination to a senior professional. Wharton pointed out he could make more money as a teacher and a league professional than he was earning at Lancashire and his suggestion that he was prepared to leave ended with the committee telling him there was no question of discipline. Just a suggestion that he might be more tactful in future. Ten years earlier, and Wharton might not have played for Lancashire again. But now, it was a triumph for the working man, the sort that was to be repeated throughout life in England, especially in industry, for many years after the war. Wharton was as good as anybody and wanted the same respect as the next man.

Geoff Edrich had a similar experience during a match away from home when the players were invited to a Saturday-night dance. There was no cricket on Sundays in those days, but at midnight Pollard started to line up the players, ready for checking before returning to the hotel. Edrich told him he had been a prisoner of war for three and a half years and nobody was going to tell him how to spend his Saturday nights. It took time for those with authority, those brought up on the teachings of pre-war England, to come to terms with the way of things after. Pollard had learned his cricket in the hard school and like others around him no doubt believed it was the right way. So the gap was wider than that of a mere generation; it was one deep-rooted in equality, in fairness of mind. It bred bloody-mindedness, too, and the ability of worker and boss to sort it all out was tested to the full.

John Kay, who was the *Manchester Evening News* cricket writer who followed Lancashire around in those days, wrote:

> Washbrook had been through a hard school and demanded the same sort of dedication, discipline and self control he himself had always practised. He never once spared himself in the cause of Lancashire cricket and expected his men sternly to follow his example so that he became, in a sense, a bogey man to the many newcomers Lancashire fielded in those rebuilding days. He tried desperately hard to see the point of view of the new generation, but instead of becoming a father figure, he assumed, undoubtedly without being aware of it, the role of all-demanding schoolmaster.

Eric Todd, who wrote for the *Manchester Evening Chronicle*, said Washbrook was a lonely man after Place and Ikin retired. 'I have nothing in common with this team,' he once told Todd, who added 'This might have explained why Lancashire won nothing under Washbrook's captaincy, although being unpopular or feared did not affect his own performances.'

Certainly, Lancashire had a good enough side to have won the title, particularly in his final year when Geoff Pullar, Ken Grieves and Alan Wharton all exceeded 2,000 runs with Bob Barber and Peter Marner getting 1,000, and Brian Statham, Ken Higgs and Tommy Greenhough all taking 100 wickets. But Lancashire were fifth that year, 20 points behind the winners, Yorkshire, which was exactly the same margin between themselves and Surrey when they finished runners-up in 1956.

CYRIL WASHBROOK was born in Barrow, the village near Clitheroe, on 6 December 1914, but by the time his cricket was developing sufficiently to attract the interest of Warwickshire and Worcestershire as well as Lancashire, he was attending Bridgnorth Grammar School. He nearly did not join Lancashire. He failed to get into Birmingham University, where he would have taken a degree in brewing, only because he had not done a written paper in art. If he had, and had gone to university, he would have joined Warwickshire as an amateur. Instead he went straight from school to join Lancashire as a professional.

When Washbrook arrived at the railway station for Old Trafford

in April 1933, he was making only his second visit to the ground. A tall man, carrying a bag, had also left the train and the 18-year-old Washbrook asked if he could tell him the way to the ground's main entrance. The man said he was going there and would show him the way. 'What are you, a batsman or a bowler?' he asked Lancashire's latest groundstaff recruit. 'A batsman,' said Washbrook. 'There's not much chance for batsmen here,' grunted the man who turned out to be Sydney Barnes, then 60 years old and a bowling coach at Old Trafford. Nevertheless, Washbrook made the sort of immediate impact that must have left the likes of Buddy Oldfield, still waiting for his debut after four years on the staff, scratching his head in wonderment. He scored 202 not out for the second team against Yorkshire, was thrust into the first team, and in only his second game there he scored 152 against Surrey at Old Trafford. He was sitting in the junior players' dressing room later when Barnes came in, patted him on the shoulder, pointed out to the wicket, and said simply 'Well played.'

Washbrook went on to become the county's finest post-war batsman and an opener to stand alongside Archie MacLaren in a Lancashire team of all time. His career spanned twenty-six years and his total of runs for Lancashire – and in all first-class matches – stands third behind only Ernest and J. T. Tyldesley. But for the war he would have been Lancashire's most prolific run-scorer. In the five years up to the war he scored nearly 8,000 runs for Lancashire alone; in the five years after he scored more than 8,000. A similar volume of runs in the six years of the war would have taken him to over 36,000 for Lancashire – against the 27,863 (34,101 in all matches) he scored – and would have given him a hundred centuries. Washbrook scored seventy-six centuries – fifty-eight of them for Lancashire – and believes he would have reached 100 regardless of the war if he had not become captain. 'I began to bat a little lower in the order to strengthen the middle of the batting,' he said. 'At that stage we were either in the cart or not going quickly enough, and I got out a number of times after getting 50 when normally, as opener, I would have gone on to a hundred.' Washbrook scored six centuries in his first two seasons as captain, but only one, against Hampshire in his last season, in the last four years. 'I was very proud to be captain of Lancashire,' he said. 'But it was a position I never coveted. I enjoyed it but I'm not sure I wouldn't have been happier just to have continued opening and scoring more runs. But I was a lucky captain. I had a decent set of chaps and I was the Boss and they knew I was the Boss.'

When Washbrook retired, he had completed exactly 500 games for the county, a figure exceeded only by Jack Sharp, Ernest and J. T. Tyldesley. He regards the high spot of an illustrious career which included thirty-seven Test matches with six centuries and 2,569 runs for an average of 42.81, as being asked to tour Australia, which he did twice. And one of the greatest moments of his career, naturally, was the 98 he scored against the Aussies in 1956 when he was recalled to the team at the age of 41 and after a six-year absence. He was a Test selector himself at the time and was asked by the chairman, Gubby Allen, to go and order the beer while they discussed him. 'He told me I had been chosen and I said "Surely the situation isn't as desperate as all that." But you don't refuse to play for England and I don't appreciate players today opting out of Test matches. I was very glad to get to 98 in that Test match but another two wouldn't have done any harm. But I was pleased not to have let my co-selectors down.' Washbrook became a member of Lancashire's committee soon after his retirement as a player and, apart from a two-year break, stayed on until 1988 when he was elected President, only the second professional player after Len Hopwood to be so honoured.

Washbrook was a magnificently aggressive batsman in the Golden Age mould, one who took the attack to the bowler, and was one of the finest cover fielders in England, following a great Lancashire tradition. He would have made just as good an amateur player as he did a professional, perhaps even better if he had been totally released from the reins in which professionalism naturally held him. He once said he would like to be remembered by people because he provided entertainment. He can rest assured he did that.

Washbrook launched his six years as club captain by scoring a century against Glamorgan at Old Trafford in the opening game of the 1954 season. By July, he had moved down the order, and apart from a game against Surrey as opener on a difficult Oval wicket in 1958, that was where he was to stay. It was a wet summer. In fact, four of Washbrook's six seasons as captain were wet and miserable. In 1954, nineteen full days were lost, eleven of them at Old Trafford where two complete games were washed out. Lancashire played at Bath again this year, scene of the one-day match the previous year when Bertie Buse's benefit was ruined and Roy Tattersall took thirteen wickets for 69 runs. Somerset were bowled out cheaply again in 1954, for 173 and 119 . . . but Tattersall, who took 113 wickets this year, did not take one at Bath.

This was the period when Surrey dominated the championship with seven successive title wins and in Washbrook's first five years of captaincy Lancashire lost six of their matches against Surrey with the other two drawn. Games against Surrey always put Lancashire firmly in their place and the 1955 game was a fine example where Lancashire lost by an innings and 143 runs after winning the toss and being dismissed for 94 and 108. Surrey, meanwhile, lost only three wickets with Peter May and Ken Barrington scoring centuries.

Washbrook's highest score as captain came in the 1955 match

against Worcestershire at Old Trafford when he scored 170 in the eight-wicket win. A last-wicket partnership put on 73, with Roy Tattersall scoring only 5 of them. An outstanding innings from Brian Statham, who scored only five half-centuries in 647 innings, was a rare occasion. And the one to savour most came against Leicestershire at Old Trafford in 1955 when he scored 62 in 31 minutes with twelve 4s, two 6s and two singles, before taking four for 34 in the innings win. Statham recalled it as a good, old-fashioned slog. 'I thought for a minute I was a batsman,' he said. 'But Cyril wasn't too impressed. "Tell that silly young bugger to get out now," he said. He wanted me to bowl for the last half hour.' Another swashbuckling innings that year was provided by Malcolm Hilton who scored his only century, 100 not out in two hours, to take Lancashire from 218 for seven to 372 for nine declared at Northampton. His bowling after that was not quite as impressive as Statham's. He took one for 137 in sixty-one overs.

One of the finest pieces of bowling against Lancashire in post-war years came that summer from Sussex off-break bowler Robin Marlar who took six for 73 and nine for 46 in his team's 87-run win at Hove. And probably the best batting by an opponent was Willie Watson's 174 which lifted Yorkshire from 37 for three to a total of 312 in the drawn match at Sheffield.

The first suggestions of the influence of televised cricket on the paying supporter were made in 1956, although Lancashire's gates were still pretty good with 134,700 paying to watch that summer, compared with nearly 150,000 the previous year and 116,000 the following summer. Washbrook was recalled by England that year for three Tests against Australia and that, plus his absence as a Test selector, allowed Edrich the opportunity of captaining the side for ten matches of which six were won. One of them created an unusual record when Lancashire beat Leicestershire at Old Trafford without losing a wicket. There was no play at all on the first day because of rain and Leicestershire, after winning the toss, were bowled out for 108 by the middle of the second afternoon with Statham taking four for 32. In the 150 minutes remaining, openers Alan Wharton and Jack Dyson scored 166 without trouble and Edrich declared first thing the following day. Leicestershire were 95 for three at lunch on the last day but after Statham had bowled Charlie Palmer with the first ball after lunch, the remaining six wickets fell for 27 runs in 49 minutes. Lancashire needed 65 and Dyson and Wharton knocked them off in 52 minutes to complete the unique feat of staying unbeaten in a first-wicket partnership in each innings.

Another piece of history was made in the following match when Edrich declared after only one ball of the second innings. This was then the shortest innings in history, but his bold tactics this time, against Nottinghamshire at Aigburth, did not bear fruit as Nottinghamshire, given two hours in which to score 98, finished at 93 for seven. Ken Grieves, whose debut was in 1949, was granted an uncommonly early benefit in 1956, making him the youngest beneficiary, at 30, in the club's history, a distinction since equalled by several players, but beaten by John Sullivan, who was 29 when he had his in 1975.

Lancashire pulled off only their second Roses win in thirteen seasons when Tattersall took six for 47 and eight for 43 in the 153-run victory at Headingley. The off spinner took 109 wickets that season, Malcolm Hilton 150, but nothing could combat the rain which ruined Lancashire's lingering hopes of the championship by not even allowing a first-innings result in their final match, against Surrey at The Oval. Lancashire needed points to maintain their challenge, but the no-result was enough to give Surrey the title for the fifth successive year. It was announced this year that there would be no Test match for Old Trafford in 1957 and the ground must have decided to make up for it by providing the most remarkable individual performance with Surrey off spinner Jim Laker taking nineteen wickets in the defeat of Australia.

Lancashire won the first five championship matches in 1957, including an innings win at Coventry where Statham produced the best bowling of his career with fifteen Warwickshire wickets for 89 runs. He took nine more wickets in the return match at Old Trafford to give him twenty-four for 157 in the two games. But Lancashire had to be content with sixth place that summer as they won only five more of the remaining twenty-three games. One of the best innings against Lancashire came from a 22-year-old Cambridge University batsman, Ted Dexter, who scored 185 after reaching his century in under two hours.

The fourth wet year out of five followed in 1958 when thirteen full days, with a total of 159 hours, were lost. Poor gates came with them, of course, and the total attendance in the season came to only 69,682 which included 14,987 who attended the Surrey match for Wharton's benefit, which raised £4,352. This was the worst total attendance since the war, 50 per cent below the previous lowest in 1954, and a total that did not even come up to the Roses match alone in 1950. Still, Lancashire had taken a lively, quick step forward by getting the premises licensed for music and dancing for winter letting of the pavilion and the first dance, organized by the Manchester and District Cricket Association, was held on 3 October. Lancashire finished seventh in the championship that year but there was some poor cricket. They were bowled out for under 100 seven times, the

297

lowest being 27 against Surrey, their lowest ever in the championship and second only to the famous 25 they scored in their first encounter with Derbyshire in 1871. Strangely, there was only one duck in the innings, by Washbrook who was run out.

The first century stand in twenty-five years for the last wicket, from Tattersall and wicket-keeper Alan Wilson, plus unplayable bowling from Statham, who took thirteen wickets, including the hat-trick, gave Lancashire an innings win over Leicestershire. Only three championship centuries were scored that year, two of them coming from Pullar and Barber against Warwickshire at Edgbaston where Lancashire lost only two wickets, and won by an innings. To counter the ignominy of being bowled out for 27, Lancashire went one better by dismissing Glamorgan for 26 at Cardiff with Statham taking six for 12 and Tattersall four for 12. Statham took 125 wickets that year, Tattersall ninety-one and Hilton ninety-four. Only Marner and Pullar scored 1,000 runs in championship matches – although Washbrook and Wharton joined them in all matches – and made great strides forward as they established themselves in the team. Ken Higgs, a fast bowler from Staffordshire, took a wicket in his first over for Lancashire and went on to take sixty-two wickets in nineteen championship matches and provide the support Statham needed. For the first time since Nigel Howard retired in 1953 Lancashire were able to call regularly on an amateur, Barber, who scored 986 runs in twenty-five matches for an average of 25.94 and was awarded his cap. One of the worst storms ever recorded hit Old Trafford after lunch on the final day of the match with Glamorgan on 22 August 1958. The thunderstorm centred over the ground for five hours, at the end of which the whole ground, including both practice grounds and the car park, was submerged underneath more than a foot of water.

After the wet summers of 1954, 1956, 1957 and 1958, it was decided on total covering of wickets. Lancashire, however, went further and bought covers to protect the entire square. But sod's law, as ever, applied and the sun shone through 1959 so that Lancashire's big covers were used only twice and the covering of the wicket, although regularly carried out, was usually unnecessary. Attendances picked up, although 114,667 in such a good summer was still disappointing, and membership was falling. But runs increased with Wharton, Grieves and Pullar all reaching 2,000 with Barber and Marner getting 1,000. Statham, Higgs and leg-spinner Tommy Greenhough all took 100 wickets and Lancashire not only finished fifth in the table, but beat Surrey twice, and each time by the handsome margin of ten wickets. Pullar had now fully emerged as an outstanding batsman and among his eight centuries in his 2,647 runs that year was one for England against India at Old Trafford in his second Test, and three in successive innings against Yorkshire, one for the Rest of England against the Champions. The high spot of Wharton's 2,000 runs was an innings of 199 against Sussex at Hove when he slipped when sent back by Jack Dyson and finished up on his hands and knees trying to crawl back to his crease as he was run out! It was the first time Wharton, Pullar or Grieves had reached 2,000 and Grieves finished off the season splendidly with 202 not out against India at Blackpool. He hit twenty-five 6s in the season, six of them against Worcestershire at Southport when he also hit sixteen 4s in his 142.

ALAN WHARTON was born in Heywood, near Bury, on 30 April 1923, and moved to Colne when he was two years old. He played for Colne, a Lancashire League club, when he was 13, but had to serve in the war, in the navy, before joining Lancashire in 1946, a happy, exciting season in which he scored two centuries. He scored 1,000 runs in every season from 1949 until he left in 1960, his best summer being that of 1959 when he, along with Geoff Pullar and Ken Grieves, all exceeded 2,000 runs. That was a marvellous season for Wharton, who was then 36, but after the following season, in which he scored nearly 1,500 runs, he was asked to captain the second team. Wharton declined and went to Leicestershire where he played for three more years. Wharton, a left-handed batsman, was also a right-arm medium-paced bowler good enough to share the opening attack many times with Brian Statham. When he left Lancashire he had scored 17,921 runs – only two batsmen since the war have scored more – at an average of 33.55, and taken 225 wickets (31.52). He played once for England, against New Zealand in 1949.

One of the emerging talents in 1959 was that of the new wicket-keeper, Geoff Clayton, who created a record for the number of victims in a match with eight catches and a stumping at Gloucester in only his eighth match. He dismissed sixty men in his first season and also scored 647 runs, with a fighting 74 not out against Middlesex, in twenty-three matches.

There were several outstanding performances against Lancashire that year, notably from Norman Hill of Nottinghamshire, Jim Parks of Sussex and Jimmy Stewart of Warwickshire. Hill followed two ducks in the match at Old Trafford with two centuries at Trent Bridge, Parks hit the fastest century ever against Lancashire in 61 minutes at Old Trafford, and Stewart hit seventeen 6s in the match at Blackpool, a record in first-class cricket. Stewart hit ten in his first innings of 155 when he reached his century in 131 minutes, and seven in the second innings when he scored 125 after reaching his hundred in 85 minutes. Nearly all his 6s were straight drives which would have carried the boundary on most grounds.

Lancashire played on another new ground in 1959 when they took the match against Worcestershire to Southport on 22 August. The game was blessed by dry weather but the clash with football affected the Saturday attendance and the match gate was insufficient, by £340, to cover the guarantee of £1,000 made to Lancashire by Southport Corporation. The wicket was excellent and Ken Grieves had the honour of scoring the first century on the ground, reaching it in 135 minutes and going on to 142 which included sixteen 4s and six 6s.

Chapter 15 1960–67

'Lancashire's centenary year was soured by the sacking of
several leading players and the special meeting of
members which overthrew the committee.'

The retirement of Cyril Washbrook threw the captaincy wide open
again. Now that the precedent of a professional captain had been
established, Lancashire could have followed it with the appointment
of Alan Wharton, 37 years old, or Ken Grieves, 34 years old, both
vastly experienced and still batting well judging by their best-ever
seasons in 1959. Other players of great experience were Brian
Statham and Roy Tattersall, but that would have meant another
precedent as Lancashire had never had a bowler as a captain. And
there was, of course, the amateur, Bob Barber, who had captained
the team on occasions when Washbrook had been away. The temptation to return to tradition was too great and Barber, 24 years old,
was appointed and strongly advised, virtually told, he would travel
and live separately from the other players. Barber was in the nets
before the 1960 season when Frank Sibbles, the pre-war Lancashire
player, now chairman of the cricket committee, said Colonel Green,
who had captained Lancashire to their hat-trick of championship wins
in the 1920s, would like a word with him. Green said to Barber
'Bob, in my view you will have a problem as captain if you stay at
the same hotel as the players. We are strongly advising you to stay
in a different one.' Barber was too young – he says naive as well –
to take on the committee and had no alternative but to follow the
suggestion which was to drive a wedge between him and his players
and lead to the captaincy being taken away from him the following
year.

Yet Barber had a successful first year, leading Lancashire into second place for the second time since the war. Yorkshire became champions, but Lancashire beat them twice, once by ten wickets. Five batsmen scored 1,000 runs and Statham, Higgs and Greenhough again exceeded 100 wickets. Greenhough, Barber, Statham and Pullar all played Test cricket but Lancashire, after being top of the table for the first half of August, missed the title only through a poor run which saw them lose four and draw two of the last six matches.

TOMMY GREENHOUGH was born in Rochdale on 9 November 1931, and played for Lancashire for the first time in 1951. In his first five years he played only twenty-two matches and took forty-five wickets and the first sign of the leg-break talent which was to take him into the England team came in 1956 when he took sixty-two wickets at a cost of less than 17 runs each. His peak arrived in 1959 and 1960 when he took more than 100 wickets each season, played in his four Tests, and toured West Indies with MCC. He had a relatively long, bouncy run, spun the ball considerably and also bowled the googly. But he became beset with injury, had a problem with his follow through, and suffered through the general decline and loss of faith in the leg-spinner. He never again bowled more than 1,000 overs, as he had done in 1959 and 1960, and left Lancashire after the 1966 season with a total of 707 wickets at under 22 runs each.

Lancashire's win that completed the double over Yorkshire was one of the most exciting ever played, the thrilling climax being set up when Lancashire were left with 125 minutes to score 78 on an Old Trafford wicket which had produced totals of 154, 226 and 149. The word had got about and spectators rushed to the ground from the city to see the closing stages which resulted in Lancashire losing wickets under the frustrations created by defensive fields. At one stage Lancashire were 43 for six before Grieves and Clayton remedied the situation. Even so, Lancashire reached the last ball needing 3, and amidst the greatest tension Jack Dyson edged it off his toes for 4 to give Lancashire a two-wicket win and their first double over Yorkshire in sixty-seven years.

Marner again gave more examples of his hitting ability that year and in the match against Nottinghamshire at Southport, hit 44 in boundary strokes – a record – with four 6s and five 4s.

The breakdown in Lancashire's cricket took hold in 1961 when much of the unrest came to the surface and Lancashire finished thirteenth in the table, their lowest position ever. It was an unhappy year and culminated in the committee deciding to replace Barber as captain. Barber himself put Lancashire's failings down mainly to a lack of leadership at the top:

Leadership is having a vision, encouraging people, getting them to walk through walls. I should have been offered a friendly hand, a listening ear, given quiet advice. I didn't get any. There was an enormous void and I also wasn't close to probably any of the young players. But we had a good team and if they had been allowed to stick together and allowed to play good cricket, I believe we could have been winning the championship for several years. Players were allowed or forced to leave, we dispersed to several places, and Yorkshire went on to win championships that could have been ours.

The young Barber also had his own problems with man management. Peter Marner had to be sent home from Folkestone after ignoring a committee edict on wearing blazers at lunch, Jack Dyson was sacked 'for a serious breach of discipline and an act of insubordination and insolence to the captain.' Controversy seemed to follow Barber. He severely criticized Colin Cowdrey's captaincy in Kent's successful effort to avoid defeat, and the committee felt obliged to publicly disassociate themselves from his remarks. And, like Howard, Barber suffered from interference such as when he was told to send Ken Higgs home because the committee thought he was tired.

Barber's right-hand man, Alan Wharton, was effectively sacked at the end of Barber's first year, being offered the second-team captaincy and left with little alternative but to resign. Barber had no say in it and again felt isolated. Roy Tattersall, too, had gone with good years left in him and Malcolm Hilton was soon to follow. Several young players were tried out and the consistency, and much of the personality, had gone from the side. With all these factors brought together it was not surprising that Lancashire's cricket was at its lowest ebb.

Lancashire's best players, Brian Statham and Geoff Pullar, played in all the Tests against Australia in 1961 and Pullar, then around the peak of his career, scored 2,000 runs. Five others, including Jack Bond – who scored a century against Sussex in 93 minutes – and Brian Booth for the first time, reached 1,000 as Lancashire played a record thirty-seven matches that year.

GEOFF PULLAR was born in Swinton, Manchester, on 1 August 1935, and first played for Lancashire when he was still only 18. He became one of the country's leading left-handed batsmen in the late 1950s and early 1960s when he played twenty-eight times for England, an opening batsman who averaged nearly 44 and scored four Test centuries, including

303

175 against South Africa. These were also his best years for Lancashire, particularly in 1959 when he scored 2,197 runs for the county at an average of 54.92 with six centuries and sixteen 50s. He also exceeded 2,000 runs in 1961, yet for such a talented player it is surprising he did not exceed 1,000 runs in a season more than nine times before he left the county in 1968. He left behind him a record of 16,853 runs at an average of 35.18 and was still only 33 years old. He went to Gloucestershire, but did little there, scoring one century in twenty-five matches before retiring through arthritis in 1970.

Lancashire's outstanding result in 1961 came at Worksop where they beat Nottinghamshire by scoring 372 for four in 300 minutes, with a century from Barber . . . and after taking only four Nottinghamshire wickets for 525 runs! Wharton had moved on to Leicestershire and, like Oldfield, got extreme satisfaction in hitting a century against Lancashire. He was one of nine players with Lancashire about this time who had moved or were to move to other counties. Most had lengthy and fruitful second careers and some, like David Green, who went to Gloucestershire, felt more allegiance to their second county than to Lancashire.

The club's decision to replace Barber for the 1962 season was followed by the strangest choice of captain in the club's 98-year history. They turned to Joe Blackledge, 33-year-old former captain of Chorley in the Northern League who had played for Lancashire 2nd for two years earlier in his career and had captained them. Jack Fallows and Ken Cranston, it is true, captained Lancashire without previous first-class experience, but they filled the gaps in the years immediately after the war when amateur captains were still the vogue. Professional captains were now acceptable and Lancashire's decision to appoint Blackledge was an awful gamble that failed and helped bring down the committee in 1964. It had been expected that Blackledge would be able to call on the experience of Ken Grieves, but the Australian decided to retire and go into league cricket. Blackledge, like Barber, had periods of isolation. He played in twenty-six of the thirty-six matches and averaged 15.37 with a top score of 68 in his opening match. Lancashire won two of their thirty-two championship matches and lost sixteen, the highest ever. Their sixteenth position in the table represented their worst season ever which was reflected in the attendances with only 65,616 people paying for admission at home games, the lowest for many years and certainly since the war.

There were encouraging signs, of course. Jack Bond scored 2,000 runs for the first time, Colin Hilton took ninety-four wickets, Geoff Clayton dismissed ninety-two batsmen, a figure exceeded only by

304

George Duckworth in Lancashire's history, and scored 833 runs. Pullar, Marner, Barber and Booth all got over 1,000 runs and there was some huge hitting with over 100 6s being struck in the season, thirty-one of them from Marner and twenty-five from Roy Collins, who hit seven in one innings at Southampton. Marner hit five 6s and fifteen 4s in 106 not out against Warwickshire at Southport and a week later four 6s and twelve 4s in the return match at Coventry. He also hit five 6s and four 4s in an innings of 59 against Sussex at Old Trafford.

Collins, who was 28 and emerging as Lancashire's best all-rounder with his pugnacious batting and useful off spin, retired this year and Barber left the unhealthy Old Trafford atmosphere for the friendlier fields of Warwickshire where he was to play by far his best cricket. Barber had decided to leave when the captaincy was taken from him:

> At first I decided I had had enough and was going to leave the club. I felt I had taken stick for other people. Then I thought it would look like sour grapes if I didn't play under Joe Blackledge's captaincy, so I decided to give it one season and then leave. Joe was a hell of a nice man but his appointment was ridiculous. I did my best to help him out without interfering but I had decided I wouldn't put up with any more of it.

BOB BARBER was the last Lancashire amateur to play in the Gentlemen v Players match and the last to play for England. He was born in Manchester on 26 September 1935, and played for Lancashire in 1954 when still only 18 and midway between Ruthin College and Cambridge where he played for the university from 1955 to 1957. He was the golden boy groomed to succeed Cyril Washbrook as captain, a position he held in 1960 and 1961 before it was taken away from him. He played one more season, under Joe Blackledge, and then left Lancashire after nine summers and 155 matches had brought him 6,760 runs at an average of 28.28 and 152 wickets at 31.36 each. By this time he had played in nine Test matches with a highest score of 86 and taken fifteen wickets which had cost 48 runs apiece. He had felt stifled at Lancashire and moved on to Warwickshire determined to express himself. Caution gave way to attack and he became one of the most attractive left-handed batsmen in the country, opening the innings and forcing the pace right from the start. He played in 124 matches in seven years for Warwickshire and scored nine centuries, one of them a brilliant hundred against the West Indians, another before lunch on the first day against the Australians. He also played in nineteen more Test matches, finishing with a batting average over 35 and including an innings of 185 at Sydney, one of the

finest in Ashes history. When his first-class career of 386 matches was over, he had scored 17,631 runs and taken 549 wickets with his leg breaks and googlies.

Ernest Tyldesley died in May 1962, and Old Trafford's Tyldesley suite, which presumably took in all the Tyldesleys from Roe Green and Westhoughton, was opened in October. And, sixteen years after the end of the war, final payment was received from the War Damage Commission.

Lancashire acknowledged the failure of another gamble when Blackledge was not asked to captain the team again in 1963 and the position went to Ken Grieves who agreed to return to the club. One distinction Blackledge had had was in being able to captain all-Lancashire teams several times and for only the second time in the club's history, following the team of 1934. His first game, in fact, against Glamorgan at Cardiff, was with an all-Lancashire team of Pullar, Booth, Bond, Barber, Marner, Collins, Clayton, Statham, Greenhough, and Hilton. More Lancastrians such as Bob Bennett, Harry Pilling, Ken Howard, Kevin Tebay and Edward Craig also helped to provide other teams composed entirely of players born within the boundary. It was just a pity that this should have coincided with Lancashire's worst season!

Grieves had an unenviable task in the atmosphere which then prevailed at Old Trafford and improvement was only marginal as Lancashire finished fifteenth and fourteenth in his two years in charge. He returned in time to lead Lancashire into the new era of one-day cricket, starting with the introduction of the Gillette Cup in 1963, a competition which quickly established itself and which brought crowds back to the game.

Only first-class counties took part in the opening year of the Gillette Cup and, to get the number down to an even sixteen, it was decided to have one preliminary match, between the two bottom teams in the championship in 1962, Lancashire and Leicestershire. This historic match was played at Old Trafford and began on 1 May 1963, a bleak, bitterly cold day when play could not start until 3 p.m. because of heavy overnight rain. Peter Marner scored a rather fine 121 in Lancashire's total of 304 for nine, Maurice Hallam scored 106 for Leicestershire, but Lancashire won easily, by 101 runs on the second day. Games then were of sixty-five overs each and bowlers were allowed a maximum of fifteen overs each. Frank Woolley, the former Kent batsman, was the adjudicator. He was nearly 76 years old but insisted on sitting behind the bowler's arm, dressed in overcoat, scarf and gloves but still frozen through. Despite their low placing in the championship, Lancashire showed the taste for limited-overs cricket when they also beat Derbyshire and Essex to reach the semi-finals of the competition. There, however, they came badly unstuck, losing by nine wickets at Worcester after being bowled out for 59.

Lancashire also reached the semi-final the following year, but lost to Warwickshire at Old Trafford in a game which spotlighted the use of defensive fields for the first time in these games. Barber, now with Warwickshire, scored 76 in their total of 294 for seven and although Lancashire were given a start of 67 in twelve overs by David Green and Duncan Worsley, they were unable to maintain the challenge against accurate bowling and deep-set fields. Lancashire, in fact, gave up, finishing at 209 for seven, and both sides were loudly barracked.

Lancashire were sorely in need of a spinner around this time and Sonny Ramadhin, the great West Indian, was specially registered and in his first year, 1964, took ninety-two wickets to support Statham's 109 and Higgs's sixty-five. This was Lancashire's centenary year, but what should have been a marvellous occasion, climaxed by a game against MCC at the end of the season, was soured by the sacking of several leading players and the special meeting of members which overthrew the committee. Cyril Washbrook, who had joined the committee in 1962, resigned in April 1964, so he could become team manager. At the end of that summer it was decided not to reappoint Grieves captain, and Marner, Clayton and Dyson were sacked. Marner and Clayton were released, the committee announced, because their considerable influence upon the team was not, and appeared unlikely to be, conducive to the sort of team-building they had in mind. In other words, they were considered disruptive. Dyson was released, it was said, because they felt his usefulness to the team was likely to disappear with the advent of Ramadhin – who, as it turned out, played only five more matches – and Ken Howard, a 21-year-old off spinner.

Matters came to a head with a special meeting of members at Manchester's Houldsworth Hall on 24 September 1964. Cedric Rhoades, a Manchester businessman who was soon to become the club chairman, led the speeches and the resolution 'That this meeting is dissatisfied with the conduct of the cricketing affairs of the club' was passed by the overwhelming margin of 656 to 48. The committee resigned en bloc at this vote of no confidence, but before the new elections were held they were to enrage the members even further by advertising in *The Times* for a new captain. Twenty-nine members stood for the twelve seats and the election brought in six new committee members, including Rhoades who played a major part in updating the running of Lancashire's affairs. It could not

307

be immediate, of course, but improvement was on the way and young players gradually felt their way into a side which was to be a force again in the early 1970s. The new committee appointed Brian Statham captain for 1965, a popular choice and one which was to start Lancashire on the right road back to respectability. He led by example, by wholehearted endeavour, and nursed young players along with the care of a father before he was to hand over to Jack Bond in 1968.

BRIAN STATHAM was born in Gorton, Manchester, on 17 June 1930, and first played for Lancashire on his twentieth birthday. He was a national serviceman in the RAF when he was recommended to Lancashire, and after a trial which impressed coach Harry Makepeace he was taken on the groundstaff in 1950. He played Club and Ground and second-team matches before making his county debut against Kent and from then until he retired in 1968 he was never dropped by Lancashire. As Statham walked down the steps for his debut and to bowl for the first time, Cyril Washbrook offered advice: 'Don't bowl short to Fagg. He's a fine hooker and he'll hit you out of sight.' Statham, always a good listener, took notice although he did have one problem. He did not know which batsman was Arthur Fagg. But ignorance can be bliss and when Statham immediately and inadvertently dropped short, Fagg mis-hit and silly mid on took the catch. He played 430 matches and ended his illustrious career with more wickets than any other Lancashire bowler – 1,816 for the county at 15.12 each, and 2,260 in all (16.36). He played seventy times for England and at one time held the world record for the total number of wickets before finishing with 252. When he started for Lancashire he was so innocent and raw – he says ignorant – that he had no idea about outswingers or inswingers, off-cutters or anything else. He just ran up and bowled . . . and bowled straight, one of his many admirable assets, which also included an unflappable nature which endeared him to everyone with whom he came into contact. 'It was all pure enjoyment for me,' said Statham. 'I was chucked in at the deep end but it didn't bother me. I was just having fun and I was successful. I think I was just mesmerized by it all. I was lucky to be playing cricket for a living and there were such a lot of nice people around.' Statham took 100 wickets thirteen times and came close on four more occasions. He headed the English bowling averages three times and was in the top three six more times, but at Lancashire he headed the averages for sixteen successive seasons. Statham was one of the game's most popular players, a genuine, honest man who did not waste time or effort on play-acting on the field . . . or off it, come to that. He was straight-forward and a man with simple needs. When the 1962-63 MCC party left for Australia, it was without Statham

who followed later to join up with them in Perth. The team had gone part of the way by ship and among the decisions made was that whatever else happened, the players would all get together for breakfast every day. The arrangement worked until Statham joined them and was told about it. 'Breakfast!' he exclaimed. 'I've never had breakfast in my life. Coffee and a cigarette, that's my breakfast.' And that was the last that was heard of it.

Len Hutton described Statham as the most accurate fast bowler he ever saw and said few bowlers shaved the stumps more often. 'But never a moan or a harsh word nor a black look at the umpire or captain could be associated with Brian Statham,' he once wrote. Cyril Washbrook admired him tremendously. 'No captain has had a more willing bowler at his command,' he wrote. 'Never once in the years I played with him did Brian ask for a single over more or show the slightest resentment when taken off or asked to bowl. He carried the Lancashire attack for years and every other Lancashire bowler ought to have been grateful for his presence in the team.'

Statham continued the slow, painful climb back up the table started by Grieves who had taken Lancashire from sixteenth to fifteenth, then fourteenth. Statham took them to thirteenth in his first year, twelfth in his second, and eleventh in his last. Now you could not get steadier, more consistent improvement than that. Significant advances were made by Harry Pilling, who topped the batting averages in Statham's last year as captain, Barry Wood, signed from Yorkshire in 1966, John Sullivan, a hard-hitting batsman, David Lloyd, a young left-handed batsman and left-arm spinner from Accrington, quick bowlers Ken Shuttleworth and Peter Lever, all of whom were going to figure in the fine side of the early 1970s. A nice, nostalgic return to Old Trafford was made in 1965 by Charlie Hallows, who, at 70 years of age, left Worcestershire and took over the coaching at Old Trafford throughout Statham's reign.

David Green's talent as an enterprising, adventurous opening batsman, shone through in 1965 when he scored 2,037 runs and created a record by becoming the first batsman ever to achieve this target without a century. His highest score was 85. But by 1967, when he played only nine matches for the county, he had finished and left for Gloucestershire where he played for four years. Geoff Pullar's Test career had ended in 1963, when he was still only 28, and he was never again to achieve those heights of the late 1950s and early 1960s when he was one of the country's foremost batsmen. He got close to 2,000 runs again in 1964 but then only twice more reached 1,000 as he was affected by injury. After scoring 33 in five innings in the 1965 season against Sussex, Surrey and Yorkshire, Pullar was dropped for the following game against Surrey at The Oval. The team was announced without him but Green, who captained the side in Statham's absence, protested successfully to have Pullar restored to a team desperately low in batting experience. Pullar duly travelled to London, opened the innings the following morning, and scored 112.

Pullar's benefit match was washed out in 1967 when he made £4,662 and in 1968 he, too, left for Gloucestershire where he played little before retiring in 1970. But before he left, he scored his fifth Roses century, a record for Lancashire.

Attendances at this time were dreadful and in 1966 only 24,669 paid to watch Lancashire's home games and the treasurer must have looked back to those halcyon years in the decade after the war when as many as 250,000 people attended home games in one season.

Nearly half Lancashire's total attendance for 1967 attended the three home Gillette Cup-ties against Gloucestershire, Yorkshire, and Somerset. The match against Yorkshire stands among the more memorable with Lancashire totalling 194 and Yorkshire reaching the final over needing 5 to win with their last pair together. Four would have done if they did not lose a wicket. But who was to bowl the last over? Statham, Higgs, Lever and Wood had completed their quotas, Green had an over left but had just bowled the previous one at the other end. Statham had got his sums wrong and turned to 22-year-old Sullivan to bowl the final over to the experienced Jimmy Binks. Sullivan had only ever before bowled two deliveries in this competition, but today that was all he needed as he had Binks lbw to give Lancashire a thrilling 4-run win. Lancashire went out in the semi-final when they were beaten by Somerset and Statham gave up the captaincy at the end of the season, although he agreed to play on . . . for a while.

One of the finest debuts ever made against Lancashire came that year, 1967, when Tony Greig, who was to captain England, scored 156 in four hours for Sussex at Hove.

Chapter 16 1968–72

*'The game developed a new dimension in Jack Bond's first
two seasons with the introduction of immediately-registered
overseas players and the arrival of Sunday cricket.'*

Ever since Cyril Washbrook had retired, Lancashire had had problems in choosing a captain. Bob Barber had been hounded out
of the job and went to Warwickshire, Joe Blackledge had been
recruited from the leagues, Ken Grieves had been brought back
from retirement, after which Lancashire had advertised in *The Times*
before turning to Brian Statham. Statham's decision not to accept
the captaincy again for 1968 produced another problem, one that
was solved by turning to a player who had spent the previous two
or three years wondering if each one was going to be his last. Jack
Bond was a surprise choice to most people outside Old Trafford, but,
and what was most important, he was a players' choice. Nobody could
have been more popular. Amateur captains had been the natural way
of things in Lancashire cricket – as in most counties – and it is hard
to think of one in the club's first seventy-five years who was not
respected. Some, like A. N. Hornby and Archie MacLaren, were the
sort who were also admired, revered, even loved by their players.
Some, perhaps all, of those feelings extended to Brian Statham,
too, but not even he won the depth of feeling that Jack Bond drew
from his players through his five years of captaincy. It is fair to
say the time was right for him. The game developed a new dimension
in his first two seasons with the introduction of immediately-
registered overseas players and the arrival of Sunday cricket.

**JACK BOND was born at Kearsley, near Bolton, on 6 May 1932,
and first played for Lancashire against Surrey at Old Trafford in**

1955, a debut that brought him innings of 0 and 1. It was 1961 before a regular place was earned in the side and that and the following year were his two best for the county. He scored 1,700 runs the first year, more than 2,000 in the second and averaged throughout the two years at a shade over 36. He broke his wrist in 1963 batting against Wes Hall, the West Indies fast bowler, and was never to get 1,000 runs in a season again. From 1963 to 1967 he was in and out of the side, uncertain of his place in the team, uncertain of his place on the staff, and frequently captained the second team. Lancashire were slow to turn to him when Brian Statham retired, but it was his captaincy which was mainly instrumental in turning Lancashire from a depressing, unsuccessful side to the outstanding team of his period in office. In his five years as captain, Lancashire won the John Player League twice, the Gillette Cup three times and twice finished third in the championship. It was a period of great excitement and interest in Lancashire cricket and was, next to the great championship years between 1926 and 1930, the best years in the club's history. The Cricketers' Association chose Bond as their Cricketer of the Year, *Wisden* selected him among their Cricketers of the Year in 1971, and when he retired in 1972 he was accepted as one of the finest captains Lancashire had ever had. His batting record was as modest as the man himself, 11,880 runs at an average of 26.51 through 345 first-class matches. But his leadership was outstanding.

The arrival of the overseas player in 1968 was the first shot in the arm for the game. Lancashire missed out on Gary Sobers who went to Nottinghamshire and drew in the crowds in great numbers. When Sobers went to Derby, he drew the biggest gate in Derbyshire's history. Lancashire signed the Indian, Farokh Engineer, who was not only a brilliant wicket-keeper but a dashing batsman who was the bedrock of a side which was to be recognized as one of the best fielding teams the game had seen. Clive Lloyd, the exciting West Indian batsman, was playing professional with Haslingden in the Lancashire League and he became qualified for the 1969 season.

FAROKH ENGINEER was a dashing opening batsman as well as a magnificent wicket-keeper, a batsman who only the previous year had come within 6 runs of scoring a century before lunch in a Test match against a West Indian attack which included Wes Hall, Charlie Griffith, Gary Sobers and Lance Gibbs. He was born in Bombay on 25 February 1938, and made his first-class debut when he was 20 and played for the Combined Universities of India against the West Indies. His Test debut came in 1961 and he had already played in half his forty-six Test matches when he first played for Lancashire in 1968 at the age of 30.

312

His wicket-keeping was dazzling and consistent; his batting exciting but eccentric and unreliable. But he was a pleasure to watch. He played for Lancashire from 1968 to 1976 and although 38 years old, he still looked to have many good years of cricket in him when he finished. In those years he played 175 matches for Lancashire, scored 5,942 runs at an average of 26.64, held 429 catches and stumped thirty-five batsmen. His best year was his last when he averaged 36.61 and failed by only 48 to get 1,000 runs for the first time in an English season. His forty-six Tests brought him 2,611 runs for an average just over 31 and he claimed eighty-two wicket-keeping victims.

Jack Bond started his five years of captaincy by leading Lancashire to defeat by Nottinghamshire in 1968 in the Gillette Cup-tie at Trent Bridge where Sobers scored 75 not out. But he soon put that behind him and spent the rest of the summer lifting Lancashire to sixth place in the championship, their highest position since finishing runners-up under Bob Barber in 1960. Two games best illustrate some of the qualities that Bond brought to his captaincy. The first came at Eastbourne in July, a match in which neither side reached even 90 and in which Lancashire needed only 71 for victory. Batting was almost impossible on the rain-affected pitch and Lancashire were 11 for three when Bond went in to play a great captain's innings. Soon they were 12 for four and 39 for six, but Bond teased and nudged and eased Lancashire towards their target, reached when he drove Allan Jones to the boundary for a two-wicket win.

The second match followed two weeks later at Northampton where, on the second day, Lancashire had reached 279 for eight in reply to Northamptonshire's 218. Bond was only seven short of his first century for three years, yet he declared so his bowlers could have the last half-hour at the Northamptonshire batsmen. He was rewarded with three wickets from his opening bowlers, Ken Shuttleworth and Ken Higgs, and Lancashire won comfortably the following day. That was the sort of sacrifice Jack Bond was prepared to make without hesitation for the good of Lancashire cricket and for his own players. It was the sort of selflessness that drew players to him and made them want to win matches – for him as much as for Lancashire and themselves. Such a quality is easily defined but not easily acquired. Lancashire's relatively high position in the table was not reflected in the individual performances. Only Harry Pilling reached 1,000 runs, the highest batting average in the championship was 26.60, from Bond, and only two centuries were scored, by Pullar, who left at the end of the season, and Graham Atkinson, a short-term signing from Somerset where he had played for thirteen seasons and scored over 15,000 runs. Higgs took 105 wickets,

313

Shuttleworth seventy-one, and Statham, in his final year, sixty-nine. Statham said farewell to first-class cricket against Yorkshire at Old Trafford in a game which finished on Monday, 5 August 1968. He said goodbye with a majestic piece of bowling, unchanged for 17.5 overs in the first innings to take six for 34. The game was drawn, but Statham had made his point and nearly 45,000 people said goodbye to a gentleman.

Somehow, Lancashire managed to slip back down the table, to fifteenth, in 1969. But they could be forgiven. They had other things on their mind. To be specific, the new one-day competition of forty overs a side, sponsored by the tobacco company John Player, played on Sunday afternoons with one game each week broadcast to the nation through television. It was the stimulation that first-class cricket needed, although many people, players included, thought it was not cricket at all, but just a Sunday afternoon knockabout. Too many players regarded the Sunday game like a benefit match; too many made no plans for it, and for the most part batting was usually in championship style or slog without anything in between. Older players tended to be suspicious of the new bit of razzamatazz and although they tried when batting or bowling, they were not going to throw themselves about like goalkeepers just to save the odd run. Bond, on the other hand, emphasized the importance of fielding to his side. He quickly realized that in an innings of forty overs, a few runs saved here and there could mark the difference between winning and losing. Lancashire quickly established their reputation as the finest fielding side in the country and that fielding alone was enough to put them head and shoulders above most other teams. Little was evident in the first two games with Lancashire winning at Hove in front of 5,000 spectators – which was an indication of the public's feelings towards the game – and losing at Chelmsford by 108 runs after Essex had scored a massive 265 for six, a total that was to stand as the highest against Lancashire for thirteen years.

That marked a turning point for Lancashire who won the next nine matches which included defending totals such as 130 (against Surrey), 179 for eight (against Nottinghamshire), and 201 for eight (against Kent). In fact, Lancashire won twelve out of fifteen matches that year – one was abandoned – without scoring more than 204 in any game. The most memorable game was that played at Southport against Glamorgan when 10,000 people were inside the ground and almost as many outside. The game was televised and probably brought home to people, more than any other, the particular magic of forty-over cricket. Glamorgan were a fine side who won the county championship that year, yet were bowled out for 112 that Sunday. Engineer positively dazzled in front of the television cameras and scored 78 not out as Lancashire won by nine wickets with nearly sixteen overs to spare. Lancashire clinched the title in the penultimate game when they overwhelmed Warwickshire at Nuneaton and went into the last match at Worcester looking for the prize of £250 for the fastest televised 50 of the season. It was decided that David Lloyd would stand firm and every other player would go for the fast 50 which resulted in Lancashire finishing up with 156 for six in forty overs, losing by 2 runs and leaving David Lloyd carrying the responsibility! Ken Higgs took twenty-six wickets in the competition, but showed his ability to contain batsmen in the more demanding county championship with two superb last overs against Warwickshire and Yorkshire.

Warwickshire needed 5 runs from the game's final over with five wickets standing. Higgs bowled Tom Cartwright and Eddie Hemmings, leaving the free-scoring Jimmy Stewart with two balls in which to get 2 runs. He could not get one and Lancashire salvaged a draw. The finish to the Yorkshire match was more incredible. Yorkshire needed one to win from the last two overs with Doug Padgett and Barrie Leadbeater together. Peter Lever bowled a maiden over to Padgett and Higgs, in the final over, took the wickets of Leadbeater, Don Wilson and Richard Hutton without conceding a run and leaving the scores level. Higgs retired that year, though only 32, and went into the Lancashire League for two years before returning to the first-class game with Leicestershire.

KEN HIGGS came from Kidsgrove in Staffordshire where he was born on 14 January 1937. He first played for Lancashire in 1958, took seven for 36 in the second innings of his debut match against Hampshire at Old Trafford, and immediately became a regular member of the side, filling a long-standing need as opening bowling partner to Brian Statham. He took sixty-seven wickets in his first season, and 113 in his second, the first of five years in which he was to take more than 100 wickets in a summer. He was a strong, accurate, fast-medium paced bowler who played twelve seasons for Lancashire and took 1,033 wickets, a figure which had then been exceeded by only eight players.

Years of consistently successful bowling brought Higgs his Test debut in 1965 against South Africa when he had the satisfaction of opening the attack with Statham not only for Lancashire, but for England as well. He played fifteen times for England and finished with one of the most impressive set of bowling figures any player has ever had with seventy-one wickets at 20.74 runs each. When he retired after the 1969 season – he was still only 32 – he had taken 1,033 wickets at 22.90 each. He played two years for Rishton in the Lancashire League before returning to county cricket with Leicestershire, playing in 165 first-class matches

315

for them up to 1982 and taking his total number of wickets past 1,500. He became a coach and just to show how fit and how accurate and sound a bowler he still was, he returned to the game in 1986, after a four-year absence because of injuries, to take five for 22 against Yorkshire. He was then 49.

When Higgs left Old Trafford in 1969, Lancashire had lost two experienced Test players – Pullar had gone to Gloucestershire – and were in the hands of probably their youngest team ever with only Bond and Engineer aged over 30 and an average age of 27. The confidence of youth overcame almost every obstacle in 1970 when Lancashire won the John Player League and the Gillette Cup, and finished third in the championship. Success in the one-day competitions spilled over into the three-day game as Lancashire had one of their best seasons ever.

The champagne of the 1969 season was still bubbling away in 1970 as Lancashire won nine of the first ten John Player matches. The title was at stake in the final match, played in front of 26,000 people at Old Trafford and against, of all teams, Yorkshire, handsomely won by Lancashire by seven wickets with 4.1 overs to spare. Lancashire completed the double six days later when they won the Gillette Cup for the first time, beating Sussex at Lord's with Harry Pilling being named man of the match after a dominating innings of 70 not out which brought victory by six wickets. Lancashire had lost at the Cup's first hurdle in each of Jack Bond's first two years as captain, but more than made up for it in his third year, starting at Bristol where they beat Gloucestershire by 27 runs after scoring 278 for eight. Hampshire were easily disposed of at Old Trafford, Somerset were beaten at Taunton, and Lancashire were now the most feared side in the land. The championship eluded Lancashire, by 21 points, after they failed to win any of their last six games. Clive Lloyd played his first full season for Lancashire and topped the batting averages in both the first-class game (46.26) and John Player League (57.88), as well as averaging 39.25 in the four Gillette matches. His maiden century came at Dartford where the houses at one end of the ground were so bombarded with sixes that an old lady called the police in an attempt to stop it. He scored 145 in 163 minutes with seven of the forty-four 6s he was to hit that summer.

Lloyd was also one of the finest fieldsmen in the world in those days as Glenn Turner, the New Zealand opening batsman, found to his cost when playing against him for Worcestershire. Turner, heading for the record number of centuries in a season by a Worcestershire player, had reached 99 in the second innings when Bond tried to help him by not having a mid-off, just leaving

Lloyd at cover. Turner pushed to mid off and ran for what should have been an easy single but Lloyd ran round, swooped and hit the stumps to run him out.

Lancashire's re-emergence as a force in county cricket was reflected in 1970 when both opening bowlers, Ken Shuttleworth and Peter Lever, were chosen to play for England against the Rest of the World before going with MCC to Australia in the winter of 1970–71.

KEN SHUTTLEWORTH, born at St Helens on 13 November 1944, made his debut in 1964 when he was 19, a tall, raw, but genuinely fast bowler with a touch of the Fred Truemans about him. He took fifty wickets in 1967 but really started to burst through in 1968 when Brian Statham was fading from the scene. His best season was in 1970 when he took seventy-four wickets at 21.60 runs each and played for England against The Rest of the World, at Lord's. He went to Australia with Ray Illingworth's Ashes-winning team and started his Test career with five for 47 at Brisbane. He played five times in all for England – four of them that winter in Australia and New Zealand, the other against Pakistan in 1971 – and took twelve wickets at 35.58 each.

Shuttleworth's career, however, never took off as it might have done and loss of form, plus persistent injuries, forced him to leave in 1975 and join Leicestershire where he played forty-one matches between 1977 and 1980. In twelve seasons with Lancashire, Shuttleworth played in 177 matches and took 484 wickets at a cost of 22.92 each. He played 105 limited-overs matches for the county and took 147 wickets at 18 runs apiece.

PETER LEVER, who was born at Todmorden on 17 September 1940, was nearly 30 when he played for England against the Rest of the World in 1970 and earned a place in the MCC side to Australia by taking seven for 83 at The Oval. He stepped up his pace to suit the conditions and played in five of the Tests and made significant contributions to England regaining the Ashes. He made his debut for Lancashire in 1960 and in his early years, 1963 and 1966 in particular, batted well enough to hold a middle-order place as well as provide energetic support for Statham and Higgs. In both those seasons he scored over 500 runs and took more than fifty wickets, but once he had become an England bowler, his batting declined, although he showed his ability in 1971 when he scored 88 not out in a Test match against India. Lever toured Australia again in 1974–75 and ended what had been a largely disappointing tour by taking six for 38 at Melbourne in the final Test, the only one England won in their 4–1 defeat. Nine of his seventeen Tests, between 1970 and 1975, were against Australia and he totalled forty-one wickets at 36.80 each.

317

**He, too, was a vital part of the Lancashire team of the early 1970s
and in 167 limited-overs matches he had the outstanding return of 256
wickets for 17.53 each. When he retired before the 1977 season he had
played in 268 first-class matches and taken 716 wickets for 26.64 runs each.**

Lancashire's success in the Gillette Cup in 1970 was the start of a
phenomenal run that was to bring them a hat-trick of wins and six
Lord's finals in seven years in this, the oldest-established limited-
overs competition in the game. Lancashire's first Gillette match of
1971 was against Somerset, their semi-final opponents of the previous
season. Once again they got away to a resounding win, followed with
victory at Worcester and then went to Chelmsford for a quarter-final
match that had them in trouble for the first time when they sank to 59
for six. But Clive Lloyd scored a century, Jack Simmons shared with
him in a partnership of 91, and Lancashire squeezed home in the last
over by 12 runs to go into a semi-final that is the most memorable,
talked-about one-day match in Lancashire's history.

The Gillette Cup semi-final of 1971 was played at Old Trafford
in front of the television cameras on 28 July against Gloucestershire,
who scored 229 for six in their sixty overs. Lancashire slipped to 163
for six in their reply but Jack Simmons helped Jack Bond to take the
score to 203 before he was out. Lancashire then needed 27 to win in
six overs with the formidable Mike Procter still to bowl in poor light
when David Hughes walked out at nearly quarter to nine. The
lights on the neighbouring Warwick Road railway station had been
switched on and Hughes decided to attack off spinner John Mortimore
in the fifty-sixth over, hitting him for 24 in an over which went
4, 6, 2, 2, 4, 6. Lancashire needed one to win and Bond got it off
Procter to end a famous, fantastic match that will live on, through
television, for ever.

Lancashire had a stiffer task this year at Lord's than in the
1970 final as they faced Kent, an outstanding side who had won the
championship the previous year and were second only to Lancashire
in one-day matches in this period. Lancashire scored 224 for seven
and reduced Kent to 162 for six, a score that was swiftly improved by
a rapier-like attack on the bowling by Asif Iqbal, the Pakistani Test
batsman who destroyed the bowling. It needed something exceptional
to end his – and Kent's – charge to glory, and it came in the shape of a
breathtaking catch by Bond. Asif drove Simmons head-high wide of
cover, but not wide enough as Bond took off like a bird to pluck the
catch out of the air and end a marvellous innings of 89. From 197 for
six Kent became 200 all out and Lancashire, from staring defeat in
the face, had won by 24 runs.

Once again, in 1971, Lancashire stayed in the running for three titles right through to the end of the season, but in the end had to be content with one as they finished third in the championship and the John Player League. They lost three of the first six Sunday games, won seven of the next eight, and with one win wanted from the last two games, both of them at Old Trafford, looked certain of a hat-trick of title wins. They lost the first to Worcestershire in a game reduced to ten overs each, and after keeping Glamorgan down to 143 on a perfect wicket before another capacity crowd, they were inexplicably bowled out for 109. Clive Lloyd had been married the previous day, so perhaps we could put it all down to Mrs Lloyd!

Attendances in the Sunday game hit their peak in 1971 with 59,166 paying for the eight games, 18,815 of them against Glamorgan and 11,114 against Kent. And for the only Gillette Cup–tie at Old Trafford, the semi-final against Gloucestershire, the gate was 24,079, which compared with the grand total of 35,703 for the championship matches.

In 1972, Lancashire slid back to fifteenth place in the championship and for the first time did not challenge for the John Player League as they finished eighth. A third limited-overs competition was introduced this year, the Benson and Hedges Cup, and Lancashire reached the quarter-final before being beaten at Leicester. Jack Bond announced his retirement this year and went out in a blaze of glory as Lancashire completed a hat-trick of wins in the Gillette Cup. But it was all becoming harder and tighter. Somerset were beaten by 9 runs, Hampshire by four wickets with nine balls remaining, and Kent by 7 runs for Lancashire to qualify for Lord's for the third year running. The final belonged to Clive Lloyd, who launched a savage attack on fast bowling with David Brown being the most heavily punished, hit for 67 in his twelve overs, as Lancashire beat Warwickshire by four wickets. Jack Bond said farewell with everybody's best wishes. He had restored Lancashire's position as one of the foremost counties in England and left his successor, David Lloyd, with the hard job of following the Lord Mayor's Show.

Chapter 17 1973–86

'There was no suggestion of an improvement in Lancashire's cricket. Instead, they settled comfortably into mediocrity.'

DAVID LLOYD was 26 when he took over the Lancashire captaincy, an experienced player with 172 first-class matches for the county since his debut eight years earlier. He was born in Accrington on 18 March 1947, and joined Lancashire as a left-arm spinner before developing into a middle-order batsman, then an opener who was good enough to score a double century for England in a Test match against India in 1974. That winter, 1974–75, he was in Australia, facing Dennis Lillee and Jeff Thomson, an experience which was to abruptly finish his Test career despite having an average of 42.46 from nine matches. He played for Lancashire until 1983, nineteen seasons in which he scored more than 1,000 runs ten times for the county with his best season coming in 1972 when he scored 1,510 runs and averaged over 47. He and Barry Wood formed a successful opening partnership and shared in three opening stands over 250. He was a more than useful bowler as his 234 wickets at under 30 runs each testifies. His best bowling return came in his early years when he took seven for 38 against Gloucestershire at Lydney. As well as playing in 378 first-class matches for Lancashire, Lloyd also took part in 273 limited-overs games, scoring centuries in all three major competitions and averaging 32.74.

Lloyd, however, was not everybody's choice of captain to follow the highly-successful Jack Bond, particularly with Clive Lloyd in the team. Every captain wants to stamp his own personality on a team, has his own ideas as to how the side should be run. But any team, like Lancashire of that period, which is so closely bonded together – if you will excuse the pun – will run on automatic pilot for a time, no matter who is captain. Lloyd took over a smooth-running engine which was to reach the Gillette Cup Final three more times during his five years as captain, winning one of them. They twice reached the Benson and Hedges Cup semi-finals, and had a specially good run in the championship in 1975 – their best season under Lloyd – when the title was still at stake in the final match. But by the time he handed over the captaincy to Frank Hayes in 1978, the engine was coughing and stalling and threatening to come to a standstill. The team that won the Gillette Cup three times and the John Player League twice changed little under Jack Bond's captaincy and usually came from Barry Wood, David Lloyd, Ken Snellgrove, Harry Pilling, Clive Lloyd, John Sullivan, Farokh Engineer, Bond, David Hughes, Jack Simmons, Peter Lever and Ken Shuttleworth. Ken Higgs made a significant contribution in 1969, Peter Lee in 1972, and Frank Hayes periodically through the years. By 1978 half the side had retired or, in Shuttleworth's case, had moved to another county and, for eleven years, starting with David Lloyd's last two years as captain, they spent their days in the bottom six of the championship table.

After winning the Gillette Cup in 1970–71–72, Lancashire came back to earth in 1973 when they lost at Lord's to Middlesex in the quarter final, ending a run which had seen them undefeated through fifteen matches. They lost only one of the first eight John Player League games, then three of the next four, and finished a creditable fourth. They moved up to twelfth in the championship and lost an exciting Benson and Hedges Cup semi-final to Worcestershire at Old Trafford. The scores ended level but Worcestershire went through to the final by virtue of having lost fewer wickets. The game, which was televised, was made all the more memorable by the first appearance of John Abrahams, later to captain the team, who took two stunning catches as substitute fielder to dismiss Basil d'Oliveira and Norman Gifford.

During his last year as captain, Jack Bond had introduced Peter Lee, a medium-paced bowler of unflagging energy and cheerful will-ingness, into the side. He was signed from Northamptonshire as back up to Lever and Shuttleworth, two England bowlers who formed the spearhead of Lancashire's attack through those years. Yet Lee was so successful he swiftly became the No. 1 bowler and in 1973 was the leading wicket-taker in the championship and finished with 101, the first to reach the hundred since Ken Higgs five years earlier. In all competitions he took 144 wickets, far ahead of Lever's 87 and Simmons's 61, and was to be the county's leading wicket-taker four seasons out of five.

Frank Hayes also burst through in 1973 after promising so much since 1970 when he made his debut by scoring 94 in his first match, against Middlesex at Old Trafford, and 99 in his second, against Hampshire at Southampton. Hayes never gave a thought to his hundred and was out at Southampton going for victory . . . and getting stumped. Yet it was 1973 before his first century arrived in his fiftieth first-class match, against Sussex at Hove. Two more followed immediately, in the next two games, and this invigorating, uninhibited stroke-maker was chosen to play for England against the West Indies the same season and scored a century on his debut.

FRANK HAYES was born in Preston on 6 December 1946, spending his early childhood there before moving to Marple in Cheshire where he played for the first team at 14. He could have joined the staff at Old Trafford when he was 18 but chose to go to Sheffield University where he gained second-class honours in physics and mathematics. So it was 1970, when he was 23, before his eye-catching debut for Lancashire arrived, an impressive start that was followed by a return to earth in 1971 when runs were not easy to come by. It took him until 1973 to become established and when he scored his century at The Oval in his first Test, it looked as if England had made a great discovery. He went to the West Indies the following winter with MCC and had a wretched tour with only 60 runs from seven Test innings and losing his Test place until 1976. Two more failures saw him dropped again, never to return, after playing nine Tests – all against West Indies.

Hayes played for Lancashire until 1984, fifteen seasons which saw him play in 228 matches and score 10,899 runs for an impressive average of 37.45. He was a hard-hitting batsman with a wide range of shots and in 1977 hit Glamorgan's Malcolm Nash for 34 in one over with 6, 4, 6, 6, 6, 6. He captained the team from 1978 to 1980 but was gradually overtaken by injury and retired, on medical advice, after playing in the first match of the 1984 season, at Oxford.

Lancashire were back at Lord's for the Gillette Cup final in 1974 and lost there for the first time when rain forced the game into Monday and Kent beat them by four wickets. They stayed unbeaten in the championship for the first time since 1930 but were still only eighth in the table with five wins in the twenty matches. They slipped down to twelfth place in the John Player League – the first time they had been in the bottom half – and for the second successive season lost in the Benson and Hedges Cup semi-finals. One of the strange things about Lancashire cricket in those years when they were playing in six Gillette Cup finals in seven years was their inability to get into a Benson's final. The only difference in the two games was that the Benson and Hedges match was fifty-five overs a side compared with the Gillette's sixty, yet Lancashire were unable to bridge those five overs. The Gillette Cup Final seemed to become their right; supporters used to book their London hotels the previous year. The Gillette brought something extra out of them; the Benson and Hedges Cup never had the same effect. But the magic of one-day cricket and the brilliance of Lancashire, though less consistent these days, continued to attract the crowds to Old Trafford. Despite their poor performances on Sundays, eight days of John Player League attendances continued to heavily outnumber thirty or thirty-six days of first-class cricket (35,117 to 25,766 paid in 1974).

CLIVE LLOYD scored 1,458 first-class runs for an average of 63.39 in 1974 but it was in the following year that he showed himself perhaps the finest, certainly the most attractive and crowd-pulling batsman in the country. Here was a lovely summer with almost unending sunshine – if one forgets the day in June when it snowed heavily at Buxton – and Lloyd responded with six first-class centuries and two man-of-the-match performances at Lord's, one in the first World Cup final when West Indies beat Australia, the other for Lancashire in their defeat of Middlesex in the Gillette Cup Final. Four of Lloyd's first-class hundreds came in successive matches. Four were reached in 130 minutes or under and the slowest, against Hampshire at Liverpool, was barely over two and a half hours. The fastest came in 118 minutes against Nottinghamshire at Trent Bridge, but his most spectacular came in the freak of a match at Buxton. He scored 167 not out in 167 minutes, the last 67 runs coming in 37 minutes as he finished with eight 6s and fifteen 4s before Lancashire's innings closed at 477 for five on a lovely, sunny Saturday. It snowed the following Monday, which was 2 June and Derbyshire, who had lost two wickets on the Saturday evening, were bowled out for 42 and 87 on the Tuesday to lose by an innings and 348 runs. One of Lloyd's centuries was against Surrey at The Oval and included an enormous hit to square leg off Robin Jackman which cleared Harleyford Road and landed in the grounds alongside Archbishop Tenison School. I measured the hit at about 150 yards, which must make it one of the biggest – if not the biggest – ever by a Lancashire player.

Lloyd was born in Georgetown, British Guiana, on 31 August 1944, made his debut for British Guiana in 1963–64, his Test debut in 1966–67 and his debut for Lancashire against the Australians while still qualifying in 1968. He became captain of West Indies in 1974–75 and as a Test captain his record stood supreme with most matches (seventy-four) and most victories (thirty-six). West Indies lost only two of the eighteen series in which he was captain and when he played for them for the last time, in 1985, he had played 110 times for

West Indies and scored 7,515 runs with nineteen centuries for an average of 46.67. A left-hander, he was one of the hardest-hitting batsmen in the world and in 1976 scored a double century in two hours against Glamorgan at Swansea, equalling Gilbert Jessop's world record which has since been overtaken by Ravi Shastri. Lloyd played in 219 first-class matches for Lancashire between 1968 and 1986, hitting thirty centuries and scoring 12,764 runs for an average of 44.94. He also played in 268 one-day matches for the county, scoring eleven centuries, fifty-four half centuries and averaging 41.24 from 8,456 runs. His final total of 31,232 runs in all first-class matches is a figure which has been exceeded by only three men who played for Lancashire, Ernest and J. T. Tyldesley, and Cyril Washbrook.

Peter Lee was again the strong man of Lancashire's attack in 1975, collecting over 100 wickets for the second time in three years, an outstanding performance which included a marvellous seven for 8 return against Warwickshire at Edgbaston.

Lancashire staged something of a repeat of their 1971 Gillette Cup semi-final win over Gloucestershire at Old Trafford when the teams clashed again that year. There were 22,000 people at Old Trafford and Gloucestershire must have thought revenge was theirs when they had Lancashire struggling at 182 for six in reply to their own 236. David Hughes and Jack Simmons put on 39 runs but Lancashire were still left needing 18 from the last eleven balls. Victory arrived with three balls to spare, which was closer than the 1971 match, when Bob Ratcliffe jubilantly drove a ball from Tony Brown for four.

There were problems in the dressing room in 1975, stemming a good deal from money, but also from principles which the players felt had to be upheld. Matters came to a head on the morning of the match against Derbyshire at Old Trafford when Frank Hayes, Barry Wood and Peter Lever, all of whom had just returned from representing England in the World Cup, refused to play in the match. The rest of the team would not follow their striking colleagues, who were disciplined by the committee, Lever and Hayes being dropped for two matches and Wood for six. The problem was soon sorted out but not until the first strike by Lancashire players had gone into history.

Clive Lloyd was with the West Indies tourists in England in 1976 and it was left to Harry Pilling, one of English cricket's most underestimated batsmen, to carry the batting in the championship that year with 1,547 runs, which was 658 more than the next highest.

HARRY PILLING was born at Ashton-under-Lyne on 23 February 1943, and joined the Old Trafford staff when he was 16. A photograph taken at the time, showing coach Stan Worthington introducing him to Old Trafford, portrayed Pilling being unable to reach the top of his locker. Pilling was never to rise above 5 feet 2 inches and was the smallest man in the game. But he was a highly-respected batsman who earned himself the No. 3 position and who scored 1,000 runs in a season eight times between 1962 and 1980. He scored more than 1,500 in 1967 and 1976, a season in which he averaged 52.30 and was talked about for England – and not for the first time. Many inferior players have represented England, and although coming close, Pilling never quite made it. He was a down-to-earth Lancastrian who fought his way through the depressions of the 1960s to become one of the most important cogs in the Lancashire side of the following decade. He became the first player to score 1,000 runs in John Player League matches and when he retired had scored 3,738 runs for an average of 25.95 in 170 one-day matches. His first-class career took in 323 matches for Lancashire and he scored 14,841 runs (32.26).

Only one bowler, Peter Lee, topped even fifty wickets in 1976, and Lancashire slid back to sixteenth place in the championship table. They were ninth in the John Player League, knocked out of the Benson and Hedges Cup in the quarter-final, but did reach yet another Lord's final when they met Northamptonshire for the Gillette Cup. No previous team had been such red-hot favourites as Lancashire were against a team which, up to then, had won nothing. But the game was as good as lost early on Saturday when Lancashire's first three wickets fell for 45 runs and Barry Wood went off with a hand injury so serious he took no further part in the game. David Hughes did hit the left-arm spin of Indian Bishan Bedi for 26 runs in the final over, but Northamptonshire, after a few nervous moments, overcame Lancashire's modest 195 for seven by four wickets. Three of Lancashire's stalwarts of the early 1970s, Farokh Engineer, John Sullivan and Ken Shuttleworth, left the county at the end of 1976 on the eve of Lancashire's worst season ever.

In 1977 Lancashire finished sixteenth in both the championship and the John Player League, they were knocked out of the Gillette Cup in the second round, and for the first time in the six years of the Benson and Hedges Cup, they failed to qualify for the knockout stages. It was a disastrous year and David Lloyd, not surprisingly, decided he had had enough.

BARRY WOOD was one of the few players who managed to rise above the mediocrity of the 1977 season, being the top run-scorer with 1,439 and having the best average (51.39). Wood was born in Ossett in Yorkshire on Boxing Day, 1942, and played five times for Yorkshire in 1964 before moving to Old Trafford where he made his debut two years later. He was a gutsy, devoted cricketer, a solid, sound opening batsman especially good against fast bowling, and a more-than-useful medium-paced bowler. He scored over 1,000 runs in his first full season in 1967, a feat he was to repeat six times in his fourteen years with the club. He played in 260 first-class matches for Lancashire and scored 12,969 runs (average 35.24) and took 251 wickets (27.52). He was good enough to play for England twelve times, although he scored only two half-centuries and averaged 21.61 from twenty-one innings. His all-round ability was invaluable in Lancashire's days as an outstanding one-day team. He played in 203 matches for them, scored 4,331 runs, took 219 wickets, and created a record by being named man of the match sixteen times. He went to Derbyshire in 1980 and in 1981 captained them to success at Lord's in the first final of the NatWest Trophy, the successor to the Gillette Cup.

The year of 1977 marked the introduction of another West Indian Test player, Colin Croft, to the Lancashire team. Croft, in his first Test series in the winter of 1976–77, had taken thirty-three wickets at 20.48 runs each with a best performance of 8–29 against Pakistan. Lancashire signed him and announced him as a left-arm fast bowler. Somebody said he was the best since Australia's Alan Davidson. He turned out to be right-handed, nothing like Davidson, and unable to live up to the reputation he had gained against Pakistan, and was released after two seasons had brought 103 wickets but not enough effort and commitment.

Frank Hayes, who was to take over the captaincy, came close to Gary Sobers's record of six 6s in an over in 1977 when he hit five 6s and a 4 against Glamorgan. By astonishing coincidence, Hayes took his runs off the same bowler, Malcolm Nash, and on the same Swansea ground as did Sobers.

Hayes was captain for three years during which there was no suggestion of an improvement in Lancashire's cricket. Instead, they settled comfortably into mediocrity, especially in the championship where they lacked, in particular, the bowlers to give them the stimulus they so badly needed. They finished fifth in the John Player League in 1978, but slipped into the bottom half of the table in the next two years, while the championship saw them cling almost jealously to positions in the bottom six. The cricket was, in general, extremely poor but a significant pointer to their lack of success was that the leading first-class wicket-taker in both seasons, Jack Simmons, and young fast bowler Willie Hogg, from Ulverston, amassed only fifty-one each.

Batting and bowling bonus points had been introduced to the

county championship in 1968 when, incidentally, Yorkshire registered 114 bowling points towards their total of 270 points in twenty-eight matches. The importance of bonus points was rammed home to Lancashire in 1980 when their playing record of four wins, fifteen draws and three defeats was exactly the same as that of Sussex. But whereas Sussex totalled 60 batting and 60 bowling points and finished fourth, Lancashire's 26 batting points was the lowest in the championship and with their 58 bowling points left them eleven positions lower in the table.

There were notable events, of course. Clive Lloyd scored a century in an hour and a half against Glamorgan in 1978, and John Lyon and Bob Ratcliffe scored the only centuries of their careers in the same match in 1979 when they shared in a partnership of 158 against Warwickshire at Old Trafford, beating the eighth-wicket record for the county which had stood for seventy-nine years. There was also an outstanding partnership between the two Lloyds, Clive and David, who put on 234 for the fourth wicket to give Lancashire yet another Gillette Cup victory over Gloucestershire in 1978. This was a record for any wicket by any team in the competition. Lancashire had a remarkable record against Gloucestershire in one-day matches at this time. They won nine of the first ten John Player matches, beat them seven times out of seven in the Gillette Cup and won one and lost one in the Benson and Hedges Cup. Between 1967 and 1978, therefore, Lancashire won seventeen one-day games to Gloucestershire's two and in the same period won four and drew eight of their twelve championship games.

In those same three years when Hayes was captain, Lancashire went out of the Gillette Cup twice in the second round after reaching the semi-final in 1978 when they lost to Sussex at Hove. They qualified for the knockout stage of the Benson and Hedges Cup only once and were then beaten in the quarter-finals.

The most encouraging feature of this period was the return of Jack Bond to the staff as manager after five years out of first-class cricket. When Bond retired as captain in 1972, he became joint coach with John Savage before being unable to resist the invitation from Nottinghamshire to return and captain their team in 1974. This was not quite the success that had been hoped for and although on a personal level Bond had the satisfaction of being an England Test selector, he then left the game and went to the Isle of Man where he was coach and groundsman at King William School. The lure of Lancashire and county cricket proved too much for him and in 1980 he returned as manager, a move welcomed throughout the county and not least of all by the players who had known and respected him. It was as if the witch doctor had been summoned. Now everybody could sit back and

327

let the man work his magic on a team which seemed to have lost the ability, even the will, to win. Bond watched and weighed up in 1980, then decided it was time Clive Lloyd, who had been captain of West Indies since 1974, should also captain Lancashire.

In his first three years of captaincy – he was to be appointed again in 1986 – Lloyd took a relatively young team of players to three Cup semi-finals, two of which turned against Lancashire in the closing stages just when they looked to have won themselves a place at Lord's. The first, in 1981, was played at Northampton and was in the first year of sponsorship by the NatWest Bank after Gillette had decided to pull out after eighteen years. After passing 100 with only Andy Kennedy out, Lancashire lost their way and had to be satisfied with the modest total of 186 for nine in their sixty overs. In a game of fluctuating fortunes Lancashire had the upper hand when they reduced Northamptonshire to 174 for nine with Tim Lamb and last man Jim Griffiths, arguably the worst batsman in England, together. Michael Holding, the West Indies fast bowler, was playing with Lancashire that season when he was not needed by Rishton, the Lancashire League club for whom he was professional. He played in seven first-class matches and took forty wickets as well as playing in six limited-overs matches. Two of the one-day games were in the NatWest Trophy and when he had overs in hand to bowl at the last Northamptonshire pair, Lancashire looked assured of victory. There were seven overs to go, and Lamb and Griffiths hung on for dear life, squeezing out runs here and there before they reached the final over needing one. David Lloyd bowled that final over when a scrambled bye off the fifth ball took Northamptonshire through and made Griffiths, who scored one not out, a hero and a television celebrity.

Lancashire reached the semi-final of the Benson and Hedges Cup the following year, a game played at Trent Bridge and a repeat of the zonal match a month earlier when Nottinghamshire had won by 22 runs after a fine all-round performance from New Zealander Richard Hadlee. Wicket-keeper Chris Maynard held Lancashire together with an innings of 60 in the total of 182 and once again Lancashire looked to be well on the way to victory when they had their opponents 116 for six. But along came Hadlee, with a marvellous innings of 55, another man-of-the-match display, to give Nottinghamshire victory by four wickets with eleven balls to spare and take them to their first Lord's final. Lancashire completed three losing 'semis' in a row in 1983 when they lost by six wickets after being bowled out for 90 by Middlesex at Lord's in the Benson and Hedges Cup. Those performances apart, Lancashire continued to rot among the dead men in the championship with positions of sixteenth and twelfth (twice).

Progress could be said to have been made in the John Player League, but it was slow and painful, never making a challenge for the title and finishing eleventh, tenth and eighth. But the years were not without incident and memories, especially for two former Durham University students and friends, Graeme Fowler and Paul Allott, who both made their Test debuts in this period and toured with England. Allott had the satisfaction of making his debut at Old Trafford in the match when Ian Botham scored his breathtaking century against Australia in the year of magic, 1981. Allott took eighty-five first-class wickets that season, seventy-five of them for Lancashire.

These were great years, too, for Fowler who scored 1,560 runs (40 average) in his first full season for the county in 1981, and followed with 1,246 (42.96) in 1982 and 1,269 (55.17) in 1983. Next to his Test debut against Pakistan in 1982, the highlight must have been his two centuries in a fantastic match against Warwickshire at Southport that same year when Lancashire won by ten wickets after facing a total of 523 for four declared on the opening day. Lancashire can have had few better wins in their history than the one in the match which started on Wednesday 28 July. West Indian Alvin Kallicharran, 230 not out, and Geoff Humpage, 254, shared in a partnership of 470 in 293 minutes, the biggest for the fourth wicket in English cricket, the highest for any Warwickshire wicket, the ninth highest ever, and the fourth best in the championship. In addition, Humpage's thirteen 6s were the most in one innings by an Englishman. On the second day, David Brown, the Warwickshire manager and former England pace bowler, became the first substitute to take a wicket in county cricket when he stood in for Gladstone Small, who was standing by for England in the morning and back in the match, in place of Brown, in the afternoon. Lancashire declared 109 behind after a century in 109 minutes from Fowler and on the third day, Les McFarlane, a pace bowler who had formerly played with Northamptonshire and who was to assist Lancashire for three seasons, had a career-best return of six for 59 to set up the astonishing win. Fowler got a second century – he batted with a runner throughout both innings except for his first 26 runs on the first evening – and he and David Lloyd scored 226 for none to produce one of the most remarkable wins ever.

This contrasted rather sharply with defeat at the hands of Cambridge University, the Varsity's first win over a county for eleven years and only Lancashire's second defeat against them since the war. Derek Pringle, who was to make his England debut that summer, was largely responsible for Lancashire's frustrations which were repeated in the home match with Surrey when Andy Needham and Robin Jackman put on 172 for the last wicket, only one run away from the Surrey record. The Lancashire batsmen had a good year in 1982 with six of them averaging more than 40, one being Clive Lloyd who scored a record sixth century in Roses matches. Former Warwickshire wicket-keeper Chris Maynard made his debut for Lancashire that year and marked the occasion by claiming nine victims in the final match, against Somerset at Taunton, to equal the Lancashire record created by Geoff Clayton in 1959. Neil Fairbrother made his debut against Kent at Old Trafford without getting to the wicket, his debut innings coming in 1983 against Warwickshire at Edgbaston. John Abrahams was captaining Lancashire in Clive Lloyd's absence and agreed with Warwickshire captain Bob Willis early in the day to close Lancashire's innings at 250, which was 146 in arrears, to set up a victory chase. Fairbrother was 94 when 250 was reached and Abrahams, having given his word, would not go back on it. Willis could have given Fairbrother the necessary deliveries to have reached a historic hundred but immediately turned on his heel at 250 and left the field, much to the disgust of several players and indignation of cricket supporters. For sure, the game died a little that day.

David Lloyd marked his retirement in 1983 by scoring a century at Northampton in his last match but Jack Simmons, now 42, just kept marching along for a fine all-round season that brought him 679 runs, sixty-eight wickets and seventeen catches.

Just when we thought the season was over, when the pies and the wine were out and the speeches were about to start, Lancashire and Leicestershire created another piece of history in the last game at Old Trafford. In the closing three hours of the season Steve O'Shaughnessy equalled Percy Fender's 63-year-old world record for the fastest century in first-class cricket, reached in 35 minutes. After the first day and a half had been lost to rain Lancashire had been put in to bat. Roger Tolchard, the Leicestershire captain, soon had his spinners operating to revive his team's flagging over-rate for the season. After taking four bowling points they needed one for batting to finish fourth in the championship. Once this had been achieved, Leicestershire declared, 86 behind, just before three o'clock on the final afternoon, whereupon David Gower and James Whitaker fed the Lancashire batsmen with long hops and full tosses in the hope of inducing a declaration. The pavilion boundary was only about 55 yards and with the right-handed O'Shaughnessy positioning himself at the Stretford End wicket and the left-handed Graeme Fowler at the City End, the openers hit 190 runs in the 35 minutes to tea before taking their stand to 201 in 43 minutes, the fastest first-class double-century partnership on record.

O'Shaughnessy's record was devalued in some quarters because of the type of bowling he received. Nevertheless, it equalled Fender's record and consisted of five 6s, seventeen 4s and three singles and needed a few recounts from the scorers before a time of 35 minutes was announced. Fowler's century, in 46 minutes, contained ten 6s and five 4s as Lancashire batted on and refused to declare. They were the two fastest centuries ever by opening batsmen and Fowler's hundred was the third fastest in the county's history behind O'Shaughnessy and A. H. Hornby (43 minutes). The partnership of 201 came from fifteen 6s, twenty-three 4s, two 3s, one 2, ten singles and a wide. A farce it might have been, but it enabled me to bring the 22-year-old O'Shaughnessy and 91-year-old Fender together at the old man's home in Horsham two days later, a fascinating meeting and one of the most memorable moments of my life in cricket.

Clive Lloyd was captaining West Indies in England in 1984 and although John Abrahams had captained Lancashire on occasions it was still a surprise – even a shock – to many people when he was named county captain in his place. Perhaps we should not have been so surprised. Jack Bond, the manager, must have seen something of himself in Abrahams. They were both players who rarely had it easy in county cricket, who must have approached a few season-ends wondering whether they would be at Old Trafford the following year. They had both known the depressions as well as the elations of the game and both, presumably, would be able to identify with fellow players at both ends of the scale. The Lancashire team of 1984 was made up of players of quite widespread age groups, with Jack Simmons, Clive Lloyd and David Hughes reaching back to the 1960s, Abrahams from the early 1970s, Paul Allott and Graeme Fowler from the late 1970s, and a whole bunch of new, largely untried young players. Abrahams, it was felt, would bridge the gap in all these age groups. Ramsbottom-born Alan Ormrod, an opening batsman who had played 22 years with Worcestershire, was signed to reinforce the batting. Frank Hayes, now 37, retired through persistent injury after one game in 1984. Abrahams's appointment met with a good deal of immediate success in the one-day game although Lancashire continued to languish in the bottom part of the championship, finishing next-to-the-bottom for the fourth time in nine years.

Abrahams's great triumph was in leading Lancashire to victory in the 1984 Benson and Hedges Cup final at Lord's, Lancashire's first success in this competition, their first trophy since 1975. A four-wicket win over Essex at Chelmsford, where Abrahams won the man-of-the-match award for a crucial innings of 53, was followed by a satisfying six-wicket win at Trent Bridge after Nottinghamshire had scored 223 for six in their fifty-five overs. Lancashire's reply was championed by 21-year-old Mark Chadwick, who opened the innings due to injury to Ormrod and rode his luck of four dropped catches to score 87. Chadwick was released after the 1987 season, by which time he had still played only that one Benson and Hedges Cup match – in which he won the gold award! Lancashire beat Warwickshire in the final, winning by six wickets with great ease in the end after an unbeaten stand of 69 between David Hughes, playing in his seventh Lord's final, and Neil Fairbrother, in his first. Abrahams scored a duck, but was chosen as man of the match by Peter May for his leadership.

Lancashire made a great challenge for the John Player League that summer, winning ten matches and finishing fourth, their highest position for eleven years. They reached the quarter-final of the NatWest Trophy, losing to Middlesex at Lord's where a raw West Indian fast bowler, 22-year-old Patrick Patterson, who was playing in the Saddleworth League, made his debut for them. Patterson was to develop into arguably the fastest bowler in the world, but in 1984 he was new and inexperienced and spent much of his time in the dressing room at Lord's gazing out of the window in wonderment at the game's most famous ground.

Team spirit was good after the 1984 season. Things had started to happen again and hopes were high for more improvement in 1985. Yet strangely the team, after taking a step forward in 1984, now took two backwards, and all the old doubts and depressions returned in a season that had to rank among the worst ever. They finished fourteenth in the championship, fifteenth in the John Player League, did not qualify for the Benson and Hedges Cup knockout stage, and went out of the NatWest Trophy as soon as they came up against first-class competition. None of the bowlers took fifty first-class wickets and only Neil Fairbrother reached 1,000 runs. Strange things happened to Graeme Fowler this year. After several good, fighting innings against the conquering West Indians in 1984, including a Test century at Lord's, he went on the tour of India where he scored 438 runs in five Tests for an average of 54.75, including a double century at Madras where he shared in stands of 178 with Tim Robinson for the first wicket and 241 with Mike Gatting for the second. His stock could not have been higher at the start of the 1985 summer, yet before it was over he had been dropped into Lancashire's second team and out of consideration for either of England's two tours that winter. Somehow, the runs simply dried up, and this, coupled with a neck injury midway through the season, left him lying thirteenth in Lancashire's batting averages with 404 runs and an average of 16.83 from fifteen matches. He, Alan Ormrod, and Steve O'Shaughnessy had each scored 1,000 runs in 1984; in 1985 they could not total 800 between them.

Lancashire won only three championship matches that year, one of them against Somerset at Old Trafford in a highly-entertaining end-of-season encounter between two teams trying to avoid the bottom position. Viv Richards hit eleven 4s and five 6s in his sixth century of the season, Ian Botham hit seven 4s and four 6s in an innings of 76 which lasted only forty-seven balls. Lancashire scored 330 for four in 104.5 overs for victory with Mark Chadwick and Kevin Hayes, two 22-year-old uncapped players, scoring what proved to be their only first-class centuries for Lancashire.

What must have made the season all the more galling for Lancashire was that Neal Radford, the Rhodesian-born pace bowler they had released at the end of the 1984 season, moved on to Worcestershire and became the only bowler in the country to take 100 wickets. Radford, a league professional for several years, first played for Lancashire in 1980. He was an overseas registered player and for four years had to compete for a place in the team with Clive Lloyd, Mick Malone, Michael Holding, Colin Croft and Steve Jefferies. He became English qualified, but instead of new horizons opening up for him, he slipped out of sight and out of reckoning and was released. In five years, he played only twenty-four first-class matches for Lancashire and took thirty-three wickets at the ridiculously high cost of 54.69 runs each. He changed almost overnight at Worcester where the extra faith in him brought out seams of talent that Lancashire had never looked like tapping. Questions, of course, were asked, but never properly and satisfactorily answered.

Lancashire took county cricket to Lytham instead of Blackpool in 1985. A dispute between the county club and Blackpool, which had first staged a county match in 1906, led to Lancashire playing Northamptonshire at Lytham, the twelfth different ground used in the county's history. Interest had now plummeted again and attendance figures showed that only 11,018 people paid to watch home championship matches in 1985 and 6,603 in the John Player League. More changes had to be made and this time the committee chose Clive Lloyd as captain again with Jack Simmons as his deputy. Again, they were selections that were not generally approved, and certainly not by the manager, Jack Bond, and the first-team coach, Peter Lever. The uncertainties of selection were shown at the start of the 1986 season when the great majority of the staff went to Hove for the opening championship game with Sussex. Lloyd and Simmons were there, of course, but choice of captain landed on Graeme Fowler, an astonishing decision that looked at first like a piece of perversity, then took on the appearance of being inspirational as Fowler scored 180 and Lancashire won by nine wickets. Lancashire won two of the first four championship matches and for a time sat on top of the championship table. But it was not long before they slid back into the bottom six for the eleventh successive year, an awful record that was matched only by Glamorgan.

Lancashire had another miserable season in the Benson and Hedges Cup, where they had the dubious distinction of becoming the first county ever to lose to Scotland when they were unable to overtake the modest-enough Scots total of 156 for nine at Perth, and lost by 3 runs. They finished twelfth in the John Player League, but lifted their game in the NatWest Trophy, reaching Lord's for the first time in ten years in the sixty-over competition. They played spirited cricket to win at Taunton, Leicester and The Oval, where their semi-final victory over Surrey was one of the most memorable of all time. Lancashire recovered from 57 for four to reach a total of 229 with half centuries from Lloyd and O'Shaughnessy and won by 4 runs when Fowler took a magnificent boundary catch to dismiss Trevor Jesty who had scored 112. A modest bowling attack had been magnificently supported by outstanding fielding, but this was not enough to sustain Lancashire through the final against Sussex who overtook Lancashire's 242 for eight (Neil Fairbrother 63) with seven wickets and ten balls to spare. Clive Lloyd sat despondently in the dressing room long after the game was over. He would dearly have loved to have taken Lancashire to another one-day success. It would have meant a lot to him. The following day he played in the John Player League match against Gloucestershire at Bristol in what turned out to be his last match for the county. Before the following season started, he had retired.

Chapter 18 1987–89

*'Lancashire turned in hope, and perhaps with a prayer,
to David Hughes and Alan Ormrod to work a miracle
on Lancashire's first team.'*

Two days after the 1986 NatWest Trophy final, manager Jack
Bond and coach Peter Lever were sacked. It must have been a
particularly unhappy moment for Bond who had been unable to bring
his captaincy qualities to the position of manager. The committee now
needed a captain and a manager and turned to the two men who had
just schemed Lancashire to the Second Eleven championship, David
Hughes and Alan Ormrod. They had forged an impressive partnership and Lancashire turned in hope, and perhaps with a prayer, to
them to work a miracle on Lancashire's first team. This did, indeed,
turn out to be inspirational as Lancashire had their best run in the
championship for twenty-seven years and almost snatched the title
from Nottinghamshire before finishing runners-up.

**DAVID HUGHES was born in Newton-le-Willows on 13 May 1947,
and played for his home-town team in the Manchester Association and
Farnworth in the Bolton League before joining Lancashire in 1967. He
considered himself a left-arm spinner first and foremost and had his best
years in this role under Jack Bond's captaincy. His peak came in 1970 and
1971 when he bowled more than 800 overs and took eighty-two wickets
each season. He took 296 wickets in the five seasons Bond was captain
but under other captains only once exceeded fifty wickets in a season.
He had taken 585 wickets for Lancashire by the end of the 1982 season
but by the time he became captain had virtually given up bowling. As
his bowling declined so his batting came to the fore and he reached 1,000
runs for the first time in 1981.**

Hughes's best all-round season came in 1982 when he averaged 48.25 runs an innings and headed the Lancashire bowling averages with thirty-one wickets at 25.45 runs each. He was unable to maintain that performance and slipped more and more into the second team so that in 1985 he played in only ten first-class matches. The end of his first-class career looked to have arrived the following summer when he played in only three one-day matches and in the middle of the season he prepared his letter of resignation. He held it back as he led the second team to their championship and within weeks found himself the captain of one of the country's foremost counties, but one which had not won the championship outright for fifty-three years. He came desperately close to achieving that goal and was chosen as one of *Wisden*'s Cricketers of the Year, following three other Lancashire players who had not played Test cricket in Jack Bond, Peter Lee and Jack Simmons.

Cedric Rhoades, Lancashire's chairman since 1969 and the driving force behind the scenes in the county's resurgence in the 1970s, was forced to resign in February 1987, by intense pressure from an action group who were intending to call a special meeting of members and threatening to overthrow the committee. Bob Bennett, a player in the 1960s, returned to the committee he had left two years earlier, to take over as chairman, and Lancashire therefore went into the 1987 season with three new faces at the head of the ship.

By the end of May, 1987, Lancashire had won three of their first five championship matches and were at the top of the table. They then won only one of the next thirteen and entered the last six games in the middle of August trailing 62 points behind the leaders, Nottinghamshire, having played the same number of games. Lancashire won those six games, starting with a 54-run defeat of Sussex in a low-scoring match at Lytham, where Mike Watkinson had the best piece of bowling in his life, seven for 25 in the second innings. They then went to Edgbaston where they won another low-scoring encounter – the highest score was 165 – by 25 runs with Watkinson taking six for 65 and Patterson six for 40. On they went to Maidstone where it was Paul Allott's turn for the bowling honours in the first innings with seven for 42, followed by spinners Ian Folley (five for 54) and Jack Simmons (four for 23) in the second. Lancashire needed 200 to win and Graeme Fowler hit a marvellous century as a six-wicket victory was achieved with eight balls to spare. Neil Fairbrother, who that year became the 54th Lancashire player to be capped by England, had been injured in this game and missed the last three matches, enabling John Abrahams to return to the side and play a significant part in the late challenge for the title. Victory over Gloucestershire at Old Trafford came by three wickets and in the penultimate match, also at home, Abrahams scored 140 not out in the first innings and 92 in the second as Lancashire chased 276 for victory in sixty overs against Surrey. Lancashire batted for much of the time in appalling light and achieved a fine, four-wicket victory with fourteen balls to spare.

Lancashire had taken 105 points from those five games and went into the last one, against Essex at Chelmsford, needing the full 24 points from the match to draw level on points with Nottinghamshire, who had completed their programme. By virtue of having won more matches – ten to nine – they would have become champions. But although they did win, by 89 runs, they were unable to take the full eight bonus points and Nottinghamshire became champions as soon as Lancashire had been bowled out for 220. But it had been a magnificent challenge in which Fowler had his best season in ten years with Lancashire, scoring 1,800 runs, the second highest in the country, yet being unable to attract the attention of the England selectors. Gehan Mendis, signed from Sussex, opened the innings and scored 1,390 runs, and four bowlers – Allott, Simmons, Patterson and Folley – all took more than fifty wickets. It was especially satisfying for Ian Folley, a former seam bowler who had turned to spin, and who bowled 753.1 overs and took seventy-four wickets, by far his best performance with the county.

Lancashire did not play so well in the limited-overs game, but made up for it the following year when they finished third in the Sunday forty-over game, now sponsored by Refuge Assurance after seventeen years by John Player, the tobacco company. This qualified them for the Refuge Assurance Cup, a new knockout tournament for the top four clubs in the league table, and won by Lancashire in the final against Worcestershire at Edgbaston in the concluding match of the 1988 season on Sunday 18 September. Lancashire had slipped to ninth in the championship but could still point to two highly satisfying years under Hughes.

JACK SIMMONS was still playing and at the age of 47 he became only the thirteenth Lancashire bowler to take 1,000 wickets – in all first-class matches. Simmons was born at Clayton-le-Moors, near Accrington, on 28 March 1941, and played for the same Lancashire League club as his father and grandfather, Enfield, making his debut when he was 14. He played for Lancashire 2nd and was asked to join the Lancashire groundstaff when he was 19, a request he turned down because he wanted to finish his apprenticeship as a draughtsman. He was told he would be invited again when he was 21 but the invitation never came and Simmons settled down to a life as a league professional. He was with Blackpool in 1968, the year before the Sunday League started,

and Lancashire's staff needed strengthening. Lancashire coach Buddy Oldfield went to watch two youngsters in an inter-league match but when he saw Simmons, he invited him to play in the second team again. His first-team debut came that year on his 'home' ground of Blackpool when he scored 1 and 0 against Northamptonshire. But he took three wickets for 44 runs with his off breaks and was taken on to the staff in 1969 when he was 28. He was wanted mainly for his bowling and batted usually at No. 8 or 9, but was still able to score five centuries for Lancashire and averaged around 23. He also had the distinction of captaining Tasmania in their first season in Australia's Sheffield Shield competition, and also led them to an astounding Gillette Cup final over Western Australia in 1978–79 when he was man of the match. Ten bowlers have taken more wickets for Lancashire than Simmons and of those, only Johnny Briggs has scored more runs.

Simmons, now 48, decided to retire at the end of the 1989 season and said farewell by helping to bring the Refuge Assurance League to Old Trafford. It was Lancashire's first success in the forty-over Sunday competition since winning it in its first two years in 1969-70, when it was sponsored by John Player. Lancashire won eleven of their first thirteen games – one was washed out and the only defeat came at Leicester – and went into the last three games needing to win only one to clinch the title. All were at Old Trafford and after the first, against Essex, was washed out with Lancashire well on their way to defeat, the second saw them beaten by Yorkshire. They came good in the third match, against Surrey, but would have won the title anyway as Essex, their only challengers after running neck-and-neck with them throughout the summer, lost their final match to Northamptonshire. Hughes's third year as captain proved Lancashire's finest for eighteen years as they also finished fourth in the championship and reached the quarter-finals of the NatWest Trophy and the Benson and Hedges Cup. Ian Folley had unfortunately lost form and faded from the scene but two young talents shone through in Mike Atherton, who had completed his studies at Cambridge University, and wicket-keeper Warren Hegg, both aged 21. Atherton played twice for England against Australia and was named vice-captain for England's second-team tour of Zimbabwe in the winter; Hegg claimed more victims than any other wicket-keeper, including eleven catches in one match to equal the world record. Lancashire, back among the front-runners in county cricket, looked in good hands as they moved into the 1990s.

LANCASHIRE RECORDS

The records, unless otherwise stated, refer to all Lancashire first-class matches since the county's first match in 1865. As far as possible the records follow the definition of first-class matches as compiled by the Association of Cricket Statisticians. All statistics are correct to the end of the 1989 cricket season.

Statistics supplied by Revd Malcolm G. Lorimer, Hon. Statistician Lancashire CCC.

Career Averages in all First-Class Lancashire Matches 1865-1989

NAME	PLAYED	Mt	Inns	N.O.	Runs	H.S.	Ave	Runs	Wkts	Ave	Best
J. Abrahams	1973-1988	251	388	52	9980	201*	29.70	2811	56	50.19	3/27
T. Ainscough	1894-1906	2	3	0	40	24	13.33				
J.L. Ainsworth	1899	4	6	1	17	11	3.40	289	18	16.05	6/84
R. Alderson	1948-1949	2	2	0	55	55	27.50				
P.J.W. Allott	1978-1989	183	208	48	2700	88	16.87	12188	517	23.57	8/48
A. Appleby	1866-1887	58	93	14	1052	99	13.31	3474	245	14.17	9/25
J.F. Arnold	1896	3	5	0	94	37	18.80				
R. Arrowsmith	1976-1979	43	40	12	286	39	10.21	2796	99	28.24	6/29
J.T. Ashworth	1871-1873	2	3	0	28	19	9.33				
M.A. Atherton	1987-1989	26	47	6	1509	152*	36.80	755	12	62.91	3/32
G. Atkinson	1967-1969	62	99	9	2468	124	27.42	24	1	24.00	1/19
I.D. Austin	1987-1989	18	25	5	428	64	21.40	948	42	22.57	5/79
D. Bailey	1968-1969	27	36	1	845	136	24.14				
G.R. Baker	1887-1899	228	350	29	7170	186	22.33	3475	138	25.18	6/18
S.T. Banham	1939	1	1	-	-	-	-				
H.W. Barber	1866-1867	3	6	0	41	15	6.83				
J.B. Barber	1874-1876	3	6	3	39	12*	13.00				
R.W. Barber	1954-1962	155	264	25	6760	175	28.28	4768	152	31.36	7/35
H.G. Barchard	1888	1	2	0	45	40	22.50				
P. Barcroft	1956	3	3	0	40	29	13.33				
R.V. Bardsley	1910-1920	7	8	0	46	15	5.75	23	0	-	-
G.R. Bardswell	1894-1902	21	28	1	429	56	15.88	342	8	42.75	4/37
A. Barlow	1947-1951	74	87	20	707	44	10.55	0	0	-	-
E.A. Barlow	1932	7	8	1	84	40	12.00	389	12	32.41	4/33
R.G. Barlow	1871-1891	249	426	45	7765	117	20.38	10010	736	13.60	9/39
J.R. Barnes	1919-1930	89	136	22	3271	123*	28.69	53	0	-	-
S.F. Barnes	1899-1903	46	58	20	452	35	11.89	4459	225	19.81	8/37
B. Barrell	1911-1923	3	3	1	45	25	22.50	135	9	15.00	3/10
W. Barron	1945	1	2	0	3	2	1.50				
F.W. Baucher	1903	1	2	0	12	8	6.00				
A.D. Baxter	1933-1934	3	1	0	0	0	0.00	208	16	13.00	6/50
F.D. Beattie	1932	5	9	1	120	36	15.00				

* Not out

NAME	PLAYED	Mt	Inns	N.O.	Runs	H.S.	Ave	Runs	Wkts	Ave	Best
A.M. Beddow	1962-1966	33	54	3	775	112*	15.19	473	15	31.53	3/10
A. Bennett	1932-1933	16	14	1	238	51	18.30	865	24	36.04	4/49
H.S. Bennett	1894	1	2	0	16	11	8.00			–	–
R. Bennett	1962-1966	49	82	3	1814	112	22.96	49	0	–	
C.H. Benton	1892-1901	29	50	6	663	68	15.06				
R. Berry	1948-1954	93	85	34	427	27*	8.37	5900	259	22.77	10/102
G.H. Biddulph	1885	1	2	0	19	18	9.50	13	0	–	–
G.A. Bigg	1887	1	1	0	16	16	16.00	13	1	13.00	1/13
G. Bird	1880	1	2	0	0	0	0.00				
M.C. Bird	1907	5	10	0	36	10	3.60	84	4	21.00	2/9
F.H. Birley	1870-1872	4	6	1	58	18	11.60	120	4	30.00	3/76
A.J. Birtwell	1937-1939	14	16	6	103	31	10.30	999	25	39.96	4/78
J.F. Blackledge	1962	26	41	4	569	68	15.37	10	0	–	–
R. Blackstock	1865	1	2	0	23	18	11.50				
W. Blake	1877	1	1	0	26	26	26.00				
E.O. Bleackley	1919	2	3	0	31	21	10.33				
R. Blomley	1903-1922	70	87	32	316	41	5.74				
R.A. Boddington	1913-1924	52	75	19	663	58*	11.83				
R. Boden	1907	1	2	0	8	5	4.00				
A. Bolton	1957-1961	40	71	6	1223	96	18.81	80	2	40.00	1/17
J.D. Bond	1955-1972	344	522	76	11867	157	26.60	69	0	–	–
A. Booth	1950-1951	4	5	0	81	49	16.20				
B.J. Booth	1956-1963	117	210	17	5075	183*	26.29	3183	106	30.02	7/143
F.S. Booth	1927-1937	140	157	25	1330	54	10.07	11180	457	24.46	7/59
E.J. Bousfield	1865-1878	12	21	2	279	32	14.68				
E. Bowden	1914	4	6	0	27	10	4.50	453	12	37.75	6/78
W.H. Bower	1885-1886	4	6	0	45	23	7.50				
J.B. Bowes	1938-1948	10	13	1	106	39	8.83	602	21	28.66	4/103
K. Bowling	1954	1	2	1	7	4*	7.00				
R. Bowman	1957-1959	9	12	1	189	58	17.18	459	11	41.72	2/28
R. Boys	1877	1	2	1	13	10	13.00				
T.F. Bradbury	1881	1	2	1	6	6*	6.00				
J. Braddock	1873	1	2	0	13	11	6.50				
W. Brearley	1902-1911	106	145	23	749	38	6.13	12907	690	18.70	9/47

NAME	PLAYED	Mt	Inns	N.O.	Runs	H.S.	Ave	Runs	Wkts	Ave	Best
T.L. Brierley	1946-1948	46	62	8	1286	116*	23.81	12	0	-	-
J. Briggs	1879-1900	391	602	39	10707	186	19.01	26464	1696	15.60	10/55
J. Briggs	1939	4	2	2	0	0*	-	391	10	39.10	4/48
J.M. Brocklebank	1939	4	4	1	5	4	1.66	279	5	55.80	3/61
F.R.R. Brooke	1912-1913	29	35	0	566	61	16.17	9	1	9.00	1/9
A.W. Brooks	1877	1	1	0	6	6	6.00				
J.J. Broughton	1901-1902	6	7	0	153	99	21.85	69	2	34.50	2/28
W. Brown	1894	2	3	0	17	7	5.66	12	0	-	-
W. Brown	1919-1922	10	17	2	239	39	15.93	474	22	21.54	4/22
L. Bulcock	1946	1	1	0	1	1	1.00	90	2	45.00	2/41
J. Bullough	1914-1919	8	8	3	24	17	4.80	573	13	44.07	5/123
W. Burrows	1867-1873	14	26	1	255	39	10.20	6	0	-	-
C. Burton	1956	2	1	0	0	0	0.00	80	0	-	-
H.R.W. Butterworth	1931-1936	25	34	5	584	107	20.13	1392	36	38.66	6/85
W.S. Butterworth	1876-1882	9	14	1	73	22	5.61				
G.A. Campbell	1866	1	2	0	18	10	9.00				
F. Carlisle	1869	2	4	0	37	18	9.25				
E.L. Chadwick	1875-1881	13	24	3	254	42	12.09				
M.R. Chadwick	1983-1987	33	56	1	1197	132	21.76	71	0	-	-
A. Champion	1886	1	2	0	4	4	2.00				
I.M. Chappell	1963	1	1	0	3	3	3.00				
J. Clarke	1905	1	1	0	0	0	0.00	35	0	-	-
G. Clayton	1959-1964	183	277	49	4382	84	19.21				
I. Cockbain	1979-1983	46	78	9	1456	98	21.10	14	0	-	-
T.G.O. Cole	1904	1	1	0	0	0	0.00				
R. Collins	1954-1962	119	181	18	3332	107*	20.44	4782	159	30.07	6/63
L.W. Cook	1907-1923	203	258	91	2051	54*	12.28	17537	821	21.36	8/39
W. Cook	1905-1907	11	17	3	307	46	21.92	946	51	18.54	7/64
N.H. Cooke	1958-1959	12	16	0	242	33	15.12	93	3	31.00	2/10
F. Cooper	1946	4	8	2	96	33*	16.00				
W. Copeland	1885	1	2	1	21	21*	21.00	23	1	23.00	1/23
S. Corlett	1871-1875	2	3	0	6	4	2.00				
J. Coulthurst	1919	1	-	-	-	-	-				
C. Coward	1865-1876	36	65	2	912	85	14.47	44	0	-	-

NAME	PLAYED	Mt	Inns	N.O.	Runs	H.S.	Ave	Runs	Wkts	Ave	Best
F. Coward	1867-1868	7	13	1	35	9	2.91				
J.M. Cownley	1962	2	4	0	45	25	11.25	36	2	18.00	2/36
F. Crabtree	1890	1	1	0	1	1	1.00				
H. Crabtree	1902-1908	5	8	0	116	49	14.50	34	0	-	-
J.S. Cragg	1908	1	2	0	10	9	5.00				
E.J. Craig	1961-1962	6	11	1	214	89	21.40				
W.R. Craig	1874	1	2	0	8	7	4.00				
K. Cranston	1947-1948	50	57	9	1928	155*	40.16	3267	142	23.00	7/43
C.E.H. Croft	1977-1982	49	50	10	433	46*	10.82	3604	136	26.50	7/54
F.J. Crooke	1865	1	2	0	55	35	27.50				
S.M. Crosfield	1883-1899	90	140	13	1909	82*	15.03	111	2	55.50	1/1
J. Crossland	1878-1885	71	109	21	1002	48*	11.38	3125	245	12.75	7/14
H. Cudworth	1900	1	1	0	4	4	4.00				
J. Cumbes	1963-1971	9	5	4	5	5	5.00	563	19	29.63	4/42
W.R. Cuttell	1896-1906	213	294	30	5389	137	20.41	14890	760	19.59	8/105
I.C. Davidson	1985-1987	2	4	0	14	13	3.50	85	4	21.25	2/24
H.D. Davies	1924-1925	11	15	0	260	46	17.33				
H. Dean	1906-1921	256	354	118	2448	49*	10.37	22828	1267	18.01	9/31
P.A.J. DeFreitas	1989	17	28	2	567	78	21.80	1687	69	24.44	7/21
J.H.G. Deighton	1948-1950	7	9	1	206	79	25.75	509	20	25.45	5/52
C.E. de Trafford	1884	1	1	0	0	0	0.00				
R. Dewhurst	1872-1875	13	22	1	267	59	12.71				
T.E. Dickinson	1950-1951	4	5	3	10	9	5.00	98	3	32.66	1/20
J. Dixon	1878	1	2	0	2	2	1.00				
P. Dobell	1886-1887	7	12	1	96	28	8.72				
H. Douthwaite	1920-1921	3	5	0	85	29	17.00				
G. Duckworth	1923-1938	424	455	170	4174	75	14.64	66	0	0	0
G.C.H. Dunlop	1868	1	2	0	17	16	8.50				
A. Durandu	1887	1	1	0	5	5	5.00				
J. Dyson	1954-1964	150	242	35	4433	118*	21.41	4447	161	27.62	7/83
A. Eccles	1898-1907	123	196	20	4179	139	23.74	30	0	-	-
H. Eccles	1885-1886	5	7	0	37	14	5.28				
J. Eccles	1886-1889	47	75	5	1787	184	25.52	38	0	-	-
P.T. Eckersley	1923-1935	256	293	45	4588	102*	18.50	145	1	145.00	1/7

NAME	PLAYED	Mt	Inns	N.O.	Runs	H.S.	Ave	Runs	Wkts	Ave	Best
C.A. Edge	1936-1938	8	5	2	2	1	0.66	759	25	30.36	4/71
H.E. Edge	1913	1	1	0	3	3	3.00	101	0	–	–
J.W. Edmonds	1975	1	–	–	–	–	–	82	3	27.33	3/52
E.H. Edrich	1946-1948	33	40	4	854	121	23.72				
G.A. Edrich	1946-1958	322	479	55	14730	167*	34.74	199	2	99.50	1/19
H. Elliott	1930	1	1	0	4	4	4.00				
J. Ellis	1892-1898	6	9	1	56	26*	7.00	240	21	11.42	8/21
S. Ellis	1923-1924	8	7	1	57	25	9.50	525	14	18.00	5/21
W. Ellis	1920-1923	36	55	4	846	138*	16.58				
F.M. Engineer	1968-1976	175	262	39	5942	141	26.64	10	0	–	–
R. Entwistle	1962-1966	48	79	4	1554	85	20.72				
N.H. Fairbrother	1982-1989	153	246	32	8284	164*	38.71	385	5	77.00	2/91
P.M. Fairclough	1911-1923	20	27	14	140	19	10.76	1158	52	22.26	7/27
J.A. Fallows	1946	25	22	1	171	35	8.14				
A.W. Farnsworth	1919	1	2	0	3	3	1.50				
H. Farrar	1955	1	–	–	–	–	–	25	0	–	–
H.L. Farrar	1904	1	2	0	28	25	14.00				
W. Farrimond	1924-1945	134	142	38	2202	63	21.17	16	0	–	–
W. Findlay	1902-1906	58	82	20	1223	81	19.72	15	0	–	–
D.J. Fitton	1987-1989	21	28	7	386	44	18.38	1618	43	37.62	6/59
I. Folley	1982-1989	132	155	48	1413	69	13.20	8336	274	30.42	7/15
G. Fowler	1979-1989	183	307	17	10939	226	37.72	178	5	35.60	2/34
F.D. Gaddum	1884	1	2	0	15	10	7.50	14	0	–	–
R.G. Garlick	1938-1947	44	56	7	753	50	15.36	2797	120	23.30	6/27
H.G. Garnett	1899-1914	144	231	17	5599	139	26.16	224	8	28.00	2/18
A.B.E. Gibson	1887	2	4	0	25	16	6.25				
P.A. Gooch	1970	4	3	1	0	0*	0.00	252	6	42.00	4/52
A.J. Good	1973-1976	8	8	2	10	6	1.66	482	17	28.35	5/62
F. Goodwin	1955-1956	11	10	4	47	21*	7.83	715	27	26.48	5/35
F.H. Goodwin	1894	3	6	1	14	10	2.80	47	0	–	–
K. Goodwin	1960-1974	122	149	42	618	23	5.77				
D.M. Green	1959-1967	135	242	10	6086	138	26.23	1849	41	45.09	3/6
L. Green	1922-1935	152	173	28	3575	110*	24.65	299	9	33.22	2/2
E.W. Greenhalgh	1935-1938	14	18	5	366	53*	28.15	282	3	94.00	2/75

344

NAME	PLAYED	Mt	Inns	N.O.	Runs	H.S.	Ave	Runs	Wkts	Ave	Best
T. Greenhough	1951-1966	241	298	79	1868	76*	8.52	15540	707	21.98	7/56
P. Greenwood	1948-1952	75	92	15	1270	113	16.49	5090	208	24.47	6/35
W.R. Gregson	1906	5	7	1	62	26	10.33	428	24	17.83	5/8
K.J. Grieves	1949-1964	452	696	73	20802	224	33.39	6769	235	28.80	6/60
G.H. Grimshaw	1868	1	2	0	11	11	5.50				
S. Haggas	1884-1885	3	5	0	59	18	11.80				
W. Haggas	1903	2	2	0	6	4	3.00				
C.H. Haigh	1879-1887	24	33	3	435	80	14.50				
A.E. Hall	1923-1924	9	10	4	11	5*	1.83	630	24	26.25	6/23
A.W. Hallam	1895-1900	71	93	25	570	31*	8.38	4063	211	19.25	6/28
T.M. Halliday	1925-1929	41	55	11	996	109*	22.63	16	0	-	-
C. Hallows	1914-1932	370	569	62	20142	233*	39.72	784	19	41.26	3/28
J. Hallows	1898-1907	138	202	27	4997	137*	28.55	6610	279	23.69	9/37
F. Hardcastle	1869	2	4	1	17	9	5.66				
W.M. Hardcastle	1869-1874	4	7	0	33	11	4.71				
F.W. Hargreaves	1881	1	1	0	0	0	0.00				
G.M. Harper	1883	1	1	0	1	1	1.00				
F. Harrison	1936	3	3	1	4	2*	2.00	118	4	29.50	2/30
J. Harrop	1874	1	2	0	5	5	2.50	14	0	-	-
F. Harry	1903-1908	69	106	9	1528	88	15.75	3795	207	18.33	9/44
A. Hartley	1907-1914	112	185	9	4963	234	28.20	61	1	61.00	1/39
C.R. Hartley	1897-1909	160	168	11	3729	139	23.75	53	0	-	-
F. Hartley	1924-1945	2	1	0	2	2	2.00	44	1	44.00	1/44
G. Hartley	1871-1872	3	3	0	37	24	12.33				
B. Harwood	1877	1	2	2	0	0*	-	16	1	16.00	1/16
C. Hawkwood	1931-1935	24	26	5	596	113	28.38	92	1	92.00	1/63
F.C. Hayes	1970-1984	228	339	48	10899	187	37.45	11	0	-	-
K.A. Hayes	1980-1986	18	24	1	586	117	25.47	25	0	-	-
A.N. Hayhurst	1985-1989	42	63	6	1185	107	20.78	1644	49	33.55	4/27
F.S. Head	1868-1869	6	10	0	75	24	7.50				
J.G. Heap	1884	2	2	0	0	0	0.00	4	0	-	-
J.S. Heap	1903-1921	210	312	41	5146	132*	18.98	9513	412	23.08	9/43
W.K. Hegg	1986-1989	65	100	13	1598	130	18.36	7	0	-	-
S. Henriksen	1985-1986	3	4	3	17	10*	17.00	105	2	52.50	1/26

NAME	PLAYED	Mt	Inns	N.O.	Runs	H.S.	Ave	Runs	Wkts	Ave	Best
J. Hewitson	1890	4	5	0	99	56	19.80	235	14	16.78	6/57
W. Heys	1957	5	7	0	74	46	10.57	54	2	27.00	2/35
H. Hibbard	1884	1	2	0	7	4	3.50	37	0	–	–
G. Hibberd	1867	1	2	1	4	2*	4.00				
W.J. Hibbert	1900-1901	14	22	4	445	79	24.72	116	3	38.66	2/41
W.E. Hickmott	1923-1924	34	35	9	272	31*	10.46	2042	82	24.90	5/20
W. Hickton	1867-1871	24	42	9	373	55	11.30	2024	144	14.05	10/46
K. Higgs	1958-1969	306	374	131	2655	60	10.92	23661	1033	22.90	7/19
E.F.W. Highton	1951	1	1	0	6	6	6.00	49	1	49.00	1/49
P. Higson	1929-1931	3	3	2	22	13*	22.00				
T.A. Higson	1905-1923	5	7	1	123	42	20.50	58	1	58.00	1/18
T.A. Higson Jnr	1936-1946	20	20	1	153	32*	8.05	302	6	50.33	1/14
L.D. Hildyard	1884-1885	8	13	1	174	39	14.50				
R.W.D. Hill	1871	1	2	0	8	5	4.00				
J.R. Hillkirk	1871-1877	30	46	4	596	56*	14.19				
C. Hilton	1957-1963	91	110	35	537	36	7.16	7039	263	26.76	6/38
J. Hilton	1952-1953	8	7	0	99	33	14.14	152	2	76.00	2/27
M.J. Hilton	1946-1961	241	294	35	3140	100*	12.12	17419	926	18.81	8/19
S.F. Hird	1939	1	–	–	–	–	–				
G. Hodgson	1928-1933	56	52	17	244	20	6.97	4107	148	27.75	6/77
G. Hodgson	1965	1	1	0	1	1	1.00				
W. Hogg	1976-1980	44	40	12	120	19	4.28	2960	122	24.26	7/84
C. Holden	1890	3	5	1	43	27*	10.75	11	0	–	–
M.A. Holding	1981	7	8	2	66	32	11.00	715	40	17.87	6/74
G. Holgate	1866-1867	8	15	1	281	65	20.07				
J. Holland	1900-1902	12	21	4	324	63	19.05				
F.H. Hollins	1902-1904	12	18	0	290	114	16.11				
J.C.H.L. Hollins	1914-1919	20	30	0	454	65	15.13	99	1	99.00	1/45
E. Holroyd	1878	1	2	0	6	4	3.00				
J. Holroyd	1927-1933	11	9	5	33	18*	8.25	652	23	28.34	5/47
J.L. Hopwood	1923-1939	397	571	54	15519	220	30.01	14905	672	22.18	9/33
A.H. Hornby	1899-1914	283	426	40	9441	129	24.45	168	1	168.00	1/21
A.N. Hornby	1867-1899	292	467	28	10649	188	24.25	94	3	31.33	1/2
C.L. Hornby	1877	1	2	0	4	4	2.00	3	1	3.00	1/3

NAME	PLAYED	Mt	Inns	N.O.	Runs	H.S.	Ave	Runs	Wkts	Ave	Best
E.C. Hornby	1885-1887	9	13	1	229	82	19.08	98	3	32.66	1/15
L. Horridge	1927-1929	3	3	1	33	11*	16.50	79	3	26.33	2/46
R. Horrocks	1880-1882	6	10	0	116	61	11.60			–	–
W.J. Horrocks	1931-1933	15	19	3	371	100*	23.18	44	0	–	–
W.H. Houldsworth	1893-1894	10	16	1	156	21	10.40			–	–
G. Houlton	1961-1963	20	33	2	688	86	22.19	6	0	–	–
B.J. Howard	1947-1951	32	45	3	996	109	23.71			–	–
K. Howard	1960-1966	61	82	35	395	23	8.40	3175	104	30.52	7/53
N.D. Howard	1946-1953	170	234	29	5526	145	26.95	23	0	–	–
R. Howard	1922-1933	8	9	2	166	88*	23.71	18	0	–	–
R. Howe	1876-1877	3	6	0	24	13	4.00			–	–
T.R. Hubback	1892	4	6	1	63	33	12.60			–	–
W. Huddleston	1899-1914	183	258	32	2765	88	12.23	12007	684	17.55	9/36
B. Hudson	1886-1888	5	6	0	207	98	34.50	59	3	19.66	2/14
G.N. Hudson	1936	2	2	1	1	1	1.00	82	0	–	–
D.P. Hughes	1967-1989	410	541	97	9778	153	22.10	17808	608	29.28	7/24
C.A.G. Hulton	1869-1882	8	12	3	80	19	8.88			–	–
H.A.H. Hulton	1868	2	4	1	13	6	4.33			–	–
J. l'Anson	1896-1908	57	76	9	986	110*	14.71	3072	148	20.75	7/31
R. Iddison	1865-1870	16	31	5	621	106	23.88	875	56	15.62	6/29
W.H. Iddison	1867-1868	4	8	0	46	19	5.75	95	1	95.00	1/33
J. Iddon	1924-1945	483	683	90	21975	222	37.05	14214	533	26.66	9/42
J.T. Ikin	1939-1957	288	431	51	14327	192	37.70	8005	278	28.79	6/21
C.W. Ingleby	1899	1	2	1	40	29	40.00	17	0	–	–
F. Isherwood	1881	1	1	0	0	0	0.00			–	–
E. Jackson	1871-1885	15	23	4	105	11	5.52			–	–
J. Jackson	1867	1	2	0	6	3	3.00			–	–
T. Jacques	1937	2	2	0	4	2	2.00	70	1	70.00	1/45
S.T. Jefferies	1983-1985	32	47	7	1167	93	29.17	2568	87	29.51	8/46
W.S. Jervis	1874	1	2	0	6	6	3.00	4	0	–	–
T.E. Jesty	1988-1989	38	65	10	1747	93*	31.76	99	0	–	–
H.C.R. John	1881	1	1	1	15	15*	–	13	0	–	–
W.T. Jolley	1947	2	2	1	21	13	21.00	132	5	26.40	4/31
C.L. Jones	1876-1888	5	10	1	52	20*	5.77	6	1	6.00	1/6

NAME	PLAYED	Mt	Inns	N.O.	Runs	H.S.	Ave	Runs	Wkts	Ave	Best
J.L. Jones	1910	4	5	4	10	7*	10.00				
J. Jordan	1955-1957	62	75	7	754	39	11.08				
G.E. Jowett	1885-1889	19	32	2	507	58	16.90	55	0	–	–
J.L. Kaye	1867	1	2	0	21	20	10.50	16	0	–	–
E.A. Kelly	1957	4	6	2	38	16*	9.50	284	4	62.00	3/77
J.M. Kelly	1947-1949	6	11	3	150	58	18.75	14	0	–	–
A.T. Kemble	1885-1894	76	112	13	1050	50	10.60				
G. Kemp	1885-1892	18	33	2	355	109	11.45				
A. Kennedy	1970-1982	149	241	20	6232	180	28.19	398	10	39.80	3/58
R.W. Kenfield	1888	2	4	0	39	18	9.75	94	2	47.00	2/52
M.N. Kenyon	1919-1925	91	127	30	1435	61*	14.79				
A. Kermode	1902-1908	76	102	22	631	64*	7.88	7260	321	22.61	7/44
J.E. Kershaw	1877-1885	33	54	3	575	66	11.27				
J.H. Kevan	1875	2	4	0	12	12	3.00				
E. Kewley	1875	1	2	0	3	3	1.50				
B.P. King	1946-1947	37	56	3	1505	145	28.39				
A. Knowles	1888	1	2	0	6	6	3.00				
G.K. Knox	1964-1967	52	92	3	1698	108	19.07	161	2	80.50	1/10
B.E. Krikken	1966-1967	2	2	0	4	4	2.00				
O.P. Lancashire	1878-1888	97	158	10	1911	76*	12.91				
T. Lancaster	1894-1899	27	40	11	554	66	19.10	1456	66	22.06	7/25
C.W. Landon	1874-1875	6	10	0	121	47	12.10	69	2	34.50	1/10
J.R. Latchford	1930-1932	7	10	0	154	63	15.40	181	4	45.25	1/6
G.F. Lawson	1979	1	2	0	19	17	9.50	88	5	17.60	4/81
A.E. Lawton	1912-1914	12	20	1	269	52	14.15	259	14	18.50	4/33
W. Lawton	1948	2	2	0	3	3	1.50	64	1	64.00	1/0
E.L.C. Leach	1923-1924	12	15	1	161	79	10.73				
H. Leach	1881	1	1	0	33	33	33.00				
J. Leach	1866-1877	5	9	0	103	34	11.44				
R. Leach	1868-1876	3	5	0	35	14	7.00				
R.C. Leach	1885	1	2	0	49	39	24.50				
W.E. Leach	1885	5	9	1	208	56	26.00				
P.G. Lee	1972-1982	152	119	54	500	25	7.69	11817	496	23.82	8/34
C.P. Leese	1911	1	2	0	16	10	8.00				

NAME	PLAYED	Mt	Inns	N.O.	Runs	H.S.	Ave	Runs	Wkts	Ave	Best
E. Leese	1880-1884	8	11	1	146	62	14.60	94	5	18.80	3/49
J.F. Leese	1865-1881	24	42	1	556	44	13.56				
J. Leigh	1887	1	2	0	2	1	1.00				
E.C. Leventon	1867	1	2	0	6	6	3.00	24	2	12.00	2/24
P. Lever	1960-1976	268	285	59	3073	83	13.59	17647	716	24.64	7/70
W.H.L. Lister	1933-1939	158	210	17	3561	104*	18.45	74	1	74.00	1/10
G.H. Littlewood	1902-1904	14	19	5	129	42	9.21	1123	58	19.36	7/49
G.W. Littlewood	1885	3	6	1	28	8*	5.60				
C.H. Lloyd	1968-1986	219	326	42	12764	217*	44.94	1809	55	32.89	4/48
D. Lloyd	1965-1983	378	605	70	17877	195	33.41	7007	234	29.94	7/38
G.D. Lloyd	1988-1989	8	14	1	464	117	35.69	55	0	-	-
R.A. Lloyd	1921-1922	3	5	0	100	51	20.00				
J.G. Lomax	1949-1953	57	78	2	1137	78	14.96	2519	81	31.09	5/18
J. Lyon	1973-1979	84	89	18	1010	123	14.22				
E.A. McDonald	1924-1931	217	215	31	1868	100*	10.15	22079	1053	20.96	8/53
L.L. McFarlane	1982-1984	35	34	18	115	15*	7.18	2563	73	35.10	6/59
H. McIntyre	1884	1	1	1	1	1*	-				
W. McIntyre	1872-1880	72	112	20	758	66	8.23	5141	441	11.65	8/31
D.W. MacKinnon	1870-1871	3	5	0	65	24	13.00	72	5	14.40	3/13
A.C. MacLaren	1890-1914	307	510	37	15772	424	33.34	247	1	247.00	1/44
F.G. MacLaren	1903	1	2	0	19	19	9.50	7	0	-	-
G. MacLaren	1902	2	4	0	7	3	1.75	13	2	6.50	1/5
J.A. MacLaren	1891-1894	4	4	0	9	6	2.25				
K.G. MacLeod	1908-1913	75	124	9	2619	131	22.77	2019	81	24.92	6/29
K.W. MacLeod	1987	6	6	0	92	31	15.33	409	17	24.05	5/8
R. McNairy	1925	1	1	1	4	4*	-	73	1	73.00	1/23
H. Makepeace	1906-1930	487	757	64	25207	203	36.37	1971	42	46.92	4/33
D.J. Makinson	1984-1988	35	39	17	486	58*	22.09	2486	70	35.51	5/60
J. Makison	1865-1873	5	9	0	131	45	14.55	73	4	18.25	4/49
M.F. Malone	1979-1980	19	16	3	181	38	13.92	1421	64	22.20	7/88
W.J. Marchbank	1869-1870	4	7	1	20	15	3.33				
P.T. Marner	1952-1964	236	391	38	10312	142*	29.21	4116	109	37.76	5/46
C.S. Marriott	1919-1921	12	16	2	78	16	5.57	967	34	28.44	8/98
P.J. Martin	1989	2	2	0	20	16	10.00	133	1	133.00	1/46

NAME	PLAYED	Mt	Inns	N.O.	Runs	H.S.	Ave	Runs	Wkts	Ave	Best
W.M. Massey	1883	1	2	0	6	5	3.00				
C.D. Mathews	1988	3	3	0	38	31	12.66	225	7	32.14	4/47
D.M. Mathews	1936-1938	7	8	0	130	46	16.25				–
J. Mayall	1885	1	1	0	0	0	0.00				
C. Maynard	1982-1986	91	120	21	1934	132*	19.53	8	0	–	–
F. Melhuish	1877	3	6	0	32	13	5.33				
J. Melling	1874-1876	3	5	0	39	20	7.80	16	0	–	–
H. Mellor	1874-1875	2	4	0	28	17	7.00				
G.D. Mendis	1986-1989	93	160	16	5626	203*	39.06	82	0	–	–
F.N. Miller	1904	1	2	0	37	37	18.50				
H. Miller	1880-1881	5	8	0	84	27	10.50	202	10	20.20	5/46
J. Mills	1889	1	1	0	1	1	1.00				
W.G. Mills	1871-1877	6	11	1	57	26	5.70	97	6	16.16	3/52
R.O. Milne	1882	1	1	1	7	7*	–				
A.W. Mold	1889-1901	260	347	114	1675	57	7.15	23384	1543	15.15	9/29
F.W. Moore	1954-1958	24	26	7	151	18	7.94	1516	54	28.07	6/45
E. Moorhouse	1873-1875	5	9	3	75	34	12.50				
L.H. Moorsom	1865	1	2	0	12	7	6.00				
R.G. Mortimer	1891	1	1	1	22	22*	–				
F.H. Mugliston	1906-1908	7	11	0	117	35	10.63				
A.J. Murphy	1985-1988	13	13	6	18	5	2.57	993	24	41.37	4/115
F.W. Musson	1914-1921	16	27	1	510	75	19.61				
Revd J.R. Napier	1888	2	3	1	48	37	24.00	102	11	9.27	4/0
G. Nash	1879-1885	54	80	24	295	30	5.26	2503	202	12.39	8/14
S.M. Nasir Zaidi	1983-1984	19	22	9	313	51	24.07	827	19	43.52	3/27
J. Nelson	1913	1	2	0	7	5	3.50				
D.V. Norbury	1919-1922	14	23	0	594	100	25.82	448	23	19.47	4/28
A.E. Nutter	1935-1945	70	90	16	2200	109*	29.72	4453	152	29.29	6/66
E. Nutter	1885	1	1	0	18	18	18.00				
W. Oakley	1893-1894	20	31	8	131	24	5.69	638	37	17.24	6/50
N. Oldfield	1935-1939	151	220	24	7002	147*	35.72	85	2	42.50	1/0
A. Ollivant	1873-1874	2	3	1	36	24*	18.00				
W.E. Openshaw	1879-1882	4	5	0	29	16	5.80				
J.A. Ormrod	1984-1985	27	47	3	1253	139*	28.47				

NAME	PLAYED	Mt	Inns	N.O.	Runs	H.S.	Ave	Runs	Wkts	Ave	Best
S.J. O'Shaughnessy	1980-1987	100	161	27	3567	159*	26.61	3947	110	35.88	4/66
S. Palmer	1879-1880	6	9	0	28	8	3.11	11	0	–	–
W. Parker	1904	2	3	0	66	40	22.00	175	4	43.75	2/47
C.H. Parkin	1914-1926	157	189	27	1959	57	12.09	14526	901	16.12	9/32
R.H. Parkin	1931-1939	20	18	4	231	60	16.50	845	23	36.73	3/52
H.B. Parkinson	1922-1923	15	18	5	34	8	2.61				
L.W. Parkinson	1932-1936	88	112	13	2132	93	21.53	5654	192	29.44	6/112
F.D. Parr	1951-1954	48	51	10	493	42	12.02				
H.B. Parr	1872-1876	10	14	0	167	61	11.92				
B.P. Patterson	1984-1989	60	57	23	182	29	5.35	4481	173	25.90	7/49
W.S. Patterson	1874-1882	7	11	1	132	50	13.20	241	24	10.04	7/30
A.G. Paul	1889-1900	95	150	15	2958	177	21.91	146	2	73.00	1/7
J. Payne	1898	1	2	0	0	0	0.00	48	0	–	–
J.H. Payne	1883	9	15	3	158	33	13.16				
E. Paynter	1926-1945	293	445	47	16555	322	41.59	1250	24	52.08	3/13
H. Pennington	1900	4	5	1	41	29*	10.25				
W. Perry	1865	1	2	0	16	16	8.00	29	0	–	–
A.W. Pewtress	1919-1925	50	73	5	1483	89	21.80	10	1	10.00	1/10
W. Phillips	1904-1908	10	18	3	109	18	7.26				
W.E. Phillipson	1933-1948	158	202	46	4050	113	25.96	13508	545	24.78	8/100
C.C. Pilkington	1895	2	4	0	38	18	9.50	100	3	33.33	3/70
H. Pilling	1962-1980	323	525	65	14841	149*	32.26	195	1	195.00	1/42
R. Pilling	1877-1889	177	258	86	1854	78	10.77				
W. Pilling	1891	1	1	1	9	9*	–				
W. Place	1937-1955	298	441	43	14605	266*	36.69	42	1	42.00	1/2
L.O.S. Poidevin	1904-1908	105	163	14	4460	168*	29.93	1786	46	38.82	8/66
R. Pollard	1933-1950	266	298	52	3273	63	13.30	22492	1015	22.15	8/33
E.H. Porter	1874-1882	17	29	1	301	61	10.75	9	0	–	–
G. Potter	1902	10	17	1	449	86	28.06				
T.O. Potter	1866	1	2	0	39	39	19.50				
W.H. Potter	1870	1	2	0	23	12	11.50				
S. Preston	1928-1930	5	4	2	46	33	23.00	212	6	35.33	2/42
A. Price	1885	1	2	0	8	8	4.00				
E. Price	1946-1947	35	36	14	305	54	13.86	2373	115	20.63	6/34

351

NAME	PLAYED	Mt	Inns	N.O.	Runs	H.S.	Ave	Runs	Wkts	Ave	Best
G. Pullar	1954-1968	312	524	45	16853	167*	35.18	305	8	38.12	3/91
G. Radcliffe	1903-1906	7	11	0	171	60	15.54				
L. Radcliffe	1897-1905	50	67	22	275	25	6.11				
N.V. Radford	1980-1984	24	33	8	549	76*	21.96	1805	33	54.69	5/95
R.B. Rae	1945	1	1	0	74	74	74.00	29	0	–	–
S. Ramadhin	1964-1965	33	40	19	151	13	7.19	2267	97	23.37	8/121
H.J. Ramsbottom	1868	1	2	0	1	1	0.50	11	0	–	–
E. Ratcliffe	1884	1	2	0	9	7	4.50	8	0	–	–
R.M. Ratcliffe	1972-1980	82	84	22	1022	101*	16.48	5411	205	26.39	7/58
E.B. Rawlinson	1867	1	2	1	15	14	15.00				
W. Rawlinson	1870-1871	3	6	0	24	10	4.00				
G.S. Rawstorne	1919	1	1	0	2	2	2.00				
B.W. Reidy	1973-1982	107	162	26	3641	131*	26.77	2508	60	41.80	5/61
F.R. Reynolds	1865-1874	38	65	20	293	34*	6.51	1823	94	19.39	6/92
A. Rhodes	1922-1924	17	25	3	382	70	17.36	475	15	31.66	2/24
C.A. Rhodes	1937-1938	8	10	4	11	6	1.83	619	22	28.13	4/37
W. Richmond	1868	1	2	0	1	1	0.50				
J. Ricketts	1867-1877	34	66	4	1120	195*	18.06	250	12	20.83	4/40
W. Rickman	1876	1	1	0	5	5	5.00				
D.M. Ritchie	1924	1	1	0	3	3	3.00				
J. Roberts	1957	2	4	2	5	5	2.50	90	0	–	
R. Roberts	1872-1874	10	16	0	100	20	6.25				
W.B. Roberts	1939-1949	114	113	39	810	51	10.94	7971	382	20.86	8/50
P.A. Robinson	1979	1	1	0	15	15	15.00	58	2	29.00	2/57
W. Robinson	1880-1888	115	186	10	3597	154	20.43	61	0	–	–
G.H. Rogerson	1923	12	20	1	340	47*	17.89				
E. Roper	1876-1886	28	47	2	586	65	13.02				
D. Rowland	1868	1	2	0	0	0	0.00				
L.S. Rowlands	1903-1910	6	10	4	27	9	4.50	23	0	–	–
A.B. Rowley	1865-1871	12	21	3	282	63*	15.66	322	16	20.12	4/29
E.B. Rowley	1865-1880	81	131	8	1626	78	13.21	603	24	25.12	5/71
E.B. Rowley Jnr	1893-1898	16	25	4	553	65	26.33	17	0	–	–
Revd V.P.F.A. Royle	1873-1891	74	120	8	1754	81	15.66	114	2	57.00	1/22
F. Rushton	1928-1929	6	5	0	59	28	11.80	362	10	36.20	4/30

NAME	PLAYED	Mt	Inns	N.O.	Runs	H.S.	Ave	Runs	Wkts	Ave	Best
T.H. Rushton	1870	1	1	0	7	7	7.00	11	0	–	–
F.J. Rutter	1868	2	4	1	15	8*	5.00		0	–	–
L. Sanderson	1884	1	1	0	0	0	0.00				
R.W.B. Sanderson	1870	1	2	0	7	6	3.50				
J.S. Savage	1967-1969	58	64	33	197	19	6.35	3051	114	26.76	5/1
C.M. Sawyer	1884	2	2	1	21	11*	21.00	65	0	–	–
J. Schofield	1876	4	6	2	27	11	6.75				
F.B. Scholfield	1911	1	2	1	17	17	17.00	2	0	–	–
S.S. Schultz	1877-1882	9	17	3	215	42*	15.35	23	0	–	–
C.J. Scott	1977-1982	46	51	13	262	27*	6.89				
W.A. Scott	1874	1	2	1	14	9	14.00				
A. Seymour	1869	1	2	0	45	25	22.50				
J. Sharp	1899-1925	518	776	70	22015	211	31.18	11821	434	27.23	9/77
G.O. Shelmerdine	1919-1925	31	45	4	980	105	23.90	97	0	–	–
C. Shore	1886	1	2	0	3	3	1.50	11	0	–	–
K. Shuttleworth	1964-1975	177	179	62	1929	71	16.48	11097	484	22.92	7/41
F.M. Sibbles	1925-1937	308	311	79	3436	71*	14.81	20538	932	22.03	8/24
W. Silcock	1899-1902	6	7	1	82	43	13.66	367	5	73.40	2/62
J. Simmons	1968-1989	429	530	142	8773	112	22.61	26489	985	26.89	7/64
A.R. Sladen	1903-1904	2	3	0	8	5	2.66	175	6	29.16	3/77
R. Slater	1865	1	2	0	0	0	0.00	3	0	–	–
J. Smalley	1869	2	4	0	24	17	6.00				
A. Smith	1867-1871	4	8	3	56	30	11.20				
A.P. Smith	1886-1894	48	76	5	1440	124	20.28	517	29	17.82	5/49
C. Smith	1893-1902	167	234	50	2248	81	12.21	18	1	18.00	1/18
C.S. Smith	1951-1957	45	55	4	768	67	15.05	2815	101	21.63	5/39
D.J. Smith	1951-1952	3	4	0	26	14	6.50	205	4	51.25	1/19
J. Smith	1865-1869	6	12	1	153	40*	13.90	290	12	24.16	4/46
R. Smith	1893	1	1	0	6	6	6.00	11	0	–	–
S. Smith	1952-1956	38	54	4	865	72*	17.30				
T. Smith	1867	2	3	0	18	12	6.00	36	1	36.00	1/8
K.L. Snellgrove	1965-1974	105	170	16	3906	138	25.36	27	3	9.00	2/23
G.J. Speak	1981-1982	5	6	4	27	15*	13.50	230	1	230.00	1/78
N.J. Speak	1987-1989	7	14	1	235	64	18.07				

NAME	PLAYED	Mt	Inns	N.O.	Runs	H.S.	Ave	Runs	Wkts	Ave	Best
H. Spencer	1914	2	3	1	5	4	2.50	139	3	46.33	1/0
A.F. Spooner	1906-1909	18	33	1	500	83	15.62				
R.H. Spooner	1899-1921	170	280	14	9889	247	37.17	554	5	110.80	1/5
K.B. Standring	1955-1959	8	14	2	110	41	9.16	375	11	34.09	3/44
H.D. Stanning	1906-1908	33	54	1	898	86	16.94	3	0	-	-
J. Stanning	1900-1903	4	7	0	97	33	13.85				
J. Stanworth	1983-1989	35	38	11	236	50*	8.74				
J.B. Statham	1950-1968	430	501	98	4237	62	10.51	27470	1816	15.12	8/34
M.W. Staziker	1970	2	2	2	1	1*	-	269	1	269.00	1/114
A.G. Steel	1877-1893	47	72	5	1960	105	29.25	3134	238	13.16	9/63
D.Q. Steel	1876-1887	22	35	1	560	82	16.47				
E.E. Steel	1884-1903	40	58	4	861	69*	15.94	2598	122	21.29	6/69
H.B. Steel	1883-1896	22	37	3	765	100	22.50				
F. Stephenson	1875-1877	2	4	1	0	0*	0.00	17	1	17.00	1/17
W.B. Stoddart	1898-1899	15	25	4	294	43*	14.00	899	37	24.29	6/121
D.H. Stone	1949-1950	6	8	2	86	46	14.33	472	9	52.44	4/30
E. Storer	1865-1868	6	11	5	46	23	7.66	245	15	16.33	5/12
F.H. Sugg	1887-1889	235	387	24	9620	220	26.50	259	10	25.90	2/12
J. Sullivan	1963-1976	154	241	32	4286	81*	20.50	2216	76	29.15	4/19
R.J. Sutcliffe	1978	1	2	2	10	10*	-	37	1	37.00	1/37
S.H. Swire	1865-1868	5	9	1	93	18*	11.62	37	0	-	-
R. Tattersall	1948-1960	277	312	128	1786	58	9.70	20316	1168	17.39	9/40
R.H. Tattersall	1971	2	-	-	-	-	-	219	1	219.00	1/44
F. Taylor	1874-1888	52	85	4	1451	96	17.91	73	3	24.33	1/4
F. Taylor	1920-1922	15	18	6	188	29*	15.66	1026	40	25.65	6/65
J. Taylor	1871-1873	3	6	0	52	33	8.66	13	0	-	-
M.L. Taylor	1924-1931	95	112	15	2216	107*	22.84	26	0	-	-
R.J. Taylor	1898	2	3	0	6	6	2.00	96	2	48.00	1/25
T.J. Taylor	1981-1982	4	4	1	2	2	0.66	238	5	47.60	2/63
K. Tebay	1961-1963	15	27	2	509	106	20.36				
A. Teggin	1886	6	8	0	31	9	3.87	176	16	11.00	6/53
H.N. Tennent	1865-1870	2	3	0	45	21	15.00				
W.M. Tennent	1867	1	2	0	3	3	1.50				
A. Thomas	1966	1	2	0	4	4	2.00	7	0	-	-

NAME	PLAYED	Mt	Inns	N.O.	Runs	H.S.	Ave	Runs	Wkts	Ave	Best
R. Thomas	1894-1902	20	22	5	60	17	3.52	28	1	28.00	1/11
H. Thornber	1874	1	2	0	0	0	0.00	7	0	–	–
S.M. Tindall	1894-1898	42	62	1	1039	86	17.03				
A. Tinsley	1890-1895	58	91	10	1348	65	16.64	94	3	31.33	2/11
H.J. Tinsley	1894-1896	4	6	0	57	18	9.50	13	0	–	–
E. Tranter	1875-1876	3	5	0	9	5	1.80				
G.E. Trim	1976-1980	15	25	0	399	91	15.96	332	6	55.33	3/33
E. Tyldesley	1909-1936	573	850	93	34222	256*	45.20	101	3	33.66	2/37
H. Tyldesley	1914-1922	4	7	3	63	33*	15.75				
J.D. Tyldesley	1910-1922	116	169	16	2885	112*	18.85	8092	309	26.18	7/34
J.T. Tyldesley	1895-1923	507	824	52	31949	295*	41.38	170	2	85.00	1/4
R.K. Tyldesley	1919-1931	374	435	47	6126	105	15.78	24139	1449	16.65	8/15
W.K. Tyldesley	1908-1914	87	137	7	2979	152	22.91	383	8	47.87	2/0
J. Unsworth	1871	2	3	0	25	23	8.33	75	3	25.00	3/52
D.S. Van der Knapp	1967	1	–	–	–	–	–	69	2	34.50	2/24
D.W. Varey	1984-1987	44	70	7	1752	112	27.80	6	0	–	–
E. Wadsworth	1871-1879	7	13	0	69	30	5.30	13	0	–	–
R. Walker	1874-1875	2	4	1	27	19	9.00				
H. Wall	1877	3	4	0	24	15	6.00				
T. Wall	1868	2	4	0	48	37	12.00				
W. Wall	1877	1	2	1	17	17*	17.00	17	0	–	–
M.A. Wallwork	1982	1	–	–	–	–	–				
G. Walsh	1874-1877	2	3	0	16	15	5.33				
M. Walton	1867	1	2	0	6	6	3.00				
L. Warburton	1929-1938	6	5	1	159	74*	39.75	217	5	43.40	3/47
A. Ward	1889-1904	330	544	47	15392	185	30.96	2380	65	36.61	6/29
F. Ward	1884-1896	47	74	6	986	145	14.50	538	27	19.92	4/14
C. Wardle	1867-1872	3	5	2	25	7*	8.33	17	0	–	–
C. Washbrook	1933-1959	500	756	95	27863	251*	42.15	268	4	67.00	1/4
Wasim Akram	1988-1989	22	37	4	832	116*	25.21	1715	84	20.41	7/53
M. Watkinson	1982-1989	139	209	29	4198	106	23.32	9530	294	32.41	7/25
A. Watson	1871-1893	283	423	88	4187	74	12.49	17516	1308	13.39	9/118
F. Watson	1920-1937	456	664	48	22833	300*	37.06	12811	402	31.86	5/31
R.G. Watson	1982-1985	2	3	0	33	18	11.00				

NAME	PLAYED	Mt	Inns	N.O.	Runs	H.S.	Ave	Runs	Wkts	Ave	Best
S. Webb	1899-1903	73	94	27	513	38*	7.65	5226	265	19.72	8/36
F. Webster	1925-1927	2	3	1	12	10	6.00	122	7	17.42	3/34
G.E. Wharmby	1894	6	8	2	29	11	4.83	209	8	26.12	3/35
A. Wharton	1946-1960	392	589	55	17921	199	33.55	7094	225	31.52	7/33
T. Whatmough	1871	2	4	2	42	28*	21.00	79	3	26.33	2/52
J.W. Whewell	1921-1927	12	13	5	19	12	2.37				
R. Whitehead	1908-1914	107	158	36	2571	131*	21.07	7260	300	24.20	8/77
T. Whitehead	1884	1	1	0	8	8	8.00	20	0	–	–
P. Whiteley	1957-1958	5	8	2	86	32	14.33	266	9	29.55	3/70
J.P. Whiteside	1888-1890	6	8	0	25	12	3.12				
D. Whittaker	1884-1888	9	14	1	128	26	9.84	46	1	46.00	1/26
E. Whittaker	1865-1868	11	21	2	232	39	12.21	125	1	125.00	1/26
L.L. Wilkinson	1937-1947	63	61	24	296	48	8.00	6091	232	26.25	8/53
A. Wilson	1948-1962	171	186	59	760	37*	5.98				
G.A. Winder	1869	2	4	0	23	9	5.75				
B. Wood	1966-1979	260	424	56	12969	198	35.24	6910	251	27.52	7/52
J. Wood	1956	1	–	–	–	–	–	103	4	25.75	3/56
R. Wood	1880-1884	6	9	2	167	52	23.85	72	4	18.00	1/23
A. Woolley	1926	7	9	0	61	24	6.77	351	11	31.90	4/56
D.R. Worsley	1960-1967	62	108	9	2508	120	25.33	904	27	33.48	4/21
W. Worsley	1903-1913	136	167	63	628	37*	6.03				
E.L. Wright	1905-1910	4	8	0	53	17	6.62				
Revd F.W. Wright	1869-1875	15	22	2	416	120*	20.80	156	3	51.66	2/44
C. Yates	1882	1	2	0	28	24	14.00				
G. Yates	1885-1894	92	135	15	1632	74	13.60	934	30	31.13	4/112

County Champions: 1881, 1897, 1904, 1926, 1927, 1928, 1930, 1934

Joint Champions: 1879, 1882, 1889, 1950

NatWest Trophy/Gillette Cup Winners: 1970, 1971, 1972, 1975

Benson and Hedges Cup Winners: 1984

Sunday League Champions: 1969, 1970, 1989

Refuge Cup Winners: 1988

Lancashire Grounds 1865-1989

CENTRE	GROUND	OCCASION AND OPPONENTS
Blackburn	Alexandra Meadows (East Lancashire CC's ground)	*First:* May 11, 12, 13, 1932 v Glamorgan *Last:* June 5, 6, 7 1935 v Glamorgan
Blackpool	Stanley Park (Formerly Whitegate Park)	*First:* July 30, 31 1906 v Leicestershire *Current Ground*
Lancaster	Lune Road	*Only Match:* July 30, 31, Aug 1 1914 v Warwickshire
Lytham	Church Road	*First:* Aug 14, 15, 16 1985 v Northamptonshire *Current Ground*
Liverpool	Wavertree Road, Edge Hill	*Only Match:* Aug 23, 24, 25 1866 v Surrey
Liverpool	Aigburth	*First:* June 13, 14 1881 v Cambridge University *Current Ground*
Manchester	Old Trafford	*First:* July 20, 21, 22 1865 v Middlesex *Current Ground*
Nelson	Seedhill	*First:* Aug 15, 16 17 1925 v Derbyshire *Last:* July 13, 14, 15 1938 v Somerset
Preston	West Cliff	*First:* July 1, 2, 3 1936 v Gloucestershire *Last:* June 18, 19, 20 1952 v Glamorgan
Castleton	Sparthbottoms Road	*Only Match:* June 16, 17 1876 v Kent
Southport	Trafalgar Road	*First:* Aug 22, 24, 25 1959 v Worcestershire *Current Ground*
Whalley	Station Road	*Only Match:* June 20, 21, 22 1867 v Yorkshire

Results of all First-Class Lancashire Matches 1865-1989

County Matches	PLAYED	WON	LOST	DRAWN	TIE	ABND
v Derbyshire	198	90	26	82	–	2
v Essex	130	42	25	62	1	1
v Glamorgan	108	35	17	56	–	1
v Gloucestershire	166	78	23	65	–	1
v Hampshire	116	52	17	46	1	2
v Kent	192	80	46	66	–	3
v Leicestershire	138	69	15	54	–	2
v Middlesex	170	49	51	70	–	2
v Northamptonshire	108	46	14	48	–	1
v Nottinghamshire	204	61	46	97	–	–
v Somerset	125	70	20	35	–	2
v Surrey	186	50	55	80	1	4
v Sussex	173	68	38	67	–	3
v Warwickshire	164	57	30	77	–	2
v Worcestershire	134	55	24	55	–	–
v Yorkshire	227	47	69	111	–	1
	2539	949	516	1071	3	27

Other Matches						
v MCC	31	11	16	4	–	–
v Cambridge University	41	12	7	22	–	–
v Oxford University	79	45	7	27	–	–
v Rest of England	6	0	4	2	–	–
v All England XI	4	0	2	2	–	–
v London County	1	0	0	1	–	–
v Scotland	5	2	0	3	–	–
v Wales	1	1	0	0	–	–
v Minor Counties	2	0	0	2	–	–
v Combined Services	2	2	0	0	–	–
v Sir Julien Cahn's XI	1	0	0	1	–	–
v Australians	42	4	17	21	–	–
v South Africans	17	5	3	9	–	–
v West Indians	15	1	4	10	–	–
v New Zealanders	12	3	2	7	–	–
v Indians	13	2	3	8	–	–
v Pakistanis	7	0	2	5	–	–
v Sri Lankans	1	0	0	1	–	–
v Australian Imperial Forces	1	0	1	0	–	–
v Philadelphians	2	1	1	0	–	–
v Jamaica	3	0	1	?	–	–
v Zimbabwe	1	0	1	0	–	–
Grand total	2826	1038	587	1198	3	27

Lancashire in the County Championship

YEAR	POSITION	PLAYED	WON	LOST	DRAWN	TIE	ABND
1873	–	7	4	3	–	–	–
1874	–	6	1	3	2	–	–
1875	–	6	4	1	1	–	–
1876	–	10	5	5	–	–	–
1877	–	10	6	4	–	–	–
1878	–	10	5	3	2	–	–
1879	1st*	10	5	1	4	–	–
1880	4th	12	6	3	3	–	–
1881	1st	13	10	–	3	–	–
1882	1st*	14	10	1	3	–	–
1883	5th	12	6	5	1	–	–
1884	3rd	10	5	4	1	–	–
1885	4th	11	6	3	2	–	–
1886	4th	14	5	5	4	–	–
1887	2nd	14	10	3	1	–	–
1888	5th	14	4	5	5	–	–
1889	1st*	14	10	3	1	–	–
1890	2nd	14	7	3	4	–	–
1891	2nd	15	8	4	3	–	1
1892	4th	16	7	5	4	–	–
1893	2nd	16	9	5	2	–	–
1894	4th	16	7	7	1	1	–
1895	2nd	21	14	4	3	–	1
1896	2nd	22	11	4	7	–	–
1897	1st	26	16	3	7	–	–
1898	6th	26	9	6	11	–	–
1899	4th	25	12	6	7	–	1
1900	2nd	28	15	2	11	–	–
1901	3rd	28	11	5	12	–	–
1902	5th	23	7	5	11	–	1
1903	4th	26	10	5	11	–	–
1904	1st	26	16	–	10	–	–
1905	2nd	25	12	3	10	–	1
1906	4th	26	15	6	5	–	–
1907	6th	26	11	7	8	–	–
1908	7th	25	10	9	6	–	1
1909	2nd	24	14	4	6	–	–
1910	4th	30	14	5	11	–	–
1911	4th	30	15	7	8	–	–
1912	4th	20	8	2	10	–	2
1913	8th	26	7	11	8	–	–
1914	11th	26	6	9	11	–	–

* Joint

YEAR	POSITION	PLAYED	WON	LOST	DRAWN	TIE	ABND
1919	5th	24	8	4	12	–	–
1920	2nd	28	19	5	4	–	–
1921	5th	28	15	4	9	–	–
1922	5th	30	15	7	8	–	–
1923	3rd	30	15	2	13	–	–
1924	4th	30	11	2	17	–	–
1925	3rd	32	19	4	9	–	–
1926	1st	32	17	2	13	–	–
1927	1st	31	10	1	20	–	1
1928	1st	30	15	–	15	–	–
1929	2nd	28	12	3	13	–	–
1930	1st	28	10	–	18	–	–
1931	6th	26	7	4	15	–	2
1932	6th	27	8	6	13	–	1
1933	5th	28	9	1	18	–	–
1934	1st	30	13	3	14	–	–
1935	4th	28	12	6	10	–	–
1936	11th	30	7	6	17	–	–
1937	9th	32	9	5	18	–	–
1938	4th	32	14	6	12	–	–
1939	6th	30	10	6	14	–	2
1946	3rd	26	15	4	7	–	–
1947	3rd	26	13	1	11	1	–
1948	5th	26	8	2	16	–	–
1949	11th	26	6	7	13	–	–
1950	1st*	28	16	2	10	–	–
1951	3rd	28	8	2	18	–	–
1952	3rd	28	12	3	12	1	–
1953	3rd	28	10	4	14	–	–
1954	10th	25	6	3	16	–	3
1955	9th	28	10	9	9	–	–
1956	2nd	28	12	2	14	–	–
1957	6th	28	10	8	10	–	–
1958	7th	26	9	7	10	–	2
1959	5th	28	12	7	9	–	–
1960	2nd	32	13	8	11	–	–
1961	13th	32	9	7	16	–	–
1962	16th	32	2	16	14	–	–
1963	15th	28	4	10	14	–	–
1964	14th	28	4	10	14	–	–
1965	13th	28	5	13	10	–	–
1966	12th	28	6	11	11	–	–
1967	11th	26	4	3	19	–	2

YEAR	POSITION	PLAYED	WON	LOST	DRAWN	TIE	ABND
1968	6th	28	8	6	14	–	–
1969	15th	24	2	1	21	–	–
1970	3rd	24	6	2	16	–	–
1971	3rd	24	9	4	11	–	–
1972	15th	19	2	3	14	–	1
1973	12th	20	4	6	10	–	–
1974	8th	20	5	–	15	–	–
1975	4th	20	9	3	8	–	–
1976	16th	20	3	7	10	–	–
1977	16th	21	2	4	15	–	1
1978	12th	21	4	8	9	–	1
1979	13th	22	4	4	14	–	–
1980	15th	20	4	3	13	–	2
1981	16th	22	4	7	11	–	–
1982	12th	22	4	3	15	–	–
1983	12th	24	3	4	17	–	–
1984	16th	24	1	9	14	–	–
1985	14th	24	3	7	14	–	–
1986	15th	24	4	5	14	–	1
1987	2nd	24	10	4	10	–	–
1988	9th	22	6	7	9	–	–
1989	4th	22	8	5	9	–	–

Lancashire Captains

1866-79	E.B. Rowley
1880-91	A.N. Hornby
1892-93	A.N. Hornby and
	S.M. Crosfield
1894-96	A.C. MacLaren
1897-98	A.N. Hornby
1899	A.C. MacLaren and
	G.R. Bardswell
1900-07	A.C. MacLaren
1908-14	A.H. Hornby
1919-22	M.N. Kenyon
1923-25	J. Sharp
1926-28	L. Green
1929-35	P.T. Eckersley
1936-39	W.H.L. Lister
1946	J.A. Fallows
1947-48	K. Cranston
1949-53	N.D. Howard
1954-59	C. Washbrook
1960-61	R.W. Barber
1962	J.F. Blackledge
1963-64	K.J. Grieves
1965-67	J.B. Statham
1968-72	J.D. Bond
1973-77	D. Lloyd
1978-80	F.C. Hayes
1981-83	C.H. Lloyd
1984-85	J. Abrahams
1986	C.H. Lloyd
1987-90	D.P. Hughes

Lancashire Players in Test Cricket

NAME	PLAYED	Mts	Runs	H.S.	Ave	100's	Wkts	Ave
P.J.W. Allott	1981-1985	13	213	52*	14.20	–	26	41.69
M.A. Atherton	1989	2	73	47	18.25	–	–	–
R.W.Barber	1960-1968	28	1.495	185	35.59	1	42	43.00
R.G. Barlow	1881-1887	17	591	62	22.73	–	35	21.91
S.F. Barnes	1901-1914	27	242	38	8.06	–	189	16.43
R. Berry	1950	2	6	4*	3.00	–	9	25.33
W. Brearley	1905-1912	4	21	11*	7.00	–	17	21.11
J. Briggs	1884-1899	33	815	121	18.11	1	118	17.74
K. Cranston	1947-1948	8	209	45	14.92	–	18	25.61
W.R. Cuttell	1899	2	65	21	16.25	–	6	12.16
C.E.H. Croft (West Indies)	1977-1982	27	158	33	10.53	–	125	23.30
H. Dean	1912	3	10	8	5.00	–	11	13.90
P.A.J. DeFreitas	1986-1989	13	204	40	11.33	–	26	49.84
G. Duckworth	1924-1936	24	234	39*	14.62	–	(St. 15, Ct. 44, T. 59)	
F.M. Engineer (India)	1961-1975	46	2611	121	31.08	2	(St. 16, Ct. 66, T. 82)	
N.H. Fairbrother	1987-1988	4	5	3	1.25	–	–	–
W. Farrimond	1931-1935	4	116	35	16.57	–	(St. 2, Ct. 7, T. 9)	
G. Fowler	1982-1985	21	1307	201	35.32	3	0	–
T. Greenhough	1959-1960	4	4	2	1.33	–	16	22.31
C. Hallows	1921-1928	2	42	26	42.00	–	–	–
F.C. Hayes	1973-1976	9	244	106*	15.25	1	–	–
K. Higgs	1965-1968	15	185	63	11.56	–	71	20.74
M.J. Hilton	1950-1952	4	37	15	7.40	–	15	33.64
J.L. Hopwood	1934	2	12	8	6.00	–	0	–
A.N. Hornby	1879-1884	3	21	9	3.50	–	0	–
N.D. Howard	1951-1952	4	86	25	17.20	–	–	–
J. Iddon	1935	5	170	72	28.33	–	0	–
J.T. Ikin	1946-1955	18	606	60	20.89	–	3	118.00
P. Lever	1970-1975	17	350	88*	21.87	–	41	36.80
C.H. Lloyd (W. Indies)	1966-1985	110	7515	242*	46.67	19	10	62.20
D. Lloyd	1974-1975	9	552	214*	42.46	1	0	–
A.C. MacLaren	1894-1909	35	1931	140	33.87	5	–	–
H. Makepeace	1920-1921	4	279	117	34.87	1	–	–
A. Mold	1893	3	0	0*	0.00	–	7	33.42
N. Oldfield	1939	1	99	80	49.50	–	–	–
C.H. Parkin	1920-1924	10	160	36	12.30	–	32	32.25
B.P. Patterson (W. Indies)	1985-1989	17	88	21*	8.80	–	59	29.81
E. Paynter	1931-1939	20	1540	243	59.23	4	–	–
R. Pilling	1881-1888	8	91	23	7.58	–	(St. 4, Ct.10, T. 14)	
W. Place	1948	3	144	107	28.80	1	–	–
R. Pollard	1946-1948	4	13	10*	13.00	–	15	25.20
G. Pullar	1959-1963	28	1974	175	43.86	4	1	37.00

364

V.P.F.A. Royle	1879	1	21	18	10.50	–	–	–
S.S. Schultz	1879	1	20	20	20.00	–	1	26.00
J. Sharp	1909	3	188	105	47.00	1	3	37.00
K. Shuttleworth	1970-1971	5	46	28	7.66	–	12	35.38
R.H. Spooner	1905-1912	10	481	119	32.06	1	–	–
J.B. Statham	1951-1965	70	765	38	11.44	–	252	24.84
A.G. Steel	1880-1888	13	600	148	35.29	2	29	20.86
F.H. Sugg	1888	2	55	31	27.50	–	–	–
R. Tattersall	1951-1954	16	50	10*	5.00	–	58	26.18
E. Tyldesley	1921-1929	14	990	122	55.00	3	0	–
J.T. Tyldesley	1899-1909	31	1661	138	30.75	4	–	–
R.K. Tyldesley	1924-1930	7	47	29	7.83	–	19	32.57
A. Ward	1893-1895	7	487	117	37.46	1	–	–
C. Washbrook	1937-1956	37	2569	195	42.81	6	1	33.00
Wasim Akram (Pakistan)	1984-1989	25	410	66	16.40	–	76	27.60
A. Wharton	1949	1	20	13	10.00	–	–	–
L.L. Wilkinson	1938-1939	3	3	2	3.00	–	7	38.71
B. Wood	1972-1978	12	454	90	21.61	–	0	–
R. Wood	1887	1	6	6	3.00	–	–	–

This list does not include players who played test cricket before or after playing for Lancashire.

* *Not out*

Ten Highest Individual Batting Scores

SCORE	BATSMAN	OPPONENTS	VENUE	YEAR
424	A.C. MacLaren	Somerset	Taunton	1895
322	E. Paynter	Sussex	Hove	1937
300	F. Watson	Surrey	Old Trafford	1928
295	J.T. Tyldesley	Kent	Old Trafford	1906
291	E. Paynter	Hampshire	Southampton	1938
272	J.T. Tyldesley	Derbyshire	Chesterfield	1919
266	W. Place	Oxford Univ.	Oxford	1947
266	E. Paynter	Essex	Old Trafford	1937
256	E. Tyldesley	Warwickshire	Old Trafford	1930
253	J.T. Tyldesley	Kent	Canterbury	1914

Centuries Scored for Lancashire

90	E. Tyldesley	15	F.H. Sugg	4	K.G. MacLeod
73	J.T. Tyldesley	14	J.D. Bond	4	A.G. Paul
58	C. Washbrook	14	J. Abrahams	4	W. Robinson
52	C. Hallows	12	N. Oldfield	4	R. Whitehead
49	F. Watson	10	A.N. Hornby	3	M.A. Atherton
46	J. Iddon	10	P.T. Marner	3	J.R. Barnes
42	H. Makepeace	9	J. Briggs	3	N.D. Howard
37	D. Lloyd	9	G.D. Mendis	3	G.K. Knox
36	E. Paynter	8	J. Hallows	3	G.D. Lloyd
36	J. Sharp	8	A.H. Hornby	3	J.D. Tyldesley
34	W. Place	8	D.P. Hughes	3	W.K. Tyldesley
32	G. Pullar	8	L.O.S. Poidevin	2	R.G. Barlow
30	C.H. Lloyd	7	R.W. Barber	2	R. Bennett
30	A.C. MacLaren	6	A. Hartley	2	R. Collins
27	J.L. Hopwood	6	A. Kennedy	2	K. Cranston
26	K.J. Grieves	5	G. Atkinson	2	J. Eccles
25	H. Pilling	5	B.J. Booth	2	E.H. Edrich
25	R.H. Spooner	5	W.R. Cuttell	2	B.J. Howard
25	A. Wharton	5	H.G. Garnett	2	B.P. King
24	G.A. Edrich	5	S.J. O'Shaughnessy	2	W.H.L. Lister
24	G. Fowler	5	J. Simmons	2	W.E. Phillipson
24	A. Ward	4	G.R. Baker	2	B.W. Reidy
23	J.T. Ikin	4	A. Eccles	2	A.P. Smith
23	B. Wood	4	F.M. Engineer	2	K.L. Snellgrove
22	F.C. Hayes	4	D.M. Green	2	D.R. Worsley
16	N.H. Fairbrother	4	C.R. Hartley		

The following have each scored one century:

D. Bailey, A.M. Beddow, T.L. Brierley, H.R. Butterworth, M. Chadwick, J. Dyson, P.T. Eckersley, W. Ellis, L. Green, P. Greenwood, T.M. Halliday, C. Hawkwood, K.A. Hayes, A.N. Hayhurst, J.S. Heap, W.K. Hegg, M.J. Hilton, F.H. Hollins, W.J. Horrocks, J. l'Anson, R. Iddison, G. Kemp, J. Lyon, E.A. McDonald, C. Maynard, D.V. Norbury, A.E. Nutter, J.A. Ormrod, R.M. Ratcliffe, J. Ricketts, G.O. Shelmerdine, A.G. Steel, H.B. Steel, M.L. Taylor, K. Tebay, R.K. Tyldesley, D.W. Varey, F. Ward, Wasim Akram, M. Watkinson, Revd F.W. Wright.

Century on First-class Debut for Lancashire

YEAR	BATSMAN	OPPONENTS AND VENUE	SCORE
1867	J. Ricketts	Surrey, The Oval	195
1890	A.C. MacLaren	Sussex, Brighton	108
1908	R. Whitehead	Nottinghamshire, Old Trafford	131

2,000 Runs in a Season for Lancashire

YEAR	BATSMAN	RUNS	AVE
1901	J.T. Tyldesley	2,633	56.02
1904	J.T. Tyldesley	2,335	66.71
1922	E. Tyldesley	2,070	46.00
1923	H. Makepeace	2,286	50.80
1925	C. Hallows	2,185	52.02
1926	E. Tyldesley	2,432	62.35
	H. Makepeace	2,340	48.75
1927	C. Hallows	2,119	73.06
1928	C. Hallows	2,564	65.74
	F. Watson	2,541	63.52
	E. Tyldesley	2,467	77.09
1929	F. Watson	2,137	46.45
1930	F. Watson	2,031	45.13
1932	E. Tyldesley	2,420	59.02
1934	E. Tyldesley	2,487	57.83
	J. Iddon	2,381	52.91
1936	E. Paynter	2,016	45.81
1937	E. Paynter	2,727	58.35
1938	E. Paynter	2,020	57.71
1947	W. Place	2,408	68.80
1959	K.J. Grieves	2,253	41.72
	G. Pullar	2,197	54.92
	A. Wharton	2,157	40.69
1961	G. Pullar	2,047	47.60
1962	J.D. Bond	2,112	37.05

Lancashire Batsmen to Have Scored Centuries Against Every Other County

J. Iddon (1924-45)
E. Tyldesley (1909-36)

Record Partnerships for Each Wicket

1st	368	A.C. MacLaren and R.H. Spooner, v Gloucestershire (Liverpool)		1903
2nd	371	F. Watson and E. Tyldesley, v Surrey (Old Trafford)		1928
3rd	306	E. Paynter and N. Oldfield, v Hampshire (Southampton)		1938
4th	324	A.C. MacLaren and J.T. Tyldesley, v Nottinghamshire (Trent Bridge)		1904
5th	249	B. Wood and A. Kennedy, v Warwickshire (Edgbaston)		1975
6th	278	J. Iddon and H.R.W. Butterworth, v Sussex (Old Trafford)		1932
7th	245	A.H. Hornby and J. Sharp, v Leicestershire (Old Trafford)		1912
8th	158	J. Lyon and R.M. Ratcliffe, v Warwickshire (Old Trafford)		1979
9th	142	L.O.S. Poidevin and A. Kermode, v Sussex (Eastbourne)		1907
10th	173	J. Briggs and R. Pilling, v Surrey (Liverpool)		1885

Highest Score Against Each County

COUNTY	SCORE	BATSMAN	VENUE	YEAR
Derbyshire:	272	J.T. Tyldesley	Chesterfield	1919
Essex:	266	E. Paynter	Old Trafford	1937
Glamorgan:	239	E. Tyldesley	Cardiff	1934
Gloucestershire:	220	J.L. Hopwood	Bristol	1934
Hampshire:	291	E. Paynter	Southampton	1938
Kent:	295*	J.T. Tyldesley	Old Trafford	1906
Leicestershire:	249	J.T. Tyldesley	Leicester	1899
Middlesex:	203*	G.D. Mendis	Old Trafford	1987
Northamptonshire:	223	F. Watson	Old Trafford	1928
Nottinghamshire:	250	J.T. Tyldesley	Trent Bridge	1905
Somerset:	424	A.C. MacLaren	Taunton	1895
Surrey:	300*	F. Watson	Old Trafford	1928
Sussex:	322	E. Paynter	Hove	1937
Warwickshire:	256*	E. Tyldesley	Old Trafford	1930
Worcestershire:	248	J.T. Tyldesley	Liverpool	1903
Yorkshire:	200*	R.H. Spooner	Old Trafford	1910

* *not out*

Batsmen Who Have Scored 10,000 Runs for Lancashire

	RUNS	AVE
E. Tyldesley	34,222	45.20
J.T. Tyldesley	31,949	41.38
C. Washbrook	27,863	42.15
H. Makepeace	25,207	36.37
F. Watson	22,833	37.06
J. Sharp	22,015	31.18
J. Iddon	21,975	37.05
K.J. Grieves	20,802	33.39
C. Hallows	20,142	39.72
A. Wharton	17,921	33.55
D. Lloyd	17,877	33.41
G. Pullar	16,853	35.18
E. Paynter	16,555	41.59
A.C. MacLaren	15,772	33.34
J.L. Hopwood	15,519	30.01
A. Ward	15,392	30.96
H. Pilling	14,841	32.26
G.A. Edrich	14,730	34.74
W. Place	14,605	36.69
J.T. Ikin	14,327	37.70
B. Wood	12,969	35.24
C.H. Lloyd	12,764	44.94
J.D. Bond	11,867	26.60
G. Fowler	10,939	37.72
F.C. Hayes	10,899	37.45
J. Briggs	10,707	19.01
A.N. Hornby	10,649	24.25
P.T. Marner	10,312	29.21

1,000 Runs in May

C. Hallows in 1928 with innings of 100, 101, 51*, 123, 101*, 22, 74, 104, 58, 34*, 232.

* *not out*

Fastest Hundreds

35 mins	S.J. O'Shaughnessy v Leicestershire, Old Trafford 1983**
43 mins	A.H. Hornby v Somerset, Old Trafford 1905
46 mins	G. Fowler v Leicestershire, Old Trafford 1983**

** *Bowling for a declaration*

J. Briggs

J. Briggs is the only cricketer who has scored 10,000 runs and taken 1,000 wickets for Lancashire, his complete figures being 10,707 runs and 1,696 wickets, and in all first-class cricket he scored 14,092 runs and took 2,221 wickets. He is the only cricketer who has scored a century and done the 'Hat-Trick' in England v Australia matches.

The Double – 1,000 Runs and 100 Wickets in a Season

		For Lancashire		All First-Class Matches	
	YEAR	RUNS	WKTS	RUNS	WKTS
W.R. Cuttell	1898	952	109	1,003	114
J. Hallows	1904	1,071	108	1,071	108
J.L. Hopwood	1934	1,660	111	1,672	111
J.L. Hopwood	1935	1,538	103	1,538	103

Bowlers Who Have Taken 500 Wickets for Lancashire

	For Lancashire		All First-Class Matches	
	WKTS	AVE	WKTS	AVE
J.B. Statham	1,816	15.12	2,260	16.36
J. Briggs	1,696	15.60	2,221	15.95
A. Mold	1,543	15.15	1,673	15.54
R.K. Tyldesley	1,449	16.65	1,509	17.21
A. Watson	1,308	13.39	1,383	13.32
H. Dean	1,267	18.01	1,301	18.14
R. Tattersall	1,168	17.39	1,369	18.04
E.A. McDonald	1,053	20.96	1,395	20.76
K. Higgs	1,033	22.90	1,531	23.04
R. Pollard	1,015	22.15	1,122	22.56
J. Simmons	985	26.89	1,033	27.18
F.M. Sibbles	932	22.03	940	22.43
M.J. Hilton	926	18.81	1,006	19.41
C.H. Parkin	901	16.12	1,048	17.58
L. Cook	821	21.36	839	21.20
W.R. Cuttell	760	19.59	792	19.59
R.G. Barlow	736	13.60	951	14.50
P. Lever	716	24.64	796	25.59
T. Greenhough	707	21.98	751	22.37
W. Brearley	690	18.70	844	19.31
W. Huddleston	684	17.55	685	17.57
J.L. Hopwood	672	22.18	673	22.45
D.P. Hughes	608	29.28	626	29.86
W.E. Phillipson	545	24.78	555	24.72
J. Iddon	533	26.66	551	26.90
P.J.W. Allott	517	23.57	620	24,86

Nine or More Wickets in an Innings

ANALYSIS	BOWLER	OPPONENTS	VENUE	YEAR
10–46	W. Hickton	Hampshire	Old Trafford	1870
10–55	J. Briggs	Worcestershire	Old Trafford	1900
10–102	R. Berry	Worcestershire	Blackpool	1953
9–25	A. Appleby	Sussex	Brighton	1877
9–29	J. Briggs	Derbyshire	Derby	1885
9–29	A.W. Mold	Kent	Tonbridge	1893
9–31	H. Dean	Somerset	Old Trafford	1909
9–32	C.H. Parkin	Leicestershire	Ashby	1924
9–33	J.L. Hopwood	Leicestershire	Old Trafford	1933
9–35	H. Dean	Warwickshire	Liverpool	1909
9–36	W. Huddleston	Nottinghamshire	Liverpool	1906
9–37	J. Hallows	Gloucestershire	Gloucester	1904
9–39	R.G. Barlow	Sussex	Old Trafford	1886
9–40	R. Tattersall	Nottinghamshire	Old Trafford	1953
9–41	A.W. Mold	Yorkshire	Huddersfield	1890
9–42	J. Iddon	Yorkshire	Sheffield	1937
9–43	J.S. Heap	Northamptonshire	Northampton	1910
9–44	F. Harry	Warwickshire	Old Trafford	1906
9–46	H. Dean	Derbyshire	Chesterfield	1907
9–47	W. Brearley	Somerset	Old Trafford	1905
9–62	A.W. Mold	Kent	Old Trafford	1895
9–62	H. Dean	Yorkshire	Liverpool	1913
9–63	A.G. Steel	Yorkshire	Old Trafford	1878
9–69	J.L. Hopwood	Worcestershire	Blackpool	1934
9–77	J. Sharp	Worcestershire	Worcester	1901
9–77	H. Dean	Somerset	Bath	1910
9–80	W. Brearley	Yorkshire	Old Trafford	1909
9–88	J. Briggs	Sussex	Old Trafford	1888
9–109	H. Dean	Leicestershire	Leicester	1912
9–118	A. Watson	Derbyshire	Old Trafford	1874

Sixteen or More Wickets in a Match

ANALYSIS	BOWLER	OPPONENTS	VENUE	YEAR
17–91	H. Dean	Yorkshire	Liverpool	1913
17–137	W. Brearley	Somerset	Old Trafford	1905
16–103	H. Dean	Somerset	Bath	1910
16–111	A.W. Mold	Kent	Old Trafford	1895

200 Wickets in a Season

		For Lancashire		All First-Class Matches	
	YEAR	WKTS	AVE	WKTS	AVE
A.W. Mold	1894	189	11.84	207	12.30
A.W. Mold	1895	192	13.73	213	15.96
C.H. Parkin	1923	186	16.06	209	16.94
C.H. Parkin	1924	194	13.38	200	13.67
E.A. McDonald	1925	198	18.55	205	18.67

Wicket-Keeping in all Lancashire Matches 1865-1989

	PLAYED	MTS	CT	ST	TOTAL
G. Duckworth	1923-38	424	634	288	922
R. Pilling	1877-89	177	333	153	486
F.M. Engineer	1968-76	175	429	35	464

Ninety Dismissals or More in a Season

		For Lancashire			All First-Class Matches		
	YEAR	CT	ST	TOTAL	CT	ST	TOTAL
G. Duckworth	1928	69	28	97	77	30	107
G. Duckworth	1929	44	26	70	58	37	95
G. Clayton	1962	86	6	92	86	6	92
F.M. Engineer	1970	78	4	82	86	5	91

Seven Dismissals or More in an Innings

7	W. Farrimond	(Ct6,St1) v Kent (Old Trafford)	1930
7	W.K. Hegg	(Ct7,St0) v Derbyshire (Chesterfield)	1989

Nine Dismissals or More in a Match

11	W.K. Hegg	(Ct11,St0) v Derbyshire (Chesterfield)	1989
9	G. Clayton	(Ct8,St1) v Gloucestershire (Gloucester)	1959
9	C. Maynard	(Ct8,St1) v Somerset (Taunton)	1982

Most Catches in a Career

CT	FIELDER	MTS
555	K.J. Grieves	452
349	A.C. MacLaren	307
341	J. Simmons	429
329	J.T. Ikin	288
322	R.K. Tyldesley	374
320	G.A. Edrich	322
311	D. Lloyd	378
311	J.T. Tyldesley	507
308	D.P. Hughes	410

Youngest Players

	DEBUT	AGE
P.T. Marner	27 August 1952	16 years 150 days
J. Briggs	26 May 1879	16 years 236 days

Youngest Century-Maker

	DATE	AGE
C. Washbrook	12 June 1933	18 years 189 days

Oldest Player

	LAST PLAYED	AGE
A.N. Hornby	12 July 1899	52 years 153 days

Oldest Century-Maker

	DATE	AGE
H. Makepeace	22 August 1929	47th birthday

Oldest Debut for Lancashire

	DATE	AGE
J.A. Ormrod	28 April 1984	41 years 129 days

Fathers and Sons Who Have Played for Lancashire

George Bird (1880) and Morice (1907)
Jeremy Ellis (1892-8), Walker (1920-3) and Stanley (1923-4)
Stell Haggas (1884-5) and Walter (1903)
George Hartley (1871-2), Charles (1897-1909) and Alfred (1907-14)
Tommy Higson (1905-23), Tommy (1936-46) and Peter (1928-31)
Albert Neilson Hornby (1867-99) and Albert Henry (1899-1914)
Rupert Howard (1922-33), Nigel (1946-53) and Barry (1947-51)
Ernest Leese (1880-4) and Charles (1911)
George William Littlewood (1885) and George Hubert (1902-4)
David Lloyd (1965-83) and Graham (1988-)
Cec Parkin (1914-26) and Reg (1931-9)
Edmund Rowley (1865-80) and Ernest (1893-8)

Gillette Cup/NatWest Bank Trophy

Played 76, won 53, lost 23
Winners: 1970, 1971, 1972, 1975; Finalists: 1974, 1976, 1986; Semi-finalists: 1963, 1964, 1967, 1978, 1981.

Highest innings total:
For: 349-6 v Gloucestershire at Bristol 1984
Against: 312-5 by Worcestershire at Old Trafford 1985

Lowest completed innings total:
For: 59 (31.1 overs) v Worcestershire at Worcester 1963
Against: 62 (45.3 overs) by Cheshire at Macclesfield 1966
          62 (44.1 overs) by Cornwall at Truro 1977

Highest individual score:
For: 131 A. Kennedy v Middlesex at Old Trafford 1978
Against: 158 G.D. Barlow for Middlesex at Lord's 1984

Best bowling:
For: 5-13 P.A.J. DeFreitas v Cumberland at Netherfield 1989
Against: 7-32 S.P. Davis for Durham at Chester-le-Street 1983

Most economical bowling:
12-9-3-1 J. Simmons v Suffolk at Bury St Edmunds 1985

Most appearances: J. Simmons (1970-89) 57
Most runs: C.H. Lloyd (1969-86) 1,920
Most wickets: J. Simmons 79

Refuge Assurance/John Player Special League

Played 336, Won 161, Lost 131, Tied 7, No Result 37 (15 were abandoned without a ball being bowled)
Winners: 1969, 1970, 1989; Refuge Cup: 1988

Highest innings total:
For: 255-5 v Somerset at Old Trafford 1970
Against: 290-4 by Kent at Old Trafford 1987
              290-6 by Northamptonshire at Tring 1987

Lowest completed innings total:
For: 71 (20.4 overs) v Essex at Chelmsford 1987
Against: 75 (26 overs) by Essex at Old Trafford 1984

Highest individual score:
For: 134* C.H. Lloyd v Somerset at Old Trafford 1970
Against: 162* C.G. Greenidge for Hampshire at Old Trafford 1983

Best bowling:
For: 6-29 D.P. Hughes v Somerset at Old Trafford 1977
Against: 8-26 K.D. Boyce for Essex at Old Trafford 1971

Most economical bowling:
8-6-4-1 D.P. Hughes v Leicestershire at Old Trafford 1972

Most appearances: J. Simmons (1969-1989) 301
Most runs: C.H. Lloyd (1969-86) 5,198
Most wickets: J. Simmons 307

The Benson and Hedges Cup

Played 88, Won 49, Lost 34, No Result 5 (One was abandoned without a ball being bowled)
Winners: 1984; semi-finalists: 1973, 1974, 1982, 1983.

Highest innings total:
For: 317-5 v Scotland at Old Trafford 1988
Against: 314-5 by Worcestershire at Old Trafford 1980

Lowest completed innings total:
For: 82 (47.2 overs) v Yorkshire at Bradford 1972
Against: 68 (36.5 overs) by Glamorgan at Old Trafford 1973

Highest individual score:
For: 124 C.H. Lloyd v Warwickshire at Old Trafford 1981
Against: 137 T.A. Lloyd for Warwickshire at Edgbaston 1985

Best bowling:
For: 6-10 C.E.H. Croft v Scotland at Old Trafford 1982
Against: 6-29 J.D. Inchmore for Worcestershire at Old Trafford 1984

Most economical bowling:
11-8-5-1 J. Simmons v Leicestershire at Old Trafford 1985

Most appearances: J. Simmons (1972-89) 83
Most runs: D. Lloyd (1972-83) 1,474
Most wickets: J. Simmons 78

Bibliography

Archie by Michael Down (George Allen and Unwin 1981).
County Cricket Championship by Roy Webber (Phoenix 1957).
Cricket All the Way by Eddie Paynter (Richardson 1962)
Cricket's Unholy Trinity by David Foot (Stanley Paul 1985).
Double Century by Tony Lewis (Hodder and Stoughton 1987).
England versus Australia by David Frith (Collins Willow 1984).
Fifty Years' Cricket Reminiscences of a Non-Player by W.E. Howard
   (1928).
Flat Jack by Jack Simmons (Queen Anne 1986).
Forty Seasons of First-Class Cricket by R.G. Barlow (Heywood 1911).
Fresh Light on 18th Century Cricket by G.B. Buckley (1935).
Fresh Light on Pre-Victorian Cricket by G.B. Buckley (1937).
Gone Cricket Mad by Chris Aspin (Helmshore L.H.S. 1976).
Lancashire by John Kay (Arthur Barker 1972).
Lancashire by Rex Pogson (Convoy 1952).
Lancashire County Cricket 1864-1953 by A.W. Ledbrooke (1955).
Lancashire Cricketers by Malcolm G. Lorimer (A.C.S. 1989).
Lancashire Hot-Pot by The Hon. T.C.F. Prittie (Hutchinson 1947).
Lancashire Scores 1864-1882 by Fred Reynolds (Heywood 1883).
The Complete Who's Who of Test Cricketers by Christopher Martin-
   Jenkins (Queen Anne 1987).
The Guardian Book of Cricket by Matthew Engel (Penguin 1986).
The Roses Matches 1919-1939 by Neville Cardus (Souvenir 1982).
Who's Who of Cricketers by Philip Bailey, Philip Thorn and Peter
   Wynne-Thomas (Newnes 1984).

Index

381

382

386

391

8